Mapping Vulnerability

Mapping Vulnerability

Disasters, Development and People

Edited by

Greg Bankoff
Georg Frerks
Dorothea Hilhorst

EARTHSCAN

London • Sterling, VA

First published by Earthscan in the UK and USA in 2004
Reprinted 2007

Copyright © Greg Bankoff, Georg Frerks, Dorothea Hilhorst, 2004

ISBN: 978-1-85383-964-1 paperback
       978-1-85383-963-4 hardback

Typeset by MapSet Ltd, Gateshead, UK
Printed and bound in the UK by Cromwell Press, Trowbridge, UK
Cover design by Ruth Bateson

For a full list of publications please contact:
Earthscan
8–12 Camden High Street
London, NW1 0JH, UK
Tel: +44 (0)20 7387 8558
Fax: +44 (0)20 7387 8998
Email: earthinfo@earthscan.co.uk
Web: **www.earthscan.co.uk**

22883 Quicksilver Drive, Sterling, VA 20166-2012, USA

A catalogue record for this book is available from the British Library

Library of Congress Cataloging-in-Publication Data

Mapping vulnerability : disasters, development, and people / Greg Bankoff, Georg
Frerks, Dorothea Hilhorst.
     p. cm.
   Includes bibliographical references and index.
   ISBN 1-85383-964-7 (pbk.) – ISBN 1-85383-963-9 (hardback)
    1. Disaster relief–Case studies. 2. Natural disasters–Case studies. 3. Human
beings–Effect of environment on–Case studies. 4. Political ecology–Case studies.
I. Bankoff, Greg. II. Frerks, Georg, 1961- III. Hilhorst, Dorothea.

HV553.M27 2003
363.34'2–dc21

                                                                        2003008344

Earthscan publishes in association with the International Institute for Environment and
Development

The paper used for this book is FSC-certified and
totally chlorine-free. FSC (the Forest Stewardship Council)
is an international network to promote responsible
management of the world's forests.

Contents

List of Figures, Tables and Boxes

FIGURES

TABLES

BOXES

List of Contributors

Greg Bankoff is a social and environmental historian of Southeast Asia. He has written extensively on the relationship between societies and the environment and has recently completed a study of the effect of natural hazards on cultural formation entitled *Cultures of Disaster: Society and Natural Hazard in the Philippines* (RoutlegeCurzon, London, 2003). Greg is associate professor in the School of Asian Studies at the University of Auckland, New Zealand, and research fellow in Disaster Studies at Wageningen University, The Netherlands. Email: g.bankoff@auckland.ac.nz, or: gregory.bankoff@wur.nl

Recent publications
Bankoff, G (2001) 'Rendering the world unsafe: "Vulnerability" as Western discourse', *Disasters*, 25(1): 19–35
Bankoff, G (2001) 'Environment, resources and hazards', in P Heenan and M Lamontage (eds) *The Southeast Asian Handbook*, Fitzroy Dearborn, London and Chicago, pp179–92
Bankoff, G (1999) 'A history of poverty: The politics of "natural disasters" in the Philippines, 1985–1995', *The Pacific Review* 12(3): 381–420

Stephen Bender is group chief for Meso America of the Unit for Sustainable Development and Environment, which is part of the Office of the Secretary General of the Organization of American States (OAS). He serves as policy adviser and programme coordinator for activities related to the vulnerability reduction of populations and economic and social infrastructure to natural hazards, and trade corridor development, as well as chair of the Working Group on the Vulnerability Assessment and Indexing of the OAS Inter-American Committee for Natural Disaster Reduction (IACNDR). Email: sbender@oas.org

Recent publications
Bender, S (2001) 'Financiamiento para la reducción de los desastres naturales (o porque se habla de desastres por diseño y como el financiamiento para el desarrollo debe representar el presupuesto para la reducción de desastres naturales)', in BCIE and CONADES, Memoria Conferencia Internacional Sobre Financiamiento del Desarrollo Sostenible, Tegucigalpa
Bender, S (2000) 'Trade corridors: The emerging regional development planning unit in Latin America', in D Edgington, A Fernandez and C Hoshino (eds) *New Regional Development Paradigms: Volume II New Regions, Concepts, Issues and Practices*, Greenwood Press, Westport, Connecticut and London

Bender, S (1999) 'Reducing vulnerability of infrastructure', in J Ingleton (ed) *Natural Disaster Management – IDNDR Commemorative Volume*, NDM Press, London

Charlotte Benson is an economist by training. She has been undertaking research on the economic aspects of natural hazard risk and disasters for over ten years. Her work has included detailed studies of the impacts of disasters in sub-Saharan Africa, Southeast Asia, the Pacific and the Caribbean, seeking to assess hazard vulnerability from a macro-economic perspective. Her other works include a review commissioned by the Asian Development Bank of its post-disaster rehabilitation assistance loans, an evaluation of the UK government's response to the ongoing volcanic activity in Montserrat, and a research study of the role of NGOs in natural disaster mitigation and preparedness, overseen by the British Red Cross. Email: cbenson321@aol.com

Recent publications
Benson, C and Clay, E J (2003) 'Economic and Financial Impacts of Natural Disasters: An Assessment of Their Effects and Options for Mitigation', Disaster Risk Management Series, World Bank, Washington, DC
Benson, C and Clay, E J (2002) 'Bangladesh: Disasters and Public Finance', Disaster Risk Management Working Paper Series No 6, World Bank, Washington, DC
Benson, C, Clay, E J, Michael, F V and Robertson, A W (2001) *Dominica: Natural Disasters and Economic Development in a Small Island State*, World Bank, Washington, DC
Benson, C, Twigg, J and Myers, M (2001) 'NGO initiatives in risk reduction: An overview', *Disasters*, 25(3): 199–215
Benson, C and Clay, E J (2000) 'Developing countries and the economic impacts of natural disasters', in A Kreimer and M Arnold (eds) *Managing Disaster Risk in Emerging Economies*, Disaster Risk Management Series #2, World Bank, Washington, DC

Kenneth Broad is currently a research assistant professor in the Division of Marine Affairs and Policy at the Rosenstiel School of Marine and Atmospheric Science, University of Miami. An ecological anthropologist, he studies the interaction between human behaviour and ecosystems in different parts of the world. His current work focuses on identifying the potential uses and consequences of climate forecasts for the South American fishing sector, forest management in Indonesia, and agriculture in the southeast US. Past projects have included studying the role of women in Spanish fisheries politics, a legal analysis of Chilean fisheries laws, and identifying illegal drug use and distribution patterns in the Caribbean.

Recent publications
Broad, K, Pfaff, A P and Glantz, M H (2002) 'Effective and equitable dissemination of seasonal-to-interannual climate forecasts: Policy implications from the Peruvian fishery during El Niño 1997–98', *Climatic Change*, 54(4): 415–438

Agrawala, S and Broad, K (forthcoming) 'Technology transfer perspectives on climate forecast applications', *Knowledge and Society*

Broad, K and Agrawala, S (2000) 'The Ethiopia food crisis: Uses and limits of climate forecasts', *Science*, 289: 1693–4

Omar D Cardona is the research director of Centro de Estudios sobre Desastres y Riesgos Natural (CEDERI) of the Universidad de los Andes in Bogotá, Colombia. He is an expert in disaster risk management with a focus on prevention mitigation measures. He has been an adjunct and visiting professor at the Architecture and Civil Engineering Schools of the Universidad Nacional de Colombia, the Universidad Politécnica de Cataluña in Spain, and of the Centro Universitario Europeo per Beni Culturali in Italy. Between 1992 and 1995 he was the national director for Risk Mitigation and Disaster Preparedness of Colombia; he was also a founding member of La RED de Estudios Sociales en Prevención de Desastres en América Latina (Latin American Network for the Social Study of Disaster Prevention in Latin America). He is currently the president of the Colombian Association for Earthquake Engineering and has been risk consultant for international organizations such as UNDP, PAHO, USAID/OFDA, the World Bank and the IADB. Email: ocardona@uniandes.edu.co

Recent publications

Cardona, O D (2001) *Estimación Holística del Riesgo Sísmico utilizando Sistemas Dinámicos Complejos*, Universidad Politécnica de Cataluña, Barcelona (http://www.desenredando.org/public/varios/2001/ehrisusd/index/html)

Cardona, O D and Barbat, A (2000) *El Riesgo Sísmico y su Prevención*, Calidad Siderúrgica, Cuadernos Técnicos 5, Madrid

Cardona, O and Barbat, A (2000) 'El riesgo sísmico de estructuras', in E Car, F López Almansa and S Oller (eds) *Estructuras Sometidas a Acciones Dinámicas*, CIMNE, Barcelona, pp369–97

Cardona, O and Hurtado, J (2000) 'Modelación numérica para la estimación holística del riesgo sísmico urbano, considerando variables técnicas, sociales y económicas', in E Oñate et al (eds) *Métodos Numéricos en Ciencias Sociales (MENCIS 2000)*, CIMNE-UPC, Barcelona, pp452–66

Cardona O and Yamín, L (1997) 'Seismic microzonation and estimation of earthquake loss scenarios: Integrated risk mitigation project of Bogotá, Colombia', *Earthquake Spectra*, 13(4): 795–814

Ian Davis has had a varied career spanning 40 years in architectural practice, teaching and research in architecture and disaster management at Oxford Brookes and Cranfield universities and international consultancy in disaster planning and management. He has been a board member of a number of NGOs, including Tearfund, Traidcraft, The Safe Trust and Intrac. He has written or edited 14 books and over 90 papers and has worked in 40 disaster situations. From 1991 to 2000 he was a member of the UK National Committee for the IDNDR. In 1996 he was awarded the UN Sasakawa Award for his contribution to International Disaster Prevention. He is currently visiting professor in the Disaster Management Centre at Cranfield University. Email: idavis@n-oxford.demon.co.uk

Recent publications
Wisner, B, Blaikie, P, Cannon, T and Davis, I (2003) (2nd edition) *At Risk: Natural Hazards, People's Vulnerability and Disasters*, Routledge, London and New York
Davis, I and Westgate, K (1999) *IDNDR Audit of UK Assests: Critical Appraisal of the Effectiveness of UK Groups in Fulfilling the Aims of the IDNDR*, United Kingdom National Coordination Committee for the International Decade for Natural Disaster Reduction, London
Davis, I, Sanderson, D, Parker, D and Stack, J (1998) 'The Dissemination of Warnings, Project 5', in United Kingdom Coordination Committee for the International Decade for Natural Disaster Reduction, *Forecasts and Warnings*, Thomas Telford, London
Aysan, Y, Clayton, A and Cory, A, Davis, I and Sanderson, D (1995) *Developing Building For Safety Programmes*, ITDG Publications, London
Clayton, A and Davis, I (1994) *Building for Safety Compendium*, ITDG Publications, London

Zenaida Delica-Willison is currently the director of the Training and Education Division, Asian Disaster Preparedness Center, Bangkok, Asian Institute of Technology, and was formerly executive director of the Citizens' Disaster Response Center in Manila, the Philippines. Her expertise is in disaster management, programme development, monitoring and evaluation, training and facilitation, and curriculum development. She has edited seven books and training manuals on disaster management and written various articles on the subject. Email: zdelica@adpc.net

Recent publications
Delica, Z (2000) 'Balancing vulnerability and capacity: Women and children in the Philippines', in E Enarson and B Morrow (eds) *The Gendered Terrain of Disaster Through Women's Eyes*, International Hurricane Center, US, pp109–13
Delica, Z (1999) 'Case study: Practical experiences in preparing a community', in J Ingleton (ed) *Natural Disaster Management*, Tudor Rose Holdings, Leicester, pp210–2
Delica, Z (1999) 'Community mobilization for early warning', *Philippine Planning Journal School of Urban and Regional Planning*, 30(2): 30–40

Timothy Finan is a professor in the Department of Anthropology of the University of Arizona in Tucson. He is the director for the Bureau of Applied Research in Anthropology (BARA) that publishes the *Journal of Political Ecology*. At the heart of BARA's approach lies a commitment to community participation, empirical fieldwork and innovative research methods. Dr Finan's research involves applied anthropology, especially development anthropology; economic anthropology; macro–micro linkages; and sub-Saharan Africa, Latin America and the Arabian Peninsula. Current interests include the impacts of policy reform on local communities; household food security; agricultural and nomadic adaptations in arid lands; and research methodology.

Recent publications

Finan, T and Langworthy, M (1997) *Waiting for the Rain: Agricultural and Ecological Imbalances in Cape Verde*, Lynne Rienne Publications, London

Maureen Fordham is senior lecturer in Disaster Management at Northumbria University, Newcastle upon Tyne, UK. She has been researching in the broad field of hazards and disasters since 1988. Her work has particularly focused upon floods and human vulnerability. It has examined definitions of vulnerability, gender analyses and socially inclusive disaster management. She is a consultant to government and non-government agencies in the UK and holds several honorary professional posts in the academic disciplines of geography and sociology. She was co-founder and is co-editor of the website Radix – Radical Interpretations of Disaster (http://online.northumbria.ac.uk/geography_research/radix/) and manages several others that also have as their objective the international distribution of disaster research. Email: maureen.fordham@northumbria.ac.uk

Recent publications

Fordham, M (2003) 'Gender, disaster and development: the necessity for integration', in M Pelling (ed) *Natural Disaster and Development in a Globalizing World*, Routledge, London, pp57–74

Fordham, M (2001) 'Challenging boundaries: A gender perspective on early warning in disaster and environmental management', Invited Paper for UN Expert Group Meeting, Environmental Management and the Mitigation of Natural Disasters: a Gender Perspective, Ankara, 6–9 November, www.un.org/womenwatch/daw/csw/env_manage/documents.html

Fordham, M and Enarson, E (2001) 'Lines that divide, ties that bind: Race, class and gender in women's flood recovery in the US and UK', *Australian Journal of Emergency Management*, 15(4): 43–52

Fordham, M, Comfort, L, Wisner, B, Cutter, S, Pulwarty, R, Hewitt, K, Oliver-Smith, A, Weiner, J, Peacock, W and Krimgold, F (1999) 'Reframing disaster policy: The global evolution of vulnerable communities', *Environmental Hazards* 1(1): 39–44

Georg Frerks is a development sociologist with experience in development, foreign policy and evaluation. He formerly worked for the Dutch Ministry of Foreign Affairs and is presently professor of Disaster Studies at Wageningen University, The Netherlands, where he specializes in the sociology of disaster, conflict and humanitarian aid. He also occupies a chair of Conflict Prevention and Conflict Management at Utrecht University. He has published on development-related subjects and humanitarian emergencies in the developing world. Email: georg.frerks@wur.nl

Recent publications

Frerks, G, Hilhorst, D and Moreyra, A (1999) *Natural disasters: Framework for analysis and action*. Report for MSF-Holland, Wageningen, The Netherlands

Frerks, G (1998) 'Omgaan met rampen (Dealing with disaster)', Inaugural Address, Wageningen University, Wageningen, The Netherlands

Frerks, G, Kirby, J, Kliest, T, Flikkema, W and O'Keefe, P (1997) 'UNHCR, the cross- border operation in Somalia: The value of quick impact projects for refugee resettlement', *Journal of Refugee Studies* 10(2): 181–90

Dorothea Hilhorst is a rural development sociologist who specializes in the sociology of disaster, conflict and humanitarian assistance in developing countries. She focuses particularly on organizations. She is associate professor of Disaster Studies at Wageningen University, The Netherlands. Email: Thea.Hilhorst@wur.nl

Recent publications
Hilhorst, D (2003) *The Real World of NGOs: Discourse, Diversity and Development*, Zedbooks, London
Hilhorst, D (2001) 'Village experts and development discourse: "Progress" in a Philippine Igorot village', *Human Organization*, 60(4): 401–413
Hilhorst, D and van Leeuwen, M (2000) 'Emergency and development: The case of Imidugudu, villagisation in Rwanda', *Journal of Refugee Studies*, 13(3): 264–280

Annelies Heijmans holds a Masters in Land-Use Planning from Wageningen Agricultural University, The Netherlands. She gained extensive experience in community-based and development-oriented disaster response as consultant with the Citizens' Disaster Response Network and the Center for Disaster Preparedness in the Philippines. As trainer and consultant she was involved in capability-building programmes for government officials, NGO staff and donors of various organizations in Asia, and promoted the grassroots approach in disaster-risk reduction. Currently, she is the Asia coordinator at the European Centre for Conflict Prevention in Utrecht, The Netherlands. Email: bbxah@yahoo.com

Recent publications
Heijmans, A and Victoria, L P (2001) *Citizenry-Based and Development-Oriented Disaster Response: Experiences and Practice in Disaster Management of the Citizens' Disaster Response Network in the Philippines*, Center for Disaster Preparedness, Manila, the Philippines
Giovacchini, T and Heijmans, A (1999) *Shaping the 'Humanitarian' Wars of the Future*, Occasional Article Series of the Philippine International Forum, Manila, the Philippines
Elegado, E, Heijmans, A et al (1998) *4B: Project Development, Monitoring and Evaluation in Disaster Situations*, Citizens' Disaster Response Center, Manila, the Philippines

Allan Lavell holds an MSc and PhD in Geography from the London School of Economics and Political Science. He has researched and taught at the University of London; Middlesex Polytechnic; El Colegio de Mexico; the National and Autonomous Metropolitan Universities of Mexico; the University of Costa Rica; the University of Buenos Aires; and the Central American University Confederation. He is currently the coordinator of the Risk and Disaster Programme at the Secretariate General of the Latin American Social Sciences

Faculty in San José, Costa Rica. Founding member of the Latin American Network for the Social Study of Disasters, he has worked on the risk and disaster theme for the last 13 years. Email: allan_lavell@yahoo.com

Recent publications

Lavell, A and Arguello, M (2001) 'Internacionalización y globalización: nota sobre su incidencia en las condiciones y expresiones del riesgo en América Latina', *Quórum: Revista de Pensamiento Latinoamericano*, Invierno, 2001–2002, pp67–80, Universidad de Alcalá, Espana

Lavell, A (2000) 'Desastres y desarrollo: Hacia un entendimiento de las formas de construcción social de un desastre: El caso del huracán Mitch en Centroamérica', in G Nora y J Nowalski (ed) *Del Desastre al Desarrollo Sostenible: Huracán Mitch en Centroamérica*, in Gartia, N and Nowalksi, J (eds) Del Desastre al Desarrollo Sostenible: Huracán Mitch en Centroamerica, BID-CIDHCS, San Jose, Costa Rica

Lavell, A (1999) *Desastres en América Latina: Avances teóricos y prácticos:1990–1999*, Anuario Social y Político de América Latina y el Caribe, FLACSO-Nueva Sociedad

Anthony Oliver-Smith is professor of Anthropology at the University of Florida and affiliate of the Center for Latin American Studies at that institution. He has specialized in anthropological research and consultation on issues relating to disasters and involuntary resettlement in Peru, Honduras, India, Brazil, Jamaica and the US since the 1970s. He has served on the executive boards of the National Association of Practicing Anthropologists (NAPA) and the Society for Applied Anthropology (SfAA). His work on disasters has focused on issues of post-disaster social organization, including class, race and ethnicity; gender-based differential patterns of aid distribution; social consensus and conflict; grief and mourning issues; and social mobilization of community-based reconstruction efforts. Email: aros@ufl.edu

Recent publications

Hoffman, S M and Oliver-Smith, A (eds) (2002) *Catastrophe and Culture: The Anthropology of Disaster*, SAR Press, Santa Fe

Oliver-Smith, A and Hoffman, S M (eds) (1999) *The Angry Earth: Disaster in Anthropological Perspective*, Routledge, New York and London

Oliver-Smith, A (1996) 'Anthropological research on hazards and disasters', *Annual Review of Anthropology*, 25: 303–28

Oliver-Smith, A (1986, 1992) *The Martyred City: Death and Rebirth in the Peruvian Andes*, Waveland, Prospect Heights, IL

Roger S Pulwarty is a research scientist at the Climate Diagnostics Center in the faculty of the Cooperative Institute for Research in the Environmental Sciences at the University of Colorado, Boulder. From 1988–2002 he served as a programme manager at the US National Oceanic and Atmospheric Administration Office of Global Programs. He is interested in climate and its role in society–environment interactions at different scales. His work has focused on hydroclimatic variability and its impacts in the Americas, societal and ecological vulnerability to environmental variations, and the role and utilization of research-based information in ecological, water and agricultural management in the western US, Latin America and the Caribbean. Email: roger.pulwarty@noaa.gov

Recent publications

Pulwarty, R and Cohen, S J (in review) 'Communicating scientific information: Moving within and beyond impact assessments', *Global Environmental Change*,

Comfort, L, Wisner, B, Cutter, S, Pulwarty, R, Hewitt, K, Oliver-Smith, A, Peacock, W, Wiener, J, Fordham, M and Krimgold, F (1999) 'Reframing disaster policy: The global evolution of vulnerable communities', *Environmental Hazards*, 1: 39–44

Pulwarty, R and Riebsame, W (1997) 'The political ecology of vulnerability to hurricane-related hazards', in H Diaz and R Pulwarty (eds) *Hurricanes: Climate and Socio-economic Impacts*, Springer-Verlag Publications, Heidelberg

Linda Stephen has recently been a research assistant at the Environmental Change Institute, University of Oxford. She now works independently as a consultant for the Stockholm Environment Institute, the World Food Program and Oxfam GB. She holds a PhD on the topic of vulnerability analysis and food insecurity in Ethiopia, and her publications reflect an expertise in methods of vulnerability analysis, with a specific focus on food insecurity. Recent projects include an emergency assessment of vulnerability and food insecurity in Namibia, and a vulnerability profile of food insecure households in Ehtiopia. Email: lsteph2001@hotmail.com

Recent publications

Downing, T E, Patwardhan, A, Klein, R, Mukhala, E, Stephen, L, Winograd, M and Ziervogel, G (2003) 'Vulnerability assessment for climate adaptation', in *Elaborating an Adaptation Policy Framework*, Technical Paper No 3, United Nations Development Programme, Global Environment Facility, http://www.undp.org/cc/apf_outline.htm

UNDP (2003) 'Drought and vulnerability in Ethiopia' (contributed by L Stephen), in *World Vulnerability Report 2002*, Bureau for Crisis Prevention and Recovery, United Nations Development Programme, Geneva

Stephen, L and Downing, T E (2001) 'Getting the scale right: A comparison of analytical methods for vulnerability assessment and household level targeting', *Disasters*, 25(2): 113–135, June

Stephen, L (2000) 'Monitoring famine and vulnerability: Lessons from international and national experiences', Proceedings from the 29th International Geographical Congress, Seoul, Korea, 14–18 August.

Downing, T E, Stephen, L, Rahman, A and Butterfield, R (1999) 'Climate change and vulnerability: Toward a framework for comparing adaptability to climate change impacts, Paper prepared for UNEP workshop on vulnerability indicators, 5–6 October

Stephen, L (1998) *Livelihoods and Food Security in Delanta: Report on Participatory Rural Appraisal of Three Peasant Associations in Delanta, Ethiopia*, Oxfam GB, Oxford

Robin Willison is director of Technical Services at the Asian Disaster Preparedness Center based in Bangkok. Originally a civil engineer, he has Masters degrees in public health, counselling/religion and studies in international development. He has worked in the fields of civil engineering, education, public health, business and the management of major humanitarian aid work. During the 1990s, he implemented a project to restore community-based primary health care in a Caucasus republic; he then spent three years directing a wide variety of projects in south Sudan. Email: rwillison@adpc.net

Recent publications

Willison, R (2001) 'Establishing community-based health care in Sudan', *Asian Disaster Management News*, 7(4): 10

Willison, R (1993) *Foundation Education: A Comprehensive Primary Education Home Study Curriculum With Complete Teacher's Manual and Student Workbook*, Foundation Education, Kettle Falls, Washington, US

Ben Wisner is a geographer who has worked for the past 37 years on development, environment and disaster management issues in Eastern and Southern Africa, Mexico, Central America and the Caribbean. He began to question the prevailing 'hazard'-dominated paradigm with an article in the UK journal *Nature* in 1976, entitled 'Taking the Naturalness out of Natural Disaster'. His work on an alternative way of thinking about natural hazards was synthesized in 1994 in a book with other authors, entitled *At Risk: Natural Hazards, People's Vulnerability, and Disasters*. He is also co-founder of RADIX, the radical disaster website (http://www.online.northumbria.ac.uk/geography_research/radix). He is research fellow at the Development Studies Institute, London School of Economics, as well as the Benfield Greig Hazard Research Centre, University College London, and also visiting researcher in the Environmental Studies programme at Oberlin College, US. Email: bwisner@igc.org

Recent publications

Wisner, B and Adams, J (eds) (2003) *Environmental Health in Emergencies and Disasters: A Practical Guide*, World Health Organization, Geneva (http://www.who.int/water_sanitation_health/Documents/emergencies/EH emergencies.htm)

Wisner, B (2002) 'Disaster Risk Reduction in Megacities: Making the Most of Human and Social Capital', Paper presented at the workshop The Future of Disaster Risk: Building Safer Cities, Washington, DC, World Bank and the ProVention Consortium, 4–6 December

Wisner, B (2001) 'Urban social vulnerability to disaster in greater Los Angeles', in S Sassen (ed) *Encyclopedia of the Life Support Systems*, UNESCO, Paris

Wisner, B (2000) 'From "acts of God" to "water wars"', in D J Parker (ed) *Floods*, Routledge, London, pp1, 89–99

Wisner, B (1999) 'There are worse things than earthquakes: Hazard vulnerability and mitigation in Los Angeles', in J K Mitchell (ed) *Crucibles of Hazard: Mega-Cities and Disasters in Transition*, United Nations University Press, Tokyo, pp375–427

Acknowledgements

The editors would like to gratefully acknowledge and wholeheartedly thank the work done 'behind the scenes' by a number of people whose names do not otherwise appear here. In particular, we would like to express our appreciation to Nynke Douma for her patience and hard work in formatting and otherwise preparing the manuscript; to Hilde van Dijkhorst for her help and good humoured support in just about everything; and to Ann Long and Chris Kendrick for their skills in rendering 'not native English' into 'good English'. Special thanks are also extended to Jos Penning for organizing the original workshop, bringing us all together and finding the wherewithal to fund it, and to the Stichting National Erfgoed Hotel de Wereld for providing the 'readies' that sponsored the whole affair that ultimately led to the publication of this book. Last, but not least, we would like to express our gratitude to Esther Velthoen and Fred Claasen for their fortitude and forbearance in seeing this project through.

List of Acronyms and Abbreviations

ADB	Asian Development Bank
ADPC	Asian Disaster Preparedness Center
AIDS	acquired immune deficiency syndrome
AKUT	Arama Kurtama Dernegi (Turkish search and rescue team)
APEC	Asia-Pacific Economic Cooperation
BARA	Bureau of Applied Research in Anthropology
CBO	community-based organization
CBSBP	community-based seed bank programme
CDMP	Caribbean Disaster Mitigation Programme
CDP	Committee for Development Planning
CDRC	Citizens' Disaster Response Centre
CDRN	Citizens' Disaster Response Network
CEDAW	Convention to End Discrimination against All Women
CORDES	Corporation for Economic and Social Development
CRED	Centre for Research on the Epidemiology of Disasters
DFID	Department for International Development (UK)
DMIS	Disaster Management Information System
DPPC	Disaster Prevention and Preparedness Commission
DRC	Disaster Research Centre
ECLAC	Economic Commission for Latin America and the Caribbean
ECOSOC	United Nations Department of Economic and Social Affairs
EHRM	Emergent Human Resources Model
ENLA	Emergency Network Los Angeles
ENSO	El Niño–Southern Oscillation
EVI	Economic Vulnerability Index
FAO	United Nations Food and Agriculture Organization
FEMA	US Federal Emergency Management Agency
FMLN	Farabundo Marti National Liberation Front
FUNCEME	Cearense Foundation for Meteorology and Water Resources
GAD	gender and development
GDP	gross domestic product
GESI	Global Earthquake Safety Initiative
GHI	Geo Hazards International
GIEWS	Global Information and Early Warning System
GIS	geographic information systems
GNP	gross national product
HYV	high-yielding varieties
IADB	Inter-American Development Bank
IDNDR	International Decade for Natural Disaster Reduction

IDP	internally displaced people
IDT	international development targets
IFRC	International Federation of the Red Cross and Red Crescent
IMF	International Monetary Fund
INPE	Institute for Space Studies (Brazil)
La RED	Latin American Network for the Social Study of Disaster Prevention in Latin America (Red de Estudios Sociales en Prevención de Desastres en América Latina)
LDC	less developed country
MRRS	Montanosa Relief and Rehabilitation Services
NAPA	National Association of Practising Anthropologists
NDVI	Normalized Difference Vegetation Index
NGO	non-governmental organization
NIC	newly industrialized country
OAS	Organization of American States
ODA	overseas development assistance
ODI	Overseas Development Institute
OECD	Organization of Economic Co-operation and Development
OFDA	Office of the United States Foreign Disaster Assistance
PAHO	Pan American Health Organization
PDRN	Pampanga Disaster Response Network
PFP	policy framework paper
PLT	Programme for Land Transference
PMP	prevention, mitigation and preparedness
PPPD	Policy, Planning and Programme Department
SAP	structural adjustment programme
SERA	strengthening emergency response abilities
SfAA	Society for Applied Anthropology
Sida	Swedish International Development Cooperation Agency
SoVCA	social vulnerability and capacity assessment
SSK	sociology of scientific knowledge
SSM	Soft Systems Methodology
SUDENE	Superintendency for the Development of the Northeast
TABI	Tabang sa Biktima sa Bikol (Help for the Victims in Bicol)
TRI	Toxic Release Inventory
TRV	traditional rice varieties
UN	United Nations
UNDP	United Nations Development Programme
UNCHD	United Nations Centre for Human Development
UNCTAD	United Nations Conference on Trade and Development
UNDRO	United Nations Disaster Relief Organization
UNHCR	United Nations High Commissioner for Refugees
USAID	United States Agency for International Development
VAM	vulnerability analysis and mapping
VCA	vulnerability and capacity assessment
WFP	World Food Programme
WID	women in development

Introduction:
Mapping Vulnerability

Dorothea Hilhorst and Greg Bankoff[1]

What makes people vulnerable? To most people today, this is an everyday question that is as simple as it is complex. At one level, the answer is a straightforward one about poverty, resource depletion and marginalization; at another level, it is about the diversity of risks generated by the interplay between local and global processes and coping with them on a daily basis. For billions of people, the nature of their vulnerability is changing and intensifying, while their ability to cope has diminished. The saddest part, perhaps, is the loss of hope for the future. As James Ferguson so eloquently pleads, the current construction of a new world order not only continues to exclude large numbers of people, but actually robs them of even the promise of development (Ferguson, 1999, pp237–8). Living with the poverty and uncertainty of their daily existence severely constrains their freedom of choice and leaves them prey to a creeping despair that the magnitude and frequency of natural and human-induced disasters only make worse. This book is an opportunity for a group of scholars and practitioners to grapple with the simple–complex paradox so manifest in the nature of vulnerability. Each contributes a different perspective to the problem, all seeking in some way to resolve the apparent contradiction of reconciling local experiences with global considerations. The nature of this complexity dictates that there can be no general theory and therefore no simple solutions. What we offer instead is a map. It delineates the landscape of vulnerability, revealing the lie of the land and the shape of its contours. While there are many possible paths on this map, there are, however, no set routes or even fixed destinations.

VULNERABILITY, DISASTER AND DEVELOPMENT

Vulnerability is the key to an understanding of risk that attempts to break from the all-too-technocratic attitudes that have characterized relationships between human societies and their environments over previous centuries, and which are often associated with Western cultural norms (Hewitt, 1983b). Instead of regarding disasters as purely physical occurrences, requiring largely technological solutions, as was widespread until the 1970s, such events are better viewed primarily as the result of human actions – as the 'actualization of social vulnerability' (Lewis, 1999, p8). Terry Cannon persuasively argues that while hazards are natural, disasters are not. Social processes generate unequal exposure to risk by making some people more prone to disaster than others, and these inequalities are largely a function of the power relations operative in every society. Critical to discerning the nature of disasters, then, is an appreciation of the ways in which human systems place people at risk in relation to each other and to their environment – a relationship that can best be understood in terms of an individual's, a household's, a community's or a society's *vulnerability*. The determination of vulnerability is itself a 'complex characteristic produced by a combination of factors derived especially (but not entirely) from class, gender and ethnicity' (Cannon, 1994, pp14–19). Since the 1980s, the dominance of technical interventions focused on predicting hazards or modifying their impact have been increasingly challenged by this alternative approach, which seeks to combine the risk that people and communities are exposed to with their social, economic and cultural abilities to cope with the damages incurred.

Examining disasters through the lens of vulnerability confers real insights at a time when both the frequency and magnitude of such events are escalating. The total number of reported disasters rose from 368 in 1992 to 712 in 2001 – an increase of over 93 per cent in a decade. More telling, however, is the doubling of the number of people affected over the same period – rising from 78,292,000 in 1992 to 170,478,000 in 2001, though the figures had already peaked at a high of 344,873,000 in 1998 (IFRC, 2002, pp185–7).[2] Vulnerability is a much more precise measurement of exposure to risk from these disasters and a more accurate concept than poverty in understanding the processes and impacts of 'underdevelopment'. Not all poor people are vulnerable to disasters, nor are the poor all vulnerable in the same way, and some people who are not poor are also vulnerable. Vulnerability, as shown by Charlotte Benson (see Chapter 11), is very much a forward-looking concept and hence more appropriate for policy-making than poverty. By linking disasters to development by way of poverty, vulnerability shares many issues with parallel, and at times overlapping, discourses in social security and sustainable livelihoods. All three are primarily engaged with the means by which individuals and the communities they constitute attempt to cope with risk, uncertainty and insecurity in their lives.

The powerful insights that vulnerability has to offer have not gone unnoticed. It has increasingly found inclusion in mainstream development jargon to identify people particularly in need of interventions and has also been widely adopted and co-opted by the expert community who tend to appropriate the term without actualizing its potential. Vulnerability is often regarded as a property and not as an outcome of social relations. However, the measure of vulnerability should not be regarded as static. Rather, vulnerability expresses changing social and economic conditions in relation to the nature of hazard and is part of a dynamic, evolutionary and accretive process (Lewis, 1999, p14). It is also important to recognize that the same social and cultural processes that give rise to vulnerability are partly subordinate to, and enmeshed in, broader processes that are expressions of international and national political and economic considerations

(Cannon, 1994, p24). Moreover, the co-optation of vulnerability as a state of affairs that development attempts to address fails to reveal how development processes actually generate vulnerability. Disasters are not simply the product of one-off natural phenomena, as Allan Lavell shows in his discussion of the Lempa River Valley in El Salvador (see Chapter 5), but are equally the result of environmentally unsustainable development projects over time. This 'development aggression' – as the outcome of these policies is sometimes termed – was identified as the single largest category of disaster itself in the Philippines according to the tabulation created by the Citizens' Disaster Response Center in 2000 (CDRC, 2001, p2).

Many people, in fact, are rendered vulnerable by development, as Annelies Heijmans' discussion of the Philippine case shows (see Chapter 8). Of the 712 disasters recorded by the International Federation of the Red Cross and Red Crescent Societies for 2001, 396 (or 56 per cent) occurred in what are classified 'medium human development countries' (that is, countries undergoing development) compared to 135 (19 per cent) in 'low' and 181 (25 per cent) in 'high' human development countries (IFRC, 2002, p185). Even well-intentioned relief operations can have unforeseen consequences and create new vulnerabilities, as Zenaida Delica-Willison and Robin Willison so tragically depict in examples drawn from African experiences (see Chapter 10). Understanding vulnerability requires taking into account people's experiences and perceptions. The current preoccupation, in practice and literature, with 'local knowledge' stems from the realization that for many people this is the only remaining asset they possess and leaves them little option but to manifest their capacity through political organization and activism. Everyday risks, often brought about as a result of the development process, share with disasters a common origin that an appreciation of vulnerability more fully reveals. And vulnerability, as Delica-Willison and Willison remind us, is all about placing the people who experience disasters, whether sudden or slow-onset ones, at the centre of research and policy agendas. In their different ways, all the contributors to this volume explore how vulnerability provides a conceptual link in improving our understanding of the relationship between disasters, development and people (thus the title of this book). Building on the critical notions of vulnerability from the 1980s, this volume explores how these notions have evolved during the 1990s as the complexity of the relationship between peoples and their environments – mediated by processes of climate change – has become increasingly apparent. In some ways, too, the authors attempt to explore new territory by moving beyond the treatment of vulnerability simply in terms of power relations to take into account people's agency.

VULNERABILITY AND HISTORY

Vulnerability is not just concerned with the present or the future but is equally, and intimately, a product of the past. A proper appreciation of the construction of vulnerability is still often hampered by the lack of an adequate historical perspective from which to understand the contexts and roots of disaster causality (Oliver-

Smith, 1986, p18; Lees and Bates, 1984, p146).[3] It is not simply the occurrence, frequency and intensity of environmental events that are significant; equally, their sequence is of critical importance (Winterhaler, 1980). The insights that refer to the 1970 disaster in Peru as a '500-year earthquake' (Oliver-Smith, 1994) and the 1975 earthquake in Guatemala City as a 'classquake' (Susman et al, 1983, p277) have their origins in an appreciation of the structural role played by external and internal colonialism in determining those disasters. Similarly, the condition of dependency created by colonialism and cash-cropping, along with climate change, is credited by some French Marxist economic anthropologists as the principal cause of drought and famine in the Sahel (Copans, 1975; Meillassoux, 1974). Certain segments of a population are often situated in more perilous settings than others due to the historical consequences of political, economic and/or social processes. History reveals that vulnerability may be centuries in the making: societies and destructive agents are mutually constituted and embedded in natural and social systems as unfolding processes over time. As Anthony Oliver-Smith so eloquently states: 'a disaster is a historical event – and the aftermath of disaster is process coming to grips with history' (1979, p96). Asking why disasters happen is a political question; but understanding how they occur is a social and historical one. Above all, it is the present condition (the outcome of past factors) that transforms a hazard into a calamity and determines whether people have the resilience to withstand its effects or are rendered vulnerable to its consequences.

Oliver-Smith talks about the mutuality that exists between nature and culture and how disasters are uniquely situated in both the material and social worlds, and in some hybrid space created at their intersection. This hybridity, however, also creates a sense of historical complexity that is decisive in the ways in which disasters occur. As the modern world becomes increasingly complex, a more holistic appreciation of the interrelation between environment and society over time is required to adequately meet the challenges posed by the processes of globalization. It is this mutuality that lies at the heart of an understanding of vulnerability and its application in both revealing the multifaceted nature of disaster and its historical roots and political agenda. Moreover, it has important implications for the manner in which disasters are 'managed': attempts to control the environment need to be replaced by approaches that emphasize ways of dealing with unexpected events and that stress flexibility, adaptability, resilience and capacity.

VULNERABILITY AND PEOPLE

No map is complete without signs of habitation. Understanding vulnerability requires more than simply understanding societies' past and present relations with regard to disasters and development. Vulnerability is also about people, their perceptions and knowledge. People's ideas about risk and their practices in relation to disaster constitute the sextant and compass with which they measure and chart the landscape of vulnerability. Perception, of course, is not knowledge, nor does knowledge necessarily translate into action. Yet, perception is important in understanding why people exhibit certain behaviours. Dorothea Hilhorst (see Chapter 4) categorizes people's perceptions according to three different social domains of knowledge that correspond to science, governance or local custom. All three are equally valuable and necessary in understanding what makes people vulnerable and how they can set about reducing that condition. And knowledge is also intimately related to issues of power, both locally and globally.

Power, in the former instance, relates to what is sometimes loosely referred to as 'local knowledge' – that is, practice borne out of necessity and based on grassroots experience. It may take the form of firsthand knowledge of the environment and its limitations and dangers that may provide a practical guide to what steps should or should not be taken in the face of the onset of a sudden or slow-onset hazard. It may equally stem, however, from a memory pool, whether traditional or invented, added to and mutated over the generations and often manifest in the form of self-help practices and mutual assistance associations at the community level. When recognized by outside agents or given consideration by Western social science, it is usually referred to in terms of a people's capacity to deal with vulnerability and their resilience in withstanding disasters. However, it rarely empowers people in any context beyond the community level and is frequently contrasted disadvantageously with a more universal and implicitly Western knowledge system (see Bankoff in Chapter 2 and Hilhorst in Chapter 4).

Less than adequate attention, too, has been directed at considering the historical roots of the discursive framework within which vulnerable people are generally presented and the particular cultural values that determine the way in which certain regions or zones of the world are usually imagined. Greg Bankoff discusses how, by depicting large parts of the globe as hazard prone, Western countries have employed the concept of disasters as a means of maintaining their socio-economic and political ascendancy in world affairs (see Chapter 2). Which areas are vulnerable, and why the people living there are considered as such, often form part of a political discourse evoked by both international agencies and national governments to decide who should receive assistance and in what manner. The politicization of vulnerability and the power relations that underpin it are manifestly evident in Linda Stephen's case example of food security in Ethiopia during the 1990s (see Chapter 7) and in Roger Pulwarty, Kenneth Broad and Timothy Finan's discussion of drought forecasting in Brazil and Peru (see Chapter 6). Perception, knowledge and power provide both the means and the explanation that link people through vulnerability to disasters and development.

THE DYNAMICS OF VULNERABILITY

Vulnerability, then, is not a property of social groups or individuals, but is embedded in complex social relations and processes. This defies the possibility of reading vulnerability from a general chart, and points to the need for more local (or regional) and more dynamic analyses of what makes certain people vulnerable to risk and through what processes they become resilient. Students of vulnerability today face the challenge of having to establish these processes at different levels of analysis, while taking into account the different dimensions of complexity involved. Principal among these processes are the need for a transdisciplinary approach, the realization of vulnerability as a differentiating process and the consideration of temporal dimensions.

First, there is the need for a transdisciplinary approach where social and natural sciences join hands in developing explanatory and policy models for dealing with vulnerability. As Oliver-Smith (see Chapter 1) rightly points out, such blending of approaches is complicated by the character of disasters that constitute material events just as much as a multiplicity of interwoven social constructions. While this underscores the necessity of interdisciplinary work, it also tends to hinder academic communication and breeds paradigmatic confusion. Second is the realization that vulnerability constitutes a differentiating process. Vulnerability is the outcome of socio-economic processes, but it is not a translation of these processes. As Ben Wisner elaborates (see Chapter 13), this can lead to ever-more nuanced definitions of specific vulnerabilities among poor people, according to markers such as age, gender, sexual orientation, parenthood, location, origin and mobility. Finally, the fact that vulnerability lies at the intersection of different dimensions of time must be considered. Vulnerability changes through time in unpredictable ways and in varying directions: increasing, decreasing, accelerating, oscillating, concentrating or diffusing. It varies with the interplay of three different time frames: long-term, short-term and cyclical change (see Holling, 2002, p9). People's vulnerability builds up gradually over time but varies immensely through rapid variations in economic, environmental or social conditions, especially when these are compounded by cyclical or seasonal patterns of change.

Yet another complication in pinpointing vulnerability relates to its spatial and organizational qualities. As Allan Lavell points out (see Chapter 5), the space where risk originates and the areas where loss is suffered are often not the same. Thus, while vulnerability to floods might be localized, the causes are manifest more widely and include the operations of major infrastructure, mismanagement of the environment leading to deforestation, and human-induced erosion. In the case of disasters that are caused by human-induced climate change, the spatial and organizational dimension is even more complex. Risks and disasters do not often respect national boundaries and are dealt with by international, regional or global regulatory bodies whose governance patterns are far from coherent. Finally, there is also the complexity of scale. Linda Stephen (see Chapter 7) develops this dimension. She points out how regional analysis of vulnerability tends to homogenize vulnerability to the effect that localized problems do not command the solutions or resources that they should. In particular, this refers to the difficulty of aggregating vulnerability data. Charlotte Benson further elaborates this problem in Chapter 11, where she critically discusses the underlying presumptions and biases in international financial estimations of vulnerability and disaster damage. As the contributors to this volume argue, drawing out these different dimensions of complexity for specific situations – such as regions, floodplains, mountain ranges or cities – involves, first and foremost, the study of people. It is only through people that the dynamics of these complexities and their interrelations make sense and are realized in practice.

VULNERABILITY AND FUTURE DIRECTIONS

All of the contributors to this book warn against simplistic notions in understanding vulnerability; instead, they stress its dynamism and fluidity. They also do not offer any easy solutions to the problem of what makes people vulnerable and how that condition is related to disasters and development. But the chapters do not stop at merely mapping out the landscape of vulnerability. They are also concerned with trying to distinguish a way forward, however tentatively that may be expressed, and exploring some of the policy and governance implications of those paths. They are all agreed, too, that there is an urgent need to break with existing patterns that maintain or enhance vulnerability: the continued expansion of human activities in the world is straining both the limits of human adaptive capacities and the resilience of nature. Nevertheless, while the complex nature of vulnerability may defy any simple solutions, and the quest for alternatives is far from complete, four future directions can be discerned among the issues raised by the contributors.

Policy reviews

Most chapters in this book entail or advocate the need for critical policy reviews. Vulnerability is political in nature in two analytically different ways. First, the material production and distribution of vulnerability is the result of political processes. Omar Cardona emphasizes that vulnerability can be understood as a lack of development (see Chapter 3). Other chapters in this volume also illustrate how vulnerability is produced in the making and remaking of underdevelopment (see also Escobar, 1995), and hence admonish development policies for creating or neglecting the conditions that breed vulnerability. Second, and not unrelated to the previous point, the labelling of vulnerable people is also a political act. In particular, Bankoff unmasks vulnerability as a Western discourse (see Chapter 2). By applying the label of vulnerability, subjects are created that can be addressed by top-down disaster management practices. Hilhorst stresses how analytic models can never fully encompass the dynamics of vulnerability and are necessarily based on selections of reality (see Chapter 4). In practice, these selections are often made in pursuit of policy ambitions. Stephen demonstrates this in showing how information gathered for early famine warnings in Ethiopia was strongly influenced by politics, including policy-making, intra-institutional competition and power struggles within the system (see Chapter 7). What she and others warn against is taking existing policies and management styles for granted with regard to vulnerability, and how they need to be constantly scrutinized for their unintended adverse effects and their possible contribution to making local actors more vulnerable.

Refining measurement

As several chapters in this book argue, in order to advance vulnerability analysis, models and measurements need to be vastly improved and refined. Cardona (see Chapter 3) complains that vulnerability has been applied so broadly that it has become useless for careful description and only serves as a rhetorical indicator to highlight areas of greatest concern. He argues that instead of taking vulnerability as a characteristic of underdevelopment, the relationship between vulnerability and hazards needs to be clarified. Benson adds to this the need for indicators and clear measurements of vulnerability for policy and planning purposes (see Chapter 11). Her discussion of the pitfalls of current measurement practices, however, leaves one wondering if this is really feasible, as well as warning one to maintain a critical stance towards figures and indicators. Reviewing several decades of disaster management, Ian Davis (see Chapter 9) commends recent vulnerability models that are based on increasingly fine-tuned tools and instruments. Although the demand for such refined models, indicators and measurements is clear, one has to be wary about the management purposes that they are meant to serve. Are they indicative of a disaster management approach that wants to 'control' complexity by combating it with ever more intricate models and measurements? Or do they contribute to policy processes that abandon the notion of control, acknowledge the political nature of vulnerability analysis and management, and seek to find different modes of disaster management or even governance? Lavell makes a strong case for the latter (see Chapter 5) when he argues that the negotiated character of vulnerability and risk should be made more visible by replacing the seemingly objective notion of acceptable risk with such notions as accepted or unwillingly accepted risk. This takes us to the third direction for change that emerges among the chapters.

Different forms of management and governance

Disaster management is notorious for its predilection for hierarchical forms of governance through the militarization of planning and responses, often, in fact, delegating such activities to the armed forces (Hewitt, 1983a). This stringent management style has been extensively criticized since the 1980s with the advocacy of more participatory forms of management for vulnerability, disaster and development. Again, most chapters in this book address in one way or another these new forms of vulnerability and disaster governance. Several contributors discuss practices and discourses of participation over the last decades. They point out how participation can be abused or made ineffective in practice. Bankoff, in his contribution, cautions against naïve applications of participation, raising some questions about the nature of the discussions of local knowledge, resilience and coping practices. He claims that advocates of local knowledge often unwittingly subscribe to notions of Western superiority. Reading through the chapters of this book, one is also given a sense of the new forms of governance that emerge or can be imagined. Working with vulnerability requires a conceptual shift that is already beginning to find methodological application in community-based disaster management programmes and multi-stakeholder platforms. Such paradigms do more justice to the complex nature of vulnerability and step away from simplistic notions of intervention in which science is juxtaposed with a homogeneous local body of knowledge. At issue are the forms of governance in which stakeholders from the domains of science and governance, and local people themselves, are involved – formally or informally – in decision-making and the management of hazards and vulnerability. Lavell's chapter presents an elaborate discussion of one such multi-stakeholder arrangement in the Lower Lempa Valley of El Salvador. What emerges from this case, and other contributions to the book, is a plea for adaptive forms of management that include a multitude of stakeholders, are based on a negotiated value system, and combine different domains of knowledge and action (Warner et al, 2002).

Local resistance and social movements

Finally, various chapters in the book express the realization that real change is not going to happen without the consistent pressure of local resistance and social movements against policies and practices that make people more vulnerable. Heijmans documents how local residents in the Philippines have become convinced that disaster mainly stems from 'development aggression'. The only coping practice they deem effective in this situation is social protest (see Chapter 8). An important component of this protest is gender 'change', as Maureen Fordham forcefully argues, that cannot be realized without strong women's movements (see Chapter 12). In addition, Oliver-Smith points to new forms of transnational civil societies that emerge partly through people's displacements and relocations, and partly through communication technologies (see Chapter 1). As Hilhorst concludes in Chapter 4, complexity can be seen as an asset rather than a hindrance when enhancing new forms of governance. Since vulnerability spans and affects different domains of knowledge and action, alliances can be forged that join hands in demanding change.

The tripartite structure of the book, with its emphasis on concepts, cases and policy concerns, reflects the various factors that the authors feel are required for an understanding of both the scope and the import of vulnerability as a concept – namely, the need to combine theoretical considerations with a discussion of developmental issues and how the two relate to the people most affected on the ground. To a large extent, this is always going to be a rather arbitrary division as much of the conceptual strength of vulnerability resides in its ability to clearly identify the relationship between factors that create risk and expose people to disasters. Certainly, the participants who attended the special workshop on the subject sponsored by Disaster Studies of Wageningen University, and from whose papers the chapters in this volume are drawn, would not want to address the question in quite such a reductionist manner.[4] As all the contributors point out in their different ways, the creation of vulnerability is a matter of great complexity. One of the strengths of this volume, however, is the degree of synergy between its sections, which confers a sense of the dynamic interplay between the more theoretical and the more practical. While none of the individual contributors would profess to have any ready solutions, collectively they do offer an insight into the nature of how disasters, development and people are intimately bound to one another in the construction of vulnerability. As such, the authors consider that this volume offers some useful paths or guidelines for mapping vulnerability along which others can travel.

Chapter 1

Theorizing Vulnerability in a Globalized World: A Political Ecological Perspective[1]

Anthony Oliver-Smith

INTRODUCTION

Vulnerability is fundamentally a political ecological concept. Political ecology blends a focus on the relationship that people have with their environment with close attention to the political economic forces characteristic of the society in which they live that shape and condition that relationship. At least from the perspective of hazards and disasters, vulnerability is the conceptual nexus that links the relationship that people have with their environment to social forces and institutions and the cultural values that sustain or contest them. Thus, combining elements of environment, society and culture in various proportions, the concept of vulnerability provides a theoretical framework that encompasses the multidimensionality of disasters. Disasters as multidimensional, all-encompassing occurrences sweep across every aspect of human life, impacting environmental, social, economic, political and biological conditions. Vulnerability can become a key concept in translating that multidimensionality into the concrete circumstances of life that account for a disaster (Blaikie et al, 1994; Comfort et al, 1999; Cutter, 1996; Hewitt, 1983b).

Considering the multiple uses of the terms vulnerability and disaster, and the multidimensionality of their expression, today it has become ever more challenging to develop theory that has application or relevance to the ever expanding concerns they encompass. As the occurrence of interactions between natural and technological hazards increases, making disasters more complex, both the practical and the theoretical challenges in turn become more complex. The multidimensionality of disasters is at the crux of the problem. Disasters exist as complex material events and, at the same time, as a multiplicity of interwoven, often conflicting, social constructions. Both materially and socially constructed effects of disasters are channelled and distributed in the form of risk within society according to political, social and economic practices and institutions. This is the essence of vulnerability.

The concept of vulnerability expresses the multidimensionality of disasters by focusing attention on the totality of relationships in a given social situation which constitute a condition that, in combination with environmental forces, produces a disaster. In that sense, conceptually it contains a wealth of linkages and relationships to explore for advancing and testing new approaches to fundamental issues of disaster causation and management, as well as social and cultural theory.

Wilches-Chaux (1989) identifies 11 different forms of vulnerability, including natural, physical, economic, social, political, technical, ideological, cultural, educational, ecological and institutional vulnerability (pp20–41). The model Blaikie et al (1994) present subsumes these different forms of vulnerability into causal chains. Blaikie et al situate ideologies of political and economic systems as they affect the allocation and distribution of resources in a society in the chain of explanation. They identify these ideologies as among the root causes of disaster. However, the linkages of ideologies to specific dynamic processes and unsafe conditions, as they readily admit, become less definite and difficult to pinpoint in the causation of specific events (Blaikie et al, 1994, pp29–30). The socio-cultural forms through which these linkages (tying ideologies, dynamic processes and unsafe conditions into causal chains) are established and maintained remain to be explored in depth. These linkages become further complicated in the context of increasing globalization of natural and social systems and their mutual interaction.

Vulnerability is conceptually located at the intersection of nature and culture and demonstrates, often dramatically, the mutuality of each in the constitution of the other. Disasters seem to be especially apt as contexts and processes that illuminate these complex relationships, particularly in the way that they challenge societies materially, socially and ideologically.

But the concept of vulnerability needs to be unpacked – not necessarily in terms of its variety of forms, as Wilches-Chaux (1989) has already ably done, but rather in theoretical terms in order to disclose its broader ecological, political, economic and socio-cultural implications. Unpacking vulnerability requires that a number of crucial theoretical tasks are undertaken to disclose the deep socio-cultural and political economic underpinnings of events that are usually understood as environmental disturbances.

If, as vulnerability theorists maintain, disasters are more a product of a society than of a specific nature, certain questions concerning the conjuncture of culture, society and nature arise. In particular, vulnerability – while linking social and economic structures, cultural norms and values and environmental hazards (and disasters) in causative chains – does little to advance our understanding of the role of those forms, organizations and beliefs in producing that environment. In that context, I want to address three questions that are relevant to the eventual formulation of a coherent theoretical framework for disaster causation, which encompasses both natural and social scientific perspectives. The first question focuses on the general contributions of the cultural construction of nature to the social production of disaster. A second question addresses how the cultural, political and economic forms and conditions that characterize vulnerability are inscribed in an environment. And a third question explores the relationship between cultural interpretation and the material world of the risk, threat and impact of disasters. Finally, a fourth question, how do we theorize the linkages among the three issues, particularly in the context of current patterns of globalization?

Disasters come into existence in both the material and the social worlds and, perhaps, in some hybrid space between them. When we have a way of theorizing that hybridity, fundamental as it is to human life, disaster researchers will have achieved a great deal, not only in our own work, but for the social sciences and humanities, as well. It is to that theoretical challenge and to the implications of the concept of vulnerability for meeting that challenge that this chapter is directed. Disasters, like few other phenomena, offer a unique context in which to pursue such a theoretical breakthrough. The concept of vulnerability may prove to be key in this effort. In addition, it will be important to bear in mind the practical implications for disaster management that can be mined from these conclusions.

CONSTRUCTIONS OF NATURE AND SOCIETY

The first question we need to ask involves the analysis of the implications of the cultural construction of nature–society relations for the production of the conditions of vulnerability and the occurrence of disaster. The concept of vulnerability developed by Blaikie et al (1994), while linking cultural and social structures and the environment in causal chains, would assign this construction to the category of ideological root causes. The relationship between society and nature is one of the fundamental, if often unexamined, pillars of any ideological system. Anthropologists have documented that society–nature relationships are expressed cross-culturally in a wide variety of forms. Although it is hard to characterize local models of nature, it is clear that many are not based on the separation of the biophysical, human and supernatural worlds. Essentially, many cultures do not construct a clear dichotomy between nature and culture as Western societies do (Escobar, 2001, p151).

Due to its historical hegemony and continued expansion, the model of society–nature relations that are dominant in the West merits special attention. The dominant Western constructions of the relationship between human beings and nature place them in opposition to each other. It was not always so. Although the opposition can be traced to classical Greece and Rome, in the medieval period nature was commonly conceived of as in partnership with humanity (Harvey, 1996). Although the Christian church was elaborating theological doctrine that set humans, like God, in transcendence over nature as early as the third century, local people were oriented by persistent pagan forms of animism that held that trees, streams, hills and other natural formations had their own guardian spirit. Before one altered anything in nature, the place spirit had to be placated (White, 1967, p1205). Human beings were seen as part of nature, part of God's creation, whose goal was to know both nature and God (Williams, 1980, p73). Many of these essentially more integrative or conservationist attitudes are sustained in Western culture over time to the present. However, Christian abolition of pagan animism altered human environment relations from mutuality between sentient beings to indifference towards the impact of human action on nature, paving the way for a more utilitarian perspective towards the natural world that eventually became dominant in the 17th and 18th centuries (Redmond, 1999, p21).

The ideological return to society's opposition towards nature and, ultimately, to society's domination over, and control of, nature reflected changes that took place both in ideology and local practice that were more compatible with the emerging global economic system. Scientific and philosophical discourses of the time began to see humans as ontologically distinct from nature. Indeed, nature provided a contrasting category against which human identity could be defined as cultural rather than natural in the work of Hobbes, Locke and Rousseau (Horigan, 1988). It is important to note here that a category composed of human beings was characterized by its association with the phrase 'in a state of nature'. Now, as then, certain people are relegated into the 'nature' category as the need arises. The nature/culture dichotomy thus becomes important in terms of vulnerability in that those put into the nature category are frequently the most vulnerable to disasters such as epidemics, genocide and forced displacement.

Furthermore, in the West, this nature as object, detached and external to humanity was constructed as a fund of resources into which human beings, regardless of social context, have not only a right to dip, but a right to alter and otherwise dominate in any way they deem fit. Moreover, the enlightenment ideal of human emancipation and self-realization was closely linked to the idea of control and use of nature (Harvey, 1996, pp121–2). Locke, for example, asserted that God had given the Earth to humanity, and since each individual was the embodiment of all humanity, each had the right to the fruits of his or her own labour in the natural world (Locke, 1965, pp327–8). Locke's assertion is only one of the clearest expressions of the linkage between an unfettered exploitation of nature and the self-realization of human beings. Indeed, it was considered that one of the tyrannies from which humankind would be emancipated was that of nature. This doctrine of natural liberty would soon become the cornerstone of Adam Smith's thought linking self-realization and societal benefit to the specific institution of the market.

The belief in social domination further specified that nature would also benefit from human action. Western ideology frequently summons up images of nature replete with savagery and violence. Tennyson's vision of 'nature, red in tooth and claw' was particularly nourished by Christian theology that saw nature as fallen and evil. From the disaster perspective, such a vision also implicitly juxtaposed the violence and disorder of nature with the order of human culture and civilization. This has led to a construction of hazards as disorder – as interruptions or violations of order by a natural world that is at odds with the human world. Its bounty or its savagery notwithstanding, nature is seen as plastic – ultimately vulnerable or malleable to the purposes of humankind.

The 'plasticity myth', as Murphy has termed it, is based on the idea that the relationship between humans and their environments can be reconstructed at will by the application of human reason (Murphy, 1994). The application of human reason is believed to impose order on a disorderly, but essentially malleable, nature to bring it into line with human purposes. Following the separation of humans and nature, human rationality is not subject to the limitations of nature because the exercise of our rationality over nature has both subjugated nature and emancipated humans. Thus, humans are 'capable of manipulating, domesticating, remolding, reconstructing and harvesting nature' (Murphy, 1994, p5). The subjugation of disorderly nature to human rationality is epitomized in the regimentation imposed on forests by German forestry during the 18th century. The clearing of species of low commercial value, the weeding and the orderly files of trees all led to the reduction in diversity of insect, mammal and bird populations, rendering the forest more vulnerable to storm felling, fire and pests (Scott, 1998, p20). Nonetheless, in both the market and the command economy, the enthusiastic application of human rationality, motivated by individual or collective productionist goals, is the primary means by which nature will be dominated and humans emancipated.

Even much of the current criticism of ecological degradation is based on the conception that society must learn to care for and safeguard nature. Other critical perspectives construe the human world as out of step with some supposed natural order, with solutions lying in bringing the human world back to harmony with the natural order. While in some general fashion it is hard to disagree with the spirit of these positions, they are still flawed in that they are constructed from a fundamentally dualistic perspective in which society exists as a collection of human constructs and relations and the environment is 'out there' waiting to be acted upon in the cause of sustaining human life. The problem is presented in terms of human beings developing the proper ways to act upon, or to act in concert with, the environment. The relationship is still expressed in dualistic terms of two separate entities in some kind of interaction, whether healthy or distorted. The result of such a conceptualization in the case of disasters, among other issues, may be policies and practices that address symptoms, even effectively, but do little to address causes, condemning us to constantly repeat the exercise since both causes and symptoms evolve with our attempts to address them. Furthermore, the inherent dualism in such a construct leads down a blind alley, or perhaps down two never-to-converge parallel alleys, as far as advancing human ecological theory, much less disaster mitigation, goes.

THE HAZARDS OF DOMINATION

To explore how socially produced vulnerabilities are expressed environmentally, the links between the increase and expansion of disasters and the dominant ideas, institutions and practices of the contemporary world must be established. It is necessary to recall that, along with the detachment of nature and society achieved by 18th-century philosophy and political economy, the fortunes of humanity were specifically linked to a set of material practices largely structured by market exchange. The market – its ego-centred ideology rapidly transforming itself into the discipline of economics – thus became constructed as the principle vehicle for individual self-realization and societal welfare. Thus, individuals were now not only free but virtually obliged to better themselves with the means that God had provided – namely, the natural world. With the reduction of nature to the status of ensuring human well-being, and the rapid expansion of market exchange driven by a productionist ethic, both the ideological justification and the institutional means were available for a relatively unfettered mastery over, and unrestrained exploitation of, the natural world. Furthermore, the mutually reinforcing pairing of ideology and the science of economics produced a set of institutionalized material practices through which human beings engaged the object of their domination for their new purposes of-emancipation and self-realization.

The material practices were oriented by a form of value obtainable only through the institution of the market. The quest for this 'surplus value' is unending and limitless, both by definition and by necessity, due to competition in the market. Since the creation of value at least starts in the exploitation of nature, capitalist economies require the justification supplied by concepts of domination over nature and the plasticity of nature, enabling the elevation of exchange value over any values that might be ascribed to nature. The results of embracing the rationality of essentially short-term gain have been unprecedented extremes of material wealth and poverty, unprecedented levels of environmental destruction and the rapid amplification of socially constructed vulnerability.

However, socialist economies have also been deeply affected by both the myth of plasticity and the productionist ethos. Although the dialectical relationship between humans and nature was a central feature in Marx's thought, he was also deeply impressed with the powers of human rationality expressed in capitalism to mobilize the forces of production in order to bring nature under control (Murphy, 1994). Socialist economic policies, though hardly a faithful enactment of the little that Marx actually said about what socialism would be like, have participated in the attempt to subjugate nature through implementing collective labour with their own expressions of the goals of human emancipation and self-realization. In effect, both capitalist enterprise and the socialist state have proceeded under the premise that nature was plastic and capable of domination by human reason. In doing so, both have rendered pollution, depletion of resources and other forms of environmental change subordinate to production goals (Murphy, 1994, p5).

The material practices of engaging the natural world, and their supporting cultural value systems, are enacted and expressed in, and through, social relations that are themselves inscribed in the natural world. Material practices transform the natural world. They produce ecological conditions and environments that not only enable survival on a day-to-day basis, but are also conducive to continued social reproduction, therefore inscribing particular systems of social relations in the environment (Harvey, 1996, p183). This process of inscription will reflect materially those contradictions that are inherent in both the social system and the relationship between the society and the environment (Cronon, 1983, pp13–14 as cited in Harvey, 1996, p27). Thus, contradictions in the social relations are expressed through material practices as contradictions within the environment (Harvey, 1996, p185). Disasters are perhaps the most graphic expression of those contradictions.

Since human environments are socially constructed, the positive and negative effects of these practices are distributed as a reflection of systems of social relations. Therefore, the instantiation in nature of certain forms of social relations creates effects that are specific to them. Social, political and economic power relations are inscribed through material practices (construction, urban planning or transportation) in the modified and built environments, and one of the many ways in which they are refracted back into daily living is in the form of conditions of vulnerability. In general, environmental security is a premium enjoyed predominately by the beneficiaries of the social relations of production and distribution; but there is not always a perfect relationship. Cultural values can complicate the relationship, convincing the wealthy that it is safe to live on hurricane coasts and on fault lines with spectacular views. Even then, superior engineering, generally only available to the well-off, reduces that vulnerability significantly. Insurance also buffers loss and induces people to occupy risky places. But both the wealthy and the poor are implicated in the construction of vulnerability. The wealthy, through the excessive consumption of market-accessed resources such as secure land and water, withdraw large quantities of resources from use by the general population. Furthermore, the rich, in the continued reproduction of their wealth, are frequently involved in despoiling public goods such as the air and the oceans, thus engendering further vulnerabilities for the general population. The majority poor, through their desperate, and sometimes inappropriate, use or overuse of the few resources available to them, both degrade their environments and place themselves in harm's way, largely through the lack of reasonable alternatives for daily survival.

Many disasters today are also closely linked to current conditions of environmental degradation (Varley, 1994; Fernandez, 1996). Social and material practices combine with natural processes and evolve into novel forms of hazard – both potential and actual disasters. Environmental degradation, driven by the quest for profit or by people subsumed disadvantageously in that quest, is now linked with accentuated vulnerability to both natural and technological hazards around the world. Much has been written recently about inappropriate natural resource exploitation that has been rationalized by Western conceptions of the nature–society relationship. However, the actual nature of the problem is not always agreed upon. Green movement critics have castigated the Western economic system for its inability to come to terms with the natural limits of environments, continually exceeding them in a relentless pursuit of economic profit. Political ecologists and economic anthropologists contend that the human–environment relationship is generated in social relations through the double nexus of production. Environmental destruction, then, is ultimately not a question of exceeding natural limits, but is socially constructed – an outcome of systems of production and social exploitation (Collins, 1992, p179). This debate clearly has relevance for furthering our understanding of disasters. Disasters instruct us in environmental limits and inform us, as well, about specific instances of conditions of vulnerability that are created and imposed by human social arrangements, structured in, and by, the production process. The study of disasters and the concept of vulnerability can contribute to clarifying the question of environmental versus socially defined limits.

There are limits, although variably elastic ones, in natural systems (Holling, 1994); but they can only be experienced by human beings in social systems in culturally constructed relations with nature. Ecological crises and disasters (if not identical) are produced by the dialectical interaction of social and natural features. Socially constructed production systems that impoverish the essential and absolute level of resources that sustain an environment will create environmental crises and, perhaps, disasters, impacting upon human populations. However, when humans are present, an earthquake as a feature of nature may represent a universal and timeless challenge to their welfare, regardless of how that goal may be organized in a social system. It becomes a disaster only in the context of a specific society and a characteristic pattern of vulnerability. Environmental imitations or challenges are natural features, but are experienced only as the result of human social, economic, and cultural arrangements. The inadequacy of purely ecosystemic approaches for understanding such major environmental disasters such as the Sahelian drought of the 1970s convinced many of the necessity of analysing environmental problems in the framework of large-scale political and economic systems (Vayda and McKay, 1975; Lees and Bates, 1990, p264). A finer-grained understanding of both vulnerability and disasters must include the dialectical interaction of the agencies of nature and society, recognizing that the environment is a socially mediated force and context experienced by people both positively and negatively, just as society expresses itself environmentally.

CULTURAL CONSTRUCTIONS OF CALAMITY

In many ways, any theoretical inquiry into the nature of vulnerability and disasters inevitably involves the tangle of ontological and epistemological questions that deal with the nature of cultural versus material realities. In some sense, this brings us full circle back to the nature–culture debate. Some scholars in disaster research suggest that disasters are entirely socio-cultural constructions. That is, the presence or activation and impact of a hazard are not necessary for a disaster to take place. All that is necessary is the public perception that either a hazard threat exists or an impact has taken place for a disaster to have occurred. This position is based on the social psychological principle that if something is defined as real, whether it is a disaster or, for example, witchcraft, its 'reality' is established by its social consequences (Quarantelli, 1985, p48). This might be termed a form of ideological vulnerability.

The linkages between concrete material circumstances and ideological structures may be directly observed as people attempt to come to terms with disasters, to construct meanings and logics that enable them, as individuals or groups, to understand what has happened to them, and to develop strategies to gain some degree of control over what is transpiring. All of the social characteristics that significantly structure people in a society will play a role in the way that those meanings and explanations are constructed, giving broad disclosure to the internal variance of a community and underscoring the difficulty in determining an absolute or objective determination of the nature of the disaster. The perception of risk and vulnerability, and even impact, is clearly mediated through linguistic and cultural grids, accounting for great variability in assessments and understandings of disasters. There is no question that the variability of interpreting the threat or the impact of disaster is extremely wide and is largely a function of social and cultural characteristics of individuals, primarily related to degrees of integration and group power relations (Douglas and Wildavsky, 1982).

For a time, cultural theory sought to extend this entirely valid conclusion reached at one level of social analysis to empower the phenomenon of language at a much higher level. Language became not only a shaper of perception but – as the essential ground in which social life was embedded, ordering all social relations – acquired determinate power over all social life. Language in this approach became hegemonic and non-referential, to the extent that the world was reduced to a text from which only relativist understandings could be drawn (Palmer, 1990, p3). More recently, there has been significant criticism of pure, idealist semiotics (Gottdiener, 1995), and a call for greater attention to exo-semiotic domains such as economic development and political conflict (Biersack, 1999). This 'reformed' semiotics explores the sign within social context and links it to the historical, political and economic domains of the world.

Hazards and disasters, constituted as they are in the society–environment nexus, offer a context in which to pursue these more synthetic understandings of the mental and the material. On the one hand, to say that disasters are social constructs to be read does not detach them from the materiality of the world. Indeed, the physical reality of disaster explicitly challenges theoretical currents that hold that nature is a purely social construction at the ontological level (Woolgar, 1988; Tester, 1991, as cited in Gandy, 1996). The physical existence of disasters establishes an agency of nature that exists independently of human perception. However, human beings are deeply implicated in the construction of the forms and scale in which that agency expresses itself. The impact of these hazards, when they are perceived and cognized, rapidly confirms this agency, but just as rapidly constructs a social text around it that may either reduce or accentuate the impact. We may 'read' the disaster as a social text as it unfolds in its particular context; but the natural forces that created it, or even hazard processes set in motion by technology, exist as independent, exo-semiotic agents that operate according to physical processes that are, ultimately, prediscursive, 'outside' the text, no matter how many texts may be constructed about them after the fact.

Disasters, because of their material expression, their emergence from human–environment mutuality and their cultural construction, belong, perhaps, to that class of phenomena that are neither purely natural, nor cultural, and that are situated between the opposing epistemological points: between the natural and social sciences (Gandy, 1996, p35). They are, perhaps, less frozen into a dichotomy than expressive of the fact that the reality that emerges from the conjuncture of nature and culture is anthropocentric, and thus both material and symbolic. That reality is based on an ecology, as Biersack says, of 'incommensurabilities, predicated on the fact that human life lies "betwixt and between", neither nature nor culture, but precisely both' (Biersack, 1999, p11).

Thus, in a directly physical as well as symbolic sense, disasters emerge out of contradictions in the mutual construction of societies and environments. And, as Henri Lefebvre (1991) notes, 'space was *produced* before being *read*; nor was it produced in order to be read and grasped, but rather in order to be lived by people with bodies and lives' (cited in Harvey, 1996, p87). Undoubtedly, our cultural life is deeply implicated in the construction of our material life and vice versa; but life does have to be produced before it can be read. Our values and orientations regarding shelter, nourishment, security and relationships both reflect and affect the material practices and systems of social relations through which they are produced, and condition our relative vulnerability within an environment that is mutually constituted by nature and society. Cultural readings cannot eradicate (or create) the existence of a natural hazard. If a cultural reading apprehends the existence of a hazard, it may or may not alter practice in such a way as to reduce or exaggerate the risk of disaster. History is littered with the rubble of societies that could not culturally come to terms with either natural hazards or the forces they themselves partially instituted in their environments through the material practices of production. Natural hazards do not exist primarily as social constructions, nor are they in some essential fashion merely the product of social discourse, which – if we stop discussing them – will cease to exist (Radder, 1992). Hazards and disasters demonstrate the exo-semiotic agency of nature. However, on the other hand, this is a nature that is mutually implicated in its construction with society through material practices and ideological discourses.

DISASTERS AND THE RE-ENVISIONING OF NATURE AND CULTURE

In the introduction to this chapter, I posed three questions that explored the relationship between nature and society, the hazards of domination of nature and the cultural construction of disaster. A fourth question addressed the need to link these three issues. To do this, we must recognize that the concept of vulnerability, with its interpretation of social forces and environmental conditions, is part of a larger effort to rethink the relationships between society, economy and nature. As mentioned earlier, alternative views of the relationship between nature and culture have begun to discard the dualism in human–environment constructs in efforts to create more synthetic approaches that can address the mutuality of nature and culture (Biersack, 1999). Some prefer to develop approaches that stress a kind of critical realism, emphasizing a balance between the social construction of nature and the natural construction of the social and cultural (Stonich, 1993), while others pursue a more anti-essentialist stance, emphasizing the social construction of nature (Ingold, 1992; Escobar, 1999). These and other approaches are part of an effort to seek a fuller recognition of the role that humans have taken in shaping, as well as being shaped by, nature by conceptualizing a 'bio-cultural synthesis' (Goodman and Leatherman, 1998).

The integration of ecological and social theory, however, does not signify the 'culturizing' of the environment and nature to the point that they disappear in a haystack of discourses. Like those who 'ecologize' culture, those who would 'culturize' ecology risk obscuring as much as they illuminate, particularly in terms of the role of disasters in human–environment relations. Disaster researchers are all too well aware that the natural forces that are present in any environment have enormous power to affect society; but it is society that actualizes the potential of a hazard. This perspective strives to recognize that the objective circumstances in which disasters occur and the material needs that they evoke are socio-historical products.

Those features of an environment that represent dangers or losses, if they are perceived as such, are also organized into an environment in the human context, through choice. That is, some societies recognize risk, take steps to mitigate them or not, as the case may be, and choose to take their chances. However, despite being basic elements of nature, many hazards do not pose sufficiently frequent threats or do not produce consistently frequent disasters, so that they may not be perceived as dangerous and therefore are often not integrated within human environments. Paine (2002) notes that risks can be culturally (and perilously) negated if realistic assessments amount to overwhelming threat. However, even when they are perceived and even frequently experienced, some elements of a society still may not be in a position to take the necessary steps to mitigate or prevent the occurrence of a disaster. Such a situation is the essence of vulnerability.

Indeed, vulnerability is one concept that allows us to bring nature in from 'out there' and facilitates reconceptualizing nature–society relations from a duality to mutuality. As Ingold (1992) asserts, environmental history and human history are inseparable, each implicated in the evolutionary life of the other, and each contributing to the resilience and vulnerability of the other. Disasters are among those phenomena whose analysis requires that the barrier between human activity and eco-systemic activity collapses, transforming a relation of difference into a relation of mutuality between the natural and social worlds. The concept of vulnerability provides one means by which to accomplish this.

If disasters cannot be defined exclusively in natural or social science terms, they may, perhaps, be seen more productively as a mode of disclosure of how the interpenetration and mutuality of nature and society, with all the consistencies and contradictions, are worked out (Robben, 1989). However, for disasters to be employed in this fashion, environmental features and ecological processes – such as earthquakes, hurricanes, floods and soil erosion – must be recognized as features of social life. Furthermore, social and cultural elements, such as commodities, land markets and money flows, must be seen as functioning ecologically (Harvey, 1996, p392). In the most direct sense, this mutual construction of human beings and environments provides a theoretical basis for asserting that we construct our own disasters insofar as disasters occur in the environments that we produce.

GLOBALIZATION, VULNERABILITY AND DISASTERS

Current trends appear to indicate that, indeed, an increase in the impact and scope of hazards and resulting disasters, already complex and multidimensional, is taking place through the combined effects of economic, social, demographic, ideological and technological factors. These effects are, furthermore, compounding their complexity many times over. Recent research indicates that greater numbers of people are more vulnerable to natural hazards than ever before, due, in part, to increases in population, but, more so, to their location in dangerous areas (Quarantelli, 1985).

In addition, we have also created new forms of disaster agents. Technology always has the capacity to malfunction, often with catastrophic effects; but the second half of the 20th century has seen the creation of completely new technologies whose mere implementation, regardless of potential or actual malfunction, has had profound environmental and, in some cases, catastrophic impacts. Many of these new technologies, ranging from toxic chemicals to nuclear power plants, have added to the list of hazards that now threaten communities, not necessarily with material destruction, but with altogether novel biologically derived hazards, creating new forms of injury (Quarantelli, 1991). Human technological interventions, while in many cases providing more security, have, in other instances, added many degrees of complexity to existing natural threats. Furthermore, natural disasters have been shown to trigger subsequent technological disasters.

The implications of such a situation have been manifested in a decade of technological catastrophes, including *Exxon-Valdez*, Bhopal and Chernobyl, to name only a few of the most prominent. The decade has also seen the effects of dominating nature in the expanded vulnerability to the impacts of natural hazards such as hurricanes Hugo, Gilbert, David, Andrew and Mitch, the earthquakes of Northridge, Mexico City, Gujarat and Colombia, as well as the droughts of Ethiopia, Senegal and Sudan – to name only the headline events among the myriad small- and medium-sized disasters afflicting the disadvantaged around the world on a daily basis. However, blaming any particular approach to the economic problem for the construction of vulnerability requires ignoring the distressing environmental record of both capitalist and socialist economies, as well as the deeply implicated role many ancient societies played in their own destruction by supposedly natural calamities (Weiskel and Grey, 1992; Redmond, 1999; Tainter, 1988).

The general culpability of human systems notwithstanding, the world is now a global system organized for the vast majority by capitalist markets. There are serious implications resulting from global capitalist expansion and the globalization process, in general, for levels of vulnerability. Markets gained pre-eminence with the rise of private property and were developed to enable the exchange of private goods, but not to regulate the use of private goods. Nor do they work especially well with public goods and, in general, have not been successful in protecting the atmosphere, the seas, rivers or, in many cases, the land (Murphy, 1994, p58). The continued expansion of human activities in the world, now almost exclusively a function of the market, is straining both the limits of human adaptive capabilities and of the resilience of nature (Holling, 1994).

Despite the unquestionable effects of human environmental alterations, the question of whether the processes attributed to globalization represent simply the logical playing out of the basic characteristics of capitalism, or something fundamentally new that alters the structure of the world, will affect the way in which societies currently address their vulnerability to hazards. A related question addresses the issue of the point at which the pace and intensity of quantitative change actually trigger a qualitative change to a fundamentally new condition, obliging a reassessment of all previous adaptive forms.

To those who have been concerned with issues of imperialism, dependency, world systems, structural adjustment and migration for some time, globalization seems a bit like a new bottle for old wine. On the other hand, the issue that the rapid accumulation of quantitative changes has produced a qualitative leap into a fundamentally different state of affairs must be taken seriously, particularly for our purposes, as it affects people's vulnerability to hazards. Assessing the relevance of globalization processes to increases in vulnerability and disaster impact is both conceptually and empirically a challenging task. To address this task, a few basic questions need to be asked:

- How do we recognize the elements of globalization that are, in fact, new?
- What processes of globalization intensify or create vulnerabilities?
- To what degree does globalization create or exacerbate systemic as opposed to specific local vulnerabilities?
- What features of globalization contribute to the reduction of vulnerability?

While a fully adequate response to these questions is beyond the scope of this chapter, I will attempt to suggest some of the areas that such a task might address. Globalization is comprised of an array of mutually constitutive economic, social and ecological flows of energy, information, material and people, intersecting densely at various points and less densely at others around the globe. These flows or currents encircle or encompass the globe; but they are not distributed evenly, particularly in terms of outcomes or impacts. They disperse according to very specific logics (Hoogvelt, 1997). The availability of advanced communication and transportation technology permits these flows of energy, information, material and people to intersect or disperse at vastly reduced time scales and space scales, producing a set of impacts that are both the logical outcomes of longstanding systems and relationships and, in many ways, fundamentally new (Appadurai, 1996; Holling, 1994).

In terms of economics, one of the more balanced approaches to globalization is offered by the sociologist Ankie Hoogvelt (1997). According to Hoogvelt, the contemporary global market is differentiated from that of earlier moments in the 20th century by the adoption of geographically dispersed productions systems by multinational corporations that exert new forms of discipline on domestic supplies of capital, labour and resources. In effect, national boundaries no longer serve to protect workers, companies or the environment, particularly in the core nations, from the competitive discipline of the global market, thus undermining their capacities to address vulnerabilities to both natural and technological hazards. Furthermore, transnational corporations are now able to organize production through subcontracting or outsourcing of both services and assembly in ways that fundamentally alter the capital–labour relation. Outsourcing all of their production activities enables them to develop 'forms of production in which capital no longer needs to pay for the reproduction of labour power' (Hoogvelt, 1997, p113). Under these forms of production, wages are pressured downward and the benefits associated with permanent employment are eliminated, thus decreasing disposable resources and the resilience of individuals and households to deal with hazards.

Finally, today, in the global market financial transactions far exceed the growth of the fundamental economic forms of production and trade, now constituting at least double the value of global production (Hoogvelt, 1997, p128). More money is now being made by manipulating the circulation of currency, rather than commerce in actual goods. Furthermore, flows of capital and commodities are intensifying in core rather than peripheral nations, which are, in effect, not even worth exploiting in global financial operations (Hoogvelt, 1997, p86). In the words of John Reed, the chairman of Citicorps, one of the largest US banks:

> *There are 5 billion people living on Earth. Probably 800 million of them live in societies that are bankable and probably 4.2 billion (84 per cent) are living within societies that in some very fundamental way are not bankable* (Hoogvelt, 1997, p83).

'Bankable' here refers to the probability of offering a safe return on investment. If societies are not bankable, investments of capital for growth and development will be made elsewhere in the global economy. Economically speaking, the societies of the developing world, roughly 85 per cent of the world's population, are rendered essentially structurally irrelevant and unlikely to warrant the kind of investments that vulnerability reduction requires (Hoogvelt, 1997, p84).

Among the salient social and cultural dimensions of globalization are increases in international migration and the intensification of the electronic mass media as key forces in the weakening of national identities, ideologies and institutions, as well as the emergence of what Michael Kearney has called 'polybians' – that is, individuals whose identities are formed out of their experiences in life spaces that the economic, socio-cultural and environmental features of globalization both oblige and enable them to inhabit (Kearney, 1996, p141). These are the people who are found in what Appadurai (1996) has called the globalized 'ethnoscape' of tourists, immigrants, refugees, exiles and guest workers. While such dislocated peoples might find themselves in extremely vulnerable circumstances, the rapidly circulating information and images facilitated by new media technologies, however, can enable them to organize. A transnational civil society is emerging, in part, through communication technologies that are developing productive social and cultural responses to the forces that displace and relocate people repeatedly across boundaries and to productive regimes that, in some cases, put them at greater risk to technological and natural hazards (Fox and Brown, 1998; Oliver-Smith, 2001).

Economic and social flows or currents expressed in the ways that human actions have impacted upon the environment have set in motion a set of ecological flows, reducing the diversity of ecosystems. This reduction in diversity contributes, according to Murphy, 'to breaking down nature's bioregional equilibrium of local ecosystems, thereby turning the planet into one big ecosystem, with ecologically (and perhaps long-term economically) irrational results' (Murphy, 1994, p18). Recently, the work of Holling (1994) has focused upon the implications of the globalization of ecological processes. He points out that the continued expansion of human activities in the world is straining the limits of both human adaptability and the resilience of nature.

Currently, a spectrum of problems is emerging, caused by human effects on air, land and water that slowly gather momentum until they trigger rapid alterations in local systems that affect the health of populations, the renewability of resources and the well-being of communities.

Furthermore, the globalization of trade and migration has led to an increasing globalization of biophysical phenomena, intensifying linkages and creating problems across scales in space through reductions in heterogeneity. For example, cargo ships, taking on ballast water in one ecosystem and releasing it in another – thereby introducing alien species who often have no predators or reproductive controls – are contributing to the creation of one global ecosystem with ecologically unpredictable results (Murphy, 1994, p18). Temporal scales have also been altered. Natural systems possess a certain level of resilience, allowing for incomplete knowledge, mistakes and recovery. However, natural resilience also provides a certain lag time during which greed or ignorance can escape responsibility. Increased levels of exploitation are reducing the natural elasticity of systems, shortening the lag time for response before irreversible damage takes place (Holling, 1994, p93). There are serious implications for continuity, change and survival of both community and culture in situations in which resilience of both culture and environment is reduced by disasters.

Today, many local problems, including disasters, may have their root causes and triggering agents – and, possibly, their solutions – on the other side of the globe. Through this globalization process problems have become basically non-linear in causation and discontinuous in both space and time, rendering them inherently unpredictable and substantially less amenable to traditional methods of observing change and adaptation. Human-induced changes have moved both societies and natural systems into essentially unknown terrain, with evolutionary implications for both social and ecological elements. As has been argued, societies and nature have always been in a process of co-evolution in local, relatively discrete, contexts. Now, people, economies and nature are in a process of co-evolution on a global scale, each influencing the others in unfamiliar ways and at scales that challenge our traditional understandings of structure and organization, with serious implications for the adaptive capacities of people and societies (Holling, 1994, pp79–81).

These findings underscore the changing nature of disasters, emphasizing that the nature of disasters is rooted in the co-evolutionary relationship of human societies and natural systems. The challenge is to specify the linkages, now on regional and global scales, that generate destructive forces within our societies and environments. In a sense, disasters are now becoming sentinel events of processes that are intensifying on a planetary scale. The interpretation of the messages brought by these sentinels remains a crucial issue.

Chapter 2

The Historical Geography of Disaster: 'Vulnerability' and 'Local Knowledge' in Western Discourse[1]

Greg Bankoff

It is not always immediately evident that when an extreme event is called a disaster, both speaker and audience are invoking a particular set of culturally determined principles used to evaluate what is or has taken place. Quite apart from being a physical phenomenon, whether natural or human-induced, the criteria used in classifying a hazard as a disaster are also a form of discourse that implicitly make certain statements about what constitutes threat and normalcy. This lack of awareness is perhaps only more apparent when it comes to discussing people's resilience in the face of such occurrences, and their ability to deal with what has happened utilizing their own physical and psychological assets. These resources are usually referred to as a community's local knowledge and are expressed in terms of its coping practices. As in the case of disasters, though, they also form part of a parallel discursive framework that shares many of the norms and values inherent in that of disasters. Both are influential in determining the way in which such events are regarded and how they are embedded in the whole literature of disaster prevention, preparation and mitigation.

How to mitigate the effects of hazards and to relieve the consequences of disasters seem destined to be major issues of academic inquiry in the new century, if for no other reason than that they are inseparably linked to questions of environmental conservation, resource depletion and migration patterns in an increasingly globalized world. However, less than adequate attention has been directed towards considering the historical roots of the discursive framework within which hazard and coping with hazard are generally presented, and how that might reflect particular cultural values to do with the way in which certain regions or zones of the world are usually imagined.

RENDERING THE WORLD UNSAFE

The process by which large areas of the globe were rendered unsafe to Europeans predates the 19th century. David Arnold describes how the growth of a branch of Western medicine that specialized in the pathology of 'warm climates' was a conspicuous element in the process of European contact and colonization from the earliest years of overseas exploration. He refers to the manner in which Western medicine came to demarcate and define parts of the world where these 'warm climate' diseases were prevalent (Arnold, 1996, pp5–6). Here, it is the role of the medical practitioner as colonial rather than simply medical expert where his long-term attitudes to distinctive indigenous societies and distant geographical environments proved instrumental in how such lands came to be conceptualized.

The very earliest European accounts describe equatorial regions in almost ecstatic terms (Columbus, 1494); but more unfavourable attitudes that accorded value only in terms of human utility rapidly came to prevail as the 17th century unfolded (Thomas, 1983). Heat and humidity were increasingly held responsible for the high death rate of Europeans, especially when compounded by the usual intemperance, imprudence, diet and demeanour of the newly arrived. As the European encounter with these regions intensified during the 18th century, so, too, did the perception that disease, putrefaction and decay ran rampant in the moist warm air of the tropics (Anderson, 1996; Curtin, 1989, pp87–90). A more scientific reasoning prevailed by the 19th century. In particular, there was a growing conviction that geo-medical boundaries restricted races to what were termed their 'ancestral environments' (Harrison, 1996). Equatorial regions were now defined as ones unsuited to Europeans, whose physical constitutions evolved under different climatic conditions and were unable to tolerate the harmful effects of the ultraviolet rays of the sun (Anderson, 1995, p89).

Arnold argues that the growing body of scientific knowledge on these regions produced not only a literature on warm climates, but also invented a particular discourse that he refers to as *tropicality* (Arnold, 1996, pp7–10). One of the most distinctive characteristics of this discourse was the creation of a sense of otherness that Europeans attached to the tropical environment. More than simply denoting a physical space, the otherness conveyed by tropicality is as much a conceptual one: 'A Western way of defining something culturally and politically alien, as well as environmentally distinctive, from Europe and other parts of the temperate zone' (Arnold, 1996, p6). In this first rendition or account of the story, then, Western medicine effectively defines equatorial regions as a zone of danger in terms of disease and threat to life and health. The medical discoveries of the late 19th century, the elaboration of germ theory and the realization that bacteria and not climate were responsible for disease, credited Western medicine with the means of effecting a 'cure' to the regions' inherent dangers, an impression that persisted throughout most of the last century. However, the reappearance of antibiotic-resistant strains of known diseases at the end of the 20th century, the spread of the AIDS pandemic and the emergence of new viruses have seriously shaken the notion of Western security (Brookesmith, 1997). Once again, those regions of 'warm climates', from which these new threats are seen to emanate, are depicted as dangerous and life threatening to Western people, giving a new lease of life to the notion of tropicality in the 21st century (Altman, 1998).

While large parts of the globe were gradually rendered unsafe and then progressively rendered safer by the conceptual geography of Western medicine, the dominant position of disease as the primary delimiting condition was superseded, though never completely replaced, by a new discursive framework, especially in the years following World War II. Cold War rivalry between the US and the former Soviet Union for global dominance led Western theorists to formulate new kinds of policies designed to solve what were deemed the pressing social and economic conditions of Africa, Asia and Latin America. But in attempting to contain the spread of communism, Western investment and aid policies effectively divided the world conceptually in two between donor and recipient nations, between developed and developing countries. Development conveys just as much an essentializing sense of otherness as the concept of tropicality. It strips peoples of their own histories and then inserts them into preconceived typologies, 'which define *a priori* what they are, where they've been and where, with development as guide, they can go' (Crush, 1995, p9). Michael Watts argues that all models of development share common 'organicist notions of growth' and 'a close affinity with teleological views of history' (Watts, 1995, p47). Regardless of their ideological persuasion, development has always been conceived of in terms of a linear theory of progress from traditional to modern, from backward to advanced. Thus, modernization theory posits that undeveloped societies evolve into developed modern nations along paths chartered by the West – economically through a stages of growth model (Rostow, 1960) and politically from authoritarianism to democracy (Huntington, 1968). Though the subject of intense criticism – most notably by the dependency school of theorists who claim that an industrialized centre has been able to appropriate the surplus of a primary-producing periphery, leading to the latter's underdevelopment (Frank, 1967) – the basic assumptions about comparable stages of development to those of the West (no matter how much the route may have strayed from the path) are not questioned even by its fiercest detractors among the Marxist mode of production model. So, the 1960s and 1970s witnessed a shift away from market- to state-centred alternatives where civil society was accorded only a minor role; the 1980s were associated with the so-called neo-liberal revolution of the new right and a period of retrenchment, austerity and protectionism; while the hallmark of the 1990s was rising levels of global indebtedness and the harsh application of structural adjustment programmes. Whatever the differences in emphasis or rhetoric, the dominant discourse remains the same. As Jan Pieterse observes, the debates are all about alternative developments and never about alternatives to development (Pieterse, 1998, pp364–8).

In particular, Arturo Escobar charts the manner in which this *developmentalism* became the predominant discourse after 1945, and how the twin goals of material prosperity and economic progress were universally embraced and unquestioningly pursued by those in power in Western nations (Escobar, 1995a, p5). As a consequence, many societies began to be regarded in terms of development and to imagine themselves as underdeveloped, a state viewed as synonymous with poverty and backwardness. As with tropicality, the discourse of development creates much the same 'imaginative geography' between Western Europe and North America and especially the equatorial regions (Escobar, 1995a, p213). Terms such as First World/Third World, North/South and centre/periphery all draw attention to the manifest disparities in material gratification between the two, while simultaneously reducing the latter to a homogenized, culturally undifferentiated mass of humanity variously associated with powerlessness, passivity, ignorance, hunger, illiteracy, neediness, oppression and inertia (Escobar, 1995a, p9).

Escobar has been criticized for losing sight of the larger issues, especially the manner in which the development discourse fits into the political context of power relations that it helps to produce and maintain, and from which it benefits. He has also been criticized for the fact that what is at stake here is not just text but a reality that has political, social and economic actuality for peoples (Little and Painter, 1995, p605). The question of development's origins has also been raised; it has a much longer pedigree than 1945. Notions of development are clearly discernible in 19th-century concepts of colonial 'trusteeship' that became central to the historical project of European empire, as well as in the measures taken to alleviate the worst of the social disorders consequent upon rapid urbanization, poverty and unemployment (Cowen and Shenton, 1995, pp28–9). In particular, Friedrich List argues in his *National System of Political Economy* (first published in 1856) that nations had unequal productive potentials and that it would be a fatal mistake for the 'savage states' of the 'torrid zones' if they attempted to become manufacturing countries. Instead, they should continue to exchange agricultural produce for the manufactured goods of the more temperate zones (List, 1856, pp75, 112). Michael Watts also reiterates this link between colonialism and development; but he argues that it has even older roots and was the product (and the problem) of the 18th-century normative ideas inherent in modernity. More importantly, he maintains that development was not simply imposed by the West upon the rest but required the existence of a non-developed world for its own production (Watts, 1995, pp48–9).[2]

However, these important qualifications do not significantly detract from the singular manner in which development as a discursive historical framework both creates and maintains a domain of thought and action that has conceptually invented the developing world. Moreover, it has achieved this feat not only in the Western imagination but also among those in the region itself who find it difficult to think of themselves in any other way than through such signifiers as overpopulation, famine, poverty, illiteracy and the like (Escobar, 1995b, p214). In this second re-telling of the story, the concepts inherent in development similarly cast most of the non-Western world as a dangerous zone. But it is one where poverty and all of its manifestations have largely replaced disease as the principal threat to Western well-being. How to achieve development and overcome underdevelopment become the fundamental problem facing most societies, and one where the 'cure' is envisaged in terms of modernization through the agency of Western investment and aid.

NATURAL DISASTERS AND VULNERABILITY

While 'natural disasters' are not a conceptual term in the same way that tropicality and development are, the regions in which such phenomena most frequently occur have been incorporated within a discourse about hazard that sets them apart from other implicitly 'safer' areas. During the 1990s, 96 per cent and 99 per cent respectively of the annual average number of persons killed or affected by hazards resided outside of the US/Canada and Europe (Walker and Walter, 2000, pp173–5).[3] However, the disproportionate incidence of disasters in the non-Western world is not simply a question of geography. It is also a matter of demographic differences, exacerbated in more recent centuries by the unequal terms of international trade, that renders the inhabitants of less developed countries more likely to die from hazard than those in more developed ones. No single term has yet emerged that defines the areas where disasters are more commonplace; but whatever the denomination, there is always an implicit understanding that the place in question is somewhere else, somewhere where 'they' as opposed to 'we' live, and denotes a land and climate that have been endowed with dangerous and life-threatening qualities.

During the 1970s, some social scientists began to question whether the greater incidence of disasters was due to a rising number of purely natural physical phenomena. Attributing disasters to natural forces, representing them as a departure from a state of normalcy to which a society returns to on recovery, denies the wider historical and social dimensions of hazard and focuses attention largely on technocratic solutions. Kenneth Hewitt argues that this technocratic approach has permitted hazard to be treated as a specialized problem for the advanced research of scientists, engineers and bureaucrats, and therefore to be appropriated within a discourse of expertise that quarantines disaster in thought as well as in practice (Hewitt, 1995, pp118–21; 1983a, pp9–12). It also renders culpable such populations (or at least their governments) who are blamed for their lack of adequate knowledge and preparedness (Varley, 1994, p3). The idea that disasters are simply unavoidable extreme physical events that require purely technocratic solutions remained the dominant paradigm within the United Nations (UN) and multilateral funding agencies such as the World Bank (Varley, 1994, p3). Far from being discredited, such views have proven surprisingly enduring and are still very influential at the highest levels of national and international decision-making, such as in the UN resolution declaring the 1990s the 'International Decade for Natural Disaster Reduction' (Hewitt, 1995, p118; Cannon, 1994, pp16–7; Lehat, 1990, p1).

More recently, critics of this technocratic approach have come to increasingly view a society's exposure to hazards in terms of its *vulnerability*. Proponents of vulnerability as a conceptual explanation take the position that while hazards may be natural, disasters are generally not. As a concept, vulnerability appears to offer a radical critique to the prevailing technocratic paradigm by placing the emphasis, instead, on what renders communities unsafe, a condition that depends primarily upon a society's social order and the relative position of advantage or disadvantage that a particular group occupies within it (Hewitt, 1997, p141). Vulnerable populations are those at risk, not simply because they are exposed to hazard, but as a result of a marginality that makes of their life a 'permanent emergency'. This marginality, in turn, is determined by the combination of a set of variables such as class, gender, age, ethnicity and disability (Wisner, 1993, pp131–3) that affects people's *entitlement* and *empowerment,* or their command over basic necessities and rights (Hewitt, 1997, pp143–51; Watts, 1993, pp118–20).[4] The observation that human and material losses from natural hazards increased over the 20th century without conclusive evidence of a corresponding rise in the frequency of such events, and that the same phenomena caused vastly different outcomes both between and even within societies, has drawn attention to the need to view disasters from a wider societal and historical perspective (Hewitt, 1997, p11). Vulnerable populations are created by particular social systems in which the state apportions risk unevenly among its citizens and in which society places differing demands on the physical environment (Cannon, 1994, p14; Wisner, 1993, p134; Hewitt, 1995, p119; Hewitt, 1983b). Central to this perspective is the notion that history prefigures disasters, and that populations are rendered powerless by particular social orders that, in turn, are often modified by the experience to make some people even more vulnerable in the future (Blaikie et al, 1994, pp5–6).

The discourse of vulnerability, however, no less than the previous concepts of tropicality or development, also classifies certain regions or areas of the globe as more dangerous than others. It is still a paradigm for framing the world in such a way that it effectively divides it into two, between a zone where disasters occur regularly and one where they occur infrequently (Hewitt, 1995, pp121–2). Moreover, the former has much the same geography as that of the tropics or the developing world. But the dangerous condition is now identified as one of hazard rather than disease or poverty.[5] Nor are the latter dangers superseded but neatly subsumed with the current paradigmatic as sub-variants. In this contemporary rendition of the story, then, large parts of world are denominated as particularly vulnerable to the effects of hazard. While this discourse is primarily about the condition or state of people, the disproportionate concentration of those vulnerable in certain regions endows their environments with qualities that make them dangerous places – threats to both Western health and assets. But the popularization of this representation through the mass media also generates a moral obligation on behalf of Western nations to employ their good offices to 'save' these vulnerable populations from themselves and to render the regions they inhabit safer for investment and tourism. As in both previous cases, the 'cure' for this menacing condition is primarily conceived of in terms of the transfer and application of Western expertise, though this time in the form of meteorological and seismic prediction, preventative and preparedness systems, and building and safety codes.

COPING WITH DISASTERS

There exists, then, a Western discourse about the historical and cultural geography of disaster that creates a particular depiction of large parts of the world as dangerous places whose menace often serves as justification for intervention in the affairs of those regions. But disaster in its various manifestations is not the only attribute associated with the non-Western world. There exists an apparent counter discourse that appears to modify the imputation of danger through casting these same areas as the abode of traditional cultures whose inhabitants are the repositories of arcane knowledge. Nor has the nature of this knowledge remained invariable. It, too, has been subjected to a series of parallel historical transformations that mirror changes in the mode and intensity of Western contacts with these regions. Yet, ultimately, it also reinforces the hegemonic discourse that denigrates non-Western peoples and marginalizes their cultural products.

The Western encounter with traditional knowledge had its roots in 'New World' contacts with peoples in the Americas and the Pacific; but its popularization in the personification of the 'noble savage' was the product of the 18th-century Enlightenment. The noble savage was a figure characterized as living in a state of nature, a childlike innocent uncorrupted by 'modern' vices and therefore possessing more nearly the God-given attributes with which humanity had initially been endowed. Certainly, there had to be stages in evolutionary development, ones that loosely equated with states of savagery, barbarism and civilization; but there was also an acknowledgement of the 'psychic unity of mankind' that credited all people with the same reason regardless of race. The noble savage was evidence of the origins of the 'civilized man', the study of whom gave birth to the comparative method in the social sciences: knowledge of the Western past was to be found among the non-Western peoples of the present who represented different stages in the progress of humanity (Stocking, 1968, pp114–5). Once more the world had been conceptually split in two, but on this occasion between 'civilized' and the 'non-civilized'.

By the mid-19th century, however, perceptions of traditional cultures had become more avowedly racist in tone. The perceived failure of many indigenous peoples to adapt to Western civilization led to a reappraisal of their origins. While Social Darwinism still considered evolution a process by which a multiplicity of human groups developed along lines that moved, in general, towards Western social and cultural forms, some people had evidently diverged, regressed or even died out along the way (Stocking, 1968, p119). Henrika Kuklick argues that there is a link between respect for non-Western cultures and the degree of colonial control: the altered relationship between colonialist and indigenous peoples supported the notion of racial hierarchy and, ultimately, of white, even Aryan supremacy (Kuklick, 1991, p284). It also gave rise to the doctrine of polygenism: the physical and mental differences separating peoples were too great to be accommodated within one species and, consequently, there must have been more than a single origin to humanity (Stocking, 1968, pp38–41). In other words, the savage was no longer necessarily noble but often ignoble, the prey to primitive instincts, unbridled sexuality and without even the capacity for abstract thought. In the process, the notion of 'primitive societies' in contrast to 'advanced societies' was born and came to dominate perceptions of the non-Western world throughout the heyday of high colonialism and its aftermath (Kuper, 1988, pp1–14).

Local knowledge may not be a conceptual term in quite the same manner as the noble savage or primitive society; but it nonetheless has been incorporated within a Western discourse that identifies certain areas of the globe whose cultural forms are not given equal weight to those in the West. Of course, the old idiom of savages and primitives has been discarded, though their ghosts perhaps linger on in the choice of which societies are selected to be the subjects of ethnographic study. Instead, the proper subject matter by the last decades of the 20th century was to call the peoples and cultures of the non-Western world collectively as the 'Other'. According to Edward Said, Western imperialism continues to exert a disproportionate cultural authority in the world through the persistence, in one guise or another, of the impressive ideological formulations that underpinned its political domination during the 19th and early 20th centuries. Former cultural attitudes that underlay the division between colonizer and colonized are replicated in the distinction between developed and developing worlds or in what is understood by the North–South relationship. Africa, Asia and Latin America are just as dominated and dependent today as when ruled directly by European powers, and their cultures are just as underrated and undervalued by the use of terms that impose limitations to their knowledge (Said, 1994, pp1–15, 31–2).

Just as people's exposure to hazard is currently assessed in light of their vulnerability, so too is their resilience to deal with its effects increasingly regarded as dependent upon what is termed their capacity. The strategies adopted by communities to reduce the impact of hazard or avoid the occurrence of disaster are known as coping practices and are based on the assumption that what has happened in the past is likely to repeat itself following a familiar pattern. People's earlier actions, therefore, constitute a reasonable framework for guidance during similar events. Variously referred to in the literature more generally as informal security systems or local capacities, and more specifically as indigenous technical knowledge or appropriate technology, such coping practices include the specialized knowledge of skilled individuals, as well as the social knowledge held by communities at large. They comprise an enormous variety of recourses, including land utilization and conservation strategies, crop husbandry and diversification practices, exploitation of geographical complementarities in ecosystems, symbiotic exchanges between communities, the development of patronage relationships, migration, the redeployment of household labour and complex dietary adjustments (Drèze and Sen, 1989, pp71–5). There are even ways of defining coping practices in terms of cognitive or behavioural responses, designed to reduce or eliminate psychological distress or stressful situations (Fleishman, 1984).

The current emphasis on the importance of this local knowledge in disaster situations is a belated recognition that non-Western peoples have historically developed sophisticated strategies and complex institutions to reduce the constant insecurity of their lives. The previous assumption that a community's own methods of coping with risk were too primitive, too inefficient or too ineffective to deal with the situation only reinforced belief in the power of the technical fix: the ability of external expertise to correctly identify the problems and introduce the appropriate solutions. The respect now accorded to coping practices forms part of a wider attempt to broaden local participation in the entire development process through bottom-up planning and to empower local people through encouraging community participation. Local knowledge is seen as the key to success as it is the only resource controlled by the most vulnerable, is already present at a potential disaster site, and in many cases constitutes a viable operational strategy. All that is required is to find the proper balance between the need for external assistance and the capacity of local people to deal with the situation.

Yet, the concept of local knowledge is still part of a Western discourse that marginalizes and demeans its possessors in much the same way as it did that of the noble savage or the primitive society. Coping practices may now be considered factors of some significance in dealing with a local disaster situation; but their applicability is largely confined to a particular type of event in a defined geographical locale. Unlike external (Western) expertise based on the scientific perspective, local knowledge, by definition, lacks universal application and only has relevance to a specific environment. Moreover, the emphasis on encouraging autarky – ensuring that local communities' ability to cope is not weakened or even undermined by outside knowledge (Anderson and Woodrow, 1989, pp81–2) and external assistance – often smacks of paternalism. In an age when the globalization of economic, social and political affairs is recognized as humanity's future for better or worse, all societies are considered as increasingly interdependent. Nor is this dependency necessarily seen as a weakness. Endeavouring to establish 'reservations of pre-modern knowledge' uncannily echoes the beliefs of Enlightenment thinkers and casts coping mechanisms in much the same light as the primitive society of the Social Darwinists. The rhetoric of coping practices may not be so obviously paternal; but it nonetheless forms part of what Eric Dudley refers to as a discourse of 'righteous imperialism' (Dudley, 1993, pp150–3).

NATURAL DISASTERS AS CULTURAL DISCOURSE

The Western discourse on disasters forms part of a much wider historical and cultural geography of risk that creates and maintains a particular depiction of large parts of the world (mainly non-Western countries) as dangerous places. More importantly, it also serves as justification for Western interference and intervention in the affairs of those regions. Of course, the matter has never been presented quite so crudely. Between the 17th and early 20th centuries, this discourse was about 'tropicality' and 'non-civilized societies', and Western intervention was known as 'colonialism'. Post-1945, it was mainly about 'development' and 'primitive societies', and Western intervention was known as 'aid'. During the 1990s, it was about 'vulnerability' and 'local capacity', and Western intervention continues to be known as 'relief'. Nor have the conditions that supposedly rendered these areas of the globe unsafe remained constant over time: the historical nature of danger has transformed once primarily disease-ridden regions into poverty-stricken ones, and now depicts them as disaster prone. Moreover, hazard also provides a useful rationale for blaming the poverty and inequitable distribution of material goods of the people living in these regions squarely on nature. It has permitted Western governments to talk and act in international fora as if disaster, poverty, disease and the environment are entirely unrelated issues that need not be tackled concurrently but that can be dealt with separately,

Table 2.1 *Dangerous regions as Western discourse*

Concept	Period (century)	Condition	Cure/Technology
Tropicality	17th–19th/early 20th	Disease	Western medicine
Development	Post-World War II	Poverty	Western investment/aid
Natural disasters	Late 20th to present	Hazard	Western science

according to a timetable largely determined by themselves. The formulation of vulnerability – or the recognition of local knowledge as a less environmentally deterministic measure of gauging the relative exposure of any particular population to hazard – does not significantly alter this perspective.

In the scientific viewpoint, the West has discovered a language of knowledge that helps to maintain its influence and power over other societies and their resources. Depicting this encounter as a clash between two opposing epistemologies does not really reflect the complex and often contradictory nature of knowledge systems and their incorporation and redefinition of outside notions (Hilhorst, 2000, p86). Nonetheless, natural disasters form part of a wider historical discourse about imperialism, dominance and hegemony through which the West has been able to exert its ascendancy over most peoples and regions of the globe. But the debate is not confined simply to geographies, however loosely defined; it is also a struggle over minds and, as such, has withstood the post-World War dismantling of extensive colonial structures (Said, 1994, pp1–15, 31–2). Nor is this Western cultural hegemony restricted to the literary imagination or the social sciences. It can be equally discerned in the theoretical underpinnings of the natural sciences that renders unsafe those same regions of the globe as *marginal environments* through a discourse of disease, poverty and hazard.

While the technological and scientific discourse of natural disasters creates marginal environments, the discourse of vulnerability appears to construct a less culturally specific geography of disaster. Yet, in the final analysis, the two are variants of the same hegemonic discourse that identifies one and the same parts of the globe as the abode of mainly disadvantaged people who dwell in poorly governed and environmentally degraded spaces. As Hewitt notes, the concept of vulnerability still encourages a sense of societies and peoples as weak, passive and pathetic, and he compares it to other 'social pathologies like, or derived from, poverty, underdevelopment and overpopulation' (Hewitt, 1997, p167). The problem, from the perspective of those outside of the dominant culture, lies in the inability of Western theory to offer an uncompromisingly radical critique of itself 'so long as its ideological parameters are the same as those of that very culture' (Guha, 1997, p11). While Ranajit Guha refers specifically to the inability of liberal historiography to escape from the limits of its own capitalist 'conceptual universe', much the same observation holds true of all epistemology. Commitment to a particular knowledge system not only predetermines the kinds of generalizations made about the subject under investigation, but also provides the means for changing the world in such a way that it maintains the interests of those who benefit most from its present condition (Guha, 1997, pp6–7). The discourses of vulnerability and local knowledge, no less and no more than that of tropicality and development, or the noble savage and primitive society, belong to a knowledge system formed from within a dominant Western consciousness. These discourses, therefore, inevitably reflect the values and principles of that culture.

CONCLUSION

Unmasking vulnerability's pedigree, however, is more than simply a matter of academic interest; it also has real practical value in terms of disaster preparedness and relief. If, as Said suggests, Western knowledge is fundamentally a means of perpetuating its cultural hegemony over the world, and if also, as Guha and others believe, no Western critique can ever fully escape the dominant consciousness within which it was formulated, then much greater attention needs to be paid to non-Western knowledge and local environmental management practices (Forsyth, 1996; Agrawal, 1995). There is a need to recognize that the ways in which we shape knowledge about the social and natural worlds largely reflects the ways in which we have shaped knowledge into disciplines; to transform the former we need to move beyond the constraints of the latter (Ferguson, 1997, p170). As Hewitt notes, a better appreciation of what constitutes a disaster and a more effective means of responding to it will require the positive and intelligent participation of those most at risk or otherwise directly involved (Hewitt, 1997, p358).

At the same time, though, there is a need to recognize that the 'space' currently accorded to local knowledge as an alternate discourse is not really so much as a critique as a reinforcement of the dominant paradigm. The capacity and resilience of non-Western people are too often incorporated into discursive practice in such a manner as to contrast the local to the universal, to the detriment of the former. But arguing that there has not really been a paradigm shift in the discourse of disaster is not meant to negate the significant conceptual advances made in the elaboration of vulnerability and the acknowledgement of local knowledge. Disasters do not occur out of context but are embedded in the political structures, economic systems and social orders of the societies in which they take place. Above all, they are historical events that occur as part of a sequence or process that determines a particular person or community's vulnerability. And, as such, people who live with the daily threat of disaster have frequently evolved certain strategies or coping practices for dealing with their effects that are quite successful.[6] Recognizing their utility can only be constructive, and empowering local people to take an active role in their management has to be beneficial. To achieve this end, however, requires according a greater equality both literally and discursively to local practice and knowledge as other types of specialist learning.

Questions of what constitutes a hegemonic discourse and whether it is Western take on an added dimension in the globalizing context of the 21st century. As recent theorists herald the emergence of a new world geography with open and expanding frontiers, without territorial centres of power and with no fixed boundaries (Hardt and Negri, 2001), it is useful to ponder on what its nature might mean to those same billions of people who have historically been depicted as living in the disease-ridden, poverty-stricken and hazard-prone regions of the globe. According to James Ferguson, this new order is constructing a spatialized inequality that not only continues to marginalize and exclude large numbers of people, but is actually robbing them of even the promise of development. What he labels 'abjection' is not mere exclusion from a status that these people have never experienced as an expulsion from that status by the formation of new or newly impermeable boundaries. The resultant state of 'disconnectedness' is as much the product of specific structures and processes that disadvantage most of humanity as is the condition of underdevelopment (Ferguson, 1999, p237–8).

Vulnerability and local knowledge as concepts have proven useful as a means of assessing disasters within their socio-economic, political and environmental context that was previously sorely lacking. These concepts have also certainly provided a helpful guide in formulating approaches and policies in hazard preparedness and relief provision. Yet, despite the undoubted conceptual and methodological advances that they represent on previous thinking, their utility and practical application are still hampered by a one-dimensional construction of the processes that transform a hazard into a disaster. In particular, the relationship between a society's vulnerability and the adaptation of its culture in terms of local knowledge and coping practices has not been adequately explained. Reducing vulnerability to a formulaic expression that explains the way in which human activities affect the physical environment and increase the impact of hazard, if not the frequency of disaster, is to ignore the important role that hazard has historically played in actually shaping human culture (Bankoff, 2002). Populations at risk are populations actively engaged in making themselves more vulnerable and who live in communities whose cultures are themselves increasingly shaped by hazard. As Susan Stonich so aptly phrases it, there is a need to 'balance the cultural/social construction of nature with a meaningful consideration (and analysis) of the natural construction of the cultural and social' (Stonich, 1999, p24). There is clearly a need for a much fuller understanding of what is meant by disaster and why and for whom it is so termed. Only then can those concerned be better prepared to minimize the devastation that it causes, as well as perhaps profit from the opportunities that it creates.

Chapter 3

The Need for Rethinking the Concepts of Vulnerability and Risk from a Holistic Perspective: A Necessary Review and Criticism for Effective Risk Management

Omar D Cardona

THE IMPORTANCE OF TERMINOLOGY

Human development has led humankind to idealise the elements of its own habitat and environment and the possibilities of interaction between them. In spite of confused perceptions about the notion of *vulnerability*, this expression has helped clarify the concepts of *risk* and *disaster*. For a long time, these two concepts were associated with a single cause: an inevitable and uncontrollable physical phenomenon. However, the conceptual framework of vulnerability was borne out of human experience under situations in which it was often very difficult to differentiate normal day-to-day life from disaster. Vulnerability may be defined as an internal risk factor of the subject or system that is exposed to a hazard and corresponds to its intrinsic predisposition to be affected, or to be susceptible to damage. In other words, vulnerability represents the physical, economic, political or social susceptibility or predisposition of a community to damage in the case of a destabilizing phenomenon of natural or anthropogenic origin. A series of extreme, and often permanent, conditions exist that make livelihood activities extremely fragile for certain social groups. The existence of these conditions depends on the level of development attained, as well as the success of development planning. In this context, development has begun to be understood as a process that involves harmony between humankind and the environment, and vulnerability in social groups could thus be understood as the reduced capacity to 'adapt to', or adjust to, a determined set of environmental circumstances.

In general, the concept of 'hazard' is now used to refer to a latent danger or an external risk factor of a system or exposed subject. This can be expressed in mathematical form as the probability of the occurrence of an event of certain intensity in a specific site and during a determined period of exposure. On the other hand, vulnerability may be understood, in general terms, as an internal risk factor that is mathematically expressed as the feasibility that the exposed subject or system may be affected by the phenomenon that characterizes the hazard. Thus, risk is the potential loss to the exposed subject or system, resulting from the convolution of hazard and vulnerability. In this sense, risk may be expressed in a mathematical form as the probability of surpassing a determined level of economic, social or environmental consequence at a certain site and during a certain period of time.

'Convolution' is a mathematical concept that refers to concomitance and mutual conditioning – in this case, of hazard and vulnerability. Stated differently, one cannot be vulnerable if one is not threatened, and one cannot be threatened if one is not exposed and vulnerable. Hazard and vulnerability are mutually conditioning situations and neither can exist on its own. They are defined conceptually in an independent manner for methodological reasons and for a better comprehension of risk. Thus, when one or two of the components of risk are altered, we are meddling with risk itself. However, due to the fact that in many cases it is not possible to modify the hazard in order to reduce the risk, there is nothing left to do except modify the conditions of vulnerability of the exposed elements. This is precisely why emphasis is frequently made in technical literature to the study of vulnerability and to vulnerability reduction as a measure of prevention/mitigation. However, what is really intended by this is risk reduction.

The term vulnerability has been employed by a large number of authors to refer directly to risk, and they have even used it to refer to disadvantaged conditions, especially in the social sciences. For instance, people refer to vulnerable groups when they talk about the elderly, children or women. However, as discussed above, it is important to ask ourselves: vulnerable to what? In other words, hazard and vulnerability are concomitant and lead to risk. If there is no hazard, it is not feasible to be vulnerable when seen from the perspective of the potential damage or loss due to the occurrence of an event. In the same way, there is not a situation of hazard for an element or system if it is not 'exposed' or vulnerable to the potential phenomenon. Even though this might seem to be an unnecessary subtlety, it is important to make this distinction since, at a certain moment in time, the adjective vulnerable might be employed in different ways in problem areas other than the field of disasters (for example, in psychology or public health). A population might be vulnerable to hurricanes, for example, but not to earthquakes or floods. Regarding the use of the term vulnerability, Timmerman had, in the early 1980s, already indicated that 'vulnerability is a term of such broad use as to be almost useless for careful description at the present, except as a rhetorical indicator of areas of greatest concern' (Timmerman, 1981). In his work on vulnerability and resilience, he concludes with a touch of irony that real vulnerability may lie in the inadequacy of our models of the social systems and concepts (Liverman, 1990).

In the same way that for many years the term risk was used to refer to what is today called hazard, currently, many references are made to the word vulnerability as if it were the same thing as risk. It is important to emphasize that these are two different concepts and their definition obeys a methodological approach that facilitates the understanding and possibility of risk reduction or mitigation.

APPROACHES AND EVOLUTION OF THE CONCEPTS

Despite efforts by social scientists undertaken since the mid-20th century (Kates, 1971; White, 1942; White, 1973; Quarantelli, 1988), the issue of risk assessment seen from the perspective of disaster risk has only been treated fairly recently. Its systematic conception and analysis was practically assumed by experts and specialists in the natural sciences with studies regarding geodynamic, hydrometeorological and technological phenomena such as earthquakes, volcanic eruptions, mudslides, flooding and industrial accidents. In other words, emphasis was centred on the knowledge of hazards due to the existing investigative and academic biases and the efforts of those who first reflected on these issues (Cutter, 1994). It is important to point out here that this emphasis still remains, particularly in the more developed countries, where due to their technological advances people try to find out in greater detail the generating phenomena of the threats. This was an evident trend during the first years of the 'International Decade for Natural Disaster Reduction' declared by the United Nations (UN) General Assembly.

If what is intended is the estimation of risk, there is no doubt whatsoever that the study and evaluation of hazard is a very important step; however, in order to fulfil such an aim it is equally important to study and analyse vulnerability. Due to this fact, various specialists subsequently promoted the study of physical vulnerability, which was essentially related to the degree of exposure and the fragility of the exposed elements to the action of the phenomena. This last aspect allowed amplification of the work in a more multidisciplinary environment due to the need for involving other professionals such as architects, engineers, economists and planners. In time, they found the consideration of hazard and vulnerability to be fundamental when considering standards for constructing buildings and infrastructure (Starr, 1969).

However, the approach is still very technocratic in the sense that it remains focused upon the hazard and not upon the conditions that favour the occurrence of crisis: ie global vulnerability – a far more holistic and encompassing concept that goes well beyond issues of physical vulnerability. In developing countries, social, economic, cultural and educational aspects are, in most cases, the cause of the potential physical damage (physical vulnerability). In contrast to the hazard, global vulnerability is a condition that is constructed, accumulates and remains over time and is closely linked to social aspects and to the level of development of the communities.

During the past few years, a considerable number of social scientists have renewed their interest in the field, inspired by the yawning gaps that impede a fuller understanding of the problems of risk and the possibilities for real mitigation. The reading of vulnerability and risk by, amongst others, geophysicists, hydrologists, engineers and planners can be a very different reading or representation than that of people in general, the exposed communities and the government authorities in charge of the decision-making on reduction or mitigation of risk. That is the reason why it is currently accepted that there is a need for greater study of individual and collective perceptions of risk and for research on the cultural characteristics, development and organization of the corporations that favour or impede prevention and mitigation. These are aspects of fundamental importance in order to find efficient and effective means to achieve a reduction in the impact of disasters worldwide (Maskrey, 1994).

Collective risk management involves three public policies: risk identification (which includes individual perceptions, social representations and objective assessment); risk reduction (or prevention/mitigation); and disaster management (response and recovery). Risk transfer (insurance and financial protection) comprises an additional policy measure, but significant advances have only been achieved in developed contexts. These different public policies imply different disciplinary approaches, values, interests and strategies and involve different social actors. In terms of most scientific disciplines, risk is a transversal notion, and without such an interdisciplinary and comprehensive approach an effective risk management is not possible. Risk reduction implies intervention in causal factors. Disaster management signifies an efficient response to risk that has materialized as disaster. Risk transfer implies risk evaluation of economic units. Therefore, risk management inevitably requires an understanding of how risk is perceived by society, how it is represented (models, maps and indicators) and how it is measured or dimensioned.

Approach of the natural sciences

The term 'natural disaster' is very frequently used to refer to the occurrence of severe natural phenomena. Events such as earthquakes, tsunamis, volcanic eruptions, hurricanes, floods and landslides have been considered direct synonyms for disaster. Unfortunately, this interpretation has favoured the belief that there is nothing to be done when faced with disasters since, given the fact that they are natural phenomena, they are considered unavoidable. Such an interpretation has also led to disasters being considered events of destiny or bad luck, or even the result of supernatural or divine causes. This could help to explain why certain communities adopt a religious viewpoint, consider that these events are unalterable and become resigned to their occurrence. In the same way, vestiges of this kind of interpretation can be found in the legislation of certain countries, where the definition of fortuitous acts or of *force majeure* are still used along with statements such as 'the occurrence of a natural disaster, such as an earthquake or a volcanic eruption'. In some cases, these kinds of events are specifially called 'acts of God', as in certain legislation of Anglo-Saxon origin.

Nevertheless, the interest of, for example, geophysicists, seismologists, meteorologists and geologists has favoured the idea that disasters are a topic exclusively associated with the physical phenomena that generate these natural events. Unfortunately, people often view disasters as if they were the same things as the phenomena that caused them. Despite technological advancement and geophysical, hydrological and meteorological instrumentation, it is generally not possible to predict with certainty and precision the occurrence of a future event. As a result, some people justify themselves to those affected by suggesting that the damages and losses are unavoidable. Some political authorities have also appealed to the religious fanaticism of certain communities in order to evade responsibilities for things that have happened due to negligence or omission.

During the second half of the 20th century, a period during which technological advancement contributed enormously to our knowledge of natural phenomena, it was commonplace to define risk as being the estimation of the possible occurrence of a phenomenon. It is still commonplace to find this idea held by specialists who study phenomena such as earthquakes, landslides and storms. During the 1970s and even the 1980s, if someone wished to refer to the probability of an earthquake they would have indicated that they were estimating the seismic risk. Towards the end of the 1980s and, particularly, in the 1990s the concepts of seismic hazard and threat became more common in referring to what was previously referred to as seismic risk.

The UN General Assembly's declaration of the 1990s as the International Decade for Natural Disaster Reduction (IDNDR) was, without doubt, directly influenced by the natural sciences. In fact, the need for this initiative was first promoted by Frank Press, a well-known specialist on Earth sciences, in the US to specifically foster the study of natural hazards.

Approach of the applied sciences

The works of Whitman in Boston and of Fournier d'Albe in Europe during the 1970s provided new elements for estimating the damages and losses due to earthquakes. Emphasis on the notion that damage was not only due to the severity of the natural phenomenon, but also to the fragility or the vulnerability of the exposed elements allowed a more complete understanding of risk and disaster.

On the other hand, the 'risk-transfer' approach employed by insurers (understood as feasible loss and the analysis of the probability of failure or 'accident' in mechanical and industrial systems) favoured the consolidation of a new paradigm with regard to risk analysis, security and trustworthiness of systems. From that moment onwards, particular attention was given to the physical properties of the system that could suffer damage or harm due to an external phenomenon or to the idea that a failure or disaster could occur in the system due to the technology employed. This could be called the epoch of the contribution of engineering and the hard sciences. The concept of vulnerability was explicitly promoted and, when seen from the perspective of disaster studies using probabilistic modelling methods, was clearly established in the report published on *Natural Disasters and Vulnerability Analysis* by the UN Disaster Relief Organisation (UNDRO) in 1980.

Disciplines such as geography, physical, urban or territorial planning, economics and environmental management helped to strengthen what can be called an applied science approach to disasters. 'Maps' became more and more common due to the ever greater participation of geologists, geotechnical engineers, hydrologists and other experts. They were able to contribute raw materials for the adequate identification of the danger or hazard zones, according to the area of influence of the natural phenomena. Computer science tools such as geographic information systems (GIS) have facilitated this type of identification and analysis.

The employment of damage matrixes, loss functions or curves, or fragility or vulnerability indices, relate the intensity of a phenomenon to the degree of harm or damage allowed for the correct estimation of scenarios of potential loss in case of future earthquakes in urban centres. This type of study or analysis of risk has increasingly been presented with the intention of contributing data on threats or risks to physical and territorial planning specialists as an ingredient within the decision-making process.

In this approach, risk calculations are the result of the probabilistic modelling of the hazard and of the estimation of the damage that a system might suffer. They may also be obtained in an analytical way or based upon empirical data. This latter possibility favours the fact that the results may be easily translated into potential losses and may then be applicable, under the concept of the cost-benefit ratio, in the elaboration of building codes, security standards, urban planning and investment projects. The possibility of quantifying and obtaining the results in terms of probability has made it easier to consolidate this approach given the idea that risk is an objective variable and may be quantified.

Approach of the social sciences

From the point of view of the social sciences, the issue of disasters gained special attention during the mid-20th century as a result of the interest of the US government in the behaviour of the population in case of war (Quarantelli, 1988). From that time on, we can state that a social theory of disasters came to life. This approach primarily involves a series of studies about reactions and individual and collective perceptions (Drabek, 1986; Mileti, 1996). Generally speaking, in the US, the social science studies and research have focused upon the reaction or response of the population in case of emergencies and not strictly on the study of risk. However, the contributions from geography and the so-called 'ecologist school' from the 1930s onwards (Burton et al, 1978) could also be considered conceptions from a social–environmental perspective (Mileti, 1999) that subsequently inspired the approach of the applied sciences. Its emphasis on the fact that disaster is not a synonym of natural events, and on the need to consider the capacity for adaptation or adjustment of a community when faced with natural or technological events, was, without any doubt, the springboard for the concept of vulnerability.

On the other hand, since the 1980s and especially the 1990s, in Europe and certain developing countries both in Latin America and Asia, social science researchers have critically discussed natural and applied science approaches. In general, their approach suggests that vulnerability has a social character and is not limited to the potential physical damage or to demographic determinants. It is stated that a disaster only takes place when the losses exceed the capacity of the population to support or resist them, or when the effects impede easy recovery. In other words, vulnerability cannot be defined or measured without reference to the capacity of a population to absorb, respond and recover from the impact of the event (Westgate and O'Keefe, 1976). This being so, for experts in political sciences, similar losses or physical effects in two separate countries with different economic and institutional conditions could have very different implications. An event that could pass relatively unperceived in a large country could mean a catastrophe in a small one due to the differential absorption capacity of each of the involved social systems. Similar damages in rich and poor countries have more serious social implications in the poor countries, where the underprivileged social groups are usually the most affected (Wijkman and Timberlake, 1984). According to Susman et al (1983), vulnerability 'is the degree to which the different social classes are differentially at risk.' This definition determines that vulnerability is established according to the political, social and economic conditions of the population. From this perspective, what is suggested is that the conditions that characterize underdevelopment (social discrimination, expropriation, exploitation, political oppression and other processes that are related to colonialism and capitalism) have made the poorest communities more vulnerable to disasters and have forced the deterioration and degradation of their own environments.

Other researchers, such as the members of the Red de Estudios Sociales en Prevención de Desastres en América Latina (La RED) – the Latin American Network for the Social Study of Disaster Prevention in Latin America – have stated that vulnerability is socially constructed and is the result of economic, social and political processes. Therefore, it is necessary to model vulnerability, taking into account – as well as the physical aspects – social factors, such as the fragility of the family and the collective economy; the absence of basic social utilities; lack of access to property and credit; the presence of ethnic and political discrimination; polluted air and water resources; high rates of illiteracy; and the absence of educational opportunities (Wilches-Chaux, 1989; Lavell, 1992; Cardona, 1993; Maskrey, 1994; Lavell, 1996; Cardona, 1996; Mansilla, 1996).

Some conceptual models of risk have appeared from the environment of political economics or neo-Marxism, such as the model of 'pressure and release' in which risk is presented as the result of the concurrence of some conditions of vulnerability and of some possible threats. Vulnerability is obtained from identifying the social pressures and relations from a global to local level. At the global level, they are called 'root causes', such as social, political and economic structures. At an intermediate level, they are called 'dynamic pressures', such as population growth, urban development and population pressures, environmental degradation, and the absence of ethics. At a local level, they are called 'unsafe conditions', such as social fragility, potential harm or poverty. In this approach, prevention/mitigation should be conceived of as 'releasing' the pressure of what is global over what is local. Risk reduction signifies intervention at each level: conditions of insecurity, the dynamic pressures and the root causes (Wisner, 1993; Cannon, 1994; Blaikie et al, 1994).

There are other conceptual models, such as the 'access model', which suggests that risk is generated as a result of the difficulties that some social groups or families have in accessing certain resources over time. What is intended here is to identify the limitations and facilities through which accumulation is achieved or the decrease in important capacities when faced with potential disaster (Sen, 1981; Chambers, 1989; Winchester, 1992). Its argument is based upon the fact that when faced with an equivalent hazard, or when facing the same potential for physical damage, the risk could be different depending upon the capacity of each family to absorb the impact. Even though there are some who consider vulnerability a synonym of poverty, those who propound the model indicate that poverty refers to basic unsatisfied needs and restrictions of access to resources, while vulnerability refers to the lack of capacity to protect oneself and to survive a calamity (Chambers, 1989). These definitions have led to some researchers affirming a link between the concepts of tropicality, development and vulnerability that, since the 17th century onwards, have made up part of the same essentializing and generalizing cultural Western discourse that denigrates large regions of the world as disease ridden, poverty stricken and disaster prone (Bankoff, 2001).

On the other hand, seen from the social communication viewpoint and considering the processes by which concepts are built individually or collectively, other authors have assumed a critical position with reference to the different approaches considered earlier. They point out in general that there exists a positivist and performative character in the different conceptual proposals, given that concepts come from experts and are subject to subjective alteration or manipulation. Most of these ideas emphasize the active role that people play in constructing the meaning of risk and in the role of communications as a transforming power, indicating the need to consider risk as an appreciation, a reading or an 'imaginary' and not as something external to people. It is important to consider perceptions, attitudes and motivations both individually and collectively (individual perception and social representation) that can vary notoriously from one context to another (Johnson and Covello, 1987; Slovic, 1992; Luhmann, 1993; Maskrey, 1994; Adams, 1995; Muñoz-Carmona, 1997).

Critique of the different approaches

Although researchers and professionals working in the disaster area may believe they use the same basic notions, serious differences do exist that impede successful, efficient and effective risk reduction. The conceptual frameworks used to understand and interpret risk, and the terminologies associated with these, have not only varied over time, but also differ according to the disciplinary perspective considered. This means that in spite of disciplinary refinement, there is in reality no single conception that unifies the different approximations or that is able to bring these together in a consistent and coherent manner.

Scientists of the social sciences such as historians, psychologists and sociologists generally draw on 'constructivist' postulates, considering risk as a 'social construction.' From this perspective, the risk notion is only graspable taking into account the analysis of the individual and collective perceptions, representations and interactions of social actors. However, engineers, geologists, geographers, economists and epidemiologists generally adopt an approach that some describe as 'realist', based on the hypothesis that risk can be quantified or objectively assessed.

The natural sciences approach is a partial view, which has undoubtedly contributed to knowledge of one main component of risk: the hazard. However, the fact that there are still those who confuse the term risk with the concept of hazard could have unsuspected implications. An intense natural event is not a synonym of disaster and, thus, risk cannot be understood exclusively as the possible occurrence of a natural phenomenon. This type of conception has contributed to a misreading or false 'imaginary' of risk and disaster by the exposed population and has been used to good effect by political authorities in order to avoid blame.

The applied sciences approach differs in the fact that it focuses on the effects of the event and not on the event itself. There is no doubt whatsoever that the contribution of engineering signified a big change of paradigm with respect to risk. Even though a more complete concept of risk is provided, the approach remains partial and physicalist. Curiously, the methodologies developed through this approach offer real risk estimations only in a few cases. In practice, the evaluation of physical vulnerability tends to replace risk evaluation, which is left as a secondary result. Through these techniques risk is evaluated in economic terms by estimating the replacement cost of the deteriorated part of the affected vulnerable system. It is even common to find, in the case of future loss scenarios, that the term 'social impact' is used for the global estimation of possible victims – the dead and injured. Despite the fact that this information is important, for instance, for emergency preparedness and response, it confirms the restricted vision and the ignorance of the applied sciences of social, cultural, economic and political aspects that should also be reflected in the estimation of vulnerability and risk.

It is important to point out here that, except in the case of seismic hazard, the vulnerability referred to in this approach has been considered a constant when used for territorial planning purposes. This is based on the notion that the elements are located in hazard-exposed zones and are thus vulnerable. Many hazard maps have unconsciously been converted into and referred to as risk maps, and vulnerability is taken as a constant and a mere function of the exposition of the elements. Thus, this approach continues to give over-riding importance to the hazard and the hazard is considered the sole origin or the cause of disaster. The use of GIS has favoured this situation and the view or vision of risk as something 'photographic' or 'frozen'. In the best of cases, the concept of vulnerability proposed by this approach is merely used to explain the physical damage and other direct side effects. Risk, seen from this perspective, has been interpreted in general as a potential loss taking into account possible damage. The disaster – by this I mean the materialization of the risk – has been restricted to a consideration of the loss represented in physical damage and not, in a more comprehensive fashion, as the overall consequences for the society. Without doubt, this approach has been fostered by the notion that vulnerability can be conceived of as simply 'exposure' or, in the best of cases, as the susceptibility to suffer damage, without really making any reference to resilience; ie the capacity for recovery or to absorb the impact.

With respect to the so-called social sciences approach, its contribution to the idea of disaster risk was initially timid, due to a marked tendency to study the behaviour of the population in situations of emergency or imminent emergency. In the developed world, social scientists have given considerable emphasis to the study of risk from the day-to-day life and human security perspectives when faced with technological incidents that could affect their health. In few cases has there been any special interest in the perception of individuals or groups regarding possible disasters but less interest shown when it comes to the implications or to the processes that contribute to the social gestation of disaster. However, some works have placed emphasis on the capacity of communities to absorb the impact or to recover after an event. These works have the merit of questioning the restricted vision of the applied sciences, indicating that vulnerability should not be considered exclusively as the possibility of physical damage.

Only towards the end of the 20th century did we increasingly witness how more theoretical constructions concerning the topic of risk consider vulnerability and hazard, at times, as the result of social, economic and political processes. Even though this approach might seem to be the more complete, on many occasions it has given such emphasis to the understanding and social modelling of vulnerability that it has omitted or ignored the fact that environmental impact and potential physical damage are very important when it comes to conceiving of and estimating risk. Vulnerability has tended to be interpreted as a 'characteristic' or as a 'feature' and not as a condition, circumstance or predisposition to damage, where this is the result of susceptibility, frailties and a lack of resilience or capacity for recovery. Some authors forget completely about the hazard and the fact that this has to be taken into account in order to establish the notion of risk. It is also important to remember that the concept of risk is linked to decision-making. This means that it has to be dimensioned in time in order to make decisions on the feasibility and convenience of doing something or not. But without hazard, without a trigger phenomenon and with vulnerability interpreted as if it were a characteristic, even though the vulnerability is ongoing, there would not be any risk and, thus, no possible future disaster. In this respect, it is not so strange that some authors have the tendency or the bias to consider poverty as equivalent to vulnerability and not as a factor of vulnerability. Some researchers who try to distance themselves from this conception say that poverty is determined by historical processes that restrict the access of people to resources, and that vulnerability is determined by historical processes that restrict people from having the resources to face hazards or to access protection or security. However, in general terms, very few works refer to risk, or they limit themselves to treating vulnerability as its synonym. Perhaps the greatest defect concerns their argument that risk is something subjective, so no attempt is made to estimate it or the techniques that are used for estimation are not very consistent.

It is necessary to transcend the epistemological antagonism between 'objectivist/positivist' and 'subjectivist/constructivist' paradigms and rely as much upon qualitative as quantitative methods for risk conceptualization and estimation. Action and decision, implicit in the definition of risk, require the establishment of relationships between subjective risk perception and the scientific need for objective measurement. Due to scientific specialization, various notions of risk exist. For this reason it has been argued that a common language and a comprehensive or holistic theory of risk is needed. The clash between 'positivism' and 'constructivism' is inoperative. Conceptually and pragmatically, it is very unsatisfactory to maintain a situation where each individual subjectively defines and assumes risk in their own particular way. This position is totally inoperable when intervention in risk becomes indispensable from the public policy perspective.

From the above, we can deduce that despite the noteworthy advances that have been made in the understanding of risk, there is still a very high level of fragmentation that does not permit a consistent and coherent theory of disasters. It is obvious that there will always be different approaches and it would be wrong to think otherwise. However, part of the difficulty of reaching an effective management of risk has been the absence of a comprehensive conception of it in order to facilitate its assessment and reduction from a multidisciplinary perspective (Cardona, 1999; 2001). In other words, the absence of a holistic theory of risk, from the point of view of disasters, has favoured, or at least partially contributed to, the problem growing faster than solutions can be found.

VULNERABILITY AND RISK FROM A HOLISTIC PERSPECTIVE

Risk is a complex and, at the same time, curious concept. It represents something unreal, related to random chance and possibility, with something that still has not happened. It is imaginary, difficult to grasp and can never exist in the present, only in the future. If there is certainty, there is no risk. Risk is something in the mind, closely related to personal or collective psychology. But a sense of objectivity is invoked in its analysis (Elms, 1992). Moreover, it is a complex concept and a composite idea. In a more integral notion of risk, three separate aspects converge: eventuality, consequence and context. These three aspects all contribute to attempts to estimate or grade risk. In risk analysis, the context (management capacity and related actors) determines the limits, the reasons, the purpose and the interactions to be considered. Analysis has to be congruent with the context and this must be taken into account when analysing the sum of the contributing factors. If not, the analysis would be totally irrelevant or useless.

Throughout history, risk analysis has been used informally in innumerable human situations. Risk has always been associated with decision-making, with something that has to be done, with the execution of an action that ranges from the most trivial to that of utmost important. The notion of risk has a performative character. In all cases, an action must be chosen. The results of these actions are in the future and this implies uncertainty. The selection of a future line of action infers possible adversity or contingency. For this reason, the risk should be evaluated so that a decision can be taken. Discussions regarding risk touch the roots of society, knowledge, values, emotions and even its very existence. These include reflections on the nature of scientific knowledge, an understanding of the visions that substantiate different arguments, and rationalization as to what we fear and as to the ways we should act. The ability to comprehend, despite uncertainties in the analysis of physical systems, is one of the circumstances that define whether a given model provides an adequate representation of the problem under consideration. It means moving from the concept of truth to the concept of control or management. This decreases the need to obtain true predictions of future scenarios, with or without the estimation of uncertainties, and encourages a move in favour of the control of future events, accepting the existence of unavoidable uncertainties. Thus, despite the fact that engineering science can make certain predictions about risk, such predictions will unavoidably be partial or incomplete. As a result, the emphasis should be placed on managing or handling security (Blockley, 1992).

During the past few years, attempts to provide a dimension to disaster risk for management purposes have been based on the calculation of the possible economic, social and environmental consequences of a physical phenomenon in a specific place and time. However, risk has not been conceptualized in a comprehensive way. Rather, fragmentation has been common and risk has been estimated or calculated according to different disciplinary approaches. In order to estimate risk on a multidisciplinary basis, we need to be aware not only of the expected physical damage and the victims or the economic losses, but also social, organizational and institutional factors that relate to community development. At the urban scale, for example, vulnerability seen as an internal risk factor must be related not only to exposure of the material context or to the physical susceptibility of the exposed elements, but also to the social frailties and lack of resilience of the prone communities. This means looking into the capacity to respond to or absorb the impact. Deficient information, communications and knowledge among social actors; the absence of institutional and community organization; weaknesses in emergency preparedness; political instability; and the absence of economic health in a geographic area, all contribute to greater risk. This is why the potential consequences are not only related to the impact of the event but also to the capacity to withstand the impact and their implications in the considered area.

Vulnerability and lack of development

It is certainly true that some social circumstances may be associated with vulnerability, but at the same time these aspects may not be considered the same as vulnerability. One example is the case of poverty, which may well be considered a factor or contributing cause of vulnerability but is certainly not vulnerability in itself. For this reason, it becomes necessary to closely study the factors that make populations vulnerable when faced with hazards. There is no doubt that many disasters are the result of economic and political factors, which are sometimes exacerbated by pressures that concentrate populations in prone areas. In most cases, the reduction of vulnerability is closely linked to the provision of basic needs. Conversely, there is a relation between social and economic marginality or exclusion and vulnerability. But, poverty is not vulnerability and the ways in which poverty contributes to vulnerability must be studied in different contexts and cases.

The vulnerability of human settlements is intrinsically tied to different social processes. It is related to the fragility, the susceptibility or the lack of resilience of the exposed elements. On the other hand, vulnerability is closely tied to natural and human environmental degradation at urban and rural levels. Thus, degradation, poverty and disasters are all expressions of environmental problems and their materialization is a result of the social construction of risk brought about by the construction of vulnerability or hazard, or both simultaneously. From a social point of view, vulnerability signifies a lack or a deficiency of development. Risk is constructed socially, even though it has a relationship to physical and natural space. In developing countries, increases in vulnerability are related to factors such as rapid and uncontrollable urban growth and environmental deterioration. These lead to losses in the quality of life, the destruction of natural resources, the landscape and genetic and cultural diversity. In order to analyse vulnerability as part of wider societal patterns, we need to identify the deep-rooted and underlying causes of disaster vulnerability and the mechanisms and dynamic processes that transform these into insecure conditions.

The underlying causes of vulnerability are economic, demographic and political processes that affect the assignation and distribution of resources among different groups of people. These reflect the distribution of power in society. Some global processes require more attention than others. These include population growth, rapid urban development, international financial pressures, degradation of the environment, global warming and climate change, and war. For example, urbanization processes have contributed greatly to the degree of damage during earthquakes; population growth helps explain increases in the number of people affected by floods; and prolonged droughts and deforestation intensifies the chances of flooding and landslides (Blaikie et al, 1994).

Adhering to the hypothesis that lack of development and vulnerability are correlated, Cardona (2001) suggests that vulnerability originates in:

- physical fragility or exposure: the susceptibility of a human settlement to be affected by a dangerous phenomenon due to its location in the area of influence of the phenomenon and a lack of physical resistance;
- socio-economic fragility: the predisposition to suffer harm from the levels of marginality and social segregation of human settlements, and the disadvantageous conditions and relative weaknesses related to social and economic factors; and
- lack of resilience: an expression of the limitations of access and mobilization of the resources of human settlement, and its incapacity to respond when it comes to absorbing the impact.

This kind of thinking attempts to integrate in a holistic way the contributions of the physical and social sciences with the idea of obtaining a more complete vision of the factors that create or exacerbate vulnerability. This approach takes into account aspects of physical resistance and the prevalent aspects of individual and collective self-protection.

LIMITATIONS AND PERSPECTIVES

Collective risk means the possibility of future disaster. It announces the possibility that a dangerous phenomenon or event will occur and that exposed elements are predisposed or susceptible to being affected. Therefore, reducing hazard or vulnerability contributes to risk reduction. And reducing risk means reducing the possibility of future disaster. However, risk and disaster are ever-increasing problems. The impact of natural or social–natural phenomena is ever greater due to the styles or models of development in vogue in many countries. Population growth and the urban development process, trends in land occupancy, increases in poverty levels, the employment of inadequate organizational systems and pressure on natural resources have continuously increased the vulnerability of populations. In general, efforts have focused on the study of natural hazards and the proposal of technical solutions. Until now, no major advances have been achieved given that these solutions are often not socially, culturally or economically applicable or adequate. Despite important technical advances, most suggested solutions have not been applied in real life due to the restrictions of available resources and the ignorance of local rationales that allow for an alternative technological handling of the situation. Sometimes, people simply reject the solutions because they do not correspond to their own reading of risk or to their image of disasters.

Disasters should be understood as unsolved development problems since they are not events of nature *per se* but situations that are the product of the relationship between the natural and organizational structure of society. Policies for urban and regional development and social and economic policies, in general, do not take into account the risk problematic; on many occasions, they increase vulnerability. Only in a few cases have the concepts of prevention and mitigation (risk reduction) been duly considered in the planning of development in poor countries.

In many places, government systems or organizations in charge of reducing risks and of drills and preparedness for disasters have not obtained effective results. This is due to the absence of political will, the feasibility or the fact that their approach has focused more upon the response and aid in case of an emergency, and less on the execution, in a systematic and organized fashion, of actions that would prevent or mitigate the disaster. These agencies are mostly centralized hierarchies that do not adequately incorporate local power bases, such as municipal governments, community organizations or other expressions of civil society.

Within the context of the UN International Decade for Natural Disaster Reduction during the 1990s, the prevention of disasters, or the idea that risk management should be a fundamental strategy for sustainable development, was promoted quite explicitly. However, despite these efforts, there are still enormous gaps in risk management and in articulating prevention and reduction activities in light of managing and protecting the environment. This is despite the fact that, clearly, in order to make society's exploitation of its natural ecosystems sustainable, it is necessary to moderate and guide human actions concerning the environment, and vice versa.

The initiative of the IDNDR at least had the virtue of catching the attention and interest of a wide number of countries, international organizations and donor agencies in the field of disasters. As a result of the initiative, different governments, organizations and institutions around the world supported projects and programmes that have already provided positive results in fields such as health and education in reducing the vulnerability of productive infrastructure. Results can be seen in the formation of institutions of a national and subregional character and in the production and diffusion of technical and scientific information. We are left with the preoccupation of what the future holds, since these advances are pretty feeble, faced with worsening conditions and factors that favour the occurrence of more frequent and more severe disasters than ever before.

CONCLUSION

All concepts of risk have a common element: a distinction between reality and possibility. If the future were predetermined or independent of present human activities, the term risk would have no significance. If the distinction between reality and possibility is accepted, then the term risk signifies the possibility that an undesirable state of reality (adverse effects) will occur as a result of natural events or human activities. This definition means that humans can and do make causal connections between actions (or events) and effects, and that undesirable effects can be avoided or reduced if the causal events or actions are avoided or modified.

An obvious concern exists due to the separation of risk evaluation and risk reduction between science and political decision. There are serious grounds for doubt regarding the effectiveness of risk management. The increase in, and accumulation of, vulnerability is truly alarming, as is the lack of consciousness and responsibility regarding this issue on the part of decision-makers, political authorities and communities themselves. This could explain why – despite many different disciplinary studies of hazard vulnerability and even risk in many places around the world – risk reduction has not been achieved. Among other factors that contribute to this lack of effective risk management, the inadequate form in which risk has been estimated or valued is very important. Some important technical contributions have been made regarding evaluation purposes, but in a specialized or fragmented way. The absence of a holistic approach to risk – in other words, the absence of a comprehensive and multidisciplinary evaluation of risk that assesses its different characteristics – seems to have contributed to a decrease in the effectiveness of risk management.

A holistic approach of risk that is both consistent and coherent could guide decisions taken within a geographic area. It should be founded on a theoretic basis of complexity that takes into account not only geological and structural variables, but also those of an economic, social, political and cultural nature. An approach of this type could assess, in a more consistent manner, the non-linear relations of the contextual parameters and the complexity and dynamics of social systems. It would also help to improve the effectiveness of management and to identify and prioritize factual and efficient measures for the adequate reduction of risk by authorities and communities, who are undoubtedly the fundamental actors in achieving a preventive attitude.

Chapter 4

Complexity and Diversity: Unlocking Social Domains of Disaster Response

Dorothea Hilhorst

INTRODUCTION

This chapter introduces a way of looking at disaster response through the study of science, governance and local knowledge as social domains of knowledge and action.[1] Social domains are areas of social life such as family, community and market whose study allows one to understand how social ordering works. The chapter starts from the premise that disaster studies during the last decade have increasingly been overtaken by a paradigm that accords central importance to mutuality and complexity in the relations between nature and society. While welcoming this shift, I am concerned about the 'system-thinking' remnant in much of complexity theory. It denies agency and diversity, and puts unwarranted boundaries around people and phenomena. Instead of conceptualizing science, governance and local responses as separate and different sub-systems of society, the study of social domains allows us to focus upon the everyday practices and movements of actors who negotiate the conditions and effects of vulnerability and disaster.

Disaster studies are often presented as constituting two competing paradigms: the behavioural and the structural paradigms (Smith, 1999, 1996; Oliver-Smith, 1996). Heralded by the work of Gilbert White, the behavioural paradigm dominated disaster studies during the 1950s. It coupled a hazard-centred interest in the geophysical processes underlying disaster with the conviction that people had to be taught to anticipate it. It is a technocratic paradigm dominated by geologists, seismologists, meteorologists and other scientists who can monitor and predict the hazards, while social scientists are brought in to explain people's behaviour in response to risk and disaster and to develop early warning mechanisms and disaster preparedness schemes (Oliver-Smith, 1996). Towards the 1980s, anthropologists, sociologists and geographers increasingly began to challenge the technocratic, hazard-centred approach to disaster. This culminated in the 1983 landmark publication of *Interpretations of Calamity from the Viewpoint of Human Ecology* by Kenneth Hewitt. He argued that disasters were not primarily the outcome of geographical processes. Especially in developing countries, structural factors such as increasing poverty and related social processes accounted for people and societies' vulnerability to disaster. The recognition of social vulnerability touched at the heart of understanding disaster. Whereas disasters used to be practically equated to natural hazards, they now became understood as the interaction between hazard and vulnerability, graphically expressed by Blaikie et al (1994) in the pseudo-formula of Risk = Hazard + Vulnerability.

Upon scrutiny, this familiar distinction of paradigms is becoming outdated. Although both paradigms continue to be used, I daresay that increased attention to environmental processes and human-induced climate change has marked the emergence of another disaster studies paradigm in the 1990s. This paradigm emphasises the *mutuality* of hazard and vulnerability to disaster due to complex interactions between nature and society. The mutuality or complexity paradigm takes the structural analysis of disaster a step further. While structural theory mainly looked at society to explain people's vulnerability to disaster, the mutuality paradigm looks at the mutual constitution of society and environment. People, in this view, are not just vulnerable to hazards; but hazards are increasingly the result of human activity. This is particularly clear in the cases of the meteorological and hydrological processes that produce high winds and floods. These hazards have become more frequent and more devastating due to environmental degradation and as a result of human-induced climate change. This has the important implication that vulnerability might not just be understood as how people are susceptible to hazards, but can also be considered as a measure of the impact of society on the environment (Oliver-Smith, 1999a, p31).

I consider the mutuality idea a new paradigm, and not just an elaboration of structuralism, because it rests (explicitly or implicitly) on different notions of causal effects, social change and possible responses to disaster vulnerability. The structural paradigm is based on the idea that causes of disaster vulnerability can be reduced to a limited number of root causes. In order to overcome disaster vulnerability, these root causes must be addressed. Even though there are many practical and political obstacles, at least there is a clear political agenda for the required radical changes. The mutuality idea, on the other hand, has much more affinity with complexity theories. These theories are characterized by the complexity of interactions between society and nature – the unpredictability of causal chains and social change. They are far less clear about the required policies to overcome vulnerability (Green and Warner, 1999).

In this chapter, I will first elaborate the outlines of a complexity paradigm and discuss its merits for disaster studies. The concept of social domains of disaster response will then be introduced using complexity theory, while taking into account diversity and human agency in responding to risk and disaster. Although the notion of social domains implies a shared repertoire of practices and languages, it is emphasized that contradictions, conflict and negotiation take place within a domain as much as in interactions with other domains.

COMPLEXITY THEORY AND DISASTER STUDIES

Complexity theory, in general terms, is concerned with stability and change in systems that are complex in the sense that they consist of a great many independent agents that interact with each other in many ways (Waldrop 1992, p11). Originating with mathematics and physics, since the mid-1980s complexity theory has encompassed the social sciences, where it has been applied in areas as widely varying as the breakdown of political systems, the working of markets and traffic jams. Complex systems are formed by a number of simultaneously acting components that each have a certain degree of local information and influence but cannot determine the whole state of the system (Possekel, 1999, p13). It makes systems inherently unstable, and causes the ways in which processes of ordering and change occur to be unpredictable and non-linear. This is expressed in the concept of self-organization, which means that through the interactions within systems and between systems and their environments, systems undergo spontaneous self-organization.

Complexity theory has been explicitly applied to vulnerability and disasters in the work of Louise Comfort on self-organization following disaster (1995) and in Anja Possekel's (1999) study of the volcano eruption in Montserrat. In addition, many developments in disaster theory have affinity with the premises of complexity. Complexity theory is highly relevant for disaster studies because it provides an entry point to describe disasters as the interaction between (sub) systems of nature and society, or hazard and vulnerability. Disasters caused by natural hazards result from the complex interactions of nature and society, and the interactions of different dimensions of space (in other words, where hazards may affect remote places) and different time frames (in other words, the conjunction of different patterns of change: short term, long term and cyclical) (Holling et al, 2002, p9). Oliver-Smith (1999b) and Comfort et al (1999) describe such complexities for the Peruvian earthquake and Hurricane Mitch, respectively. Floods can originate from the unlucky coincidence of a number of contingent variations and interactions in social, natural and meteorological elements. Although these variations may each be insignificant and fall within perfectly normal ranges, usually not resulting in floods, at particular junctions they result in dramatic flood events (Linde, 2002; Perrow, 1984).

Complex system approaches can, I believe, have a major impact on the study of disasters caused by natural hazards. In the first place, the approaches enable the study of the impact of the environment and society on disasters in a symmetrical fashion. Disaster could be portrayed as resulting from interactions between several subsystems in the geophysical and climatological environment, on the one hand, and subsystems of society, such as science systems and local knowledge systems, on the other. In the second place, complex system approaches remind us of the profound impact of disaster risks on society and environmental relations. All too often, disasters are still considered aberrations from the normal situation, or a temporary interruption of development. A major disaster such as the 2000 floods in Mozambique are invariably followed by statements of politicians and experts outbidding each other on television with estimates of the number of years that the country has been 'set back' in development. These comments disregard the fact that disasters may result from, rather than impinge upon, development. They also fall back on a notion of linear development as the norm of temporal change, disregarding the multidirectional ways in which societies evolve. Hence, complexity can provide an alternative for erroneously putting disasters in a linear time frame of development.

Since complexity theory may offer a major contribution to disaster studies, it is especially important to realize that different approaches are developed under the heading. Complexity theory has the potential to bridge natural and social sciences; but, in practice, it often reanimates divides between, for instance, positivist and social constructivist notions. These differences can remain hidden in the use of similar abstract vocabulary, but can have important implications for dealing with risk and disaster in policy and practice. It is impossible to discuss the enormous body of emerging theory on complexity. However, to elaborate this point, I want, at least, to briefly discuss the ways in which change is appreciated in different strands of complexity theory.

Stacey et al (2000) distinguish three strands of theory based on chaos, dissipative structures and adaptive systems, respectively. In the chaos theory, change occurs because of the many ways in which different elements of an open system interact upon each other, resulting in unpredictable patterns of change. Chaos is often exemplified by referring to the possibility of a butterfly flapping its wings in Amazonia causing a storm in Chicago, although at other times there will be no effect, depending upon its interaction with other conditions. Although the interactions between components of a system or between subsystems follow predictable patterns, chaos stems from the unpredictability of the combined interactions where small variations in each of them can accumulate into large consequences. Note that unpredictability here refers especially to the 'inability of humans to measure with infinite accuracy' (Stacey et al, 2000, p89). It is a mathematical approach, where complexity becomes equivalent to the computer time needed to analyse a system (Possekel, 1999, p16). The term 'dissipating structures' stems from the Nobel laureate Ilya Prigogine, who demonstrated the imbalance of chemical and physical systems by proving how changing conditions (such as supply of energy) leads to the spontaneous formation of new structures. Self-organization, in this case, is a property of systems that is triggered by interaction with external factors.

The third strand of complexity theory identified by Stacey et al (2000) centres on the notion of complex adaptive systems. The difference between this compared to those discussed above is that adaptive systems have the potential to learn by experience, specifically to process information and adapt accordingly. Here, self-organization means agents interacting locally according to their own principles or intentions in the absence of an overall blueprint of the system (Stacey et al, 2000, p106). Adaptive systems do not just passively respond to events; they actively try to turn whatever happens to their advantage (Waldrop, 1992, p11). This strand leads to a more radical kind of unpredictability than, for instance, the unpredictability of chaos that contains the promise of becoming predictable once mathematics and computers are up to the task. The unpredictability of adaptive systems stems from the creative interaction of sense-making and diverse agents. This way of thinking offers a venue for understanding vulnerability and disaster in terms of multiple realities and has many implications, among others, for the relationship between scientists and lay people.

If complexity is defined as a multitude of systems, agents and interactions, the challenge becomes to devise models to capture and control it. Indeed, according to Shackley et al (1996, p221), much of complexity work (in natural and social sciences) still seems 'largely inspired by the commitment to discover the principles of predictability [and thus of control, or theological reassurance?] only at a meta-level'. However, some scientists use a different notion of complexity based on sense-making agents. Complexity, in this view, can be defined as a function of the number of ways in which we can interact and the number of separate descriptions required to describe these interactions (Mikulecky, 1997, p4, in Possekel, 1999, p15). In this view, complexity becomes the need to select. Complexity requires people and scientists alike to reduce their interactions and interlinkages. Because of the many possible ways that this happens, situations of multiple realities emerge. Instead of capturing and controlling complexity, the challenge then becomes to acknowledge multiple realities (shaped by culturally and politically informed 'selections') and to 'embody the realization of complexities in developing institutional relations, mediations and identities' (Shackley et al, 1996, p221).

These two views of complexity lead to different kinds of science and policy. Given the dire need to reduce vulnerability to disaster and the history of top-down disaster management styles, it is likely that many disaster students and institutes would be attracted by the prospect of controlling complex systems. The alternative of acknowledging multiple realities is more insecure. It is still difficult to imagine disaster policies that are not based on the aim to control and are, nonetheless, effective. However, since they more accurately reflect disaster realities, in the end this may be the more fruitful road to take.

FROM COMPLEX ADAPTIVE SYSTEMS TO COMPLEX SOCIAL DOMAINS

While further exploring the possibilities embedded in reflexive strands of complexity theory, I would like to step away from the concept of systems. The notion of systems or subsystems does no justice to the dynamics of societies' disaster response. The very idea of a system supposes that the elements of the system relate in functional and predictable ways. This runs against the notions of agency and diversity. People are social actors who do not merely react to what happens around them; they have the capacity to process social experience and to respond accordingly (Long, 1992). Because people and institutions, acting from diverse histories and life worlds, have different interpretations of situations and events, they develop differential responses to similar conditions and processes, thereby changing the meaning of institutions and the course of events in unpredictable and multidirectional ways. This property of especially human systems has, to some extent, been acknowledged in systems theories and has resulted in qualifications such as open, adaptive systems or soft systems (for the latter, see Chapter 7).

However, the more open systems remain problematic because of the implicit assumption that elements or people belong to one particular (sub) system. This overlooks the possibility that actors may belong to different systems at the same time and relate with each other in different capacities, and that they have the ability to integrate and rework knowledge derived from different systems. As a result, even the softest system thinkers risk overestimating the commonalties within systems and the differences between them. The difference this can make to our understanding of disaster is so substantial that I would rather avoid the concept of systems altogether. Instead, I prefer to work with the notion of social domains.

Social domains can be defined as areas of social life that are organized by reference to a central cluster of values, which are recognized as a locus of certain rules, norms and values implying a degree of social commitment (Long, 2002, p59; Villarreal, 1994, pp58–63). In social domains of response to risk and disaster, ideas and practices concerning risk and disaster are exchanged, shared and, more or less, organized because of a certain proximity (physical or discursive) in the ways in which people refer to disaster and risk. The concept of social domains explicitly departs from the idea that domains would be composed of functionally relating elements. Although domains imply a shared repertoire of practices and languages, it is emphasized that contradictions, conflict and negotiations take place within the domain as much as in interactions with other domains. Differential interpretations are often concealed because people use the same language. 'Domains for people represent some shared values that absolve them from the need to explain themselves to each other – [but] leaves them free to attach their own meanings to them' (Cohen, 1987, p16 quoted in Long, 2001, p59).

Working with the concept of social domains, rather than systems, may redirect our gaze and lead to a different way of analysing disaster. It can make the analysis more sensitive to social change within domains. Domains are not just changing in response to interaction with, or penetration of, other systems. Due to ongoing negotiations over the meanings of, and responses to, everything happening within and around these domains, they are subject to social change from within. It will also better tune the analysis to the fluidness of domain boundaries. Although a notion such as open systems takes into account the softness of the boundaries of systems, the concept of social domains gives more central attention to the movement of people, resources and ideas between domains. And it provides handles on studying how social and symbolic boundaries that separate domains are created and defended (Long, 2001, p59).

The three main domains of response to risk and disaster are the domain of science and disaster management, the domain of disaster governance and the domain of local responses. They are the respective domains of scientists and managers, bureaucrats and politicians, and local producers and vulnerable people. As will be elaborated, each of these domains of knowledge and action represent notions and relations of nature–society interaction, vulnerability, risk and disaster response. They are associated with particular discourses through which meaning is given to phenomena. They are, for instance, characterized by different ways of experiencing and producing nature (Escobar, 1999, p5). On scrutiny, however, these domains turn out to be differentiated and constitute multiple realities. At the same time, there are more common aspects in different domains than apparent at first sight. As will be elaborated, this property of domains leads to more complexity, but may also hold the key to developing alternative ways of making policy about disaster.

THE DOMAIN OF INTERNATIONAL SCIENCE AND DISASTER MANAGEMENT

The domain of disaster science and management is dominated by a hazard-centred paradigm. This paradigm is embedded in a general discourse of capitalist modernity where nature and society are seen as separate, and nature is considered a commodity that can be appropriated and controlled through expert knowledge and modern administration (Escobar, 1999). Disasters seem to pose a challenge to this paradigm since they are made up of moments where nature clearly escapes human control. Disaster management, however, brings hazards under control as far as possible. Because disasters primarily happen in developing countries, moreover, Greg Bankoff demonstrates how disasters actually reinforce the dominant paradigm. Disasters are mainly considered phenomena of tropical areas whose insufficiently modernized relationships with nature make their populations vulnerable as a matter of course. Western technology, then, provides the remedy to this vulnerability to the whims of uncontrolled nature (see Chapter 2).

The modernity discourse can clearly be recognized in the central assumptions, notions and priorities of hazard-centred disaster science and management. Keith Smith (1999/1996) summarizes these as predominantly interested in the geophysical processes underlying disaster, geared to developing technology for monitoring and predicting these processes, and preferring to contain nature through engineering works such as flood embankments or avalanche sheds. This scientific approach is coupled to modern forms of governing disaster through disaster plans and emergency responses according to a military-style organization, often, in fact, delegated to armed forces (Hewitt, 1983a). It is modern organizing to the extreme, based on notions of intervention as linear processes, where empirical complexity is divided into a series of independently given realities (Long and van der Ploeg, 1989, p229).

Although this paradigm may dominate the field of disaster science and management, it by no means forms a hegemonic claim conditioning scientists and disaster managers into predictable and uniform actors. The paradigm is contested by rival approaches – in particular, the structural approach that was discussed in the introduction to this chapter. This rival approach is invariably presented as a critique from the margin, but has, in fact, made a considerable dent in the majority point of view. In the case of flood management, for instance, Smith and Ward (1997) consider that a structural development paradigm – where floods in developing countries are considered as being rooted in civil war, foreign debt, uncontrolled urbanization and poor building constructions – has largely overtaken earlier paradigms in the 1970s and continues to dominate flood theories and practice – where the emphasis has increasingly focused upon sustainable solutions rather than expensive constructions.

Further differentiation in paradigms is found when considering the specific approaches of the 30 or more disciplines concerned with disaster (Alexander, 1997). The question is whether these differences are more than variations within the discourse of modern capitalism, since they all continue to rely on expert knowledge and modern interventions. However, the extent to which they are reliant differs. The development paradigm has brought with it a call for participation and the reliance on local knowledge, which represents a move away from the so-called dominant paradigm. Likewise, The Netherlands has recently embraced a new paradigm where the reliance on dikes is abandoned in favour of a policy to give water space and to have water dictate landscape planning, rather than the other way around. This is a significant step for a water-engineering country *par excellence* towards a more holistic approach to nature normally considered exclusive to people in the South (Rijkswaterstaat, 2002).

Portraying the Western hazard paradigm as hegemonic not only dismisses rival, parallel or previous discourses and paradigms; it also ascribes too much consistency and homogeneity to the paradigm. Natural science is in many respects as local, parochial and cultural as folk or local knowledge. Numerous definitions compete over the meaning of concepts such as risk, disaster, hazard, vulnerability and mitigation, and work often rests on scientifically groundless assumptions. Bruno Latour (1997) showed how making science is a social endeavour, whereas enrolling people into accepting certain truths depends more upon the social relations and status of institutions than upon the use of scientific methods. Hence, social networks, political rivalry, career considerations and personal characteristics such as age and social background may better account for ongoing paradigm schisms than the value of the arguments raised. In other words, we should not conclude from the forceful way in which the idea of Western rationality is advocated (or attacked) that organizations in 'the West' (whatever that may be) actually operate according to this image (Herzfeld, 1992, p47).

These considerations are more than cracks in a hegemonic scientific bastion. It means that the analysis of empirical situations requires more than a 'dominant science versus local perspectives' binary. Rather than representing some exceptions to a solid rule, they imply that we have to revise our explanatory framework for understanding disaster intervention. Instead of assuming that the field is ruled by a uniform, hegemonic paradigm, we have to base our analysis on the notion of complexity and contradictions within the domain of disaster science and management. It means that we have to study how actors in this domain make sense of risk, vulnerability and disaster through their everyday practices, how rival scientific narratives are being formulated and through what processes particular narratives gain the status of truth.

THE DOMAIN OF DISASTER GOVERNANCE

The domain of disaster governance is the disaster response domain where society's priorities regarding risk and vulnerability are defined. It is the domain where disaster knowledge and management is mediated and altered through political and bureaucratic governance practices and institutions. In a broader sense, the domain of disaster governance is also the domain in which it becomes apparent how disasters affect state–society relations and, vice versa, how state–society relations affect responses to risk and disaster.

The official policies of disaster governance are often derived from the domain of disaster science and management; but in actual decisions and practices, they take on a different nature. In developing countries, where disaster science and management is often imported, the question of how it works in practice and articulates with governance is especially relevant. However, such gaps between science and governance occur, to some extent, in every situation. Politicians and civil servants weave their own narratives, explaining the relations between hazards, vulnerability and disaster, and picking bits and pieces from science as they deem fit according to their own beliefs. These narratives reflect political interest and motivations, but are also informed by cultural patterns of governance, including the governance of risk. Mary Douglas and Aaron Wildavsky postulated in 1982 that societies selectively choose risks for attention, and that this choice reflects beliefs about values, social institutions, nature and moral behaviour. As Wildavsky (1991) remarked: 'Every survey study of risk perception, including among risk professionals, concludes that knowledge of actual dangers makes no difference whatsoever'. It is the 'adversarial context', and not whether people are likely to be harmed, that matters most.

Writing in the early 1980s, Douglas and Wildavsky thought that it was possible to identify particular risk cultures for societies. More recent work has left intact their basic notion of the social constructed nature of risk, but started to point to the variability between and within domains of risk regulation. Therefore, leaving aside the search for *the* risk culture of a society, these works have come to analyse how risk regulation is shaped in an amalgam of many possible dimensions (Hood et al, 2000). A single government, for instance, can take different attitudes towards different hazards. The same country that would command forced evacuation for prospective victims of a volcano eruption could be much easier and reactive to, for instance, the monitoring of brakes on cars even though traffic accidents may be a much larger killer than volcanoes. While some hazards are regulated by specialized risk bureaucracies and militarily structured operations, others are regulated by generalist agencies, left to local governments, or to people to cope for themselves, or are dealt with by a multiplicity of agencies.

The complexity of risk and disaster governance becomes more pronounced when taking into account the international dimension of risk governance, and when we consider the everyday practices of disaster management. The international dimension is important because risks and disasters do not respect national boundaries and need to be dealt with by international, regional or global bodies of regulation. The resulting governance patterns may be far from coherent. Everyday practices of disaster management may substantially diverge from official policy and reflect more the historically developed patterns of bureaucrat–client relationships. For instance, after the floods in Mozambique, students of disaster studies found that managers of relocation camps charged people contributions to get access to the camps, effectively excluding the vulnerable people whom the camp was meant to shelter (Holla and Vonhof, 2001). These practices were probably the effect of years of post-war construction programmes where low-income bureaucrats who handled foreign-funded projects had grown accustomed to getting paid for services that were supposed to be given free. Hence, risk cultures do not form an invisible infrastructure of risk regulation. Instead, patterns of risk governance evolve in the everyday practices of risk and disaster management.

The domain of disaster governance is also important because it allows for the analysis of the mutual impact of risk and disaster response and state–society relations. When disaster looms or strikes, social actors (local people, bureaucrats and scientists alike) grapple to understand the reality around them. Narratives that people create about risk, vulnerability and disasters are not just statements about nature, but are also statements about state–society relations. True or false, the ideas that people have of the state in relation to society shape their interpretations of, and responses to, disaster. In Turkey, for instance, the 1999 earthquake shook people's confidence in the state because it strongly brought out the fallacy of the dominant discourse promoted by the state that 'father State would take care of everything' (Arkel, 2000). Alternatively, vulnerability to disasters may be seen as the delayed outcome of colonial policies or international adjustment programmes. This underlies, for instance, Grace Machel's accusation after the Mozambique floods in 2000 on BBC World that international donors failed in their *duty* to deliver adequate humanitarian assistance. In some countries, disasters are increasingly seen as the implicit breach of a social contract where states should protect their citizens from vulnerability to disaster.

Responses to risk and disaster also affect state–society relations. Where disaster is frequent, such as in the Philippines, disasters can be seen as one of ordering elements that, over centuries, shape state–society relations and the differentiations within societies (Bankoff, 1999). Single-disaster events can accelerate, reverse or change the way in which state–society relations evolve. Disaster in Nicaragua speeded the downfall of dictator Samosa and the Armenian earthquake in 1988 accelerated Glasnost in the former Soviet Union (Benthall, 1993, pp108–21). The direction of disaster impact is not always the same: disasters can enhance radical change or bureaucratic reform, bringing about the potential for change by exposing conditions that need alteration (Hoffman and Oliver-Smith, 1999, p10). However, disasters also often reinforce existing power relations when resourceful people manage to profit from the potential for change over more vulnerable people, or provide an opportunity for military factions to strengthen their grip on democratic institutions.

Shackley et al noted that complexity resides especially in the social relationships within and between institutions and agents (Shackley et al, 1996, p201). The domain of disaster governance is clearly no exception to this rule. It is highly complex because it is in the interactions within governance institutions and at the interfaces between these institutions and scientists and managers, on the one hand, and vulnerable people, on the other, that disaster responses are shaped. The domain is particular to local histories, governance patterns and state–society relations and it is hardly possible to define its characteristics, actors and dimensions beyond meso-level analyses at country, region or river-basin levels.

DOMAIN OF LOCAL KNOWLEDGE AND
COPING PRACTICES

The domain of local disaster response is constituted by the manifold ways in which local people cope with emergencies, maximizing their own capacities, resources and social networks. People anticipate disaster and rely on themselves and their community for survival. It has been estimated that no more than 10 per cent of survival in emergencies can be contributed to external sources of relief aid (Duffield, 1993, p144). In recent decades, several publications have pointed to the extensive knowledge that people avail themselves of to cope with crisis, such as ingenious practices to regulate the size of herds by nomadic peoples to overcome periods of drought (Toulmin, 1995; see also Blaikie et al, 1994, pp64–9; Curtis, 1993, pp4–7; Frerks, 2000).

Local knowledge domains are different from the other two mentioned because they are rarely self-referential. With the exception of some indigenous movement actors, people refer to their local knowledge as knowledge. It is rendered local because outsiders – in particular, intervening experts – label this knowledge as local, a status that, no matter how admiring, is ascribed to them by people from a superior position of universal knowledge. The use of the notion is not homogeneous. Kees Jansen (1998) distinguishes three approaches to local knowledge in development practice that can be recognized, as well, in disaster management. The first is a utilitarian or instrumental approach that views local knowledge as a barrel of information that can be tapped for disaster management. The second stems from a critique of modernization and stresses the different character of local knowledge. It is assumed that local knowledge overcomes the separation of nature and culture and can thus inspire to 'decolonize' our minds (Apffel-Marglin, 1996, in Jansen, 1998, p165; Fairhead, 1993). The third approach to local knowledge also criticizes the modernist approach, but stresses local knowledge as a source of political-economic empowerment of local people. It points to the need for an alternative development agenda based on self-reliance, ecological soundness and popular empowerment. This approach can be recognized in structuralist approaches to disaster, calling for participatory societal change to structurally address vulnerability.

The three lines of thinking share the same assumptions that there exists a growing body of homogeneous local knowledge that is community-owned and can be separated from extra-community knowledge. These assumptions are problematic. First, local knowledge cannot be represented as an accumulating and homogeneous community stock. It is often not shared in the sense that everybody possesses the same knowledge. It could even be said that the only one knowing all is the outsider who collects the knowledge taxonomy. In addition, people in communities do not need to have the same ideas about nature, vulnerability and disaster. In the smallest communities, alternative discourses prevail around the same concepts, such as, for instance, development (Hilhorst, 2001). These discourses are partly distributed along gender or other locally relevant categories of people; but people also adhere to conflicting discourses simultaneously and use them according to the contingency of the situation. Hence, the same people may hold on to holistic notions about society–nature relations and to notions that nature can be used and destroyed (Bruun and Kalland, 1995).

Second, local knowledge does not emerge in isolation. It is shaped at interfaces with other domains of knowledge, such as scientific or bureaucratic knowledge (Arce and Long, 1992). Local knowledge is made up of a blend of bits and pieces of information and insights from different perspectives. Local producers may thus anticipate extreme weather by reading signs from animal behaviour, but may just as likely have heard the forecast on the radio. Following Arce and Long, 'rather than premise one's view of knowledge on a binary opposition between Western and non-Western epistemologies and practice, one should attempt to deal with the intricate interplay and joint appropriation and transformation of different bodies of knowledge' (Arce and Long, 2000, p24). This conclusion brings us back to the question of how people in situations of complexity make sense of knowledge and select what is relevant to them.

This brings me to a third point regarding the way in which local knowledge is produced. Using the category of local knowledge implies that it stands apart from non-local or modern and universal knowledge. Local knowledge, as is often suggested, would be holistic, unlike science, which seeks (causal) relations. However, local knowledge may be more varied in nature. Agricultural producers experiment, combining information in ways that are often highly rational. Paul Richards (1989) speaks in this respect of 'people's science' and points to the capacity for people to improvise. Experimenting and improvising are usually social activities, fed by things heard on the radio or in a shop and discussed with neighbours. This means that knowledge gets constructed in social processes, including the role of social networks and power relations (Long and Villarreal, 1993). In these processes, some people become much better positioned to obtain knowledge and make their interpretations of events and processes authoritative in the community (Hilhorst, 2001).

Like the other two domains, the domain of local knowledge is also diverse and conflictive. What local knowledge constitutes can, as a consequence, only be gathered in community studies that acknowledge the heterogeneity and power differentials in communities and step away from viewing communities as isolated units. Local knowledge is not a stock of knowledge, but constantly evolves through the social negotiations, accommodations, exchanges and power struggles of local actors.

DOMAINS AND PEOPLE

The interpenetration and internal diversity of domains of knowledge and action become evident when we take into account the multiple identities and movements of people. Domains overlap partly because of the simple reason that some people belong to more than one domain or because they travel between domains. Scientists and bureaucrats are also community members. Even in the most remote communities, one might find a retired meteorologist, repatriated migrants with some particular expertise, people with social networks able to mobilize high-level government officials, or international knowledge centres. Hence, people can operate within different domains, according to what they are thinking or doing. Two categories of people and institutions are particularly apt to surf between the different domains: non-governmental organizations (NGOs) and the media.

NGOs are often lumped together as one category sharing the same characteristics, value orientation and interests. In reality, this is not the case: NGOs are highly diverse in all kinds of ways. Some combine different approaches, whereas others fit into one of the distinguished domains. For instance, the Turkish NGO Arama Kurtama Dernegi (AKUT: search and rescue team) grew from the volunteer rescue work of amateur mountaineers during the 1999 earthquake. Ever since, this NGO has been active during earthquakes across the world, offering their rescue expertise (Arkel, 2000). Another disaster-oriented NGO is the Philippine Citizens' Disaster Response Centre (CDRC; see also Chapter 8). This NGO adopts a participatory approach to identify, with a community, the hazards and vulnerabilities that they are exposed to in order to work out community preparedness plans. The first NGO would belong to the disaster science and management domain, whereas the second would identify much more with the local domain of knowledge and action. NGOs may be in a very good position to bridge domains of knowledge and action. National Red Cross organizations, for instance, are sometimes considered government agencies and sometimes NGOs. They bridge the governance and the scientific domain, and in some countries are also reaching out to the local domains of knowledge and action.

The media can also take different positions. From a content analysis of three Dutch newspaper reports about three disasters, it was found that reporters normally adhere to the dominant view of *natural disasters* as caused by nature, and have a fascination for the hardware of rescue operations, especially the use of helicopters, as well as representing affected people as hapless victims (Belloni et al, 2000). However, there was variation in the way that reports were made. Background features or analysis would usually take a more structural position on disaster, and the general news clippings would become more sensitive of root causes and vulnerability after some time had elapsed. Remarkably, reporting on Mozambique and Honduras would be more likely to adhere to the dominant view, perpetuating disaster myths, than reporting on Turkey. This was explained because, unlike the other two countries, Turkey is closer to The Netherlands and is not considered a developing country. While in Mozambique and Honduras the vulnerability of the countries to 'the cruel side of nature' were taken for granted, in Turkey reporters immediately speculated about root causes, mismanagement and other social explanations for the disaster. Media, then, can also be associated with different domains, and it may be said that good reporters manage to straddle them all.

CONCLUSIONS AND IMPLICATIONS

This chapter began by identifying the emergence of a new paradigm in disaster theory that focuses upon the mutuality and complexity of environment–society relations in creating vulnerability and disaster. Complexity theory is a promising field for disaster studies, and its implications for disaster management have only begun to be explored. It is already clear, however, that complexity theory can involve radically different ways of thinking, alternating between identifying complexity as a multiplicity of relations and interactions waiting to be described and controlled, and identifying complexity in the reflexive agency that makes systems inherently unpredictable.

Taking on the second line of thinking, this chapter has introduced the notion of social domains as one way of accommodating the effects of human agency and actors' movements across systems of disaster response. These domains are obviously different from one another: a university or research centre has other modes of organizing and operating than disaster committees and operational structures. Both are very different and remote from the coping practices of local communities. Yet, the domains are diverse and may have more in common with each other than meets the eye. One of the reasons why they apparently stand apart may be because they are described and analysed through different perspectives and accorded different rationale and status. For instance, the universal status of scientific knowledge may blind observers to some of the more mundane dynamics of knowledge production, while romantic notions about the holistic nature of local knowledge may stand in the way of observing the rationality of people's science or conflicts at the community level.

What are the major conclusions to draw from this chapter for the conception of social domains of disaster response? First, it will be clear that none of the domains are distinguished as being decisively more trustworthy. The domains, as I argue, are equally tainted by parochial concerns; are constrained by historically grown patterns of disaster response; are challenged by rival discourses and meanings attached to vulnerability; and are riddled by political intricacies. Second, if there is more analogy than assumed between the knowledge generated by scientists, bureaucrats or local farmers, this has implications for how we consider the ranking of knowledge. Instead of assuming that scientific knowledge is superior to local knowledge, or the other way around, a more open and critical eye needs to be cast on each approach. Third, and most importantly, it means that the domains can only be understood in relation to each other. Disaster responses come about through the interaction of science, governance and local practices, and they are defined and defended in relation to one another.

What does a focus on complexity, agency and social domains imply for the research of disaster response? First, case studies are important. Meso-level analyses at country, region or river-basin level may yield the best results for accumulating knowledge on disasters, even when these are global in nature. Second, ethnography is important in order to grasp how actors in different domains attach meaning to disasters and disaster response and how they influence each other. Ethnography should not be limited to local domains but can be equally suitable and insightful when performed in and between other domains of disaster response. Recent developments towards multi-sited ethnography and studying-up ethnographies (ie looking into social groups that are more powerful or have more status than the researcher) are interesting to take into account (see, for instance, Burawoy et al, 2000; Schrijvers, 1991). Finally, we have to find ways of representing the social domains in a meaningful way that provides handles for systematic discussion and, possibly, action without downplaying the complexity involved.

Some promising methods are stakeholder analyses, the use of narratives where conflicting notions are outlined in rival narratives without necessarily judging their objective truths (Roe, 1991), and the use of multiple scenarios in projecting risk and disaster response (Possekel, 1999).

Finally, an approach that focuses upon the social domains of disaster response also has implications of a practical vein. Such an approach can draw out the relationships between actors in different domains. Current stakeholder approaches reinforce the idea that social domains of knowledge and action stand apart from each other and each have different perceptions and interests regarding vulnerability and disaster. By focusing on contradictions within domains and possible analogies between them, it is possible to identify alliances between actors from different domains. For instance, rather than collapsing the collaboration of radical scientists, NGOs and organized local people into a local domain of knowledge and action, such collaboration can be viewed as an alliance between parts of the different domains. Such a view enhances questions of how knowledge and power differentials between the partners evolve, acknowledging that alliances between domains may constrain relations or enlarge gaps between different parties. It also enhances the search for complementarity and win–win situations that alliances can entail. In the latter case, such alliances can be seen as one of the ways of reducing people's vulnerability to disaster.

Chapter 5

The Lower Lempa River Valley, El Salvador: Risk Reduction and Development Project

Allan Lavell

INTRODUCTION

Between July 2000 and April 2001, the author had the opportunity to coordinate a group of consultants working on a project aimed at promoting disaster risk reduction and sustainable development in the Lower Lempa River Valley, El Salvador. This work was undertaken for the Ministry of the Environment and Natural Resources and financed by the Inter-American Development Bank (IADB). The project called for the elaboration of an integral diagnosis of the zone and the proposal of an integrated intervention strategy that could lead to substantial flood disaster risk reduction, improvements in human welfare indicators and new opportunities for overall sustainable development.

The principal objective of this chapter is to provide a succinct analysis of some of the major conceptual and methodological tools used in project implementation and a review of some of the major results achieved in the search for risk and vulnerability reduction in the intervention zone. Particular interest will be paid to the role played by the local population and their organizations in the measurement and understanding of risk and in discussions and decisions regarding the proffered risk-reduction strategy. The active, participatory role of the local population was considered a cornerstone to project success and was a dominant focus in project concept and methodology.

Risk, or the probability of future damage and loss, has an objective dimension and may be scientifically and technically estimated where adequate information on hazards and vulnerabilities is available. However, this objective dimension of risk must be evaluated socially in order to contribute to decision-making processes regarding the promotion of acceptable and feasible intervention strategies and instruments. This subjective dimensioning of risk may legitimately be undertaken by diverse social actors/outsiders and affected populations. However, success in identifying the need for, and creating the will and opportunity for, reduction measures requires dialogue and, hopefully, consensus between different actors. The attitudes, evaluations and strategic parameters of external actors may not, and often will not, coincide with those of the local population. Different visions or considerations regarding risk and risk levels, and their 'acceptability' or 'unacceptability', will be made according to different social perceptions and contextual factors. Acceptable and unacceptable risks cease to be technical dimensions and become socially determined variables that are influenced by different cultural, economic, social, political, institutional and organizational conditioning factors. Many times the notion of 'acceptable risk' will have to be traded in for the idea of accepted risk or unwillingly accepted risk. This is particularly true amongst poorer, resource-limited populations, such as those inhabiting the Lower Lempa River Valley in El Salvador.

In order to fully understand the project concept and intervention strategy, we will begin our discussion with a brief introduction to the Lower Lempa River Valley. This is of critical importance given that the dimensioning of risk and the design of risk-intervention strategies may only be adequately achieved where these activities are fully cognisant of the real social and human context subject to intervention. Experience has shown that, despite the apparent similarity in many risk contexts, there is no homogeneous way of looking at and designing risk-reduction strategies. Rather, these will vary from context to context and must closely take into account the particular social, economic, cultural and political conditions prevailing in different risk zones. Homogeneity or preconceived intervention packages tend to be the fodder of risk professionals and technicians and many times deny the social heterogeneity that typifies populations at risk throughout the world (Maskrey, 1989).

THE LOWER LEMPA RIVER BASIN:
BASIC CHARACTERISTICS

The Lempa River Basin is a multinational hydrological unit covering parts of Guatemala, Honduras and El Salvador. The Lower Lempa River Valley covers some 850 square kilometres and is located between the Salvadoran coastline and the Littoral Highway that runs from San Salvador to the Honduran border, crossing the Lempa River using the Golden Bridge (*el Puente de Oro*) at the town of San Marcos Lempa. According to estimates carried out during fieldwork undertaken by the consultancy team, the area has an estimated total population of between 30,000 and 40,000 individuals (without a census it is impossible to accurately report the real population of the zone), distributed in nearly 90 villages and small towns.

The area is, in good part, a highly fertile alluvial plain and nowhere does the area rise much above 200 metres. The coastal limit comprises a bay-land area populated by the country's principal mangrove swamps and other saline plant types.

A portion of the river's left bank is occupied by the Nancunchiname Forest, one of the very few areas of lowland tropical woodland left in the country. Covering some 1000 hectares, this woodland was severely deteriorated in the 1980s during the country's civil war due to deforestation and burning by woodcutters, croppers and illegal hunters. This process has continued although major attempts have been made to control degradation of this unique resource.

Until the end of the 1970s, the area was commonly referred to as the 'breadbasket' of El Salvador. Historically occupied by large-scale land holdings, the area produced *añil*, basic grains and cotton for the export market. These products occupied part of the floodplain; but settlements and housing were generally located out of the major flood-prone areas. Although seasonal flooding was a regular feature of the zone, few reports of disastrous flooding were recorded in the area until the 1990s. The large landholders had achieved a reasonable balance between production, settlement and flood amelioration, using adequate land-use practices and the selective use of well-built and maintained dikes.

During the early 1980s, the area was subject to an agrarian reform programme that led to the break-up and redistribution of many of the large land holdings. Then, with the advent of the newest phase of the country's civil war, the area became a natural route for arms movements to the guerrilla forces of the Farabundo Marti National Liberation Front (FMLN) and a zone of conflict between the guerrilla forces and government troops. This inevitably led to large-scale population migration from the zone. By the end of the 1980s, very few individuals permanently occupied the area.

With the end of hostilities in 1992 and the signing of the peace agreement between the FMLN and the government, the area was included in the so-called Programme for Land Transference (PLT). By means of this programme, land was allocated to combatants from both warring factions, and poor and very poor families were relocated to the area in previously established and newly created population centres. Many of these persons came from urban centres and had little previous history of agricultural work or fishing and shell collection, the principal activities of the zone. Even in the case of previously agricultural populations, many came from highland zones and had little experience of lowland tropical agriculture. Given the absence of other alternatives, the newly located population dedicated itself primarily to agriculture and fishing. Grains, particularly maize, plantain, root crops and fruits were produced for basic sustenance. Coastal communities attempt to eke out a living by fishing and extracting shellfish for commerce.

Many of the new communities were located in areas that are highly prone to flooding due to extreme periods of river flow and the effect of coastal tidal movements, or a combination of both. This was simply the result of a lack of concern or consideration for flood hazards, the speed in assigning land and the decisions made on the location of infrastructure and villages. With this, and the floodplain location of cropping and rural settlement, the area started to make the headlines more frequently when struck by regular flooding incidents that severely affected a predominantly poor population with little resilience and few opportunities for self-protection.

In October 1998, the area was severely hit by flooding associated with tropical storm Mitch. The flooding, to be expected with a storm of this magnitude, was complicated due to the opening of the sluice gates at the '15th of September' hydroelectric facility upstream from the area with little previous warning to the downstream population. Although few deaths were reported, the damage suffered reached new heights and led to increased demands from the population and interest by government and international intervention in flood-risk reduction.

Non-governmental organizations (NGOs) and population associations in the zone articulated a good part of the demand for protection from flooding. In particular, the Corporation for Economic and Social Development (CORDES), a development NGO predominantly working on the right bank of the river, and the co-ordinator of communities in the Lower Lempa Valley – the Coordinadora – working on the left bank, played a dominant role. CORDES was particularly vociferous in calling for levee construction whilst the Coordinadora had traditionally favoured early warning and evacuation systems, accompanied by improvements in agricultural productive capacity and the welfare of the population. In fact, both organizations had promoted different schemes for improved agricultural production over recent years. CORDES had successfully promoted agricultural diversification into new commercial products and industrial processing of some of these (cashew nuts, milk and honey). It also promoted increased use of irrigation and organic growing methods. The Coordinadora had favoured diversified agricultural plots for home consumption with limited commerce of crop surpluses, and the increased use of dispersion-type irrigation schemes.

These two organizations are representative of the highly organized population base to be found in the area. Almost all of the organizations in the area are of FMLN affiliation and are linked to the different factions that compose this now formally established political party. In fact, these FMLN origins help to explain the present highly developed level of organization in the zone. Various communities comprise individuals who lived together in other parts of the country or abroad during the war and had already developed strong organizational links.

However, despite the common FMLN base of the dominant organizations in the zone, this had not guaranteed cohesion and collaboration. In fact, the more important organizations had many times been at loggerheads regarding strategy, philosophy and ideology. The principle left- and right-bank organizations had very little previous history of mutual collaboration. The river divided rather than united this natural geo-ecological zone. Today, the four municipalities with a presence in the Lower Lempa Valley are also controlled by the FMLN, while the right-wing ARENA party controls the national government. The combination of FMLN-oriented organizations and municipal governments in the zone, along with an ARENA-run national government, made it very difficult for central government ministries to play an active, peaceful and visible role in the zone during the 1990s. Finally, it is important to point out that the zone is symbolic of many of the outstanding conflicts in Salvadoran post-war society. Ex-combatants are to be found living in poverty in one of the most potentially productive areas of Central America. The area is dominated by left-wing opposition political forces in a country governed by the right wing and tied to neo-liberal principles and tenets.

In many ways, the existence of these conflicts and contradictions may help to explain why the zone has received so much attention from national and international agencies and organizations. This had occurred despite its relatively small population and a flooding problem that is no more severe than in many other areas of the country that have received much less attention. During the post-Mitch period, the area was the recipient of relatively large-scale finance, executed particularly by numerous national and international NGOs, in coordination or liaison with local organizations. Little coherence and coordination characterized much of this investment.

THE CONCEPTUAL FRAMEWORK FOR THE LOWER LEMPA RIVER PROJECT: RISK, DEVELOPMENT AND SUSTAINABILITY

Perhaps the most critical aspect of project implementation relates to the conceptual and methodological framework employed and its unquestioned acceptance by the project stakeholders – the major local organizations, the government and the Inter-American Development Bank (IADB). The conceptual framework was developed by the consulting team following notions and ideas developed over the last ten years by the Latin American Network for the Social Study of Disaster Prevention in Latin America (La RED). This network was established in 1992 to promote multidisciplinary and transnational research and debate on risk and disaster topics in the region and has had considerable influence in the way that risk management has developed in Latin America over the last ten years. (Access to many of the publications produced by La RED and its members may be found on the website www.desenredando.org.)

The framework may be synthesized by taking into account a limited number of central concerns and ideas. This section briefly introduces the reader to the essential components of this framework. The real importance and relevance of the concepts presented will be taken up or become apparent in the discussion offered in the main body of this chapter.

Disaster risk, the probability of future loss and damage associated with adverse physical events comprised one central conceptual and practical issue that informed the planned strategy intervention. Hazard (the probability of a damaging physical event occuring) and vulnerability (the propensity to suffer loss and to find difficulties in recovering from this) were considered dependent concepts or categories in achieving an understanding of risk. Interaction between these two types of factor leads to the existence of varied levels of disaster risk. Specific 'disaster risk' (which can be defined in terms of 'exceptional' losses) was seen, however, to be but one component of global societal risk. The other major component introduced into the project concept relates to what may be called 'life style' or 'everyday risk'.

In this case, we are essentially referring to the more or less permanent living conditions of poor populations that constitute a permanent threat to their physical and psychological security. These conditions include health problems, malnutrition, unemployment and income deficits, illiteracy, social and domestic violence, drug addiction and alcoholism. In other words, this comprised a series of conditions that, in many ways, define poverty and limit development conditions and opportunities. Some have stated that the sum of these conditions signify that the poor or destitute live under permanent conditions of 'disaster' and that disaster related to environmental extremes is only one impermanent and irregular component of this (see Maskrey, 1989; Wilches-Chaux, 1998; Blaikie et al, 1994). Given this context, exceptional losses associated with environmental extremes attain the category of disaster precisely because the population is in a previous state of near destitution, and not necessarily because of the absolute size of the losses incurred. Disaster risk was thus seen to be conditioned and determined by the everyday risk faced by the population in the zone, over 70 per cent of which live in conditions of poverty or extreme poverty. The perceptions, interpretations and prioritization given to disaster risk by such population groups are inevitably conditioned by their levels of everyday risk and the constant struggle to deal with them.

The linking of disaster and everyday risk in a single, integrated holistic framework helps us to understand why the project considered 'risk' the central concept and not vulnerability (or hazards) as such. Disaster risk reduction can only convincingly and permanently be achieved where intervention deals not only with the particular components that contribute to exceptional loss, but also with those that explain and feed everyday risk. Vulnerability is a concept that can be used with regard to both of these linked risk contexts, although it assumes different connotations and characteristics for each of them. And, although the major argument put forward over the last decade is that reduction of disaster vulnerability and risk must be achieved in order to prevent the constant erosion of development gains and the spiralling of poverty in many developing nations, the project argument worked from the opposite premise. That is to say, only by reducing everyday risk and vulnerability may we expect significant advances in the reduction of disaster risk. The roots of this risk lie in poverty, social exclusion and inadequate development practices (Blaikie et al, 1994; Hewitt, 1997).

Despite the insistence on placing risk in the centre of analysis, it is also true that vulnerability inevitably ends up being the principle topic of analysis and concern. Attempts to reduce risk will almost inevitably privilege the reduction of the diverse forms of social and environmental vulnerability that contribute to the overall risk equation. This is so because there is little, really, to be done with the natural physical extremes that contribute to a good part of disaster risk. Furthermore, many of the pseudo or 'socio-natural' hazards that result from inadequate environmental and resource-use practices derive from distinct forms of everyday vulnerability of poor populations. This is the case, for example, with increased flooding and drought related to deforestation by the poor, shoreline instability due to mangrove cutting, and unstable slopes due to different destabilizing and mining activities. Other socio-natural hazards such as the flooding associated with the opening of dam sluice gates are related more closely to competing interests and inadequate planning and institutional processes (Lavell, 1996). Vulnerability to disasters and life style vulnerability are part of the same package and must be tackled together in the search to reduce overall human insecurity or risk.

A practical corollary of the notion of global risk can be seen with regard to the objective of 'disaster-risk reduction'. Where we consider the idea of disaster risk in a restricted fashion, risk-reduction activities may be seen to basically include those that reduce the possibility of loss during times of disaster, with no explicit consideration of how this loss relates to the overall social conditions of the population. Loss is seen in absolute terms. However, if we consider risk from a holistic perspective, linking and analysing this in everyday and disaster contexts, we arrive at other conclusions.

Thus, for example, it is possible to conceive of important reductions in risk where nothing is done to reduce the physical hazard *per se* via direct actions. This could be achieved where policies, strategies and actions foster overall development and increases in local productivity, incomes and welfare, which, in turn, increase population resilience, capacities and local economic reserves. Under such circumstances, if loss is suffered during sporadic or intermittent damaging events (I deliberately do not use the term disaster here), this will not assume the same significance and importance as under previous conditions, where loss may constitute total loss and real disaster. Adequate development will automatically reduce the levels of relative or total risk. The more holistic the approaches we use, the less likely we are to run into problems that ensue from a false fragmentation of reality. Separating disaster and everyday risk is one of these false divisions. Continuity more adequately captures the notion of everyday life and disaster than discontinuity (Hewitt, 1997).

A final consideration regarding the conceptual framework relates to the territorial dimensions of risk-construction processes. As is very obvious, risk is most precisely manifested at a micro-social or micro-territorial scale. As we aggregate and work at more macro scales, precision is lost. Risk is expressed and can best be measured at the local level or below, on the geographical and social scales.

However, a good part of risk is not constructed at the local level, although certain local processes will add to it and help to define its final form or expression. Models such as the pressure and release or access models of vulnerability described by Blaikie et al (1994) reveal the complex nature of the social processes that lead to risk or insecure conditions at a local level. Many of these processes are macro-level processes, the product of social actors that see the world as their action scenario. Others are more circumscribed but, nevertheless, not local. Therefore, populations under risk are many times divorced in time and space from the social actors who are helping to mould their local risk scenarios. One result of this is that although disasters are experienced and attended at the local level, risk reduction as such requires changes in processes and policies that emanate from the regional, national and international levels. This signifies a major problem for local actors due to the problem of actor identification and the inability to subject these actors to control due to jurisdictional limits for action. The causal space of risk and the territories where loss is suffered are rarely the same (Lavell, 1996).

THE PROJECT'S PROCESS AND METHODOLOGY

In order to develop activities for the Lower Lempa River Valley project, certain basic criteria were established in order to translate the conceptual framework into methodological dictates. At the start of the process, six basic criteria or premises were set out:

1   Disaster risk must be analysed and dealt with in the light of the everyday risk and life style insecurity experienced by over 70 per cent of the population who live below the poverty line.
2   The diagnosis of risk conditions in the zone must take into account local perceptions, and variation in these between different areas, population groups and organizational representations.
3   Local risk conditions and notions on intervention strategies must be analysed, taking into account external causal factors and social actors.
4   Strategic interventions must simultaneously take on the challenges of everyday and disaster risk.
5   The project process should actively involve local population and organizations in the diagnostic, strategy formulation and decision-making process, alongside government and project personnel.
6   Project personnel should maintain their status as external agents and adhere to clear principles of impartiality when dealing with different local organizations and competing interpretations and demands.

Let us now succinctly examine some of the major defining characteristics of the methodology in view of the fact that this was a critical facet of the project, and the applicability of project results rested on the success of this process.

The diagnostic phase

Utilizing existing published information sources, extended interviews with local organizations, NGOs, government ministries and local population, and direct observation *in situ*, a preliminary diagnosis was elaborated during the first six weeks of the project. This preliminary diagnosis was intended to:

*   outline the major problems and challenges in the zone;
*   help to identify significant information gaps in order to complete an integral diagnosis;
*   provide an approximation to an internal socio-economic and environmental sub-zoning of the area;
*   provide a preliminary organizational 'map' of the zone, identifying allegiances and conflicts; different attitudes regarding development, risk reduction and popular participation; the strengths, opportunities and weaknesses of organizations; and the territorial affiliations or presence of organizations.

With the preliminary diagnosis in hand, a justification was presented to the environmental ministry and IADB authorities regarding the need for an extensive, highly participatory, full-scale diagnosis, utilizing specialized consultants, workshop training sessions on local-level risk management, group consultation sessions and in-depth interview and observation techniques. Originally, little support had been forthcoming from government for an extensive diagnostic phase given the dominant notion that diagnoses abounded on the area, that these normally got shelved away on completion and that what was important was to get on with the job and design the intervention strategy. Moreover, certain government sectors, outside of the environment ministry and the IADB, were not overly enchanted with full popular participation in the process. This could be explained by the conflictive nature of the zone and conservative, right-wing notions held by some influential government sectors.

However, as a result of discussions between the project stakeholders, total support was finally given for extending the diagnostic phase beyond the originally conceived time frame and for extensive popular participation and consultation. Ministry and IADB authorities fully supported the work team's notion that any well-conceived intervention strategy should be based on a thorough diagnosis, where local ideas, opinions, needs and capacities were considered of prime importance. Moreover, somewhat surprisingly – and never really explained – a central government dictate at this time insisted on popular participation in the project process. The positions adopted by the different stakeholders and an understanding of these should be the objective of a separate study, as the team never completely understood the route by which government finally came to fully support the project concept and methodology. Hypotheses could include the notion that the consultant team was seen to be facilitating a process by which government gained more legitimate access to a zone that was previously 'out of bounds', but, at the same time, of significant political currency.

Following on from the preliminary diagnosis, three months were dedicated to achieving an integral diagnosis of the zone. This was undertaken using a combination of technical studies and various popular consultation methods.

On the technical side, studies were contracted on:

• the hydro-geomorphology of the river, potential flooding patterns, and the strengths and pit falls of existing and projected flood control levees;
• the ecological and woodland status of the area;
• the agricultural, mangrove and saltwater production systems, including existing industrialization and commercial practices;
• basic infrastructure and housing, and the territorial organization of the zone;
• the legislative and organizational framework for development promotion in the zone;
• the organizational and planning structures for early warning, alert and emergency management systems.

With regard to popular participation and consultation procedures, discussion sessions were held with different organizations, and interviews were undertaken with leaders throughout the zone. Care was always taken to consult all competing or confronted groups and organizations and to be impartial in the process. This was of fundamental importance in a zone where confidence and impartiality were among the key pillars of any successful intervention. As far as possible, smaller and less influential organizations were given an equal hearing. Project members were present in the zone as long as possible throughout the process, thus avoiding the idea that the project was being run by consultants who live in the capital city and just visit the zone on occasions. This procedure, in addition to being absolutely necessary, also permitted the forging of confidence between the principal local organizations and the project group. Here it should be pointed out that consultants are always external agents and 'intruders', and total impartiality is never possible. However, the group always attempted to maintain the maximum possible level of impartiality and not to succumb to the particular wishes or pressures of the different local organizations when these occasionally emerged. In general, this was successfully achieved and these organizations were highly collaborative in the process. At no time did they make their own internal differences a problem for implementing the project methodology. The level of confidence in the consultant group could be corroborated when the local organizations requested that they also run the second stage of the project, once the diagnostic and strategic phases had been completed.

Two three-day workshops on local-level risk management were organized for organizational representatives from the different communities and sub-zones as part of the popular consultation procedures. Members of La RED ran these workshops, using the training methodology developed by the organization between 1996 and 2001, and implemented in more than 15 countries throughout Latin America and the Caribbean (Wilches-Chaux, 1998).

The workshops allowed for conceptual clarification and a firmer understanding of risk-construction processes, knowledge on methods for constructing local risk scenarios, the development of notions on strategic intervention and the construction of sustainable local-development scenarios, as well as basic expertise in techniques for putting together and implementing local plans. Over 70 local community representatives participated in the workshops. None of the representatives dropped out of the sessions during the three days. This occurred in an area where many individuals had to get up at 4 am, walk relatively long distances to the bus collection point, journey up to an hour to the workshop venue, and return home at 6 pm to domestic and agricultural labouring tasks. This was a tribute to the organizational base in the zone, the social appropriation of the risk and development problematic and the commitment of the population. No attempt was made at this time to mix populations from different sides of the river, or from competing organizations from left-bank communities due to the still existing levels of antagonism between different areas and organizations, features that have been discussed earlier in this chapter. Here, it should be emphasized that while the consultancy group made it clear to local organizations that the existing divisions could not be taken as a valid reason for pressures regarding segregation of groups, respect for the arguments in favour of this – and apprehension about the possible outcomes of ignoring it – led to the conclusion that caution was the best possible course to take.

On completing the draft diagnostic document, a series of three, two-day popular consultation meetings were organized for local representatives. During these meetings, participants were presented with a summary of the major preliminary findings of the diagnosis. Using talks on key risk and development issues, game playing and work group discussions, the participants analysed the formal conclusions of the diagnosis, and modifications and additions were made incorporating the results of their deliberations. Following on from this, a similar exercise was undertaken but this time considering and prioritizing a series of postulated solutions for the major risk and development problems identified in the diagnosis. These solutions had been put together by the consultants, taking into consideration the technical studies undertaken and the expressed priority needs of the local population.

The results of this exercise were incorporated within the formal diagnosis document and offered an important basis for the elaboration of the final intervention scenario presented to the ministry and the IADB in the final project report.

Putting the intervention scenario together

Once the diagnostic phase and the popular consultation process had been completed, the team put together an integrated intervention scenario. This closely took into account the series of problems identified in the diagnosis and evaluated in the consultation meetings with local population, NGOs and government. The scenario went well beyond the possible investment opportunity offered by the IADB as a follow-up to the project. This was done deliberately as a need was seen for a fully integrated scenario that could guide any other future investments beyond the IADB's particular short-term commitment which, at the time, had been estimated at some US$8 million to $10 million. Projects identified as possible IADB ventures were to be of a strategic nature and facilitate subsequent linked investments. The projects presented as part of the strategy sought a balance between territorial integration and sectorial development goals.

Adjustments were made to the project portfolio and a consensus was arrived at regarding projects to be further elaborated for potential IADB financing. The project portfolio sought to cover projects of general relevance to the whole zone, while at the same time satisfying the needs, priorities and requirements of the different organizations and sub-zones. A mix of broadly based development projects, along with more precisely defined disaster-risk projects, was achieved. The final project portfolio included the following projects, developed at a logical framework level:

- A proposal for the development and management of riverside and coastal bay woodlands. The prime objective would be to develop a socio-productive culture in harmony with the flooding and drought environments that typify the zone, as well as to utilize the woodlands as a natural buffer to flooding. Community participation in developing product diversification schemes and natural regeneration of woodlands, accompanied by the strengthening of local organizations and schemes for natural resource conservation, would offer natural protection from the river and new research, eco-tourist and production opportunities. Employment creation and increased welfare levels would be expected to follow.

- A training programme on local-level risk management for local organizations and population, and the strengthening of the local early warning systems.
- Territorial planning and community reorganization schemes, leading to an increase in the density, territorial concentration and interconnectivity of communities and basic services. Improvements in the access to public services and in the efficiency of links between housing and work, as well as improved road access for commercial and emergency operations, were proposed.
- Housing construction, including the provision of environmentally adequate housing to disaster populations, individuals in areas of high risk and the destitute. Relocation of certain high-risk communities was proposed, including those affected by liquefaction in the coastal areas during the January and February 2001 earthquakes.
- Potable water supply systems and environmental hygiene projects.
- Monitoring, improvement and renovation of existing dikes. The extension of existing dikes towards the coastal area would be followed by national governmental institutions using other funds.

SOME MAJOR TRANSITIONS IN IDEAS EMANATING FROM THE DIAGNOSTIC PROCESS

The project diagnosis and associated problem prioritization exercises provided extensive information and analysis on diverse topics and contexts relating to the risk and vulnerability problematic and their relationships to the overall objective of identifying lower-risk, sustainable development options. This included considerations regarding attitudes, perceptions and the social 'reading' of risk and vulnerability. This section provides a summary of a number of the more important issues diagnosed and debated in the dynamic process established between external actors and local individuals and organizations. In particular, it concentrates on the transitions achieved in terms of understanding the risk problematic and regarding conceptions on intervention and change. This is so because we became increasingly convinced as the project proceeded that local self-awareness and consciousness, empowerment, organizational strength and the ability to construct integrated options and strategies were key factors in reducing vulnerability and in promoting project sustainability.

Disaster and everyday risk

The notion that disaster risk cannot be separated from the ongoing contexts of daily risk associated with the extremely high levels of poverty and social deprivation prevalent in the area was fully supported by local groups. This permitted an easy understanding that disaster-risk reduction was a facet of development planning and not an autonomous goal with its own independent set of strategies and instruments. When faced with the task of prioritizing diagnosed problems, the vast majority of the representatives present in the consultation meetings proffered a varied gamut of projects that broached diverse aspects of disaster risk and vulnerability. These included:

- improvements in, and extension of, potable water systems in order to reduce the incidence of disease vectors, such as mosquitoes and water-borne bacteria;
- expansion of the lateral, secondary road systems, allowing the movement of products and people under normal environmental conditions and also when flooding required evacuation and temporary housing in refuges;
- environmental sanitation measures in order to reduce the problems associated with stagnant floodwater and inadequate control of animal populations;
- housing adapted to the local physical and ecological conditions;
- permanent monitoring and repairs to the existing dikes, and the extension of dikes to the southern-most coastal area;
- increased opportunities for agricultural production using irrigation systems, including the possible inversion of the planting and harvesting seasons, allowing cropping in the dry season and not at the time of maximum flood risk;
- provision of commercial infrastructure and services, thus allowing the elimination of entrepreneurs who take advantage of the limited commercial options of the population in order to buy at low prices (locally known in Spanish as coyotes or prairie dogs);
- increased surveillance and security in the area;
- environmental conservation and planning, including the preservation and extension of existing woodlands and increases in their productive potential;
- selective relocation of very high-risk communities;
- improvements to the existing community-based early warning and evacuation schemes.

Of these projects, maximum priority was finally given to potable water systems, housing with selective relocation of certain high-risk communities, ecological management and recovery, alternative production options and commercial practices and local-level risk management expertise, including upgrading of early warning systems. These priorities were translated in good part into the short-term intervention scenario presented for IADB and government consideration, as outlined in the previous section.

The diverse components of vulnerability

An increased understanding of the varied components of vulnerability allowed for the identification of priority actions and an awareness of the need for linking external resources with local capacities and opportunities in the search to reduce the different manifestations of risk and vulnerability. A consideration of the varied components of vulnerability allowed the local population to comprehend the diversity of different complimentary approaches that could help to reduce overall risk. More easily understood notions relating to economic, social and ecological vulnerability were accompanied by an increased awareness of subtler but no less important facets. In particular, this included an increased awareness of the dangers of unilateral views of disaster-risk reduction based solely on technological interventions as opposed to broader-based interventions using land-use planning, agricultural diversification and adaptation, ecosystem management and increases in life style resilience. Moreover, discussion and analysis allowed participants to clearly perceive the fundamental importance of organizational development and cooperation and the creation of social capital in providing a basis for risk reduction.

Organizational development and organizational harmony: keys to the development of social capital

Although the zone had been the object of numerous previous interventions by external actors and of important efforts in terms of infrastructure, housing and production opportunities, many schemes implemented post-Hurricane Mitch were ecologically, structurally and socially flawed. The lack of a unified or harmonious organizational base depleted the negotiating capacity of local actors and left the zone prey to the (well-intentioned) decisions and criteria of many external actors. During the local-level risk management workshops, many local actors, in fact, identified external actors as a major 'hazard', while the incapacity to negotiate and demand adequate solutions was seen to be a major vulnerability in the zone. Many insisted that on a number of occasions the population had been obliged to take or leave what was offered. The immense demand for housing, water and sanitation systems and new production options in the zone made this possible. Various external actors simply sought out other demand sectors if those approached showed dissatisfaction with what was offered. Commonly agreed upon development criteria, parameters and goals were perceived to be a prerequisite for increasing the negotiating strength of local organizations and in helping guarantee adequate and coordinated solutions to problems and needs. This conclusion, reached by the major organizational actors during discussions, was pivotal in achieving an acceptance of the virtues and needs for a single integrated strategy document for the zone.

Moreover, as a result of the project and the wide-ranging opportunity for discussion and negotiation that it offered, the levels of confidence between the project team, local leaders and government personnel, and between local organizations themselves, allowed the formation of an embryonic local development committee. This was established with representatives from the two competing umbrella organizations, municipalities and national government. Never previously had the two major umbrella organizations sat down together to discuss and arrive at common agreements. The formation of this committee was of great importance due to the confidence it generated in terms of the real possibility of future local participation in implementing new projects financed by the IADB or others. Decentralization with local participation was considered a keystone to future success with risk reduction and sustainable development.

Understanding environment and reducing risk

Transformation in consciousness levels on risk and risk reduction, and a fuller understanding of risk construction processes were of particular importance in the Lempa Valley where many people are recent migrants to the zone and have little experience with tropical lowland environments and agriculture. This aspect is relevant in many different contexts where migration places people in unfamiliar environments. Technological solutions are far more palpable to population groups with little experience of lowland agricultural environments, and where the opportunities offered in terms of environmental management, land-use planning and alternative agricultural schemes and practices are not immediately obvious. This aspect of vulnerability, discussed above, led to discussions regarding alternative non structural methods of risk reduction and the creation of a flood-zone 'culture', as opposed to a disaster prevention culture *per se*.

The fallacy of relocation

Despite prevailing attitudes in government circles that massive relocation of population was the only real solution for the zone, this was increasingly seen to be neither a real or viable proposition. The generalized opposition by local groups and organizations to relocation comprised a fundamental part of local ideology and reflected diverse interpretations, fears and reticence regarding government motivations for such a policy. These included the idea that government was in favour of relocation in order to reoccupy areas of higher productivity, large-scale agriculture. Any idea of massive relocation would be strongly resisted by a population who saw the land that they now occupied as a prize for their struggles and sacrifice during the civil war years.

THE CURRENT STATUS OF THE PROJECT

Perhaps the single most important indicator of project success is not its immediate short-term results, but, rather, what it leaves in place and its sustainability in the medium and long term. The immediate results of this project can be gleaned from the discussion offered above: an integral consciousness and awareness-raising diagnostic elaborated with wide-scale participation of local organizations and interest groups; a single commonly agreed upon intervention scenario and local development strategy document; and the formation of an embryonic local development committee.

With regard to continuity and consolidation, the project has had an encouraging outcome.

On the basis of the positive results and the level of cohesion and collaboration achieved within the zone, the IADB made a bridging loan available to the environment ministry to further carry project aims and goals forward. This consisted of a near US$0.5 million-finance package provided by the British and Japanese governments in order to consolidate project results and to finalize the preparation of the investment strategy.

In particular, UK funds have been channelled to strengthen the local organizational base and to promote local-level risk management strategies. Through this finance, the embryonic local development committee has been formally institutionalized and strengthened, incorporating new representatives from other local organizations. This committee plays a joint role with government in the running of the project extension phase and is being prepared to fully participate in the future implementation of new development and risk-reduction projects. Japanese funds are being used to undertake the fully fledged feasibility studies for the projects identified in the intervention scenario and strategy document elaborated during the first stage of the project. IADB, in agreement with the Salvadoran government, is committed to providing a minimum US$8 million loan to commence implementation of the projects once the feasibility studies are successfully completed.

On another front, the strategy document elaborated during the first stage has been firmly appropriated by the local organizations and was reproduced in summary form and distributed and discussed throughout the zone in community- and zonal-based meetings. Agreement exists that this document will be used by the major local organizations in negotiating and determining future investments in the area. Moreover, the environment and housing and public works ministries have also agreed that future projects and investments in the area will closely take into account the strategy dictates included in the document.

CONCLUSION

This chapter has attempted to illustrate the importance of concept and method in achieving positive results with regard to risk reduction. Moreover, it has highlighted certain issues about vulnerability that may be considered fundamental in terms of intervention and change.

The overall components or facets identified regarding risk and vulnerability in the zone are initial well-being, strength and resilience; livelihood resilience; self-protection; societal protection; and social capital. Moreover, the intervention scenario components developed in the strategy document also showed a balanced mix of projects that address these varied levels of vulnerability. Here, there is a clear sign that where the population is cognizant of the relationships between the differing facets of everyday and disaster risk, the obvious thing to do is to simultaneously tackle these apparently different problems. Cognizance of the fact that both disaster and everyday risk have similar origins is a starting point for promoting integrated sustainable and environmentally secure development schemes. As long as disaster is seen as externally imposed, little advance will be achieved. The appropriation of the idea of social risk construction and risk as an unresolved development problem are critical factors in increasing awareness and empowering communities. Empowerment and increased and strengthened social capital are major factors in reducing vulnerability and an unavoidable starting point for risk reduction.

Chapter 6

El Niño Events, Forecasts and Decision-making

Roger S Pulwarty, Kenneth Broad and Timothy Finan

The future is not what it used to be (Anonymous).

INTRODUCTION

This chapter explores the concepts of vulnerability and equity in the context of the production and use of scientific information as tools in mitigation and for responding to climatic events. 'Vulnerability' has been defined in terms of risk and exposure (likelihood of a particular event and attendant economic loss), root causes and dynamic pressures that produce unsafe conditions and the capacity to act (Wisner, 1993; Pulwarty and Riebsame, 1997; Comfort et al, 1999). Equity here is taken to relate to rules and rule-making processes, and to the exchange and distribution of material or non-material resources in a specific context. Much insight has been provided by political ecologists and others regarding vulnerability as a result of actions prescribed at different scales (international, regional, national, and sub-national) over time. As has long been known, reducing social vulnerability does not depend upon the precision of forecasts of particular physical hazards alone. However, as evident in the case of El Niño-related risks, both preparedness and exacerbation of vulnerable conditions may be influenced by forecasts of events (for example, information about an impending event) as much as by the occurrence of the events themselves. Thus, the decision-making process into which such information is placed, and the associated benefits and inequities created require careful attention.

As a result of changes in funding since the end of the Cold War, there is an increasingly common trend towards justifying scientific research on its societal relevance. The post-Cold War years are witnessing an ascendant rhetoric of a 'culture of accountability', where research-funding agencies have been increasingly transformed from institutions primarily responsible for maintaining basic science in universities and labs into instruments for attaining national technological, economic and social priorities through the funding of research projects and programmes (Nowotny et al, 1999). The result is an increasingly distributed knowledge production system in which communication and alliances increasingly develop across existing institutional boundaries (Gibbons, 1999). Nowhere is this ascendance more visible than in the international set of activities that result in forecasting El Niño events and their impacts at local levels.

Based on extensive fieldwork, this chapter draws upon concepts of social justice and technology management studies to show that, while there may exist significant potential benefits, 'knowledge-based' interventions can and do simplify complex situations and strengthen existing assumptions and myths about the 'powerlessness' of impacted people. As is well known, governments at different scales are usually already aware of problems exacerbated by local climate anomalies but their practice does not always reflect this awareness (Glantz, 2001). Interventions undertaken under such conditions can continue or can accelerate existing processes of social differentiation through differential access and the use of information. 'Inclusion' is increasingly viewed as a means to overcome distributional inequities. However, for the most vulnerable groups, inclusion in many cases usually means accepting only subordinate positions based upon distribution within the power structures, without an increase in rights or responsibilities. As we hope to show below, clarifying the nature of, and barriers to, effective procedure and participation requires renewed attention from students of social vulnerability.

Cases are drawn from the 1997 to 1998 El Niño event as it affected Peruvian artisanal fisheries and water and agricultural management in Northeast Brazil (see Figure 6.1). These were amongst the earliest regions settled by Europeans in the New World. In both locations, the relative climatic experiences have been documented over long periods. Spanish Conquistadors recorded the occurrence of El Niño in Peru in 1525. Northeast Brazil was the site of the original Portuguese settlement 500 years ago. In addition, Peru and Brazil have been two of the most studied regions in terms of climatic impacts (especially related to El Niño) in the world (Diaz and Markgraf, 1992).

We discuss how technology-based knowledge about potential hazards (for example, the forecast of an El Niño event and its projected impacts) interacts with existing vulnerabilities. We identify discourses that legitimize dominant representations of society and the environment. The study further outlines important differences among local, national and international decision-making processes in responding to actual and forecasted El Niño-related impacts. It highlights the homogenizing assumptions about culture, history and capacity that are engaged in strictly technocratic approaches to risk assessment and management. Emphasis is placed on how the relationships between political and 'expert'-derived power determines which actors are seen as 'legitimate' developers of risk messages and whose view of reality is represented, pursued and secured. These processes have distinct influences on post-event claims of the 'success' of international programmes. We investigate why such technocratic responses prevail even when there has been long-established work on the social construction of vulnerability. We argue that studies of dynamic pressures and

Figure 6.1 *Locations of cases: Peru and Northeast Brazil*

'capacity' should include assessment of impediments to flows of knowledge and information and assessments of the policies and practices that give rise to these impediments. A plea is made for a stronger interpretative and participatory role for analysts of vulnerability in unwrapping and making transparent the particular decision contexts and organizational processes in which knowledge is developed and used.

EL NIÑO AND FORECASTING: RECENT DEVELOPMENTS

An El Niño event occurs every four to seven years and has been associated with extreme climatic events around the world (Davis, 2001). The term 'El Niño' will be used throughout this chapter to refer to the fully coupled oceanic and atmospheric phenomena of the El Niño–Southern Oscillation or ENSO event (see Glantz, 2001). The extraordinary 1982 to 1983 El Niño, which influenced inter-annual climate variation around the globe, catalysed government and scientific interest in developing an El Niño forecast capability. Estimates of global loss range from US$32,000 million to $96,000 million (IFRC, 2002). Since then, the scientific community, through large resource investments, has produced marked improvements in monitoring, understanding and forecasting the El Niño phenomenon and its climatic impacts. As a result of this work, international and other agencies developed outlook policies and selectively projected their activities for many parts of the world during 1997 to 1998. The 1997 to 1998 event was one of the two strongest such events on record. It was a major international focusing event drawing worldwide attention and calls for response to forecasted impacts while the event itself was developing.

As documented in Glantz (2001), the United Nations (UN) General Assembly took note of the intensity and global extent of 'natural disasters' and requested the secretary-general, as reflected in Resolutions 52/200 and 53/185, to develop a strategy within the framework of the International Decade for Natural Disaster Reduction (IDNDR) to prevent, mitigate and rehabilitate the damage caused by the El Niño phenomenon. As a response, the Inter-Agency Task Force on El Niño was created in December 1997. It provided a platform for combining efforts to improve the general understanding of the El Niño phenomenon, for disseminating early warnings and for channelling technical assistance and capacity-building resources to member states threatened or affected by El Niño- and La Niña-related disaster impacts.

As discussed above, the development of seasonal-to-inter-annual climate predictions has spurred widespread claims that distributing forecasts will yield benefits for society. Indeed, forecasts of El Niño events have been called 'science's gift to the 21st century' (Glantz, 1994). The assumption is that the ability to anticipate how climate will change from one year to the next will lead to better management of agriculture, water supplies, fisheries and other resources (Pfaff et al, 2001). Furthermore, the expectation, held by many scientific researchers, is that by incorporating predictions into management decisions, humankind is becoming better adapted to the irregular rhythms of climate. While *ad hoc* interventions using scientific information, to some extent, help to address immediate humanitarian emergencies, they usually do not address, and may even increase, the underlying structural problems that create disasters. As will be discussed (in the context of drought management in Northeast Brazil and fisheries in Peru), the relative gaps in our understanding include not only the identification of affected categories of people and how they are affected, but also whether such groups have the capacity or are likely to use forecast information beneficially, if at all.

DROUGHT AND RESPONSE IN NORTHEAST BRAZIL

Northeast Brazil (the Nordeste) is a semi-arid region comprised of nine states that represents approximately 10 per cent of the national territory and 30 per cent of the population. In 1877, an extended drought (as defined by a climatic season with insufficient quantity or distribution of rainfall to secure an agricultural harvest) occurred throughout the region, resulting in over 500,000 fatalities and totally disrupting rural society (Da Cunha, 1902). Extreme drought also occurred in 1932, 1958, 1983 and 1998. In 1959 (following the then 'worst drought of the century'), the Superintendency for the Development of the Northeast (SUDENE) was created by the federal government to concentrate development efforts and to coordinate investment programmes. Its role in drought relief was (and still is) to organize and oversee the programme of 'work fronts' – in essence, an emergency public works programme comprised of labour gangs drawn from the families of drought victims. In this programme, politics and policy became inextricably enmeshed, as local politicians used the available funds to spread the gospel of clientilism and patronage (Pessoa, 1987; Goldsmith and Wilson, 1991). In the state of Ceará, 10 per cent of the landowners own 90 per cent of the land and the large landholders regularly directed relief funds towards improvements on their *fazendas* (estates). Through this and other avenues, public relief funds were converted into actual income for large holders or an army of labour that became a source of private (no cost) investment for their *fazendas*. This widespread exploitation of intense misery has been labelled the 'drought industry', considered one of the most lucrative in the Northeast (Reis, 1981; Dia, 1986; Glantz and Magalhaes, 1992; Greenfield, 1992).

It is within this context that climate forecasts based on El Niño were introduced during the 1990s by international and national research and aid organizations. In the next section, we focus on the impacts of such interventions in Ceará.

Science and drought in Ceará during the 1990s

The first major public effort to combat drought in Ceará occurred with the 1977 to 1979 crisis that included nearly half the population of the state (Souza and Filho, 1983, p34). In 1972, the Cearense Foundation for Meteorology and Water Resources (FUNCEME) was created first as a centre for cloud seeding and then restructured in 1987 as a regional centre for meteorological applications (see Orlove and Tosteson, 1999, for an excellent history of the institution). At the beginning of the 1990s, FUNCEME became a key element in a wider government effort to combat the drought. It tied forecast information, first, to a programme of seed distribution called Hora de Plantar (Time to Plant) that provided quality bean, rice and corn seed to farmers; second, it established a programme of short-term production credit that was meant to give farmers the resources to purchase inputs and to cover labour costs. The timing of both seed and credit release was based on the climate predictions, which, in effect, mandated when the agricultural campaign would begin (Lemos, 2002). The scientific basis of the policy was solid; but the assumptions that farmers do not already know when to plant or that government could solve the problem of drought reinforced the clientilistic environment in which such policy was formulated.

FUNCEME gained international attention in 1992, when, during the previous December, it announced the likelihood of drought based on a forecast. According to legend and literature (Finan, 1999; Orlove and Tosteson, 1999), this forecast unleashed a set of measures that included the provisioning of 'drought-tolerant' seed, the opening of credit lines, and a bandwagon journey throughout the interior by the then-governor Ciro Gomes to urge farmers to participate in the programme. The purported result of this effort was a table of numbers published in the international literature comparing two drought years, one with forecast, one without, both with similar levels of precipitation, but with 85 per cent of average harvest in the forecast year compared with only 15 per cent of average in the other. These figures were consequently cited regularly by regional and international organizations to promote the value of climate information. However this 'success story' laid the groundwork of a major crisis for FUNCEME and diverted attention from the areas of environmental policy-making where climate information could be the most valuable. Even if the numbers are accepted, however, there are alternative explanations for the differences. As all climate scientists warn us, the semi-arid tropics are characterized by high levels of spatial and temporal variability in rainfall. For the years in question, 75 per cent of average precipitation is a meaningless figure if the distribution of rainfall is not taken into consideration. The phenomenon of 'green drought' in the *sertão* is well documented, when total regional rainfall can exceed the average, but farmers actually experience drought, as defined by harvest levels.

Where, however, policy became mere demagoguery was the assertion that the government's effort to direct planting, symbolized by the governor's pilgrimage to the interior, actually made a difference in farmer behaviour. Every farmer selects the most vigorous plants from the previous harvest as the household seed bank. This system of seed selection, as well as the farmer's tendency to acquire improved seed from neighbours, has produced seed varieties adapted to regional climatic conditions. Thus, it is not producer ignorance over when or what to plant that is responsible for the impacts of drought. Rather, it is the essential vulnerability of these families to drought and the lack of real alternatives to buffer their livelihoods against climate extremes.

During the last half of the 1990s, state (and regional) drought policy has maintained the two-pronged approach (Hora de Plantar and short-term production credit) that seeks a preventive solution in science and a mitigation solution in emergency relief. With a strong team of scientists from around Brazil, technical support of INPE, Brazil's prestigious Institute for Space Studies, and a substantial investment in computing and data-gathering infrastructure, FUNCEME developed the capacity to issue seasonal climate forecasts based on several sources of data, including ENSO. The dissemination of seasonal forecasts would begin annually in November/December, the period just preceding the expected arrival of the rains, and would project the likelihood of adequate precipitation for the winter.[1]

The presence of the rain prophets (*profetas de chuva*) and the many natural 'signs of rain' to which rural people attribute great significance are testimonies to the psychological anxiety that the threat of drought engenders. Against this background, the FUNCEME forecasts, associated with science, were seen as competing with or even expropriating divine design, as if the state had gained special access to sacred knowledge. Instead of dispelling this notion, policy-makers exploited the forecasts to promote their own legitimacy and to solidify their power positions as benefactors of the people. In the public discourse, the policy-maker in possession of 'science' became one with the saints' intercessionary power. The FUNCEME 'success story' was never repeated in a decade that subsequently produced four more droughts. The international community has yet to assess whether the influence of forecasts continues to be detected in maintaining higher levels of production. In the eyes of the international climate community, FUNCEME provided important proof that climate forecasts could have applications of great social value. From the perspective of policy-makers and politicians, the forecasts demonstrated that science '[makes] it possible for the Cearense farmer to live with drought and "this is not an accident", confirmed [Governor] Ciro'.[2]

The forecasts became more a legitimization of the government and its leaders than a mere science product. From the perspective of rural farmers, the forecasts were associated with another government promise of solutions to end the misery of their lives. When betterment was not forthcoming, resentment followed.

In December 1996, FUNCEME issued a forecast of winter rains 'beneath the average', which was interpreted by the media in terms of the dreaded word *seca* (drought). During this year, the below-average forecast delayed the release of seeds under the programme and virtually cancelled the credit programme (which, in reality, was more affected by the macro-economic situation nationally). Consistent with the variability of semi-arid climates, certain regions in the state experienced early rains, seemingly contradicting the forecast. The fact that the seed and credit programmes were not launched despite adequate rains was presented in the media as a crisis of confidence, not only in FUNCEME and science but also in the government, in general. The discourse quickly became political and was debated in the state assembly. In fact, the early rains halted in most *municípios* (municipalities) of the state, and the final verdict was that the season, indeed, had been below normal. From a production perspective, many regions did experience drought, although a major relief effort was not launched.

El Niño 1997 to 1998: information sources and provision in Ceará

The inevitable fall of FUNCEME in the eyes of its stakeholder public occurred during 1997 and 1998 and resulted in a redefinition of the agency's mission. During the 1998 drought, an estimated 80 per cent of the harvest (based on average annual production) was lost. The state government, through its civil defence agency, coordinated the widespread emergency relief effort throughout the state. The role of FUNCEME in the relief effort was to report on the amounts of rainfall in each *município* since the level of precipitation was one of the eligibility criteria for emergency assistance. As early as March and April 1998, municipal governments began to declare local states of emergency and to use political representation in the state assembly to pressure the governor's office. However, FUNCEME credibility had been severely damaged. Among people in the rural areas, it was common to hear the opinion that whatever FUNCEME says, act as if the opposite is true. During 1997, the pronounced El Niño signal was monitored by FUNCEME and in January an International Climate Outlook Forum was held in Fortaleza. The consensus of the forum was a strong probability of a weak winter. At the same time, a conference of rain prophets was held in a rural centre and was widely publicized as the 'alternative forecast'. The rain prophets concurred that the existing signs pointed towards a normal or even above average winter (*I Encontro Estadual de Profetas Populares*, 1998). FUNCEME issued its forecast in January, again predicting below-average levels of rainfall. The final outcome of this public debate was that the climate information system itself had virtually no influence on any public preparation for the most severe drought in memory. The argument made here is that the legacy of the politicization of science had reached its inevitable conclusion: the potential value of the forecast became a victim of the demagoguery of the early part of the decade.

The vast majority of households were aware of FUNCEME and the climate product it offered; but there was also near unanimity that its forecast was wrong, that FUNCEME could not substitute for God, and that this was just another government ploy.[3] In several *municípios* in the study area, local radio stations assumed the mantle of responsibility for the crusade to discredit FUNCEME and its forecast, and these media sources have an important influence in forming public sentiment. The sample of households was also able to identify several traditional signs that forecast the winter rains, such as star positions, rings around the moon, birds' nests, ant and armadillo behaviour and the flowering of certain *sertão* plant species (Finan, 1999). The major insight from this inquiry, however, was not in terms of access to climate information, but, rather, the use of such information. It became clear from interviews that, even if FUNCEME's credibility had not been challenged, these farmers, for the most part, were unable to use climate information because their levels of vulnerability are so limited in terms of technology choice. Stated simply, even with perfect information, there are no science panaceas – no escape from the reality of drought for the majority of the population. It is this fact that policy has ignored in the interest of clientilistic politics.

The exceptions to these conclusions are twofold. Firstly, those households in the survey that have access to irrigated land (about 14 per cent concentrated in three *municípios*) are generally the least vulnerable and, in fact, can take advantage of increased prices for food crops that result from a lost harvest. In the *município* of Limoeiro do Norte in the Jaguaribe Valley, irrigated producers shifted quickly to bean production in anticipation of price increases early in the 1998 season. The other category of stakeholder that showed a potential to use climate information is the large ranch-holder, who has the option of moving the herd to other, less affected pastures or of bringing in purchased feed and water. This strategy was again observed during the El Niño 1998 event.

It is not an exaggeration to affirm that from the perspective of some farmers, FUNCEME was not the messenger but the cause of the crisis. Ironically, the FUNCEME forecasts were essentially accurate over the three years that the research team monitored the system, even though, in the eyes of the public, they were completely wrong. As Orlove and Tosteson note, FUNCEME has changed its mission during the last two years and has taken steps to de-politicize its climate information provision policy. Firstly, the linkages between the seasonal forecast and seed and credit programmes have been sundered. Those programmes are now implemented independently of the forecast. The dissemination of forecasts has now become a low-visibility activity, with FUNCEME working closely with the rural extension services and *prefeituras* (prefectures) to spread the forecast information. Secondly, FUNCEME has turned its research capacity to focus more on the long-term impacts of frequent drought – for example, desertification. The move to integrate long-term resource degradation with current agricultural practices and drought is a promising development. FUNCEME now promotes a philosophy of adaptation to drought.

CLIMATE AND FISHERIES IN PERU

The Peruvian fishery was fuelled by the increased post-World War II demand for fishmeal and the collapse of the California sardine fishery during the 1950s that made boats and machinery cheaply available. The Peruvian industrial fishing boom began during the mid-1950s and lasted until the early 1970s (Schaefer, 1970; Paulik, 1971). In the context of weak regulations and technological advances, its catch increased to more than 12 million metric tonnes (primarily anchovy) by 1972. Overfishing combined with the 1972 to 1973 El Niño contributed to the collapse of the fishery. It was not until the early 1990s that the anchovy fishery recuperated to pre-1973 levels (see Figure 6.2). Throughout much of the 1990s, the Peruvian fishing sector accounted for over 10 per cent of the world's catch (consistently ranking second to China) with over 90 per cent of that going to fishmeal production. Second only to mineral products, fishmeal is of appreciable importance to Peru's economy, representing more than 4 per cent of the gross domestic product and generating over US$1000 million in foreign exchange earnings in 1996.

The fishing sector can be roughly divided into artisanal (about 50,000 small-scale producers) and industrial groups employing about 26,000 persons. These two groups catch different species using different methods of capture, are subject to different regulations and occupy different socio-economic strata. Inter-annual climate variations, generally related to El Niño events, shift the spatial availability and relative abundance of the variety of harvested species (Barber and Chavez,

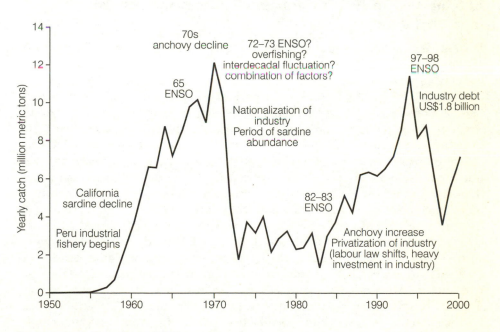

Source: adapted from Broad (1999)

Figure 6.2 *Annual catch of small pelagics (including Anchoveta* Engraulis ringens*) and key events in fisheries management off Peru*

1983). As different groups and sub-groups specialize in the extraction of different species, a given event may benefit one group or set of sub-groups, while harming others. Moreover, throughout the period of commercial fishing, the industrial subsector has wielded strong political influence (Thorp and Bertram, 1978; Baltazar, 1979; Zapata, 1998).

At present, labour union power has significantly diminished in the fishing sector due to the large number of short-term contract workers and the removal, in 1996, of regulations that protected worker security during *vedas* (closed seasons). During the mid-1990s, the largest fishing firms began diversifying into canned fish products, agriculture, mining and other industries. The financial sector is linked to the fishing sector through banks, many of which have invested heavily in the industrial fleets and plants. Currently, regulations are made by the Ministry of Fisheries. Its decisions, in theory, are informed by the recommendations of the board of directors of the governmental scientific agency in charge of fisheries and oceanographic studies, as well as expert advice from the UN Food and Agriculture Organization (FAO). This board of directors is made up of representatives from the navy, the industrial fishing sector, a scientific agency, and the Ministry of Fisheries. The board members are, in turn, informed by the agency's scientists. Regulatory mechanisms include species as well as minimum size restrictions, closed seasons or bans, spatial and gear restrictions, and statistical reporting. Regulations are inconsistently enforced.

El Niño 1997 to 1998: information sources and provision in coastal Peru

Reluctance by a range of decision-makers to act upon early forecasts of the 1997 to 1998 El Niño was influenced by their memory of the characteristics of prior El Niño events and the existence of multiple conflicting forecasts of the event. For example, the 1997 to 1998 event manifested early in the year compared to the last big event of 1982 to 1983, contributing to the debate over how the present event would develop. Similarly, some fishermen, firms and bankers recalled the 'false starts and finishes' of the El Niños of 1991 to 1995 and were also hesitant to take significant proactive measures well in advance (for example, cancel plans to build new boats and plants, buy new nets, divestment, etc). Finally, biological indicators that accompanied the 1982 to 1983 event, such as the arrival of massive numbers of jellyfish to the coastal areas, did not occur during 1997 to 1998, discouraging procurement of different equipment in anticipation of the arrival of other commercially valuable tropical species. As mentioned above, uncertainty surrounding the development of the event was further compounded by conflicting forecasts. The first official announcement of an impending event came from the Peruvian meteorological service in June 1997, though it was heavily disputed by other local agencies. The first government measures, which included forming a multi-sectoral task force led by the head of the national oceanographic agency, took place shortly afterwards, in July 1997.

Towards the start of the event (April 1997), the small pelagic fish stocks composed primarily of anchovy (*Engraulis ringens*) moved closer to shore in search of cooler, nutrient-rich waters. These conditions led to a short-lived increase or 'spike' in catch, which the Peruvian oceanographic agency realized was related to the anomalous warming and changing biological conditions of the waters. Based on the recommendations of the oceanographic agency, the Ministry of Fisheries implemented a fishing ban (*veda*) in the central-north sections of the coast in April; but it was retracted just a few days later due to industrial pressure. The high catches declined rapidly as fish began to migrate both vertically below the range of the nets (over 70 metres), and southward into Northern Chile. The oceanographic agency increased their monitoring of biological indicators and began efforts at coordinating this monitoring with their Chilean counterparts.

Despite industry pressure to continue fishing, the Peruvian oceanographic agency recommended a *veda* in the south (from 16° south to the Chilean border), a virtually unprecedented measure. Again, due to political pressure, the *veda* period was cut short; but, in reality, fishing had already dropped to very low levels, imposing what fishermen called a '*veda natural*'. Pending the results of monitoring cruises, the Ministry of Fisheries set a low preliminary quota on anchovy for the upcoming period (September to March) and enacted special decrees that allowed the extraction of non-traditional species, as well as the use of smaller-size net mesh to fish traditional species (despite protests from some local scientists and some international agencies).

By mid-1998, oceanic conditions very slowly began returning to 'normal', and the fish that 'survived' the extreme conditions were now concentrated in the few pockets of water that supported the nutrient base on which to feed. Despite the fact that stocks were comprised of mixed species with few juveniles (indicating possible failure of recruitment of an age class), rendering selective harvest of fish by size and species nearly impossible, and that they had biological indicators of a stressed stock (low fat content, underdeveloped reproductive organs), many days of 'experimental' or 'exploratory' fishing were permitted, leading to an increase in landings (Broad, 1999).

In keeping with recent market-oriented reforms of then President Fujimori, and in contrast to government reaction following the 1973 collapse, there was no nationalization of the industry or government subsidization. In addition, the government did not take advantage of the situation to buy out vessels and retire them as recommended by FAO advisers in late 1997 as an option for reducing the capacity of the overcapitalized fleet prior to the return of the diminished stock. The artisanal sector experienced a boom in the availability of tropical species such as mahi-mahi (*Coryphaena hippurus*) and shark (*Isurus oxyrinchus*), the growth rate of octopus (*Octopus* spp), scallops (*Agropecten purpuratus*) and other species. However, there was virtually no government aid to these fishermen for switching to appropriate gear and finding new markets for potentially valuable species. The majority of government aid arrived in the form of repairing port infrastructure damage and foodstuffs.

Widespread coverage of the developing El Niño event took place in newspapers, television and the radio, with special sections and shows devoted to the topic. There were complaints, however, of an overabundance of conflicting information, attribution of any weather anomaly to El Niño and sensationalistic reporting (Broad, 1999). Some valid information was undermined by the perception that there were individual, institutional or private incentives influencing the content. Other formal information sources were widely publicized meetings.

The first, an emergency meeting, was held by the Comisión Permanente Pacífico del Sur in early July in Lima. The consensus at this meeting was that it was too early to tell the severity of the event and it would not be until October that its magnitude could be known. It was also acknowledged at the time that the predictive model that seemed to best capture the evolution of the event was the US National Oceanic and Atmospheric Administration's coupled model, although it seemed to underestimate the event's severity. It is noteworthy that there was virtually no artisanal sector representation at this meeting, while the industrial representatives played central roles in shaping the focus of the fisheries working group and general sessions.

A second major regional conference with attendance by international experts and, in part, supported by national, US and international organizations took place in Lima during late October 1997. Entitled 'Is This the El Niño of the Century?', it was intended to produce a consensus forecast of the event. Fearing business losses because of the forecast, comparisons to the severe impacts of the 1982 to 1983 event were strongly discouraged by the Peruvian government. There was a difference in opinion regarding the potential impacts of the event among the three major Peruvian scientific agencies. The national meteorological service was predicting an extreme event on a par with that of 1982 to 1983; the geophysical institute, which had previously been considered the leader in climate prediction, was insistent that the impacts of this event (referring primarily to precipitation) would be much less severe than 1982 to 1983; and the oceanographic agency was predicting a weakening of the event, with only a moderate impact on marine species of primary economic interest. Based on interviews and observations following this event, most decision-makers in the fishing sector were left confused by the mixed opinions that resulted and by discrepancies in the forecasts that allowed alternative constructions of uncertain information in self-serving manners. Again, there were no artisanal representatives at this conference, at least in part explained by an exorbitant entrance fee for the public presentation of information. Many scientists and policy-makers claim that there was pressure by central governmental officials and the private sector to play down the severity of the event in their public statements for fear that it would lead the banks to stop lending (which they did) and to discourage foreign investment in the country.

Given weak labour laws and unions in Peru (for example, no minimum wage during closed seasons), management may lay off workers in response to a prediction of an El Niño event. If such responses to the forecast are not considered, then these outcomes may not be anticipated. Even if anticipated, however, forecast outcomes and rational choice may be viewed negatively depending upon providers' interests and goals. We argue that both a clear, appropriately detailed definition of societal benefit and some understanding of the existing institutional constraints on forecast use and value are crucial elements in a process that leads to the best choices regarding the dissemination of climate forecasts. We discuss these implications in detail in the following section.

CONCLUSIONS: IMPLICATIONS FOR 'VULNERABILITY' IN THEORY AND PRACTICE

The importance of forms of interactions and participation that permit forecast issuers (or, more generally, researchers and international and state agencies) and forecast users (those at risk) to recognize each other as legitimate and trustworthy remains under-appreciated. Public and private groups appear to demand accurate and precise information, while scientific groups compete for channels of dissemination, credibility and social acceptance for information of varying accuracy. As pointed out by Orlove and Tosteson (1999), such pressures can lead scientific institutions to downplay the uncertainties and make categorical forecasts. FUNCEME's ensuing difficulties were, in part, the overstating of certainty in an earlier forecast that led the public to be highly critical of future ones, especially if they are seen to be 'incorrect'.

As discussed above, emphasis on 'authority' and 'expertise' alone can reduce contending perspectives and lead to unanticipated consequences. The critique offered here complements, to some extent, Habermas's notion of the colonization of the public sphere through the use of instrumental technical rationality (Habermas, 1970). In this sphere, complex social problems are reduced to technical questions, effectively removing the plurality of contending perspectives. One outcome, as noted by Lavell (1999), is that the use of economic criteria and cost-benefit analyses for justifying risk mitigation reap benefits for the modern sector economies but not for the poor and traditional sectors that make up the majority of the impacted. Thus, industrial fisheries in Peru become *de facto* the most likely to benefit from forecast information. The reduction of risk in terms of reducing exposure to economic loss becomes confused with the reduction of societal vulnerability.

The need to understand 'usability' of scientific information has received much attention from a communications perspective, but little from an organizational perspective. Research-based knowledge (from physical as well as social sciences) is increasingly viewed as important, but is still divorced from an understanding of how such knowledge is framed within different research communities, socialized within development agendas and gains precedence over local problem definitions. 'Framing' refers to the way in which a particular problem is presented or viewed. As observed in Ceará, cultural frames have a deeper impact on decisions and choices, or lack thereof, than the analytical tools with which policy-makers seek to characterize environmental stresses and problems (see Douglas and Wildavsky, 1983). These frames shape the organization of knowledge that people have about their world in light of their underlying attitudes towards key social values (for example, nature, peace and freedom), their notions of agency and responsibility (for example, individual autonomy and corporate responsibility) and their judgements about reliability and relevance (Jasanoff and Wynne, 1998). Thus, problems of 'framing' are issues not only for those who are affected but exist across research disciplines, institutions and development agency professionals as well. Our discussion strongly supports the integration into analyses of vulnerability and the extent to which knowledge is produced, framed and applied.

Table 6.1 *Selected values used to frame the forecasting enterprise from technical, applied and procedural perspectives*

Technical frame	Application frame	Procedural frame
Quality	Relevance	Access
Consistency	Compatibility	Legitimacy
Economic potential	Usefulness	Usability
Dissemination	Communication	Capacity
Efficiency	Efficiency	Equity
Expert	Consultative	Co-produced

Table 6.1 summarizes some of the various values used to frame the forecasting enterprise from technical applications and procedural perspectives.

Knowledge that is socially robust is the product of an intensive (and continuous) interaction between data and other results, between people and environments, and between applications and implications in which the authority of science will need to be legitimated repeatedly (see Gibbons, 1999). The opportunity and capacity of those affected to question information and to expose untested assumptions and unarticulated values that often underlie expert assertions require ongoing and long-term facilitation. As pointed out by Finan (personal communication), the very discussion of the climate forecast within potentially impacted communities has served as a vehicle for democratizing the drought discourse in Ceará.

Many scientific researchers (physical and social) hope to encourage or enhance democratic processes or to support public interest by providing 'rigorous' information about a particular situation and about different consequences of action. As argued above, attempts to secure the public interest must include recognition of the differing forms of agency and of notions of equity. From the standpoint of the international community and, particularly, the scientific community, we note the emphasis on distributive justice or how benefits and burdens are distributed. State entities, instead, focus on corrective justice or punishment (for example, by withholding seeds) and compensation based on liability. As shown by Jamieson (1999), justice is not limited to these two forms. Marginalized communities, assisted by those who purport to speak in support of such communities, are increasingly demanding procedural mechanisms to guarantee effective participation. As was the case for artisanal fishing communities in Peru, people objected not to the fact that they were exposed to climatic risk, but that decisions about the role and use of information about risk (in other words, forecasts) occurred without their consent and without institutional mechanisms that would allow them to articulate their opposition. 'Participation' is increasingly seen as a means to implement procedural justice. Such attention should be focused not only on the institutions of participation, but on the ways in which science, technology and information are contextualized. As pointed out by Gibbons (1999), the strongest indications that contextualization is occurring is the place accorded to people in the production of knowledge and as recipients of policies.

As noted in numerous studies, the societal conditions (development, land use, inequity) that shape vulnerability are dynamic. Repeating calls for increased dialogue and cooperation between disciplines and between research and decision-making continue to ring hollow without guidance as to how such processes may be best structured, implemented and evaluated. We argue that unwrapping the contexts within which problems are defined and information is created, legitimated and used involves understanding the nexus within which these 'hidden values' emerge and become socialized into development agendas. As in the case of Ceará, problems arose from the ways in which international institutions defined equitable principles and how equity was formulated and functioned within the community historically. Because of the contextual nature of personal networks, unofficial communication processes can satisfy a variety of local and personal needs beyond the scope of official systems (Parker and Handmer, 1997).

In conclusion, analysts of vulnerability must move beyond the assessment of social, demographic and environmental trends as end products and engage and analyse decision-making and participatory processes, as well as the consequences of information use. We offer the following recommendations for analysts as first steps in this direction:

1   Articulate the difference between risk as a construct of probabilistic return periods and the likelihood of economic losses, and vulnerability as a social condition resulting from ongoing cross-scale, social-political decisions, ranging from the global through to the day-to-day activities of the household.
2   Transcend the immediate context of application and consider the consequences and impacts that such interventions of information, if left uncontested, can generate.
3   Integrate an understanding of local contexts and contending perspectives with an understanding of how new information becomes framed and socialized within agendas.
4   Assess impediments and opportunities to the flow of information, including issues of credibility, legitimacy and acceptability.
5   Assess policy- and decision-making practices that can undermine procedural, as well as distributive processes (see below).

Assessments of societal stresses and dynamics that condition vulnerability should be complemented with a focus on how institutional and procedural contexts in which decisions are made can discount procedural equity, marginalize existing capacity, and undermine the expectations of many agencies and researchers. Moving beyond strictly technocratic applications of research-based knowledge (physical or social) and utilitarian responses will require engaging international and community-level participation in order to provide an understanding of the decision-oriented context within which most interventions takes place. Who participates? What are their perspectives? In which arenas do they act? What is being valued? What strategies are employed? What outcomes are generated? Secondly, participatory mechanisms (for example, beyond simple 'stakeholder' assessments) that articulate the views of the future among decisive and non-decisive partners (for example, researchers) must be facilitated.

From a practical perspective, it is important for researchers to address the following two questions about equity. What are the desired outcomes? How do we actually respond? Even in the context of the devastation associated with ENSO in Northeast Brazil and Peru, there are international and national pressures to return to a society as it was, even though one's position in society may not have been an advantageous one. Given the above arguments, the danger for participant observers in such settings lies in inadvertently shaping the very processes and outcomes that they wish to study. The actual benefits, furthermore, may outweigh the academic projections.

Chapter 7

Vulnerable Regions versus Vulnerable People: An Ethiopian Case Study

Linda Stephen

INTRODUCTION

Assessments of vulnerability to various types of global change carry an implicit assumption that people are 'equally' vulnerable, as one often hears of vulnerable people in the context of regional analyses. It is common to read of the effects of the El Niño–Southern Oscillation (ENSO) on farmers in Southern Africa, for example. It is also not unusual to hear of Ethiopia's north central highlands as chronically food insecure or of the centre as food sufficient. The 'regionalization' and 'homogenization' of vulnerability forms part of a global process in which ideological, economic and political tensions polarize the positions of countries in the North versus the South, of rich countries versus poor countries, and of national interests versus sub-national and local ones. A disadvantage is that localized problems do not command the solutions or resources that they should. Wisner (1998) and Uitto (1998) provide case examples where localized social-vulnerability analyses were ignored in favour of global, technological and scientific assessments of vulnerability to disasters caused by natural hazards. This leads to the marginalization of the most vulnerable people. In this chapter, I maintain that the emphasis on broad-scale vulnerability is detrimental to good analyses and is shaped by international and national discourses. This is discussed in the Ethiopian context during the middle and late 1990s. Hence, the following sections are structured around three elements: the influence of global discourses, how this affects policy and discourse in the Ethiopian national early warning system, and spatial-scale issues present in food-aid targeting and interventions. This is followed by a final comment linking these elements to specific activities and reports produced by early warning institutions in 1997, 1998 and 1999 and a proposal for an alternative discourse to guide future vulnerability analysis.

Regional themes and local analysis in the Ethiopian vulnerability analysis

The rationale for the Ethiopian generalizations are founded on a history of famine that affected the north, particularly during 1974 and 1982 to 1984, and on calculations based on the number of times during the past five years that people in a region experienced hunger (DPPC, 1998). There are also socio-economic similarities amongst people in specific areas in terms of income and economic constraints. Yet, the findings in a study done by Clay, Molla and Habtewold (1999) lead one to question whether subregional variability is of high relevance to decision-makers. They have shown that the actual relationship between food availability and food aid receipts in Ethiopia is not conditioned on localized need. This chapter furthers the argument that an issue for targeting food aid is the amount of local variability that is lost among the broad descriptions.

A constraint to current vulnerability analysis in Ethiopia is collecting data on food security. This includes limited financial and staff resources, the contrasts between climatic zones and the poor road infrastructures that make many communities inaccessible (DPPC, 1998, p21). Despite this, the government's Disaster Prevention and Preparedness Commission (DPPC) manages to detect the major food problems throughout the country. The DPPC's five-year plan mentions the difficulty of describing vulnerability to famine and food shortages, bringing attention to the complexity of the problem. At the same time, the real texture of vulnerability remains hidden in regionalized problem descriptions such as the following:

> *The most drought-prone areas of the country are its northern, eastern and southern parts. [These] areas are characterized by high rates of land degradation, low agricultural input, poor agricultural technology, etc, which all have contributed to increasing the vulnerability of the rural population to food shortages* (DPPC, 1998, p3).

While this characterization is true, it ignores the fact that rural people are not affected in the same way. They experience drought differently depending upon what socio-economic group they belong to, their economic and social-political resources or even the altitude at which they live. Alone, the climatic communities within a *wereda* (the second smallest administrative subdivision where data is collected) can produce highly diverse circumstances.[1] Moreover, the ranges in area and demographics subscribed to Ethiopian *weredas* are dramatic. In the Amhara region, there are more than 100 *weredas*. The smallest is 6 square kilometres in extent and the largest is 8181 square kilometres. The population of the smallest is around 25,000 and the largest, 228,772 (Central Statistics Authority, 1994). Often the method of summarizing problems distances the reality of livelihoods where coping measures are regularly employed to mitigate disasters.

The government described the 1998 crop prospects for Delanta, Ethiopia, and surrounding *weredas* as poor to very poor (DPPC, 1998, p5). In contrast, an analysis of household survey data (Stephen, 2002a) on crop production indicated that it was more variable than these classifications suggest, and this was across

Table 7.1 *Crop production and sales in Delanta, Ethiopia, 1997–1998*

Peasant Association /Altitude	Less crop production than previous years (percentage)	Total sales (in Ethiopian birr)
Lowlands	34	261.2
11	13	167.7
29	52	93.5
Midlands	52	250.5
3	91	68.7
4	0	67.1
13	52	114.7
Highlands	55	95.0
32	30	22.4
39	92	72.6

Note: 1 birr = UK£0.8 and US$0.12 in 2001

altitudes and peasant associations in Delanta.[2] People living in Peasant Association Number 4 had no reduction in production compared to those in numbers 3 (91 per cent less production) and 39 (92 per cent less production) (see Table 7.1). Similarly, the study showed that during the period, people received various types of aid quite generically, regardless of whether they had produced more or less than previously (see Table 7.2).

Figure 7.1 presents a vulnerability profile of the assets among rural people in Delanta. These profiles reveal many nuances between the five groups of people (as indicated in Table 7.2). The two main economic activities among the five were crop and dairy farming; thus, the five groups consisted of people involved in either one or other activity or a mix of the two. However, the different levels of income and assets that they possessed distinguished these groups. It was clear that the low-income crop farmers had the highest levels of vulnerability. In addition to income, their labour supply, land holdings, food aid, livestock holdings and sales in difficult years were well below those in other groups. Conversely, the middle- and high-income crop and dairy farmers showed a comparatively moderate level of vulnerability because they had greater access to the assets and resources identified as important for food security.

There was also a great deal of variance between members of the vulnerability groups in terms of frequency of meals. 75 per cent of the families in the survey said that they ate only one meal a day during hard periods. This was true for 73 per cent of those classified as extremely food secure in our vulnerability profile

Table 7.2 *External aid versus production in Delanta, Ethiopia, 1997–1998*

	Percentage of Households Receiving Assistance				
	General aid	Food aid	Food for work	Food aid and food for work	Credit
Quality of Harvest					
Less production	98%	59%	20%	17%	11%
More Production	100%	44%	22%	33%	6%

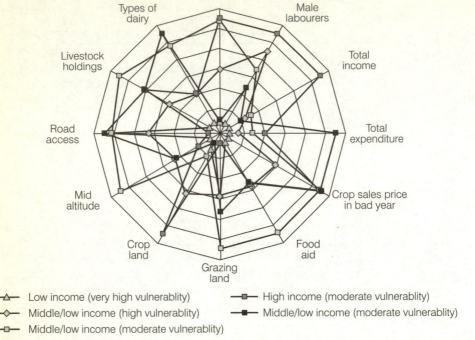

Figure 7.1 *Vulnerability profile for Delanta Dawunt, Ethiopia*

and 64 per cent of the moderately food secure. This variability in vulnerability to food security was found amongst people living in a very small subdivision in Ethiopia. One could reasonably expect there to be similar diversity among other communities of farmers across Ethiopia.

A wealth-ranking exercise conducted in three peasant associations of Delanta also revealed different levels of assets that were spatially dependent upon altitude and village. Table 7.3 indicates that those holding the most assets (category 1) were resident in the lowland villages of Kess and Wohaw Mender. The lowest asset holders (categories 3 and 4) resided in the midland village of Firja Mareja.

Table 7.3 *Percentage of population in four qualitatively ranked categories, by altitude and village, in Delanta, Ethiopia, 1997–1998*

Village	category 1	category 2	category 3	category 4	cross-categories	Total
Highlands:						
Tina	7.8%	31.9%	36.1%	11.3%	13%	100
Millawa	5%	35%	45%	15%		100
Midlands:						
Firja Mareja	13%	31.2%	36%	18.4%	1.4%	100
Lowlands:						
Kess/ Wohaw	22%	27.8%	27.8%	20.8%	1.6%	100
Kiltu	20.4%	24.4%	43.8%	10%	1.8%	100

Given the importance of scale and diversity among families as factors affecting variability in vulnerability, the scale at which institutions in Ethiopia operationalize interventions may be seen as pre-described statements of certain political objectives. Marston (2000, pp219–42) notes that scale is not necessarily a pre-designed, hierarchical ordering of the world; it is the outcome of tensions existing between structural forces and the practice of agents. Drawing from theories of scale, I propose that early warning decision-makers conceptualize the spatial dimensions of food security as aggregated because it serves their own and international agendas. In contrast, peasant farmers necessarily hold to a concept of food security that is more immediate and local. The evidence from research aimed at effective analysis, measurement and targeting strategies validates that the farmers' localized concept of food security is more than a self-centred viewpoint.

FRAMING THE REGIONAL ANALYSIS

There are different ways of deciphering the 'generalized', regional framework of vulnerability in Ethiopia. One way is to frame analysts' discussions within the context of the sociology of scientific knowledge (SSK), which, according to its proponents in environmental studies, says that at policy levels, scientific claims are often intermingled with policy claims (Wynne, 1994). In a food vulnerability assessment, the SSK framework advances the argument that the socio-economic impact of drought on vulnerability to food insecurity is obscured by the broad-scale scientific data and by the *quantitative* needs estimates that decision-makers debate. SSK shows how the demands for rationalism and objective science facilitate the formulation of some beliefs and values, while defining others as irrelevant (Wynne, 1987). A limitation of this view, however, is that it accounts for the persistence of objective truths, such as the reliance on quantitative assessments of vulnerability. However, it does not fully explain the interplay of other voices and the power struggle whereby some claims gain advantage over others. Discourse analysis offers the analytical tools to investigate the framing of the food aid discussion, and allows us to show the ways in which food insecurity is homogenized to fit within the prevailing socio-political setting.

Two relevant contributions to discourse analyses are Foucault (1977) and Hajer (1993). Foucault argued that societal and institutional practices and interactions bring to life the dialogues that structure policy and action, and that these practices often run contrary to stated goals. Hajer (1993) showed us how discourses dominate the definition of environmental problems, and that the ensemble of concepts, ideas and categorizations are always being produced, reproduced and transformed through a particular set of practices. Discourse analysis explains why stated policy and theory so often differ from practice.

The influence of global vulnerability and food security discourses

Some of the most influential global ideologies that affect Ethiopian policies on vulnerability and food security during the 1990s gained prominence through historical precursors and international mechanisms. A first example was the World Food Summit of 1996 that articulated a human rights agenda, ultimately aimed at ensuring the right to food and the reduction by 50 per cent of malnutrition by 2015.[3] Secondly, the summit came in the wake of a decline in international food aid, and this had an important impact on national food security policies. Finally, the end of the Cold War, which ushered in an era of capitalist restructuring among socialist economies such as Ethiopia's, promoted greater attention to acquiring economic capital and reshaping policy to suit this aim.

These frameworks had particular outcomes. Vulnerability to food insecurity framed within the concept of global rights to food presented a myth of vulnerability as a globally shared challenge and implied that conditions for individual households could improve through institutional collaboration. In contrast, the operational rules of this rights-based framework, in which there was a hierarchical division between global and national responsibilities for assistance and conditional international economic arrangements, suggested that household-level vulnerability to food insecurity would be alleviated, primarily, by the efforts of national governments. The burden on national governments was enhanced by the decline in overseas development assistance and in food aid for development purposes, which began during the 1980s. Much of the food aid decline, however, has been in bilateral food aid.[4] Multilateral commodity assistance, the majority of which is provided through the World Food Programme, has shown a much lower rate of decline because this was mainly targeted for emergency relief efforts (Eele and Stephen, 1998, p2; ODI, 1998). Ethiopia's overseas development assistance (ODA) actually increased between 1980 and 1996 because of repeated famine and food insecurity (World Bank, 1999). Apart from these particularities in the Ethiopian case, the decline in aid meant that, for most developing countries, there would be the administrative task of juggling food security programmes with competing poverty issues, national economic considerations and significant decreases in international aid.

GLOBAL DISCOURSES AND THE POLITICAL DISCOURSE IN THE NATIONAL EARLY WARNING SYSTEM

In Ethiopia, both international agreements and government ideology played significant roles in setting national priorities for famine early warning. The political channels of international assistance (in the form of food aid, expertise or technology) deliver the agendas represented at the summit and the possibility for entry into global markets to national policies and the early warning system. The government's programme for responding to chronic food insecurity during the 1990s came as a result of decreases in overseas development assistance and restructuring under a new administration. A few years after the end of their civil war, in late 1991, the Ethiopian government initiated a major reform, moving from a command to a market economy. Their programme has since been supported by the International Monetary Fund (IMF) and the World Bank. Ethiopia's reform programme also received strong endorsement from donors at three consultative group meetings in November 1992, March 1994 and December

1996. Early in 1997, Paris Club creditors granted Ethiopia debt relief based upon Naples terms.[5] In autumn 1997, Russia reached an agreement with the Paris Club creditors on more favourable treatment of ruble-denominated debt to countries such as Ethiopia that had formerly been supported by the Soviet Union (IMF/World Bank, 1998, p1).[6]

The government's policy framework paper (PFP) for 1998 to 2001 articulated its strategy:

> *The overriding objective of the government is to attain a relatively fast, broad-based and more equitable economic growth with macro-economic stability. A rapid increase in agricultural output sparked by productivity gains and rural development programmes to upgrade infrastructure and social services is expected to be the cornerstone of economic growth and poverty alleviation...agricultural development would provide the springboard for higher export earnings of farm commodities and agro-industrial goods* (Government of Ethiopia et al, 1998, III).

In addition to aid, foreign direct investment played an increasingly critical role in Ethiopia's development, both in terms of financial resources and technological and managerial know-how. The strategy involved creating a favourable and credible environment for investment, while opening up foreign investment to all but a few sectors. In that regard, the government has already permitted foreign entry in hitherto restricted areas, such as in telecommunications and power generation (Government of Ethiopia et al, 1998, III). Food aid was a way of accumulating development assistance and strengthening the country's agricultural base, and this was planned to lead to economic growth.

Nevertheless, structural reform and democratic forms of governance were not, in themselves, a sufficient guarantee of food security in Ethiopia during the 1990s because they were instituted to satisfy external mandates; those external sources did not necessarily feel accountable to developing countries; and Ethiopian national aims continued to be given the highest priority over localized issues. During the governmental transition from the 1980s to 1990s, various forms of nationalistic behaviour were employed to build solidarity and support. Having vulnerability profiling as an aim was therefore needed to understand vulnerability and to extend government credibility amongst the people. It also complied with the role and responsibilities that donor countries envisaged for government and nationally based international institutions. The vulnerability concepts present in Ethiopian early warning policies such as the Food Security Strategy or the National Policy on Disaster Prevention and Management reflected the new government's initial reshaping of its ideologies and economy to show consistency with global concepts and a commitment to Ethiopian people. These policies held the stated aim of naming target groups and of identifying and articulating who vulnerable people were. Consequently, the naming and identification of vulnerable target groups was set within a framework where separate and unequal responsibilities between international and national bodies had already polarized the issue as one of North against South, rich versus poor, those who were vulnerable and those who were not. This translated sub-nationally into scaled divisions in analysis:

national versus regional versus local. In line with its global role, the Ethiopian government and early warning institutions, who were based at the national level, placed greater emphasis on measuring vulnerability in aggregate. They calculated vulnerable people en masse to produce the need estimates that donors and early warning institutions frequently debate. Regional and local interactions between early warning personnel and local people were largely non-participatory exercises used to elicit and extract information, not to engage. This form of information gathering is better suited to emergency situations and not to assessments of vulnerability over the long term. This type of 'extractive' vulnerability assessment in Ethiopia followed a historical precedent in which the importance of short-term relief measures outweigh long-term development ones.

Socio-political processes affecting information in the national early warning system

By applying the Soft Systems Methodology (SSM), I was able to view the Ethiopian early warning system holistically. At the same time, the approach had the flexibility that allowed the system to be broken into individual contributing factors. The principle behind SSM is that people's perceptions of the real world yield ideas and concepts within a system; these, in turn, create new perceptions of the world that may be observed in the activities in which people engage (Checkland and Scholes, 1990). To facilitate the method, the staff in four institutions active within the Ethiopian early warning system in 1998 were interviewed, and government and international institutions' policy documents, plans and reports were consulted. Six of the persons interviewed (46 per cent) had more than five years' experience working on food security or vulnerability. Few had more than ten years' experience on the subject.

SSM supported examining the organizational culture of the institutions interacting in the early warning system. This showed that the institution that led much of the methodological development of vulnerability assessment in the Ethiopian early warning system was the World Food Programme (WFP), particularly the vulnerability analysis and mapping (VAM) unit. According to SSM, this made them the *problem solvers*. Early on in developing vulnerability assessment methods, they used their expertise in technology and WFP resources to steer the outcomes of the analysis. A dialogue between WFP and the government, in which there was a mutual exchange of data for funding and skills, was fundamental to the government's role as *problem owners*. The government shaped the early warning and vulnerability assessment agendas through policy and decided the roles of the other institutions in early warning. They subordinated non-governmental organizations (NGOs) to further their own national food security strategies. Farmers were the *intended beneficiaries*; but, in practice, they were not the *real clients* of early warning activities.

From the government's perspective, the comparatively greater wealth of donor organizations was an asset to the national early warning system. International organizations introduced the latest computer technologies to analyse crop data, while remotely sensed data and geographic information systems (GIS) provided a national and regional view of farmers' problems. Those who owned the most technology and expertise generally were the strongest decision-makers. It was no coincidence that they were also donors and affiliated organizations. For the DPPC, donors and international organizations would be the key users of early warning information and vulnerability profile data as they funded the greatest proportion of relief efforts (DPPC, 1995, p9; SERA, PPPD and DPPC, 1999). Based on the interviews and activity reviews conducted, those donors and international institutions that were active in Ethiopian early warning during the 1990s were engaged in preliminary localized vulnerability-profiling activities, but were, at the same time, largely involved in producing broad-scale computer-generated assessments of vulnerability.

In addition to cultural factors, SSM assumes that there is an internal logic to these interactions and, importantly, to the policies, methods and interventions pursued. This logic would be evident from the way in which vulnerability and food security were treated and the activities taking place.

Early warning policies, plans and activities often cite the World Bank's and the World Food Summit's food security definition as adequate access to food for all at the household level. During the 1990s, the people shaping the definition were:

- the government, whose main interests were to acquire foreign aid;
- the donor organizations, who were forced to justify their position in the presence of declining aid and have been suspicious since the Mengistu regime inflated famine mortality figures during the 1980s; and
- the NGOs, who have had to walk the balance between their own mandates and courtship with the government in order to maintain a voice in decision-making.

At the time of interviewing, famine and food insecurity were being defined by staff as both environmental and socio-economic. However, the environmental factors, such as poor rainfall or land degradation, could be measured quantitatively while there was controversy over how socio-economic factors should be measured and there was no systematic method for doing so. One technician in the government's office for disaster preparedness saw 'food security [as] a relative term, its definition depended on the aim of the definer. If the aim was to match resources to need, then it could be defined from a "resources" standpoint' (Stephen, 2002b). In this light, the diverse estimates and the practice of analysing regional figures of vulnerability could be framed by a worldview in which famine strategy translated as a nationally aggregated head count for food aid.

There were a number of constraints to realizing the aims that these definitions suggest. The most frequently mentioned constraints were politics, information and system inflexibility. Information (quality, timeliness, use, interpretation, etc) was the most frequently mentioned. A review of the antecedents to the problems associated with information, drawn from the issues that people raised, showed that information was strongly influenced by politics (including policies, decision-making and intra-institutional competition) and the power struggles within the system.

The primary information used and produced by the Ethiopian early warning system comprised needs assessments. This arrived through two distinctly separate processes and sources: one local, the other national and global. The 'local' way was to gather crop production data, which formed the basis of needs assessments and, ultimately, came down to the number of people who had a production shortfall in a given year. 'Development agents', who were employees of the Ministry of Agriculture, collected data. These figures were passed from one layer of bureaucracy to the next: from peasant association, to *wereda*, to zone, then region and finally to national DPPC. Socio-economic information behind the figures was assessed at the local level; but this was not reflected in the final documentation of need. They were mainly used for targeting once aid was distributed. The 'global' way of gathering crop information was to analyse Normalized Difference Vegetation Index (NDVI) measurements and satellite images of crop growth.[7]

Thus, information was routinely transformed from its input stage (the crop assessment) to its output stage (a calculation of food needs), a process that was shaped by different interpretations. Any one interpretation could be paired to a worldview about food insecurity and famine. For instance, among the people actively engaged in analysing crop production data, only one of them mentioned vulnerability as a component of food insecurity. They largely held a view of food insecurity as related to socio-political and environmental issues, such as access (to food, services), rainfall and land size. The determinants of access to food were not clearly articulated in their analysis. Approximately one half of the people analysing crop data connected it to poverty.

Furthermore, there was a pattern of information gathering and analysis that spatially and symbolically demonstrated the disjuncture between locally situated food insecurity and nationally based decision-making. The majority of the decision-making activities took place at the national level, where the bulk of the qualitative discussions and the final analyses occurred with little further engagement with the farmers from whom crop data was initially collected.

SCALE

An indication of the disjuncture between food aid/early warning regional analyses and the farmers' position is the way in which early warning decision-makers conceptualize the scale of the problem. An issue that is seldom addressed in the debates about measuring vulnerability to food insecurity is the issue of scale. I argue that many approaches to vulnerability analysis and intervention may have the theoretical intention of placing vulnerability at the household level; but institutional and systemic constraints force users to apply them to higher geographical scales. As a result, a selected methodology may merely be an action through which the discourses within early warning are reproduced.

The problems facing most early warning systems in Africa are multi-variant. Hence, many individuals have superficially sought a post-modern methodology following the prevailing theories emerging during the 1980s and 1990s. These methods for evaluating vulnerability suggest that space, scale and time matter particularly from a socio-political perspective. Post-modern social thinkers have argued that human behaviour varies intrinsically across space, and therefore locality frames an intimate picture of behaviour.[8] Many of the underlying assumptions about vulnerability to famine in current operational models emphasize the nature of vulnerability as dynamic. They focus on specific variables such as gender inequities in access to food, local trading patterns, ethnicity and seasonality of rainfall. Together, these aspects are understood to be leading indicators in vulnerability and food insecurity. These concepts are applied in analytical models that attempt to interpret the interacting details of the problem: the socio-economic and environmental patterns that determine vulnerability to famine and inform the choices vulnerable people make. Thus, such models appear to conform to the current view that disaggregation yields a better analysis of famine. Nonetheless, there is an inconsistency between the low volume of studies of local areas and the evidence that data at the lowest scales of analysis adds value to the vulnerability analysis.

In geographical and environmental studies there are two issues that are related to scale. Social theorists are interested in the social construction of scale, in which scale is not seen as an objective category, but something that is 'produced' by socio-political processes (Marston, 2000; LeFebvre, 1991). There are also the empirical issues of spatial resolution, where the central issue is whether information about a phenomenon occurring at one scale can be applied to another scale.

The social construction of scale offers an important explanation regarding the political limitations for vulnerability analyses. Brenner's (1997) research on state territorial structuring in Germany serves as a good example of how political and social processes influence policy. He showed that the reconfiguration of space was a spatial tactic used by the state to best maximize capital. Smith (1995) wrote that different societies produce different kinds of geographical scale for containing and enabling particular forms of social interaction. In the Ethiopian early warning system, for example, the spatial analysis of famine at high levels of aggregation has been a tactical measure, exercised by the state and international funding bodies through both their own organs and non-governmental agencies. It is a policy designed to control the dispersal of scarce resources, but also to preserve the status quo. In an appraisal of Ethiopian famine policy during the 20th century, Mesfin Wolde-Mariam (1986) demonstrated that government self-interest and a disinterest in the prospects of the poor, led to untimely and insufficient responses and policies. It is possible to hypothesize that where there have been similar policies of exclusion, this has limited the development of conceptual views within the national early warning systems to only superficial parts of the analysis.

In addition to the conceptual issues of scale, there is also the technical difficulty of interpreting data from one scale to another. Lam and Quattrochi (1992, p90) showed that the processes that appear homogeneous at a small scale could be heterogeneous at larger scales. Using the example of coniferous forest infested with pine bark beetle blight, they discussed how the patterns of infected individual or infected small groups of trees are not evident at small spatial scales. At large geographic scales, however, groups of infected trees appear as patches of dead trees and can be easily distinguished from the others. The reverse can also be true, particularly in the case of socio-economic phenomenon. The factors contributing to poverty are often interpreted homogeneously at broad spatial dimensions, which is assumed from aggregated census data. Instead, the patterns that identify 'who' could be poor (small farmer, single females, etc) are more visible at smaller scales. The importance of analysing at 'local' levels has greater meaning when dealing with multivariate and complex problems, as local statistics help to understand points of error in spatial analysis (as discussed in Fotheringham, 1997). Lam and Quattrochi's studies of fractals in the mapping sciences emphasize that most of the real world is not constant at all scales, but there are techniques whereby the dimensions and changes in patterns at different scales can be summarized.[9] For example, using geographically weighted regression allows local rather than global parameters to be estimated (Fotheringham, 1997). Another statistical technique is mathematical flow modelling, which can encompass social processes such as migration, residential choice, retailing and recreational behaviour. Other techniques employ regression models in which smaller-scale patterns are nested within larger-scale ones (Morris, 1996).

In 1992 the Food and Agricultural Organization's Global Information and Early Warning System (the FAO's GIEWS), in collaboration with Save the Children Fund (UK), used techniques for integrating socio-economic data within a global-scale analysis that had previously relied considerably on remotely sensed data. Apart from this effort, there have been few applications for bridging scales. Some of the reasons are directly associated with a policy focus on aggregated information. The famine assessment and alleviation strategies that dominated early warning 15 and 20 years ago (in other words, the wide reliance on national food balance sheets) are still present today.

The problem of accurately linking analyses drawn from different scales presents a difficulty for targeting food aid; but tackling this problem is not readily a top priority for policy-makers. Hoddinott (1999) noted that the principal considerations in targeting have been to increase the overall impact of an intervention on improvements to food security and to reduce the overall costs of providing the intervention. Administrative costs reduce the amount available for interventions; therefore, the administration of village- and household-level targeting, which can be more costly than broader geographic levels, is less favoured. However, Hoddinott also indicates that, in the first instance, geographic targeting may be relatively cost-less, and is also easier and less expensive to administer. Geographic targeting works best when the geographic units are relatively small districts as opposed to states. The geographic or administrative boundary is widely accepted as an indicator of the location of vulnerability, especially as vulnerability is variable across a country, region or even a village (Webb et al, 1994; Downing, 1991). This is also true in emergency situations. Jaspers and Shoham (1999) advise that in emergency targeting, and where there are scarce resources, targeting of needy people should be done on the basis of geography and nutritional status. Often, however, one single targeting method is applied generically to situations of diverse context. The effect of food insecurity at all scales becomes 'generalized' when data are collapsed into regional and national analyses. There could also be a greater impact on food security if resources are concentrated on fewer units, such as the district, village or household (Hoddinott, 1999).

Lam and Quattrochi (1992, p90) sum up the scale issue well by saying that, ultimately, the focus will depend upon the analyst's objectives, the type of environment under consideration and the kind of information desired. When early warning systems fail to conduct vulnerability analyses, or even to use data, at the level that is most appropriate for accurate analysis, it is partly a result of their remit. An early warning system that remains emergency-focused will have different constraints and goals than one that incorporates a developmental approach. However, where there are sufficient resources and interests in incorporating small scales in analyses, the effort will be made to conduct more localized studies.

COMMENTARY

Global discourses, political interactions in the early warning system and the scale at which vulnerability is conceptualized bias vulnerability assessments, especially targeting, in significant ways. Sharp (1998) drew attention to the fact that ineffective targeting strategies in Ethiopia were as much to do with local authorities resisting the general principles for targeting the needy as other factors. Who else might be implicated in poor targeting and the conceptual biases that work against farmers?

If we consider the activities of the larger and more influential aid institutions in Ethiopia, such as the WFP and the US Agency for International Development (USAID), we would note that their written policies support good targeting; but some of their methodologies do not. They show an interest in working within current knowledge of vulnerability and food security. Their policy reflects the global vulnerability and food security concepts, such as food security as 'access to food'. To this end, some have designed methods for vulnerability profiling within villages, which considers the socio-economic determinants of vulnerability in individual subregions. The dominant methodology, however, continues to be an assessment of national needs, using technological equipment whose purpose is to provide a broad view. These methods of analysis fall in line with the greater demand for information in emergencies and resources available for relief, as opposed to long-term development. This is also consistent with the type of report regularly provided by the Ethiopian government. Furthermore, it caters to the needs of a donor and government ministerial clientele, not the local farmer. Donors and the government were the primary financiers of vulnerability profiling and assessment.

Turning to NGOs, we would note that – while their efforts are more grassroots than other institutions in the Ethiopian early warning system, and therefore they are generally more informed about locally specific vulnerability – their activities are largely controlled by the government. They must comply with an NGO code of conduct, prepared and enforced by the government and two key NGOs that the government works closely with. They do not command the type of financial resources that has been shown to influence decision-making. Therefore, the government's framework for operation has had an enduring influence on what they do and how they do it.

As for the government, one would observe that the DPPC is skilled at deflecting blame for ineffective targeting away from itself and towards local people. It has said that it is the local *wereda* administration who is responsible for selecting beneficiaries, along with a committee of elders and community representatives. Ultimately, however, the national DPPC is responsible for establishing the overall framework in which targeting is conducted by developing vulnerability profiles and guidelines for area targeting. A lack of flexibility in the DPPC's famine early warning system is reflected by the fact that food aid continues to flow to the same areas as before – areas known for chronic drought and food shortfall. It has been slow in its efforts to create a deeper understanding of spatial and temporal changes in vulnerability. During the 1995 to 1996 harvest period, for example, 63 per cent of the regions were at or above the requirement of 1680 kilocalories per person per day; yet, food aid distributions bore no relationship to this fact.[10] This has been documented by Clay et al (1999), who also showed that food aid increased in relation to the greater number of years during which regions and households had received aid in the past.

Many DPPC reports give the impression of making a fair appraisal of each *wereda's* need, which helps to satisfy the conditions for the continuation of aid. Yet, the focus remains somewhat superficial with respect to what farmers actually experience. It is useful to note the government's language in relation to food needs in the Amhara region, North Wollo zone and in Delanta. Table 7.4 shows the descriptions of regions and zones to be quite specific and quantitative, while those of the Delanta *wereda* give a vague impression of need. On a GIS map in the DPPC's report, Delanta is shown as risking a 'medium' decline from normal food consumption; yet, the report never explains what is meant by a 'medium' decline.

One might assume from this report that medium decline refers to a mid-level drop in cereals available, affecting the achievement of a minimum of 1680 kilocalories per day. What one cannot assume is how that might impact upon the consumption of different groups of people, like the different household groupings in the Delanta vulnerability profile (see Figure 7.1). One may not expect the prospects for the middle-income crop farmers who have a high level of vulnerability to differ greatly from the low-income crop farmers who are also considered to be highly vulnerable; but without the proper analysis, one cannot automatically assume this. Another assumption one might make with caution is that a single alleviation strategy suffices for both the vulnerability crop and dairy farmers in Delanta. It is likely that their different livelihood strategies require different interventions. Yet, it has been demonstrated that although production, type of income (crop, livestock, both or other) and altitude were variables between

Table 7.4 *Government descriptions of need for Amhara region, North Wollo zone and Delanta weredas, 1998*

DPPC descriptions	Amhara region	North Wollo zone	Delanta wereda
People affected	2,854,800	482,900	
Population needing relief	2,121,100		Risk of medium decline from normal food consumption in 1998
Food needs	287,198 metric tonnes	68,672 metric tonnes required	Crop prospects 'poor'

villages and peasant associations in the Delanta Ethiopia case, such variables did not greatly affect who was selected for participation in government-administered food aid programmes (a more extensive case is presented in Clay et al, 1999).

The issue of ineffective targeting and differences between regional analysis and local realities in Delanta and Ethiopia illustrates the cross-purposes of national and regional governance and the governance of localities. Yet, the nexus of control and, certainly, the responsibility for fair distributions exists at the national level, where the motives for aid-giving are shaped by many factors peripheral to farmers' needs.

Vulnerability science: framework for an alternative discourse

In helping decision-makers and practitioners to address the issues presented in this chapter, it may be useful to consider vulnerability as a scientific project in its own right. New academic frameworks may never fully change the way in which governments and international institutions operationalize a vulnerability intervention, as it has been shown here that they can be considerably more influenced by how the world of food policy and food assistance works. Nevertheless, viewing vulnerability as a science could alter the way in which they approach the subject.

Understanding vulnerability within a scientific approach encompasses a definition of the nature of the problem, a theoretical framework and suitable methods for collecting data to test our theories. The nature of vulnerability could be defined as a place-based issue affected by global and local climatic and environmental conditions, and by various administrative levels of social, economic and political issues. The theoretical framework for dealing with vulnerability would conceptualize the significance of its diversity and would account for the varied and sometimes conflicting socio-political and scientific components. The methods for information gathering would explore the socio-political, economic and institutional questions – particularly how these shape policy and interventions and the environmental questions. Specifically, why do certain climatic and human-induced patterns trigger certain problems? Each of these factors has been considered independently within many bodies involved in assessing vulnerability to global change, including those dealing with food policy. Few have brought the elements together within a comprehensive strategy. Climate change and environmental researchers are beginning to make advances by finding ways of merging scientific research and social science methods to deal with socio-natural issues (Downing et al, 1999). This has furthered the understanding of human adaptation to changes in the environment. However, the scientific approach has not yet been applied to make a comprehensive assessment of vulnerability to food insecurity. The advantage to be gained from approaching vulnerability as a science would be to understand why and how these issues coalesce to affect livelihoods in some areas and not others. This brings considerable weight to place-based local analyses that will only strengthen regional- and global-scale research, increase our knowledge of human adaptation in different contexts and help us to design appropriate interventions.

CONCLUSION

The decline in global foreign aid donations set the tone for debates at the World Food Summit and for national planning committees. Aid reductions forced people to justify their importance in the scramble for dwindling resources. It could be argued that shrinking development capital forced the Ethiopian government to take a pragmatic approach, limiting aid to including only those who needed it most. Given the need to comparably assess all regions within a country before deciding where aid should be targeted, such strategies could be considered the best way of allocating resources. However, it is important to consider that Ethiopia thrived during a period in which aid to all countries declined, and at some stages their share increased. Furthermore, while the actual delivery and targeting of households for aid lies with local administrations and communities, the real information that could inform better targeting (in other words, socio-economic differences) is subjugated to different priorities that arise out of the internal struggles and management of the early warning system. A strong indication of the underlying basis to regional analyses are the policy debates to reduce dependency on food aid, while maintaining a hold on the capital that comes with aid every year.[11]

In a study of the government's food-aid targeting policies and strategies, Sharp's (1998) observations suggest that a re-evaluation of policy would be in order. Sharp noted two things. First, the Ethiopian government's area-level targeting is essential as a *first layer* in the distribution system and is where the greatest potential gains in effectiveness and efficiency could be made. Second, the impact of schemes for channelling food aid (such as through employment-generation schemes) would be improved by a 'system for monitoring and evaluating its impacts and record-keeping that focuses more on the people involved than on the physical outputs and sacks of grain moved' (Sharp, 1998). In my view, to improve the effectiveness of area-wide targeting, greater attention should be given to data at the *second layer*: the communities. There ought to be a stronger linking of information between the two geographic scales.

As illustrated in the Delanta vulnerability profile, relying on the regional analyses produced by the government or the national perspectives offered by international institutions could lead to wrong assumptions. This would particularly apply to areas such as Wolayta, where there has been vulnerability in an area traditionally classified as food secure. The absence of localized information is a disadvantage to our knowledge of the dynamics of vulnerability and of societies' adaptation to environmental and socio-political change. Bankoff's (2001, p31) comment underscores the issue: 'adaptations are not characterized by *homogeneity* but by their own singular interpretations of hazardous uncertainty and by their own context'. A vulnerability science might bring the structure needed to attend to the variability of vulnerability in local settings.

Chapter 8

From Vulnerability to Empowerment

Annelies Heijmans

INTRODUCTION

Disaster response agencies increasingly use the concept of 'vulnerability' to analyse processes that lead to disasters and to identify responses. Because no common definition of 'vulnerability' exists, agencies use the concept in the way that best fits their practice – in other words, focusing on physical and economic vulnerability. In most assessments, however, the stories of the affected communities are not included.

Local people view disasters as part of 'normal life' and develop coping strategies to adjust to a fast-changing environment. It appears, however, that in the context of globalization, these coping strategies are no longer effective. In Southeast Asia, construction of hydropower dams, mining operations, land conversion for plantations and other development programmes, which are here referred to as 'development aggression', often involve displacement, military activity and violation of human rights. This trend particularly highlights the political vulnerability of local people, since they can hardly influence or block decisions on laws, policies and programmes that harm them.

Political vulnerability requires a specific response, such as advocacy, alliance-building and work on human rights. These responses might be valuable in addressing physical and economic vulnerability since their root causes often lie in political processes.

VARIOUS VIEWS ON 'VULNERABILITY' AND ITS USERS

Concerned by the increasing number and impact of disasters, the International Decade for Natural Disaster Reduction (IDNDR) was initiated during the 1990s to serve as a catalyst for disaster reduction. One of its major goals was reducing vulnerability to *natural disasters*, 'requiring concerted and coordinated efforts of government, UN-system organizations, the world's scientific and technical community, volunteer organizations and educational institutions, the private sector, the media, and individuals at risk. Vulnerability assessment…[is] essential' (UN IDNDR, 1992). The international community was alerted to the fact that if it ever wants to control and prevent disasters, it must be able to assess and identify vulnerabilities in order to design timely, affordable and effective strategies for reducing the negative effects of disasters (Anderson, 1995). Most disaster response agencies now use the concept of 'vulnerability' to analyse the various factors and processes underlying the impact of disasters on society. Most of the agencies further recognize that vulnerability is a bigger concern for the poor, and that the most vulnerable sectors in society need special attention. This does not mean, however, that disaster agencies share a common understanding or definition of 'vulnerability'. The definition attached to 'vulnerability' largely depends upon the user and the role of vulnerability in the society concerned.

Various authors have come up with historical overviews on how the understanding of vulnerability has shifted and enlarged, or how different actors perceive disasters and vulnerability (Cuny, 1983; Anderson and Woodrow, 1989; Cannon, 1994; Anderson, 1995; Smith, 1996). In short, three different views and resulting strategies to address vulnerability are being distinguished:

1   Nature as cause → technological, scientific solutions: This view blames nature and natural hazard as the cause of people's vulnerability, which fluctuates according to the intensity, magnitude and duration of external events. Vulnerability results from hazards (including intensity) and risk (exposure to events, measured in terms of proximity). In order to reduce vulnerability, systems for predicting hazards and technologies to enable human structures to withstand negative impacts are designed and applied (equipment to monitor seismic activity, weather forecasting, remote sensing for drought and fire monitoring, water control systems, and code regulations for buildings).

2   Cost as cause → economic and financial solutions: In spite of increasing technological and scientific capacity, people continue to suffer because prediction and mitigation technologies are costly. Economists develop and improve methods to assess the costs of losses from disasters to calculate whether, when, how and where reducing vulnerability is viable. In this view, vulnerability will be reduced if national governments adapt safety nets, insurance and calamity funds, and provide financial assistance to build up people's assets (World Bank, 2001, p135).

3   Societal structures as cause → political solutions: This view observes that disasters have a differential impact on people who live in hazard-prone areas. It is not only the exposure to hazards that puts people at risk, but also socio-economic and political processes in society that generate vulnerability. These create the conditions that adversely affect the ability of communities or countries to respond, to cope with or to recover from the damaging effects of disaster events. These conditions precede the disaster event, contribute to its severity and may continue to exist even afterwards (Anderson and Woodrow, 1989, p10; Blaikie et al, 1994, p9). 'Reducing the vulnerability of the poor is a development question, and such a question must be answered politically' (Cuny, 1983, p7). In this perception, a safer environment can only be achieved

if disaster response changes the processes that put people at risk. The long-term solution lies in transforming the social and political structures that breed poverty and the social dynamics and attitudes that serve to perpetuate it (Heijmans and Victoria, 2001, p16).

These three views are not exclusive. In big aid agencies more than one view exists among policy-makers and implementers. The first two views are dominant in the analysis and actions of most disaster response agencies, including international humanitarian organizations. They perceive 'vulnerability' as the result of both external dynamics and the lack of financial capacity. In their analysis, poor people are plagued by critical trends, shocks and seasonal problems, which lie far beyond their control. 'Vulnerability' here means 'people being potential victims', or 'people in need and crisis'. To help them, support focuses on relief and disaster prevention, such as scientific forecasting and warning equipment to give vulnerable populations time to move out, and on financial assistance to build up people's assets, including insurance (DFID, 1999, sheet 2.2; Annan, 1999; Bender, 1999). Vulnerability, with emphasis on physical and economic vulnerability, is addressed only in aspects that are susceptible to technical solutions (Cannon, 2000). It is regarded as politically neutral.

The third view, primarily supported by environmentalists and activists, highlights that vulnerability reduction and targeting the most vulnerable groups are, in fact, related to social order and politics. Therefore, Bender (1999) argues that there is little reason to expect that the IDNDR would have dealt with disaster reduction in a serious way. For many countries and donors, vulnerability reduction is too political.

At this point, I would like to raise some issues regarding 'vulnerability' that need further clarification and discussion. The first issue is how communities (repeatedly) affected by disasters view and respond to 'vulnerability'. This issue is relevant since most of the aid agencies just make assumptions regarding local people's needs and priorities, and treat them as recipients or beneficiaries of their programmes, not as creative actors in disaster risk reduction. The second issue is what are the consequences of local people's perceptions and actions for disaster policies, in general, and assessment tools, in particular. The third issue is of a different level and relates to the political nature of the concept: if most disaster management agencies and governments ignore the social and political origin of disasters, how can disaster risk reduction ever be accomplished?

ABSENCE OF PEOPLE'S PERSPECTIVE IN VULNERABILITY ASSESSMENTS

Although most actors agree and recognize that poor people are the most vulnerable and require special attention, none of the three categories mentions explicitly how people at risk experience and understand disasters. This invisibility will be illustrated by the case of the Indonesian fires of 1997 to 1998 that explains the various actors' perceptions of the fire hazard, its causes and their proposed solutions (see Box 8.1).

Box 8.1 Interpretation of the 1997–1998 fires in Indonesia and its consequence for disaster response

During the El Niño drought during 1997 to 1998, fires devastated Indonesia's forests, creating a vast shroud of smoke that reached as far as mainland Southeast Asia. The Indonesian government, international donors, environmental activists and local communities interpreted the causes of the fire differently; therefore, their solutions for responding to the fires also varied.

The majority of the Indonesian government officials blamed El Niño and global warming – caused by industrialization in the developed world – for the disaster. They saw fires as a result of unpredictable and uncontrollable nature, and of insufficient development, suggesting that if the government had more modern technology, it could predict nature more precisely and respond more quickly. Government, therefore, emphasized the need for better technology to predict, monitor and address fires. This interpretation of the fires was blind to the human factors that caused the fire and lacked the political will to address them.

International donors conducted wide-spread damage assessments, primarily through remote sensing (satellite photos showing area, thickness and content of smoke, and the location of fire hotspots). Their interest was to estimate the impact on wildlife and natural resources. No one had collected any systematic field data of impacts on local communities or investigated the cause of the fires. In fact, they kept silent about the role of the plantation sector in the fires, unwilling to mix in 'local politics'. Instead, they constructed an analysis showing that Indonesian forests are of global concern, a source of priceless biodiversity. Nature was seen as most vulnerable in this case. People who inhabit the forests are poor and degrade their environment in order to survive. Therefore, the Indonesian government requires modern technology, such as geographical information systems, (GIS) to slow the process of environmental degradation and to protect valuable resources. This interpretation blames poor local people for the fires, not the wealthier plantation sector.

The local non-governmental organization (NGO) community revealed – also using remote sensing – that the majority of hotspots originated on logging and oil palm plantation land. Since the 1960s, Suharto's economic development initiatives, supported by the International Monetary Fund (IMF) and the World Bank, promoted capitalization of large-scale 'natural resource production'. Government policies allowed plantation owners to use fire as a cheap and effective means of clearing land to establish plantations. This process of forest exploitation contributed to the outbreaks of fires, more so since the government lacked the political will to enforce the 'zero burn' legislation enacted in 1995, prohibiting the use of fire in commercial land clearing. This process created ecological and social landscapes vulnerable to fire. The NGO community blamed the plantation sector for the fires, as well as the inequitable government forest practices. Although the NGO sector advocated local indigenous control of resources, it represented 'the forests that cannot represent themselves', rather than the local people. In this context, NGOs envisioned reforms of forest management policies to address fires and environmental degradation.

While the rest of the world focused upon the smoke visible from satellites, farmers on the ground endured the hardship caused by the fires. They lost both their gardens and fallback resources. The fire destroyed everything, including their life savings invested in the land. Farmers blamed the land clearing activities of adjacent oil palm plantations for the fires. They even believed that they were victims of arson, a means employed by plantation owners to displace farmers from their land in order to stake claims to locally held lands. In cases where timber or oil palm plantations caught fire, the owners could not count on local help to extinguish the flames, indicating that the roots of the disaster lie with struggles over ownership of land and forest resources. It is not poverty or the 'slash-and-burn' practices of poor farmers that set the degradation of nature in motion, but the greedy and unjust behaviour of concessionaires, politicians and law enforcement officers involved in the conversion of forests to plantations. This created the vulnerable ecological and social conditions for the fire disaster.

Source: Harwell (2000)

The case of the Indonesian fires reveals that the responses, forecasting technology, remote sensing and reforms of the government's forest management policies ignore the role of the palm-oil and timber sectors and related government departments that are, in fact, responsible for creating the onset of the disaster. The International Monetary Fund (IMF) even included, as a condition of its 'rescue package' loan (following the 1997 financial collapse), the further expansion of the oil-palm sector and the inclusion of foreign investment in the forestry sector (Harwell, 2000, p325). In this way, existing relations of power are being reproduced. None of the actors involved considered the local people's views and their situation important, since it would only pour more 'oil' on the conflict (and fire). Fires in Indonesia will continue to happen if economic and political power relations do not change.

LOCAL PEOPLE'S PERCEPTION OF 'VULNERABILITY'

Hazards have always been part and parcel of the world's reality, and populations inhabiting hazard-prone areas adapted strategies to deal with extreme events, using their own capabilities, skills, talents, knowledge and technologies. Learned from their ancestors and their own experiences, these adaptation strategies are made part of their traditions and culture (Blolong, 1996, p15). When hazards strike, people have always been ready to cope and did not rely much on support and assistance from outsiders, such as government. In this historical perspective, local people have no concept of 'vulnerability'. In local dialects, there is seldom an appropriate translation for the term.

Unfortunately, this picture is disappearing. Political, demographic and global economic processes have put adaptation strategies under great pressures and given rise to vulnerability (and reproduction of vulnerability over time), affecting the allocation and distribution of resources between different groups of people (Blaikie et al, 1994, p24). The farmers in Kalimantan, Indonesia, who were affected by the fires in 1998 have lived there for generations, making their living from a combination of subsistence and commercial agroforestry, including swidden agriculture, rubber, pineapple and rattan gardens. In times of drought, excessive rains or pests, they have always had other resources to fall back upon. With the arrival of the oil-palm plantations in the area, competition for land and forest resources intensified. Arson, allegedly applied by plantation owners, resulted in the destruction of farmers' savings and their inability to cope with extreme pressures. All of this was unprecedented (Harwell, 2000, p328).

Similarly, communities in the uplands of the Philippines have been increasingly exposed to the negative impact of typhoons and drought since the 1970s. They blame the government's logging policies, mining operations and the construction of hydroelectric dams for the increasing occurrence of flashfloods, landslides, pollution of water and fish kill. Nowadays, local people also observe that even normal monsoon rains trigger adverse disastrous events such as landslides and floods, which never occurred before. In their view, the conceptual difference between a typhoon (*hazard, extreme event*) and monsoon rain (*normal climatic condition*) has become negligible since effects at community level have become similar. The increasingly vulnerable condition, in which people live, can now turn not only extreme events, but even normal events, into disaster situations.

In a fast changing environment, local people find that traditional coping strategies are no longer effective. They continuously look for new ways of adjusting their livelihood strategies with the aim of reducing risk, sustaining their livelihood and avoiding entering irreversible strategies – in other words, strategies that undermine the basis of their means of survival (Walker, 1989, p50). Although local people do not use the concept of 'vulnerability' to describe their worsening situation, they feel the stress, face difficulties, talk about 'risks' and make risk-taking or risk-avoiding decisions. Box 8.2 illustrates how local people perceive risks and what they do to reduce them. They do not only take into account the possible exposure to danger and future damages (in other words, what outsiders generally refer to as 'vulnerability'), but also their capacities, options and alternatives, and the implications of their decisions. It is important that outsiders understand both sides that make up local people's perception of risk, rather than analysing and measuring their vulnerability with outside criteria. Outsiders might label two households who live in similar conditions equally vulnerable. But the two households might still perceive risk differently and, as a consequence, prefer different risk-reduction measures.

Box 8.2, which provides examples of people's responses to drought, shows that there is not one universal response to a particular disaster, even if communities are located in apparently similar conditions. They explore coping strategies that provide for immediate food availability, combined with strategies that ensure long-term livelihood security (Mula, 1999, p138). They 'calculate' risks in a multidimensional way based upon personal circumstances. These include available resources to feed the family; the farming calendar (planting season, harvest time, etc); family composition (age and gender) to consider off-farm work; location and escape routes; education and skills of family members; past experience; and fall-back mechanisms. They will make a choice from which they expect optimum benefit and less risk even if they do not know all of the consequences of their choices. Coping strategies are also the result of a process of experiments and innovation through which people build up the skills, knowledge and self-confidence necessary to shape and respond to their environment. This provides people with a sense of 'safety'. Maxwell argues that the choice of certain coping strategies over others may provide insights into perceived security and risk, and may enhance understanding of levels of vulnerability (Maxwell, 1996, p301).

Local people approach their circumstances beyond the disaster and emergency paradigm. Even if they are not confronted with disasters, they face many risks, such as food shortage, diseases, malnutrition, or eviction from the land that they till. Hazard events aggravate such living conditions.[1]

The following examples further show the different perceptions of both hazard 'victims' and hazard managers and how they may respond to disaster risk in different ways according to their personal understanding and experience (Smith, 1996, p66). This difference often creates tension when, for instance, provincial government gives evacuation orders to local communities without prior consultation with local authorities or people at risk (see Box 8.3).

Box 8.2 Risk-reducing behaviour to deal with the changing environment of various upland community members in Panay Island, the Philippines

Upland communities in Panay used to grow traditional rice varieties (TRV) and corn in their *kaingin* ('slash-and-burn') farms. During the early 1980s, these communities began experiencing drought periods, which became more frequent during the 1990s. They all blame the large-scale logging activities by the elite lowlanders for the landscape's increasing vulnerability to drought. To a lesser extent, they think that forest also disappeared because of the influx of more settlers from the lowlands due to land scarcity. The uplands of Panay were never exposed to the damaging effects of typhoons; but since the mountains have become more denuded of trees, strong typhoons now damage crops and bamboo. Although upland communities were confronted with similar events and processes, they developed different strategies to respond to these developments, as presented below.

Settlers in Maasin district, Iloilo Province, Panay

This area is relatively accessible from the lowland and nearby Iloilo City, the political centre of the island. This explains why the area is almost denuded. Farmers no longer practice slash and burn, but have shifted to permanent farming (TRV and corn). During the 1980s, they 'discovered' that through making *kahon* (literally, 'box', referring to a local version of rice terraces without canals but constructed in such a way that they can hold and maximize rainwater for rice production) they could better cope with drought conditions. Farmers developed these boxes where suitable, and grow a combination of TRV and high-yielding varieties (HYV). The advantages of growing HYV is that they produce faster than TRV, and by optimizing the available water in *kahon*, a second crop is sometimes possible. They practice direct seeding because there is insufficient water for seedbeds. Farmers make risk-taking decisions to optimize usage of their resources, considering the occurrence of drought and typhoon. TRV signify less expensive inputs but only one harvest after six months. HYV signify more expensive inputs, such as fertilizers, pesticides and herbicides; but farmers can gamble on two harvests during the same period. Most farmers risk growing HYV; on land unsuitable for *kahon*, they continue to grow TRV and, increasingly, corn. If it does not rain for the second HYV crop, they plant mung beans and corn. For additional income, families are involved in bamboo weaving and charcoal production. Drought and typhoons are perceived as part of normal life. People use all of their resources to fight hunger.

Although this description of people's coping strategies is typical, different versions of these strategies exist among community members, depending upon family situation and available resources at household level. These elements influence risk perception and decision-making on how communities can best reduce risk:

- Families who are relatively better off and own livestock and working animals cultivate a relatively larger area of corn. Corn is used to feed animals, which can be sold in times of crisis (a form of savings).
- Families with grown-up sons prefer to earn income through seasonal migration and do not plant HYV, which is considered more risky than out-migration.
- A female single parent with six grown-up children plants only HYV because she has control over sufficient labour, and it is the fastest way to produce rice. Additional

income comes from three children working in Iloilo City (bakery) and from bamboo weaving.

- A young couple with small children grows HYV, TRV and corn. Farming is their main source of income. For additional income they get involved in (illegal) charcoal making (male occupation) and bamboo weaving (female occupation) rather than out-migration. They do not like to leave small children behind.
- A sharecropper family with small children only grows TRV and corn. The family has no resources to buy herbicides needed to grow HYV. The father provides paid labour on other farms.

During 1990 to 1991, farmers experienced a drought period of more than ten months, causing their coping strategies to fail. They received assistance from a local non-governmental organization (NGO) who perceived the drought problem as a problem of shortage of seeds. A community-based seed bank programme (CBSBP) was conceptualized and implemented to enable farmers to save seeds for the next planting season. The NGO failed to analyse the nature and behaviour of drought in the past, and how farmers have developed strategies to mitigate the effects of drought. Furthermore, the NGO did not recognize the farmers' HYV strategy as viable: it condemned the farmers' solution as environmentally and economically unsustainable. Besides, HYV are not drought resistant, like TRV, corn, peanuts or other alternative crops. Farmers would have preferred assistance to develop a marketing strategy for their bamboo products. However, they cooperated with the NGO, since they also desperately needed seeds to plant. However, the CBSBP was not a success. In only 1 out of 18 communities were farmers able to store seeds after the harvest. However, even these were used to feed the family before the next planting season.

Internal refugees in Barangay Osorio, Remegio, Antigue Province, Panay

The farmers in Osoria used to practice the same farming system as the farmers from Maasin district in order to cope with drought. However, in 1985, when military operations intensified, farmers left their original community and evacuated to Osorio, which is a day's walk away. During 1988 to 1989, a military detachment came to Osorio and imposed a curfew and food blockade. People were not allowed to cultivate their farms and became dependent on wage labour and seasonal migration to Negros's sugar plantations. In 1999, the farmers still lived in Osario because, despite the departure of the military detachment, it was still not safe to return to their original farms. Only one third of the families, whose farms are located four hours' walk away, were farming again; but they were not able to fully restore their farms, since they lacked working animals and tools. Most of the families depend on wild crops for their meals, such as *kayos*, and seasonal farm work in the lowlands of Antigue and on sugar plantations in Negros. For most of the year they try to survive on one meal a day. Almost all children are malnourished. Under such circumstances, addressing drought is not a priority for people. Their priorities are pro-tection against the greater risks of disease, child mortality and achieving peace and order.

Source: Heijmans, Personal notes taken during several monitoring missions to disaster

Besides differences in risk perception between local community people and disaster managers, politics also play an important role in the selection (or withholding) of disaster mitigation measures. Filipino elites, who support the government, often manipulate crisis situations to further consolidate their power

Box 8.3 Risk perception of farmers residing on the slopes of Mount Mayon Volcano, Bicol, the Philippines

Mount Mayon is the most active volcano in the Philippines, with 46 eruptions since 1616. The last major eruptions occurred in 1984, 1993 and 2000, while threats occur almost yearly.

Living on the slopes of Mount Mayon volcano in Bicol gives marginalized farmers the opportunity to produce food, even without secure land titles. Although Mount Mayon is a very active volcano, the simple fact of earning a livelihood increases the level of tolerable risk of being exposed to a possible volcanic eruption. This is one of the main reasons why people tend to ignore evacuation orders when the likelihood of eruption increases and an incentive of relief is offered in evacuation centres. People only move if they actually see smoke, ash falling, lava flowing and stones coming down the slopes (that is, when the highest alert level is reached). In most cases, people are prepared for evacuation and have arranged for transportation in advance, but postpone moving as long as possible because they know that living conditions in evacuation centres are even worse (congested, lack of water, insufficient food and livelihood options). More people die in evacuation centres because of poor conditions than due to the immediate effects of the eruption. Therefore, the benefits of each day's work on the farm near a 'trembling' volcano are perceived as less risky than the physical exposure to the actual eruption, as well as 'being safe' but hungry in the evacuation centres.

While governments put emphasis on scientific methods for predicting volcanic eruptions in order to improve 'safety' and on relief assistance (here, the response focuses on natural hazard), poor residents would be better off if the government provided them with land security in safer areas (here, the response focuses on vulnerable conditions and root causes). In this case, they would not need to farm on the volcano's slopes that are prone to mudflows every rainy season (the risk of mudflow and crop damage is much higher than the probability of volcanic eruption). But the political will of governments to genuinely reduce disaster risks is lacking.

Source: Heijmans, Personal direct observations and interviews with local residents during several monitoring visits to the area as project officer of the Citizens' Disaster Response Centre (1996–2000)

and to serve their personal economic interests (Bankoff, 1999). For years, displaced families in evacuation centres and communities threatened by *lahar* flows from Mount Pinatubo in the Philippines protested against the construction of the mega-dike and other dams. These costly structures were supposed to protect roads connecting important economic centres and the free-trade zones of Subic Bay and Clark Airbase in Central Luzon. However, the dams were washed out yearly due to lack of feasibility studies and proper designs, but were a source of profit for contractors and politicians. Local people were not consulted and lacked the capacity to influence government decision-making on disaster mitigation. This particularly highlights their political vulnerability, which seems to be crucial when assessing their ability to cope with disasters in the long term (years after the actual natural hazard hit their communities) and in identifying an appropriate strategy to address their overall vulnerability.

'DEVELOPMENT AGGRESSION' AS EMERGING
HUMAN-MADE DISASTER

So far, people's risk perceptions and coping strategies have been discussed in the context of 'natural' disasters and increasing vulnerability due to political, demographic and global economic processes. However, since the 1990s, voices from grassroots organizations have become louder when their livelihood and basic means for survival are directly threatened and affected by development projects. In the Philippines, local communities perceive government's 'development' projects, such as dams for electricity generation and irrigation, mining operations, plantations and recreation areas that require conversion of prime agricultural land to industrial and commercial uses, as more disastrous than natural hazards.[2] These projects might favour national and global interests; local communities, however, are not consulted. Instead, they are displaced, losing not only their homes, livelihoods and rights to cultivate (ancestral) lands, but also their identity and roots. The San Roque Multi-Purpose Dam Project, currently under construction in Benguet Province, the Philippines, will displace 61,700 individuals (IBON, 2000). These kinds of projects with immediate negative effects on local poor communities are referred to as 'development aggression'.[3] The Philippine Alliance of Human Rights Advocates sums up the meaning of 'development aggression' as follows: 'Development is development aggression when the people become the victims, not the beneficiaries; when the people are set aside in development planning, not partners in development' (Casiple, 1996, p43). Development or modernization projects result in fully fledged disasters when a state adopts a high-modern ideology with an excessive optimism and self-confidence regarding scientific and technological progress; when it is willing to use its full power (including military force) to implement the projects; and when a civil society lacks the capacity to resist state repression and to channel opposition (Brand, 2001, p961). These factors hold true for the Philippines and, unfortunately, for many other Asian countries. According to the International Rivers Network, roughly 2 million people are displaced yearly by large dams. In almost all case studies, the majority of people evicted are usually poor farmers and indigenous people (IBON, 2000; Wong, 2001).

Local people perceive this kind of development as human-made disasters. It is much more difficult to cope with the adverse effects of development aggression than with those of a typhoon; typhoons destroy crops, houses and infrastructure, but do not necessarily undermine the basis of people's means of survival. Displacement, as a result of development aggression, deprives people of their land, which is the most crucial resource to sustain their livelihood. People seldom leave their homes voluntarily, but are forced by continuous harassment, or by the actions of private armies, police or military. Government or private investors offer compensation that is far below the amount needed to rebuild a livelihood elsewhere, and land is not made available. Unlike some of the effects of natural hazards or wars, displacement for development purposes is always permanent (Brand, 2001, p962).

It is commonly accepted among researchers and disaster managers that development creates new forms of hazards – for instance, technological hazards and pollution. But development aggression, causing displacement of people, is not yet recognized as a human-made disaster except by the affected communities themselves and a few supportive local non-governmental organizations (NGOs). Discussing the issues usually results either in a political debate or in a conceptual discussion of terms and definitions.

In the 'disaster-pressure model', Blaikie et al (1994) extensively explain the progression of vulnerability from root causes through dynamic pressures, resulting in local unsafe conditions. In this model, government policies and programmes are considered the result of unequal power relations that create vulnerability and unsafe conditions at the local level. These deprive people of the resources to cope with extreme events (Bankoff, 2001, p7). According to the disaster-pressure model, the *decision* to construct a dam might be considered a root cause of creating unsafe conditions at a local level, particularly the threat of flashfloods if the dam breaks. But the actual forcible *eviction* is a disaster, according to the affected families – even more so because no decent and permanent relocation settlement is provided.[4]

In this situation, people's usual coping strategies have become irrelevant. The only valid and appropriate response local people see is political activism to oppose the kind of development that violates their human rights in all dimensions – economic, social, cultural and political – and to promote an alternative development agenda. They seek the assistance of NGOs to address both their immediate basic needs and to defend their human rights in the long term. The Citizen's Disaster Response Network in the Philippines, for instance, supports at-risk communities to develop functional grassroots counter-disaster plans. These include warning systems, evacuation plans, and the formation of disaster-response committees, but also the development of skills for negotiation and speaking in public, knowledge about laws, procedures and human rights, as well as advocacy and alliance-building with other communities in similar circumstances. Disaster management is increasingly linked to human rights work.

LOCAL PEOPLE'S PERCEPTIONS AND CONSEQUENCES FOR DISASTER-RESPONSE POLICIES: SUMMARY AND CONCLUSIONS

Vulnerability to disasters is a matter of perception, and in the perception of most aid agencies no consideration is given to the view of local people. Many agencies tend to think on behalf of the victims, not realizing that disaster-prone communities might interpret their circumstances differently. Assessing vulnerability is just one side of how people take risk-related decisions. If we want our disaster responses to be meaningful, we need to give affected communities a voice and to recognize their risk perception, as well as their active role in exploring strategies that ensure livelihood security in the long term. The latter means that we should strengthen these strategies in order to address the root causes of their vulnerability, and to broaden our perspective beyond the disaster response framework. Part of this involves supporting alliance-building among communities at risk, as well as with organizations and groups in society that advocate justice, peace and responsible governance. After all, addressing vulnerability is a political issue.

More concretely, and based on my experiences in the Philippines, I would like to recommend the following:

- Shift from a disaster-cycle model towards a disaster risk-reduction framework. The disaster-cycle model encourages us to look at disaster problems by dividing them into smaller entities, such as emergency response, rehabilitation, reconstruction, mitigation, preparedness and early warning. The focus is still very much on the hazard event itself, and organizations and funding agencies specialize in one of the entities, independent from each other. Contrary to what most disaster managers do, poor communities do not perceive disaster preparedness, emergency response, rehabilitation, recovery and mitigation as separate phases of a cycle, but as integral parts of their survival and development process. Poor communities accumulate knowledge and skills from previous experiences and manage their resources and capacities to deal with the ongoing process of mounting vulnerability. Disasters are part of that process, either as the result of natural hazard events, or as the result of 'development' that went wrong and does not benefit the people at risk.

   Communities at risk would benefit from a framework that shifts from managing disasters as a temporary interruption to development towards linking poverty, disaster risks and vulnerability to development. The aim of disaster response is not to bring things back to how they were before the disaster, but to increase people's capacities and to strengthen their coping strategies in order to deal more effectively with adverse events. However, this alone would not be sufficient.

- Participation of people at risk, which is essential for effective disaster risk reduction. Local people have knowledge about their locality, the history of local disasters and how vulnerability to disasters has changed over time. They have the right to participate in decisions that affect their lives directly. People's participation is basic because safety, stability of livelihood, well-being and disaster management are their concern, and not solely that of 'experts' such as government, scientists and aid agencies. However, the knowledge of scientists and experts is still relevant and needed, especially regarding rare and new types of (human-made) hazards. Scientists and disaster managers should recognize the value of people's perceptions; local and outsiders' perceptions should be considered as complementary. The success of participatory risk assessments depends upon the ability of the different actors in the locality to discuss, to reason and to plan together.[5]

- Making local communities aware about root causes of vulnerability and what they can do about it. People's participation is not just the process of consultation and providing information to outsiders during assessments, intervention selection and implementation. If we are serious about addressing vulnerabilities, then people's participation should be made part of an empowerment process: joint assessment of capacities and vulnerabilities builds awareness. The disaster-pressure model, developed by Blaikie et al (1994), is a very effective instrument to encourage local people to analyse their conditions, and to discover root causes of why they endure hardship. It raises, in particular, people's awareness about the political origins of a disaster and their vulnerability. In the Philippines, this also means that lawyers often become involved in this process, explaining to community people the new government's acts and laws that affect them. On paper, these news acts offer possibilities for villagers to express themselves and even to make more effective use of the judicial system to defend their rights. However, support from concerned lawyers to help local people to really participate in procedures, to file cases and to express their objections and interests is crucial. Communities who are aware and supported can then be mobilized for action. This can lead to the formation of new local institutions or to the strengthening of existing ones. Disaster vulnerability can only be reduced if conscious and organized communities and the public can pressure governments in such a way that their interests are no longer ignored in government's decision-making and planning (Heijmans and Victoria, 2001, p16).

- Linking disaster risk reduction and human rights work. There is a considerable overlap between disaster risk-reduction efforts and human rights work. Since 1948, there have been hundreds of conventions and other legal instruments developed to protect human rights. The definition of human rights has also broadened, including more domains of human life: intentional pollution or degradation of environment can now constitute a violation of the human rights of the people affected (Handmer and Wisner, 1998). Therefore, exposure to disasters should also be perceived as a violation of human rights. Every human being or community has the right to a certain quality of life and to anything that enhances the quality of life – for example, economic growth, improved access to resources, or social and political empowerment. In fact, since the end of the 1990s, there is an increasing trend for a rights-based approach in disaster management. In 1997, the Sphere project was launched to develop a set of universal minimum standards in core areas of humanitarian assistance, linking disaster response to the Humanitarian Charter (Oxfam, 2000). However, these documents, despite their good intentions, will have limited impact without the presence of a strong grassroots movement that is alert and able to pressure institutions to avoid, once again, translating these standards into technical solutions.

By linking disaster risk reduction with human rights work, we recognize people at risk as powerful claimants with rights, rather than poor victims or passive recipients. We can no longer ignore their voices, but must genuinely respect and implement declarations and laws to make the world a safer and more just place.

Chapter 9

Progress in Analysis of Social Vulnerability and Capacity

Ian Davis

INTRODUCTION

In April 1993, I was asked to speak on 'Assessing Community Vulnerability' (Davis, 1994) at a conference at the Royal Society in London on Medicine in the International Decade for Natural Disaster Reduction (IDNDR). Preparing this chapter has presented a useful opportunity to revisit that original paper to observe any significant developments in social vulnerability assessment during the intervening years. It has also provided the necessary incentive for me to reflect on my own changing perceptions of a subject that has become a central aspect of disaster management. The structure of this chapter is built around six key issues that I raised in the original paper. These are restated, followed by quotations drawn from the original paper. The issues include comments on almost ten years of change. Each issue then concludes with a summary of actions required to make progress in risk assessment and management.

Issue 1: Has social vulnerability and capacity assessment (VCA) been established and institutionalized as a key element in disaster management?

Community vulnerability has only recently been recognized as a key element in a holistic appraisal of who or what is exposed in the threat of a disaster. It had been neglected for four main reasons:

- the general bias in the planning process to the physical sciences;
- bias of political concerns;
- since community or social vulnerability is a late arrival, there is the need to develop an agreed methodology or assessment of risk factors;

- the lack of assessors from a professional background best suited for this demanding role (Davis, 1994, p11).

All of these factors remain firmly in place despite the concentrated efforts of the IDNDR and the dramatic growth in disaster management budgets for relief activities. For example, in the risk assessment field, the negative bias that favours the physical sciences is still present, and may even be expanding as societies become ever more intoxicated with optimistic expectations of science and technology as a panacea for their manifold problems. This confidence is reflected in the vast majority of disaster managers who still appear to hold the simplistic notion that disaster risk assessment is synonymous with scientifically generated 'hazard mapping'. Such a view grows from a technocratic and fundamentally false assumption that once hazards are mapped in terms of their location, duration, frequency, severity and impact characteristics, then the risk assessment process is complete.

Nevertheless, there is plenty of evidence of clear progress in certain areas. For example, there has been the development of the vulnerability and capacity assessment (VCA), particularly by the Red Cross, who has played the lead during the past decade. A useful overview of this progress is set out in the *World Disasters Report 2002*: 'Assessing vulnerabilities and capacities during peace and war' (IFRC, 2002). This report highlights the fact that VCAs are now routinely undertaken as an essential part of their disaster assistance and development planning. They have adopted a dual approach to assess the capacities and vulnerabilities of their member organizations, as well as the communities in which they work. This policy and practice was certainly not the case a decade ago.

The political realities that inhibit the promotion of social vulnerability assessments remain in force due to political sensitivities; but there is a growing and discernible recognition of the need to address vulnerability in governmental circles. For example, in 2002, the UK government's House of Commons International Development Committee reported on global climate change and sustainable development. One of the committee's findings is likely to be the first official endorsement of the importance of promoting vulnerability assessments in relation to disaster management. The report includes a proposal that:

> *The Department of International Development (DFID) should sponsor vulnerability assessments in developing countries and use the information to help target work on adaptation where vulnerability is greatest* (House of Commons, 2002).

In 1993, I noted that there was still the need to develop an agreed methodology to assess risk factors. Some progress has been made on this; but an agreed inter-agency or inter-governmental methodology for social vulnerability assessment remains elusive other than the growing general acceptance of the need to firmly link vulnerability to capacity. One reason is the lack of data concerning the different assessment approaches used and defining their relative effectiveness as assessment tools. This gap will only be closed by applied interdisciplinary research to rigorously compare assessment approaches across different hazard categories within different country and cultural contexts in order to identify key variables that are needed relative to different hazards. From this process, it will be possible to identify elements of 'best practice'. Such an evidence-based approach is urgently needed to replace the ad hoc process that currently prevails.

A further gap is the link between pre- and post-disaster assessments. For example, there are obvious benefits in the same person or agency collecting, storing and analysing data from both contexts. Pre-disaster VCAs are inevitably speculative, comprising projections concerning likely damage and casualties; however, post-disaster needs and damage assessments are the acid test of vulnerability and capacity. Both processes need to be merged within an integrated Disaster Management Information System (DMIS).

Summary of actions needed

Actions that are required comprise the following:

- Conduct comparative internationally based research to discover what VCA processes have been completed or are being undertaken in relation to varied hazards.
- Develop an agreed methodology with key non-governmental organizations (NGOs) and governments by sitting down together to develop templates for assessments based on best practice.
- Authorities need to explore the links between social vulnerability and capacity assessment data, assembled prior to a disaster, with social needs and capacity assessment data collected after a disaster. This data needs to be built into an integrated Disaster Management Information System (DMIS).

Issue 2: What has been the value and impact in linking vulnerability assessment and capacity analysis?

The type of information that is needed comprises, for example, aspects of knowledge, attitudes, economic status and occupations in relation to:

- perception of risk;
- risk adjustment (for example, the capacity of people to modify their lifestyle or the capacity of buildings to cope with the threat);
- coping mechanisms, including kinship ties, religious observance, social obligations and emergency reserves operating at individual, family and community levels;
- links between hazard potential and occupational factors (Davis, 1994, p12).

In the spring of 1973, I visited Professors Henry Quarantelli and Russell Dynes of the Disaster Research Centre (DRC) in Ohio State University. The visit was en-route to the devastated city of Managua following the 1972 earthquake. During the course of two days of intensive learning, seeking to grasp some of the key results of approximately 25 years of social research into disaster response and behaviour conducted by DRC staff and students, Quarantelli briefed me on what I might expect to observe in Managua:

In over 25 years experience of disaster situations, we have observed that in most disaster situations there is a tendency for all concerned to exaggerate *the scale of damage and dislocation and to greatly* underestimate *the capacity of the affected population to resolve their own problems* (Quarantelli, 1973).

The expectation proved to be correct on both counts. In Managua, there had been a gross exaggeration of damage, deaths and injuries in a largely successful attempt to secure enhanced aid from foreign sources. The requested support was particularly in the form of cash in order to line the pockets of Dictator Somoza and his ruling elite. Three months after the disaster, the coping abilities of the survivors were in sharp evidence; but these were often squashed by the delivery of paternalistic and, generally, inappropriate aid from governments and NGOs. All too often, this merely duplicated the actions that the survivors were better able to provide themselves (Davis, 1985).

It took a full five years for the corrupt dictatorship to eventually be deposed. One of the reasons for Somoza's overthrow in 1978 was his loss of support from the corrupt ruling elite, who were denied their own share of the rich reconstruction pickings that he allegedly pocketed or passed on to his family. To this date, Managua has not been rebuilt, a tragic legacy of corrupt leadership, incompetent governments and an inability to mobilize local capacities.

It also became evident in other situations that coping strategies could be found in all contexts, both before and after disasters, as well as in relation to the capability of 'survival artists' to deal with chronic deprivation and poverty. Thus, it was encouraging to note a positive development in disaster management and risk assessment that emerged during the 1980s with the link between the negative and the positive or, in current terminology, with the link between vulnerability and capacity.

An expression of the change in emphasis can be seen in the way that the formula, used in describing disasters during the early 1990s, has now developed. The original equation was:

$$\text{Disaster} = \text{Hazard} \times \text{Vulnerability} \ (D = H \times V)$$

This has now been expanded into an equation that adds 'capacity' to the equation. This is expressed as a key element to reduce disaster risk where capacities are strong or, where they are absent, to increase the threat of a disaster:

$$\text{Disaster} = \frac{\text{Hazard} \times \text{Vulnerability}}{\text{Capacity}} \ \left(D = \frac{H \times V}{C} \right)$$

Whenever I have introduced this equation in a disaster management training course, a predictable question concerns how these relationships, embracing such a wide range of variable elements, can begin to be quantified? The answer is that, if the various elements of the equation are fully covered, it is possible to undertake a 'loss-estimation scenario' for a given situation, with specific projections concerning casualties and both direct and indirect physical, economic and environmental losses. The level of accuracy depends upon the quality of the assessments and analysis, and there is always the problem that the projected scenario will not precisely match any future disaster in terms of its timing, location, severity and secondary impact. These complexities emphasize that risk assessment is, inevitably, an 'inexact science' and is likely to remain so. But such inherent uncertainties should never be allowed to become an argument for omitting a vital process that aims to reduce the uncertainties as a prelude to reducing risks.

The equation proposes that the greater the capacity, the smaller the disaster impact, and experience decisively endorses the point. However, it is not always easy to provide probing public officials or political leaders with the concrete proof that they seek concerning the direct relationship between strengthening capacity and a measurable reduction in the impact of a hazard in order to save lives and to protect livelihoods and property. An example of persuasive evidence of the positive impact of capacity-building in reducing vulnerability in Honduras came during Hurricane Mitch:

> *One example is the municipality of La Masica, on the Caribbean coast of Honduras, where a series of capacity-building activities were initiated with technical support from local agencies, along with an early warning flood system. In contrast to neighbouring communities, not a single life was lost in La Masica* (Maskrey, 1999).

This positive–negative, capacity–vulnerability relationship was an influential theme in Mary Anderson and Peter Woodrow's *Rising from the Ashes*, first published in 1989 (Anderson and Woodrow, 1989). The authors developed a *Capacities and Vulnerabilities Analysis Matrix*. This was a simple, yet ingenious, six-box matrix (or template) to aid risk assessment (see Table 9.1). Users of this matrix were invited to fill in appropriate boxes to describe their situation, often finding that the same element might be repeated in both the 'vulnerability' as well as the 'capacity' box. For example, within the 'social' category, elderly persons would often be cited as a 'vulnerability' due to their susceptibility to disability, immobility or general lack of resilience. However, the elderly might also appear in the 'capacity' box, being regarded as a powerful community asset, with their memories providing vital links between present threats and past experience or with useful, yet neglected coping abilities.

Linking vulnerability with capacity has been increasingly seen as a key element in building a concern for development into the vast and ever expanding disaster-relief community, who are often unfamiliar with the process. The relationship between vulnerability and capacity is also being increasingly expressed in risk assessment methodologies that include vulnerability and capacity assessment (VCA).

Examples of the linkage are now all pervasive. The International Federation of Red Cross Societies published a guide entitled *Vulnerability and Capacity Assessment* in 1999, and the link is implicit in the title selected for an Oxfam Working Paper: 'Risk-Mapping and Local Capacities; Lessons from Mexico and Central America' (Trujillo et al, 2000). Thus, an isolated and innovative approach to the analysis of capacities and vulnerabilities in 1989 had become an accepted working methodology within many enlightened international NGOs and their partners by 2000.

Table 9.1 *Capacities and vulnerabilities analysis matrix*

	Capacities	**Vulnerabilities**
Physical/material What productive resources, skills and hazards exist?		
Social/organizational What are the relations and organizations among people?		
Motivational/attitudinal How does the community view its ability to create change?		

Source: Anderson and Woodrow (1989, p12)

While patterns of vulnerability have undoubtedly increased since 1993, it is also clear that the *perception* of capacities and *actual measurable* capacities have also grown during this period. These strengths, coping abilities or resilience can be found in social, administrative, physical, economic and environmental realms. These capacities are now being routinely assessed in tandem with vulnerabilities on similar lines to Anderson and Woodrow's 1989 model.

Where this occurs, it can become a vital therapeutic process in which increasing numbers of highly vulnerable people assess and build up their own abilities and resources to cope with the threats that they face. Thus far, VCA has been restricted to social factors in most of the VCAs that have been undertaken by agencies. However, the approach needs to be routinely adopted at a macro-level to physical elements, such as buildings, the natural environment and the economy. In each of these categories, there are vulnerabilities to be assessed, as well as capacities. For example, a study of any urban environment in relationship to risks will reveal an inventory of vulnerable as well as hazard-resistant buildings. From such a detailed assessment, it will be possible to indicate possible evacuation options so that residents of unsafe structures can be rapidly relocated to safe buildings. Similarly, a vulnerability and capacity assessment of a local economy will reveal which livelihoods are at risk from a potential hazard, while the parallel economic capacity assessment will identify the likely resilience of the economy by considering the existence of income diversification.

Summary of actions needed

Actions that are required comprise the following:

- Build a detailed understanding of the scale and nature of the 'coping strategies' of communities 'at risk' within all disaster plans, at all levels from national to local.
- Provide much needed encouragement; document and widely disseminate examples where vulnerability has been reduced by strengthening capacities.

- Expand the VCA process to cover all key sectors: social, economic, physical and environmental elements. To underline the various processes and to avoid future confusion, the name of VCA should ideally be replaced with a prefix of 'social' (SoVCA), 'economic' (EcVCA), 'physical' (PhVCA) and 'environmental' (EnVCA). In time, additional elements may need to be included such as political vulnerability and capacity assessment.
- Develop and test an agreed methodology for this wider application of VCA to all of the above sectors.
- Take the data collected in hazard mapping and VCA and develop *loss-estimation scenarios* to provide authorities with an indication of what social, physical, economic and environmental losses they can anticipate in future disasters.

Issue 3: How can VCA expand from the narrow concern of improving safe conditions to embracing the root causes and pressures that give rise to such conditions?

> *People are not generally at risk by accident. Many are exposed due to the highly complex web of causes and pressures that include exploitation to serve commercial, racial or political ends. Thus, to remove vulnerability it would be essential to address such causal factors by raising political or ethical awareness and mounting pressure for change. If this is not undertaken, then vulnerability will persist and recur even if symptoms are rectified* (Davis, 1994, p12).

Throughout the past decade, there have been numerous examples that indicate that vulnerability is politically motivated. Therefore, given patterns of multiple causes, it follows that a wide diversity of 'tools' is needed to reduce entrenched risks. I worked with Piers Blaikie, Terry Cannon and Ben Wisner in writing *At Risk: Natural Hazards, People's Vulnerability and Disasters* (Blaikie, Cannon, Davis and Wisner, 1994; the second revision is due for publication in 2003). This book developed a pair of models to describe the cause and effect of vulnerability. One of these models maintained that vulnerability is traceable to three linked realities that operate in a progressive manner, starting with root causes that create dynamic pressures and lead to unsafe conditions. The premise of this 'crunch model' is that if actions are confined to addressing the cosmetics of unsafe conditions, without tackling fundamental pressures or addressing the root causes that generate the patterns of vulnerability, then patterns of acute vulnerability will keep returning.

This hypothesis raises a major challenge to the system of vulnerability and capacity. Future assessors of vulnerability will need to expand their data collection by encouraging their informants to be much more probing. In suggesting this wider frame of reference for the assessment, it may be helpful to relate this to an imagined scenario, as presented in Box 9.1.

The SoVCA scenario presented in Box 9.1 highlights three issues. First, if the SoVCA had been confined to addressing Stage 1, then the consequent measures to address the needs of the family would have failed to consider or address the underlying reasons of why they were in Delhi in such a precarious situation.

Box 9.1 A social vulnerability and capacity assessment (SoVCA) in Delhi, India

Let us assume the following: an Indian NGO is conducting a social vulnerability and capacity assessment (SoVCA) in a vulnerable flood-prone area of Delhi.

Stage 1: Vulnerability and capacity – unsafe conditions

A careful vulnerability assessment has identified a range of 'high-risk groups', including a high-risk family comprising a single parent family with several small children and several elderly dependent relatives. The family secures an intermittent income from the mother's and eldest child's labour, but lacks a regular income. The family is at risk from multiple causes, including seasonal flooding, fires due to acute urban congestion, varied health threats, including epidemics, and the ever present threat of eviction for living illegally on government-owned land.

The capacity assessment has identified a local NGO who provides this family with welfare assistance and another that offers micro-credit small loans. The mother of the family is attending a training course and may qualify for a loan to expand her work in washing clothes for neighbours.

Stage 2: Vulnerability and capacity – dynamic pressures

The assessment probes further in an attempt to identify why this family finds themselves in this situation. It determines that they migrated to Delhi following severe flooding on the Ganges River two years ago that destroyed their home, assets and livestock. At that time, they were destitute following the death of the husband from tuberculosis and decided to move to Delhi as a 'last resort' survival strategy. Their own 'capacity assessment' had identified an uncle who assisted them in their move to Delhi. Despite their fragile foothold in the city, it appeared that they were probably far better off living in this congested floodplain when compared to their relatives who had remained behind. The difference lay in better income opportunities, access to improved medical care and schools and some institutional support from local NGOs. Thus, their urban migration could be regarded as an effective family survival strategy or 'capacity'.

However any positive gains to an individual family at the micro-scale certainly contributed in a negative manner at the macro-scale to the acute urbanization problem of Delhi.

Stage 3: Vulnerability and capacity – root causes

The root causes of this particular family's plight relate to a range of macro- 'push' and 'pull' factors. These include the 'push' in attempting to escape from the grinding poverty in the countryside. The 'pull' factor that generated their move to Delhi was precipitated from believing overoptimistic reports of work opportunities in a booming economy in the capital city. Further fundamental causes relate to the failures of the government to introduce effective disaster preparedness, including an effective flood early warning scheme.

Second, confining attention to Stage 1 with an analysis of the unsafe conditions is a tempting option since it is probable that most agencies will lack the vision or resources to address the problems and root causes of the urbanization process or of corrupt administrations.

Third, the scenario moves from examining vulnerability and capacity at the micro- to the macro-scale and as such indicates that it is essential for the national government to become the lead player in the overall VCA approach. An effective local NGO may be able to run a micro-credit programme at a community level, but will not be able to organize an early warning flood system or provide enhanced rural opportunities to counter the process of urbanization. This underlines the importance of government/NGO collaboration as discussed in the section 'Issue 5: Who should undertake vulnerability assessment and analysis?'

Summary of actions needed
Actions that are required comprise the following:

- Unless there is a rapid and radical expansion of VCA to move far beyond the cosmetics of addressing unsafe conditions to addressing the reasons why they exist, there will be minimal progress in risk reduction. This will require a wider vision among NGO leaders, as well as among national governments, to become centre stage in the process. They will need to sit down together to work out how to undertake integrated assessments and operations.
- As VCA moves towards causal factors, it will inevitably enter the political world and encounter powerful political and commercial forces that will resist such enquiries. Thus, the assessment of root causes will lead to the need for political advocacy in order to strengthen some policies and to reverse others.
- The value of the VCA approach lies in its focus on 'unmet needs' and, thus, provides assistance to groups in understanding their role, building upon the strength of local capacities.
- Recognize inherent dangers in the development of the VCA approach. The possibility exists that cynical government officials will become aware of the strength of capacities and thus give even less attention to addressing patterns of vulnerability than would have been the case before.

Issue 4: Is there any progress in the development of comprehensive, integrated risk assessment?

The analysis of vulnerability is a vital element in risk assessment and involves three broad areas, all of which are closely interrelated:

- *physical*: vulnerability of buildings, infrastructure agriculture, etc;
- *economic*: vulnerability of economic assets, incomes and industrial production; economic vulnerability can be further broken down into 'direct loss potential' (for example, the loss of a coconut crop in a cyclone) and 'indirect loss potential' (for example, the economic consequences of the time taken for newly planted coconut palms to produce).
- *social*: vulnerability of livelihoods, incomes, community resilience and coping mechanisms.

The merging of differing forms of spatial data has become a reality through the development of geographic information systems (GIS). In 1992, I assisted in the leadership of a disaster management course in China. One of the topics that the authorities requested for inclusion in the course was an overview of 'best practice' for disaster risk assessment. They specifically requested a presentation on the application of GIS for risk assessment. A specialist was found from Los Angeles who had developed a complex, wide-ranging GIS for disaster management within that city. It embraced layers of data on, for example, various hazards, vulnerability assessment information, disaster impact data, the location of critical facilities and evacuation routes. All of this data was regularly inserted into the Los Angeles Risk Assessment/Disaster Management System to maintain a comprehensive data bank. The Chinese disaster managers were obviously in awe of the system. In response to their perceived overconfidence in the power of technology and the ability of such computer-based information systems to solve their problems, the visiting US planner repeatedly sought to remind them of the human constraints on such computer-based systems, for all the benefits they might yield. He insisted that each GIS was only as good as the data that was inserted into the computers.

During the late 1980s, I recall visiting Professor Nick Ambraseys, professor of earthquake engineering at Imperial College, to discuss a model that we had been jointly developing to analyse urban-scale vulnerability to earthquakes. The project was to analyse urban seismic risk reduction in Mexico City following the earthquake of 1985 (Aysan et al, 1989). Ambraseys's main concern was about the quality and comparability of data on urban vulnerability that was being entered into our computers. When it was explained that the data was collected by various assessment teams, he then asked what steps we had taken to verify its accuracy since the data was derived from various assessors who might have been using different criteria for collection purposes. Unable to give him the positive assurances that he was looking for, the conversation ended rather abruptly. Ambraseys explained that in his own research he had made it a practice never to enter data that he had not personally collected or directly supervised.

These anecdotes serve as a reminder that the essence of any effective assessment system is the collection, insertion and analysis of *accurate* data. This concern is a particular issue in the processing of qualitative data on capacities and vulnerabilities that may be collected and analysed by varied assessors, who may not always be using comparable survey techniques. This basic point is particularly important since most officials I have met are far more excited and interested in the increasingly magical qualities of computer technology than in the 'hard grind' of painstakingly securing, and maintaining accurate and consistent data.

One of the major concerns in the development of VCA is that agencies that have embarked on the gathering of data appear to regard this activity to be the sum total of risk assessment. They do not emphasize that effective VCA can only begin when hazard mapping has been undertaken. They have also made minimal progress since 1993 in linking social vulnerability and capacity assessment to economic, physical and environmental vulnerability and capacity assessment. They also fail to see the opportunities to take the results from hazard mapping and social, economic, physical and environmental VCAs and use them in order to develop loss-estimation scenarios.

A vivid indicator of the dangers of narrow sectoral thinking came in an important ongoing international programme called the Global Earthquake Safety Initiative (GESI) (Geo Hazards International and UNCRD, 2001). The pilot programme, completed in 2001, examined the seismic safety of 21 cities. In order to define the seismic vulnerability of each city, the project team defined a five-part methodology, with data being collected on the following topics:

- *'building fatality potential'* (soils/building stock/building construction and materials/building occupancy rates);
- *'landslide fatality potential'* (landslides triggered by earthquakes);
- *'search and rescue life-saving potential'* (numbers of people available to participate/levels of training, etc);
- *'fire fatality potential'* (fires induced by earthquakes);
- *'medical care life-saving potential'* (casualty management).

It is notable that this list inexplicably omits a range of critical key factors that also have a decisive impact on vulnerability and capacity:

- *'the level and effectiveness of public awareness programmes'* (particularly those that are focused on school children);
- *'the level and effectiveness of disaster plans'* (disaster plans at all levels, from national to local);
- *'high-risk social groups'* (social vulnerability and capacity assessment);
- *'economic assessment'* (urban seismic vulnerability is intimately related to an identification of any industries/commerce and individual livelihoods that are at risk).

Explanations for such gaps may include the fact that the project is primarily the work of civil engineers for whom such concerns as public awareness, disaster planning, and social and economic vulnerability may be unfamiliar territory. However, as this project expands with a new range of international urban studies, it is vital for the organizers of GESI to radically expand their assessment criteria and to build interdisciplinary teams in order to undertake the necessary work in each city that is investigated. Without this wider multidisciplinary and interdisciplinary frame of reference, the project is fundamentally flawed in its current design since the results will fail to provide the necessary holistic picture of urban vulnerability.

Reasons for such gaps probably lie in the interdisciplinary and multidisciplinary problems in creating integrated actions, and the lack of leadership in assembling a total picture. If risk assessment is likened to a jigsaw puzzle, there are often missing pieces because the individuals assembling the picture lack an awareness or understanding of the elements that are needed to comprise an integrated 'whole'. Assessors from social backgrounds can typically lack an understanding of engineering aspects of vulnerability; economists are unfamiliar with environmental considerations, and so on. Therefore, improved interdisciplinary education and integrated teamwork are required at all levels to tackle problems and to synthesize issues. But for this to occur, there is a need for inspired leadership to grasp the totality of the problem and the opportunities. In addition, there is a need for improved publications and better field-based training in assessment methodologies that will cover both manual, as well as GIS, applications.

There is minimal evidence of systematic vulnerability analysis in which the physical, economic and social data are comprehensively integrated together. Furthermore, where vulnerability assessment takes place, it is normally seen as a specific process in measuring what is certainly more tangible and static than all the complexities of people within communities which are undergoing dynamic change (Davis, 1994, p11).

This quotation still applies ten years after it was written. Integrated and expanded VCA is rarely happening, and the only progress in integration across sectors has come from the use of GIS as an effective tool to merge data; but its application as a powerful risk assessment tool is still largely confined to wealthy countries.

Summary of actions needed
Actions that are required comprise the following:

- VCA needs to be expanded from a narrow concern with unsafe conditions to addressing the reasons of why they exist. This will require a wider vision among NGO leaders, as well as among national governments, to become centre stage in the process. They will need to sit down with key NGOs to work out how to undertake integrated assessments and operations.
- The political consequences in assessing the sources of vulnerability will need to be recognized and addressed, with a focus on advocacy in order to create the necessary changes in policies.
- A multidisciplinary and interdisciplinary approach to vulnerability and capacity assessment is essential in order to merge social, technical, economic and environmental data.
- GIS information technology will have to become more affordable and accessible for use in poor developing countries where its application is most needed.
- Those who undertake risk assessment and risk management need to pay much closer attention to the collection of accurate and consistent data.

Issue 5: Who should undertake vulnerability assessment and analysis?

The first requirement is to find people who are very familiar with the local situation. The second requirement is to find people who are trained in how to organize sample surveys and who also have some understanding of simple interviewing techniques. The third requirement is the necessity that the teams assessing social vulnerability must not be the same personnel who dispense assistance (Davis, 1994, p13).

In 1993, the concern was raised over the lack of assessors from a professional background to undertake the demanding VCA role. The issue still remains as a challenge to be resolved. On a consultancy visit to a large Caribbean country in 2001, I asked the national disaster management director whether any progress had been made in risk assessment during the past decade. She replied that there had been extensive progress in hazard mapping for floods, landslides and hurricanes but no progress in social vulnerability assessment. The reason she gave echoed my 1993 statement concerning 'a lack of professionally qualified assessors to undertake the task'.

However, on returning to the UK, I recall pondering whether this national director and I were correct in holding such a narrow view. If there is one vital lesson from the past decade, it is the importance of de-professionalizing the assessment and risk-reduction processes wherever this can be achieved for three vital reasons: to cut costs; to expand and accelerate the urgently needed process of mapping vulnerability and capacity; and to strengthen community learning to enable any given society to protect their citizens. For example, if a community leader has systematically assessed social risks, determining precisely who is at risk, where and why, then that leader will likely be a strong advocate in pressing the authorities, as well as the affected community, for improved disaster protection.

While it may require a competent engineer or architect to assess the vulnerability of a major building, or an economist to assess the vulnerability of livelihoods at risk from a potential disaster, it is likely that many key leaders can assess the vulnerability of people within their communities in an effective manner. Such people can be found in most communities, and some locations may also contain others who are particularly well equipped to undertake participatory surveys at the community level. But for any of these groups to undertake vulnerability and capacity assessments, they will need the support of effective leadership and good assessment checklists, as well as simple training in mapping techniques.

Mobilizing such grassroots resources requires the support of good community development and social workers. They are needed to train community workers, to establish assessment methodologies, and to monitor the process and analyse the data. However, these experts are thin on the ground in most developing countries. Therefore, it is vital to use their skills in a strategic manner, rather than use them to conduct routine tasks such as collecting data. Within each community 'at risk' (whether they are urban or rural), there is likely to be a range of able persons to collect such essential data.

Three founder figures of international disaster studies – Gilbert White, Bob Kates and Ian Burton – have commented on the developments in reducing disaster risks as a result of the increasing focus on vulnerability, as well as the 'added value' of community mobilization:

> *The concept of vulnerability also helps in the promotion of the involvement of community and citizen groups in the planning and development process, and contributes to the goals of empowerment, democratization and the advancement of human rights* (White et al, 2001, p86).

In many societies, progress with VCA has been made through locally based NGO actions, rather than through government initiatives. However, it is vital that NGOs work in close partnerships with government officials in undertaking the VCA process in order to incorporate a better understanding of vulnerabilities that may have come about as a result of past governmental actions or of past neglect. Such working partnerships need to extend to the entire spectrum of risk assessment, risk reduction and risk management processes.

While this need is a prerequisite of genuine sustainable programmes, it is alas elusive in so many contexts where the one thing that appears to unite the local NGO community – who is working to provide disaster assistance – is a dislike or even active contempt of *national* governments. Significantly, the attitude does not also apply to the *donor* governments who so often faithfully support them. It is, of course, a wild generalization to assume that this value is universally held, and there are major exceptions. But such an attitude is often expressed verbally in discussions and can even be enshrined in agency approaches or policies. In one particularly memorable training course for disaster intervention for staff teams working for a large international NGO in the UK in 1995, there was barely a single mention of the role of government by the participants in a full two weeks of intensive study and training. In the final session, I noted the gap, reminding the participants that they and their organizations were essentially 'guests' in a given country and that the national government was their host. The suggestion fell on deaf ears. Such a blinkered vision, party spirit or prejudice can also appear when governments display jealousy of the international resources that NGOs can command or are dismissive of the value role or significance of NGOs working within their countries.

Therefore, an aspiration for the coming century is that NGOs and government officials will cooperate more constructively in undertaking actions for risk assessment and risk reduction, recognizing that they share common causes of concern. They also need to be reminded that there are powerful *real* enemies to development in the form of public apathy and the policies of some multinational companies as well as certain governments. To attack public indifference or ignorance, as well as unsafe policies and practices, requires the united and integrated effort of all concerned.

Summary of actions needed

Actions that are required comprise the following:

- The process of VCA needs to be de-professionalized to include a range of skilled and experienced persons who can be found in most communities.
- Leadership is also needed where experienced professionals will train local assessors and develop the templates for assessment.
- NGOs and governments need to work together in conducting VCA and in developing risk reduction and risk management measures that follow effective risk assessments.

Issue 6: How is vulnerability and capacity assessment contributing to disaster risk reduction?

Social vulnerability assessment is diagnostic. It identifies who is at risk, from what and in what location. It tends towards the next stage which concerns protective planning and embraces both preparedness and mitigation measures (Davis, 1994, p13).

It is probable that the improvements that have taken place in reducing disaster risks have resulted, in part, from improved risk assessment. It has always been a source of wonder to find that major risk reduction programmes have been undertaken without an essential diagnostic risk-assessment process. This reckless process is analogous to conducting major surgery without first undertaking the routine diagnostic processes of X-rays or body scans to identify the problems needing attention. A senior disaster management officer in West Samoa casually informed me that his country simply lacked the resources for risk assessment and that disaster preparedness was largely a 'matter of common sense'!

In future, it is likely that the way to evaluate progress in risk assessment will be through a diagnostic process that has supported improved risk-reduction measures that are based on strengthening existing capacities, as well as on addressing vulnerabilities, and that are holistic: based on the integration of physical, social, economic and environmental capacities and vulnerabilities.

Summary of actions needed

Actions that are required comprise the following:

- Donor bodies should always insist that a comprehensive risk assessment is conducted prior to the design or funding of any preparedness or mitigation programme.
- Research is needed to see how risk assessment data is used in the development of risk reduction measures.

CONCLUSION

The six sets of 'Summary of actions needed' form the conclusions of this chapter. Since writing the 1994 paper, there is evidence of some progress, as is demonstrated by the bibliographies in Box 9.2. However, there remains a clear need to apply the expanding pool of knowledge of VCA within both useful and usable assessment methodologies.

Progress has been painfully slow in certain key areas of human resource development, such as in developing interdisciplinary teamwork, building productive relationships between NGOs and governments and in de-professionalizing the assessment process. These and other gaps will have to be closed if there is to be any hope of coping with mounting disaster threats. However, by far the most positive development since 1993 has been the process of looking at capacities, and, thus, unlocking powerful forces from within vulnerable communities to address their own vulnerabilities.

BOX 9.2 SUMMARY OF BIBLIOGRAPHIES THAT RELATE TO SOCIAL VULNERABILITY AND CAPACITY ASSESSMENT

Reducing vulnerability at community levels

Bethke, L, Good, J and Thompson, P (1997) 'Building Capacities for Risk Reduction', UN Department of Humanitarian Affaires (UNDHA) Disaster Management Training Programme (DMTP), Geneva

Jaspers, S and Shoham, J (1999) 'Targeting the vulnerable: A review of the necessity and feasibility of targeting vulnerable households', *Disasters,* 23(4): 359–72

Maxwell, D (1999) 'Programmes in chronically vulnerable areas: Challenges and lessons learned', *Disasters*, 23(4): 373–84

Sharma, V (1998) 'Strengthening vulnerable communities for natural disaster reduction', *South Asian Series in Vulnerability Reduction*, No 10, Disaster Mitigation Institute and Durog Nivaran, Ahmedabad

Tobin, G (1999) 'Sustainability and community resilience: The Holy Grail of hazards planning', *Environmental Hazards*, 1(1): 13–26

Community-based disaster management and preparedness

Mileti, D (1999) *Disasters by Design,* Joseph Henry, Washington, DC, pp209–40

NDO (1992) *Australian Emergency Manual: Community emergency planning guide (second edition)*, Natural Disasters Organization (NDO), Canberra

Quarantelli, E L (1997) 'Ten criteria for evaluating the management of community disasters', *Disasters*, 21(1): 39–56

WHO (1999), Chapter 3 'Vulnerability Assessment', *Community Emergency Preparedness: A Manual for Managers and Policy-makers*, World Health Organization (WHO), Geneva, pp30–68

Ethical aspects of vulnerability reduction

Boyce, J (2000) 'Let them eat risk? Wealth, rights and disaster vulnerability', *Disasters*, 24(3): 254–61

IFRC (1994) *World Disasters Report: Knowledge Power and Need in Disasters, How the Misuse of Power Creates Vulnerability?* International Federation of Red Cross Societies (IFRC), Geneva

Livelihood security

Carney, D (1998) 'Sustainable rural livelihoods:What contribution can we make?' in F Ellis (ed) *Livelihood Diversification and Sustainable Rural Livelihoods*, Department for International Development (DFID), London, pp53–66

Parasuraman, S (1995) 'The impact of the 1993 Latur-Osmanabad (Maharashtra) earthquake on lives, livelihoods and property', *Disasters*, 19(2): 156–69

Theoretical framework

Bankoff, G (2001) 'Rendering the world unsafe: "Vulnerability" as Western discourse', *Disasters*, 25(1): 19–35

Blaikie, P, Cannon, T, Davis, I and Wisner, B (1994) *At Risk, Natural Hazards, People's Vulnerability and Disasters*, Routledge , London and New York

Oliver-Smith, A and Hoffman, S (1999) *The Angry Earth, Disaster in Anthropological Perspective*, Routledge, New York

Vulnerability and capacity assessment

Bhatt, M (1999) 'Mapping vulnerability: Participatory tool kits' in J Ingleton (ed) *Natural Disaster Management*, Tudor Rose, Leicester

Bethke, L, Good, J and Thompson, P (1997) *Building Capacities for Risk Reduction*, UN Department of Humanitarian Affairs (UNDHA), Geneva

Coburn, A, Spence, R and Pomonis A (1991) *Vulnerability and Risk Assessment*, UN Disaster Management Training Programme (UNDMTP), Geneva

Davis, I (1994) 'Assessing community vulnerability' in UK IDNDR Committee *Medicine in the International Decade for Natural Disaster Reduction (IDNDR) Research Preparedness and Response for Sudden Impact Disasters in the 1990s*, UK IDNDR Committee, London, pp11–3

Davis, I and Hall, N (1999) 'Ways to measure community vulnerability' in J Ingleton (ed) *Natural Disaster Management*, Tudor Rose, Leicester, pp87–9

IFRC (1999b) *Vulnerability and Capacity Assessment: An International Federation Guide*, International Federation of Red Cross and Red Crescent Societies (IFRC), Geneva

IFRC (2002) 'Assessing vulnerabilities and capacities during peace and war' in *World Disasters Report, Focus on Reducing Risk*, International Federation of Red Cross and Red Crescent Societies (IFRC), Geneva, pp129–47

Morrow, B H (1999) 'Identifying and mapping community vulnerability', *Disasters*, 23(1): 1–18

Stephen, L and Downing, T (2001) 'Getting the scale right: A comparison of analytical methods for vulnerability assessment and household level targeting', *Disasters*, 25(2): 113–35

Trujillo, M, Ordonez, A and Hernandez C (2000) *Risk-Mapping and Local Capacities: Lessons from Mexico and Central America*, Oxfam, Oxford

Chapter 10

Vulnerability Reduction: A Task for the Vulnerable People Themselves

Zenaida Delica-Willison and Robin Willison

INTRODUCTION

Vulnerability has been associated with poverty, powerlessness, weakness, limited capacity and lack of resources. As such, people who are considered poor, weak, incapable and with little resources are labelled as vulnerable. They then become the objects of planning by the various stakeholders in poverty reduction and development. We are living and working at a time when there is a significant level of interest in vulnerability reduction. Governments, non-governmental organizations (NGOs), private agencies, universities, donors and banks are increasingly devoting attention and activities, and, in some cases, announcing major commitments to vulnerability reduction.

Despite the interests and initiatives on vulnerability reduction, the vulnerabilities of people continue to increase in many developing countries. Among the factors that have contributed to the rise of vulnerability are the rapid spread of urban settlements into high-risk areas; the use of inappropriate technologies; the lack of enforcement of building codes; the architectural and construction designs that pay little attention to disaster risks; the lack of vulnerability analysis; and the usual non-consideration of the views and perceptions of the vulnerable groups. Strategies that link scientific and technical research to management and decision-making are missing in state/national development plans.

There is an increasing incidence of hazards accompanied by a corresponding increase in the number of people affected (CRED, 2001a). Extreme natural phenomena and conflicts are integral components of the physical, socio-economic and political environment. When combined with the vulnerability of groups and locations, these forces result in damage and destruction. The magnitude of damage caused by this combination is, to a large extent, a result of the decisions made, activities undertaken or not undertaken, and technologies applied in the course of a society's development. In most cases, the extent of destruction produced by an extreme event is preventable. Had the vulnerable physical and social conditions in Gujarat (India), Izmit (Turkey) and Baguio (the Philippines) been addressed long before these hazards, then the massive destruction could have been significantly lessened.[1]

This chapter will discuss experiences of people in their local communities who, because of their exposure to certain hazards and limited resources to cope with hazards, have many vulnerabilities. Their experiences proved that they were primarily the ones who had to address their vulnerabilities and had to help each other in building their capacities.

POVERTY ALLEVIATION/VULNERABILITY REDUCTION IN RETROSPECT

During the past, the focus of development initiatives was more on poverty eradication than on vulnerability reduction. Development assistance to poor countries had always looked at poverty as a challenge to economic prosperity and treated disasters as mere abnormal occurrences that disrupt economic growth. Hazards were understood as temporary interruptions of the linear development process. Disasters were considered as one-off events and responded to by governments and relief organizations without due consideration of the causes, and without taking into account the social and economic implications. Thus, disastrous situations were faced with emergency actions and immediate social welfare assistance, followed by rehabilitation and reconstruction. After these activities, it was believed that poverty alleviation or development work would resume immediately.

Since it is now understood that vulnerability and poverty are social conditions that mutually reinforce each other, it is worth briefly tracing the course of action taken to reduce poverty. This correlation assumes that the alleviation of poverty would result in a significant reduction of vulnerability. Have these development strategies really alleviated poverty? Has there been a consequent vulnerability reduction?

For almost all of the latter half of the 20th century, development efforts have been guided by an economic paradigm that, in simple words, attributed the problem of countries' poverty to a 'lack or shortage of capital' combined with abundant labour. In order to change the situation, this view advised that capital should be transferred to these countries in the forms of loans and aid. Financial capital was transferred from richer to poorer countries, where it was transformed into physical capital, largely in the form of public infrastructure (Duncan, 2001).

Modifications to this economic theory occurred along the way and included the need for health and education programmes to 'upgrade' labour during the 1960s; the need for policy changes to foster and sustain 'import substitution strategies' among borrowing countries during the 1970s; and the 'endogenous' growth models that focused upon technological changes as economic engines to ensure sustained progress, allied to a view that research and development is the external factor required to aid economic development during the 1980s and early 1990s (Duncan, 2001).

Transfer of capital in the form of aid and loans did not work, as both borrowers and lenders acted irresponsibly. Money borrowed was used to purchase oil and weapons, to construct environmentally destructive projects such as dams and nuclear power plants and to import foreign goods. As a result, more people became poorer and poorer in most of these indebted countries. Poor countries were unable to repay their foreign debts and these debts and interest continued to grow during the early 1980s. In attempts to make the main development theory work, new policies were imposed by the lending institutions on indebted countries. These impositions are incorporated within the structural adjustment programmes (SAPs) which involve austerity measures (Bruin, 1996).

As a condition for further development assistance, recipient countries must generate foreign exchange so that they can repay their debts. International development agencies and individual country donors that encouraged economic reforms in developing countries channelled development assistance in this manner and direction. Meanwhile, recipient countries of aid had difficulty in meeting other conditions imposed by the lending institutions. Instead of improving their socio-economic conditions, these countries have actually either stagnated or deteriorated. For example, in 1998 the World Bank estimated that even if a 6 per cent growth rate in the Philippines was maintained, massive poverty would remain (World Bank, 1998).

Reforms that were necessary to affect the poverty situation have not been actualized. In fact, in 1994 the United Nations (UN) secretary general, in his report to the Commission on Human Rights, pointed out that recent findings reveal that present actions by development agencies are not effective because the measures undertaken have failed and the structural adjustment programmes are based on flawed development models (UNHCR, 1994). The Development Assistance Committee of the Organisation of Economic Co-operation and Development (OECD) concluded, after reviewing the projects funded by international agencies and bilateral donor agencies, that 'there is very little evidence that the projects have been particularly helpful, or effective, in reducing poverty' (DAC, 2000, p45). In this case, development assistance has, by and large, been unable to significantly affect poverty. The developing countries are still below the poverty line and their people remain mostly poor.

Cuny (1983) states: 'It is the poor who suffer most in disasters...they are vulnerable in the most complete sense because they are poor'. Therefore, with poverty still very much on the horizon, vulnerability to hazards seems to be the lot of most of the billions of the poor.

CONTEMPORARY THINKING ON VULNERABILITY

While poverty is identified as a major factor of increasing vulnerability to hazards, and the poor are more exposed, it is an oversimplification to deduce that poverty and vulnerability are one and the same. However, the correlation is very evident. For example, a poor family who does not have sufficient income cannot afford to buy land in a safer place or even improve its dwelling. Thus, when a major cyclone hits the poor family's area, there is a high probability that their house will be damaged, which will make its members poorer. Poverty will therefore always be a problem. Poor people's economic standing limits their ability to mitigate the debilitating consequences of hazards (Watts, 1983).

Poor people, having no adequate resources and opportunities for earning a reasonable income, have many vulnerabilities to hazards. But the impact of hazards on vulnerable people is a factor in producing more poor people: poverty and vulnerability can be considered as two sides of the same coin. Therefore, addressing vulnerability also necessitates addressing poverty.

Traditionally, vulnerability to hazards has been viewed as more of a physical threat. As such, there was a dependence upon technological fixes to face disasters. Attempts to control floods have been in the form of the construction of dams, reservoirs, levees, embankments, and flood-protection structures. However, there are other views that perceive vulnerability as more than being restricted to merely the physical or material dimension. Anderson and Woodrow (1989) introduced the vulnerability capacity analysis framework. In this framework, vulnerabilities are identified in the social/organizational and the motivational/attitudinal realms as well as in the physical. This describes not only the visible aspects of vulnerabilities in societies, such as poor location, low income and lack of resources, but also other aspects, such as community organization, social relations, attitudes and motivations. In a different perspective, this framework looks at how to reduce vulnerability by increasing the capacity of the community in physical, organizational and attitudinal realms (Anderson and Woodrow, 1989).

Vulnerability, like disaster, has been defined in varied but not in contradictory ways. The Asian Disaster Preparedness Centre (ADPC) defines vulnerability as 'a condition which limits or reduces people's ability to mitigate, prepare for, withstand, respond to or cope with a hazard' (ADPC, 1999). It is weakness in the face of strong forces; it is susceptibility to danger. Periperi, a southern African NGO, defines vulnerability as a 'set of prevailing or consequential conditions composed of physical, socio-economic and/or political factors that adversely affect ability to respond to events. It can be physical, social or attitudinal' (Holloway, 1999). Piers Blaikie et al (1994) offer a working definition that states that vulnerability is:

> ...the characteristics of a person or group in terms of their capacity to anticipate, cope with, resist and recover from the impact of a natural hazard. It involves a combination of factors that determine the degree to which someone's life and livelihood is put at risk by a discrete and identifiable event in nature or in society.

The vulnerability of people refers to a certain level of exposure to hazard that derives from the social and economic condition of the individual, family or community concerned. High levels of vulnerability to a hazard indicate that the impact of this hazard would also be high.

Vulnerabilities to hazards are not static but dynamic situations. Blaikie et al (1994) describe the progression of vulnerability from the invisible root problems to the visible unsafe condition. This progression may be understood through a chain of explanations that begins with the root causes of the current unsafe conditions. The emphasis is on unsafe or vulnerable conditions that do not happen overnight. Instead they can be traced back to the underlying causes and linked with the socio-economic political processes and people's limited access to power, structure and resources (Blaikie et al, 1994).

Other factors contributing to vulnerability include political instability, insecurity and high levels of stress. Political instability is a major factor leading to the increased vulnerability of large populations. It can lead to sudden changes of vulnerability in any sector of society and, in the case of civil war, make large sections of a population suddenly vulnerable. The Solomon Islands group in the Pacific has had a long history of people mixing from the different islands; but they still maintain their identity. Two islands, Guadalcanal and Malaita, comprise the majority of the population. Now that the population has rapidly increased, rapid urban growth has not been handled properly, educational facilities are lacking, there has been inequitable development, and the population from Guadalcanal resents the influx of many people from the other principal island, Malaita. Hence, political and economic factors lead to conflict between the two main groups. The majority population group wants to dominate senior civil service positions, so that many of those from other islands, even technically well-qualified people, are thrown out of work without future prospects and become vulnerable (Solomon Islands Government, 2000).

Vulnerability can also be associated with general insecurity. Insecurity raises the stress level in a population and renders individuals more vulnerable to hazards. The increased stress can derive from a wide variety of related factors. It is sometimes partly attributable to intense and emotional media coverage of events, as the media exploits disasters, whether natural or human-induced, by luridly depicting the suffering of individuals who may not be representative of the affected community as a whole. This attracts people to media reportage; but, as they observe close-up pictures in print and on television that highlight human suffering, both physical and mental, this heightens their feelings of fear, insecurity and vulnerability.

A multiplicity of factors are leading to greater civil instability in many countries today all over the world. On one hand, climatic conditions seem to be becoming more extreme; on the other hand, arms are becoming all too available as many nations support their economies by manufacturing arms and selling them to any bidder. It has been estimated that 86 per cent of the world's arms are being manufactured by the five permanent members of the UN Security Council, whose task is to preserve peace. For instance, in a recent assessment of landmines found in South Sudan by a UN mine assessment team, there were landmines from Belgium, China, the former Czechoslovakia, Egypt, Iran, Israel, Italy, the former Soviet Union and the US (Human Rights Watch, 1998, p20). Ethnic tensions, religious differences, political ineffectiveness, economic pressures, population and factional strife all contribute to greater insecurity, stress, and less ability to cope with hazards and, hence, to increased vulnerability. These stresses, when combined with the free availability of weapons, are far more likely today to rapidly deteriorate into crime, bloodshed, social disruption and overt armed conflict, leading to inevitable social and material disruption and loss.

When assessing a population's vulnerability, the perceived stress of these factors must be taken into account.

Take, as an example, Zimbabwe in Africa. For political reasons, President Mugabe faces waning popularity and considers that race and the distribution of land may be used as tools to restore his image among the voting public. After 40 years of independence, landless people are encouraged to take property from the descendants of former immigrants who have farmed it successfully for the economic benefit of the country (and their own) for many generations, and to redistribute its use by resettling the national poor on it. Some of the supreme court judges are also from former immigrant stock from several continents, and are now threatened with violence by the same political leaders for making legal decisions that declare these political actions illegal and unconstitutional. Suddenly the rich and influential become vulnerable. Farms are taken without recompense, homes are attacked and people are killed. Even though the political violence has led to many more of their workers being killed than the landowners or judges, vulnerability is now widespread and is associated with high stress levels.

Increasingly, views on disaster are also changing from 'disaster as natural' to 'disaster as a question of vulnerability'. Disasters could be reduced if the socio-economic condition of the people is improved, if the environment is protected and preserved, and if preventive measures are undertaken. Hazards are now seen to be different from disasters, as hazards become disasters only when they strike vulnerable people who are at risk.

While discussions on poverty, disasters and vulnerability have developed a more progressive understanding, addressing these issues in a complete sense that will really alleviate poverty, prevent disasters and reduce vulnerability has not been successful. To accept that every community has capabilities for self-protection and for group action is to approach the problem of vulnerability with more effective and permanent solutions. Recognizing these capabilities means believing that people can do more than cope or adjust to crisis situations.

VULNERABLE PEOPLE'S VIEWS ON THEIR VULNERABILITY

Vulnerability has traditionally been discussed and defined by non-vulnerable people with an interest to help reduce the vulnerability conditions. Definitions are most often constructed by well-educated Western men and women who strongly believe in the merits of scientific, expert knowledge rather than the local knowledge system. They prefer to be entrenched in their own profound ways of knowing and understanding. As discussed above, people's vulnerabilities are determined by social, political and economic structures and relations within a given society. However, 'from the point of view of local vulnerable people, vulnerability is a difficult term to grasp. Instead, they use the term "weakness", "problems" and "constraints"' (Heijmans and Victoria, 2001).

In a detailed study on vulnerability in South Sudan, it was found that local people considered vulnerability to be 'weakness', and those whom they considered to be vulnerable or weak in their community, they divided into two categories – those who were weak through their own actions and those who were weak through no fault of their own. Hence, in their context, vulnerability may be caused by war; flood or failure of the rains; hunger; disease; pests; or insecurity; or it may be due to loss of close family members; the death or sickness of the mother or father; lack of daughters to bring bride wealth into the family; laziness in making preparation for hazards; and a multitude of other factors that reduce traditional reserves needed for times of stress or uncertainty. Clearly, these factors of vulnerability are very individual, although major events affect the whole population. It is the sum total of these individual vulnerable situations that defines the vulnerability of the whole (Harragin and Chol, 1998).

Mistakes have been made by aid agencies that have not assessed the multiplicity of contributing factors to an emergency, or the local culture and concept of vulnerability and coping, and have tried to simplify or generalize vulnerability from an external stance. For instance, if a population is suffering from lack of food, and a needs assessment is to be made for food supplementation, how should it be done? In the experience of one of the authors, a small team is usually sent out to assess how many needy families are to be found in an area to which food can be delivered. This team seldom travels widely; rather, it sends out a call and expects people, particularly local leaders, to come to tell them the situation. Not understanding the local culture, how such delegates are chosen and how food is shared in that culture, an assessment is made of how big the average family is, how many families there might be in the designated population who require support, and the magnitude of the needed supplementation from these selected interviewees. The food is then ordered and distributed according to the assessment findings.

In an example witnessed in Eastern Upper Nile in South Sudan at the end of 2000, the arrival of several thousand internally displaced people (IDPs) had put pressure on local food resources to cope. Such a general appraisal was made, and the message was soon carried that food would be available at a certain site. Large numbers of people began to converge from a wide area beyond that surveyed. They rejoiced when the food was dropped from the aircraft and when the distribution began several days later. Everything went well to start with as people thought that food would be available for all, which would be distributed in the normal way among their families. Then the assembled people began to realize that it was being distributed according to a pre-set plan that would leave many people excluded. When they saw that if they waited, many were not going to receive any food, they pulled out their guns and distributed the food according to their own plan. Thankfully, no shots were fired.

The food agency personnel fled and called for immediate evacuation, saying that the local people had turned their guns on them. That location was then taken off the list for food assistance for several months until everyone, including higher officials far away in Nairobi, where the aid for Southern Sudan is coordinated, had apologized for what happened and promised that it would never be repeated. Meanwhile, the hunger situation there deteriorated drastically and people began to die. But whose fault was it that there was a potential threat of violence? A lack of understanding of the local culture and of their view of vulnerability and coping mechanisms had led to what happened but the local people were then blamed and punished for it.

A key factor within a community in determing its perception of vulnerability is the stress level in individuals who comprise the population. Stress derives from the way in which a person perceives the situation, in all its complexity, and how he or she reacts to that perception. In psycho-social terms, it is primarily concerned with a person's perception of their ability to survive the future. If people feel uncertain of being able to survive, they feel a heightened internal stress that makes them less able to prepare for, to mitigate against, and to survive hazards when confronted by them. Others may reflect on all the support mechanisms surrounding them and may feel more confident of the future, having a lower stress level. Still others may be acutely aware of the precariousness of their situation and the uncertainty of being able to cope with the future; feeling highly stressed, they may worry over what will happen next.

A significant influence on the stress level that increases vulnerability is the social structure of the community and the situation of particular families. If the family and the community have strong supportive relationships, where they jointly care for the weaker members of their community, that society tends to be less vulnerable than other factors might lead one to assume. They can survive much external stress from hazards if they support each other, share their feelings with each other and know that they will cope with hazards together. A strong emphasis on family structure in a culture or a shared and active religious life are strong cohesive forces for communities. The more fractured a society is, the more vulnerable are the individuals who compose it (Harragin and Chol, 1998).

Conversely, if people are outcasts from their society, or if they do not have many close family members nearby for any reason, this increases their stress level and makes them more vulnerable. As a result, even if the whole population is subjected to the same hazard such as war, famine, flood and earthquake, the influence of the immediate family is a significant factor for individuals. Those families who have lost many members due to death or displacement, an infertile, sick or dead husband or wife, or an aged parent with no relatives living close by become vulnerable because they cannot rely on a pool of support to help them. In some societies, marriages create a network of important supportive bonds, welding the community together through their interrelationships and laying obligations on relatives for mutual support. This contributes to a greater ability to withstand stresses and, hence, lessens vulnerability. If individuals for any reason do not marry or cannot have children, they may have less of a supportive framework around them and may become more vulnerable. In these societies, a large family is beneficial because it can call upon a large pool of people to assist with coping strategies.

A disaster produces an intense social crisis. There is intense stress as the affected people adjust to the loss of shelter, food, water, income-generating activity or the support of family members. These losses, according to the intensity of the disaster experienced, will test the strength of the society. The way in which it functions under adversity will largely depend upon its pre-disaster condition.

Closely allied to the stress level is the perception of the security situation. Outside agencies that initiate interventions, which they deem appropriate from their external evaluations, may increase stress levels in a population and may destabilize their perceptions of security. This can lead to greater vulnerability.

An example of this is compulsorily relocating people to a 'safe' place – putting them into a refugee camp in another area, or relocating them where they are physically removed from the current danger. Are they less vulnerable in this more controlled situation? Reactions were observed about the attempt to do this during the recent flood emergency in Mozambique, where some people had been forced by rising floodwaters to live in trees and on small pieces of land in rivers. Their plight was highlighted in some very emotive journalism, particularly the scenes carried worldwide of a mother giving birth while swaying in a tree surrounded by floodwaters since there was no safe land below upon which the baby could be delivered. Then they were taken to 'safety' by helicopter.

An appeal went out from government and aid agencies for helicopters to transfer people to a 'safe' place away from the flooded area. When the threatened people heard that the helicopters were coming to relocate them rather than to give them food and to minister to their temporary needs until the floods subsided, they refused to leave (Shukman, 2001). With no history in the new place, with new hazards to face, with everything new – the food, the accommodation, the environment, the water supply, the social situation – and with no certain way to return home, the stress this induces can be immense. Here, they become vulnerable to other stresses and hazards. Some hazards may have been eliminated; but individuals face new ones with which they have no experience and to which they may be vulnerable. They may therefore experience a net loss by relocation. External forces or conditions that pressure people into doing something that they do not want to do contribute to stress and vulnerability. This is an important factor that should be realized by aid workers in the planning and implementation of all projects to assist the vulnerable.

Another example is the situation of people in the Naxcivan Autonomous Republic, Azerbaijan, among whom one of the authors worked as director of an aid project to establish a new primary health care system during 1997 and 1998. Armed struggle continues between Armenia and Azerbaijan over the contested territory of Ngorno Karabakh and other areas regarded by Azerbaijan to be its territory occupied by Armenia. Meanwhile, families continue to live and even prosper in their traditional, but vulnerable to war, home areas in Naxcivan despite occasional disruptions. Families were visited living in places within range of enemy artillery that had fired on them before killing relatives and fellow villagers. When questioned why they continue to live under such unpredictable security, they replied that they would not live in any other place. This is their home that they have known for generations, and they refused to move. They feel less stressed here than if they relocated and had to face a new set of challenges.

Interaction with vulnerable people by the authors in different parts of Asia reveals that people consider powerlessness in the face of the powerful as the most appalling manifestation of vulnerability. For them, it is emotionally and psychologically draining. When strong and powerful landlords demand a major share of their harvest, they feel very weak and vulnerable. They say that when they cannot argue their case in front of a powerful person, even if they know that they are correct, they feel that they are oppressed and vulnerable. The fact that they cannot design the course of their future renders them weak and susceptible to abuse by stronger individuals.[2]

Local people believe that they have been manipulated by outside interventionists, whether these are real benefactors or exploiters. They cannot identify a single reason for their vulnerability. A combination of interrelated factors is involved. For example, individuals relate their malnutrition to landlessness and their limited capacity to earn more income with lack of education. They live in unacceptable, unsafe dwellings because of a lack of choice to live in a better place. They are poor because they do not receive all of the fruits of their labour, as in the case of a farmer who is given only a certain percentage of his harvest by the landowner.[3]

In Cambodia, local trainers who are working with poor and vulnerable communities refer to poverty, marginalization and lack of knowledge about the hazard as vulnerable conditions. They believe that those who are most vulnerable are the individuals with no other sources of income or who have no economic diversity. They have no or little savings at all to be able to stockpile food, buy medicine or strengthen and improve their houses. The poor people in a Cambodian village said that they have chronic diseases even before the disasters, and they have limited options and expectations. They considered themselves vulnerable because they have no information as to the probable impact of the coming hazard and they lack adequate support from the government to cope with it (ADPC Training Report, 2001).

In a *char* in Bangladesh during a training session conducted by one author, a poor woman said that 'she has many *bipodepenneta*' (vulnerabilities) because she has no means to buy even the basic necessities of life; so how can she even think of preparing for a flood? But she stressed that when floods occur, she knows where to go and what to do.[4] In a village in the Philippines, poor urban men and women identified their weakness and problems as having no regular income, making them dependent on 'five-six' to send their children to school.[5] They also mentioned that they constantly fear demolition of their shanties. They have been in this condition since they were born and have learned to adapt and cope. In fact, they would rather discuss their strengths than their weaknesses, and their capacity and coping abilities, than their vulnerabilities.[6]

Sometimes, those factors that lead a community to feel vulnerable are not what the outside observer would expect. A population in India lives in a shantytown along both inner sides of a river levee in Delhi where individuals have found enough room to build their houses, without needing to pay for land, but where rising flood levels often threaten them and they have to evacuate and sometimes lose their houses when this happens. A government team went in to persuade them to move to a less vulnerable location, onto free land provided for them elsewhere. But when the team went to ask the community to move to what they regarded as a much less vulnerable and more valuable location, they found that the population had no desire to move to the safer environment offered. Some had lived in that place for 28 years. They worked near to where they lived, many wives were also working, their children were in school, and they lived with their friends. Their main stresses were not the floods that plagued them, but the fear of being compulsorily moved away and losing their livelihood since they were squatters and had come from many backgrounds. Some feared being thrown out of the country since they were not legal immigrants. As the team investigated, they found that it was this fear that made them feel vulnerable, not the fear of floods.[7]

VULNERABILITY REDUCTION BY VULNERABLE PEOPLE THEMSELVES

In past developmental undertakings, the role of the vulnerable people themselves did not substantially feature when addressing their vulnerable conditions. Their role was obscured in most discourses because of lack of substantial documentation regarding their achievements. Studies and analysis of vulnerable conditions were primarily focused upon describing the vulnerable within society: estimating how many they were and defining them in terms of location, occupation, gender, age and health, including access to assets, markets and public services. Currently, more attention is being given to questions of why they are in this condition, why they have very limited access to income-earning assets such as land, credit, education and health, and why they have poor access to markets. How to reduce vulnerabilities is also a central issue in current discussions.

Powerlessness has been identified as one of the manifestation of a vulnerable condition. Organizing poor and vulnerable people is a direct counter-measure to powerlessness. The cornerstone of efforts to reduce vulnerability is self-organization of the vulnerable at the local or community level. Organizing themselves is an effective antidote to powerlessness, which is a major source of vulnerability.

The experiences of community-based organizations (CBOs) in the Philippines during and after disaster events reveal that they are capable of meeting some of their immediate needs by applying community resources. They do not totally rely on government emergency response, as it takes some time before government services reach devastated areas.[8] The different units of the organized communities undertook the functions of designing local-level early warning, evacuation, public awareness and mitigation systems, which are usually the domain of government entities (Delica, 1999).

The organization of vulnerable people to tackle their own vulnerability is a step in the right direction because this arrangement enables the poor to create community bonding through which to perform needed services, especially during emergencies; to exercise and experience social values that are important in developing an economic enterprise and system; to obtain a social entity that is effective in enlisting the support of elements from the wider society for transactions that may require such assistance; and to own a social entity that the poor can directly influence for other purposes related to vulnerability reduction, thus minimizing the problem of encountering serious resistance to such changes. Furthermore, these organizations are able to act as value initiators and sustainers for the purposes of cooperation, trust and concern for others.

Through networking with other social groups and through forming broad-based coalitions, the organized poor can have a voice and can influence local government, holding it accountable for efforts geared towards reducing susceptibility to hazardous events.

The experience in community-based vulnerability reduction is also the basis for successful economic enterprise. Cooperative enterprises have been successful in some villages in Batangas City, the Philippines. Starting as small self-help groups, these later combined to form larger area-based institutions. Such larger groups have been successful in influencing local governments and even the private sector. A community-based co-operative of farmers in Barangay, Soro-soro, Ibaba, has been able to improve the living condition of its members from destitute farmhands to middle-income families.[9] The creation of income-earning opportunities and ownership of assets have inspired the formation of similar co-operatives in other villages, such as the ones in Barangay Talumpok and Conde Itaas.[10]

Formerly vulnerable and poverty stricken, these farmers-turned-agrobusiness entrepreneurs are much less vulnerable. They have the power to decide the direction of their enterprises. As a well-worn cliché goes, the future is in their hands. These experiences and lessons show that certain goals, especially short-term goals, are realizable. This then becomes the foundation for achieving medium- and long-term goals.

The requirements for a successful community-based organization of vulnerable people demand strict adherence to certain principles and methods, among which are participatory approaches and techniques, and an honest and effective leadership. Participation of the vulnerable is a *sine qua non* because it is through such approaches that people's access to knowledge, skills and technology increases. The acquisition of these capacities has actually been identified by the community members as their highest priority.

It is, of course, not simple to make a community-based organization function without difficulties. There are many challenges and constraints that the organized groups have to face and solve. First and foremost is the social truth that anything that will introduce change, such as empowering the vulnerable, will be suspect to the existing powers in society because such movements could disturb the status quo. Those who benefit from the status quo will definitely refuse and stifle change that will bring about the needed and desired results in favour of the poor. This first problem is already extremely difficult to surmount.

Organized vulnerable groups have then to seek the support of sectors outside of their (vulnerable) circles, which can be referred to as less vulnerable groups. They could be within or outside of the vulnerable communities and may have their own organization, which can be categorized as civil-society organizations. They play an important role in providing necessary assistance and in extending essential goods and services. While they cannot directly represent the poor, they could be effective in policy advocacy or in influencing national programmes in favour of the vulnerable groups. Thus, it is important to forge partnerships with these groups. Poor people can rely on this partnership to advance their interests, especially when national and local governments are unresponsive to their needs. Civil-society organizations should not take over the legitimate functions of the state; but it is important to forge alliances for vulnerability reduction strategies. These alliances will increase the 'ownership' of desired reforms. A broad-based 'ownership' could make change more acceptable to the existing social structure. Networks that include both the vulnerable and less vulnerable sectors have been successful in many endeavours already started.

Box 10.1 People's participation in saving the community

The *barangay* of Talba, in Central Luzon, the Philippines, with a population of 779 families, or 4674 people, was situated along a river through which *lahar** from Mount Pinatubo had flowed. The possibility of an overflow in the near future was a real danger.

Municipal and *barangay* authorities were in constant communication through handheld radios to monitor the *lahar* flows from the volcano. The existing Barangay Disaster Coordinating Council had a chairman and committee heads in the *barangay* captain and the councillors, respectively. However, the different committees had no members and the *barangay* officials did not know how to operationalize the structure.

A non-governmental organization (NGO) focusing on disaster management was requested by a health-service NGO working in Talba to assist in the training and setting-up of a disaster management group in the community. The NGO complied with the request and established a community-based group, known as Barangay Disaster Response Organization. The participation of a *barangay* councilman in this group facilitated the interface of the Barangay Disaster Coordinating Committee and the people's organization by making the members of the latter group members of the committees of the former group. The Barangay Disaster Response Organization, however, maintained its identity by holding regular meetings with other organizations and stakeholders in the village.

Among the first activities of the community's disaster mitigation plan was sandbagging along the river banks and the construction of an 'uplifted' walk path for the residents, which was also made of sandbags. The sandbags along the banks were intended to slow down the flooding of the area if a rampaging *lahar* flow struck the village.

In 1995, a *lahar* overflow destroyed the village of Talba. As a result, the government communication system was disrupted and failed to give proper warning to residents. It was the parallel warning system developed by the community that warned them on time to vacate the area, thus avoiding any loss of life. Community resources, such as privately owned small boats, jeeps and a truck, were used to move the village's population to safety.

At the evacuation centre, the Barangay Disaster Response Organization members augmented the national government's health personnel in the delivery of services to the survivors of the *lahar* rampage.

In the new area where the affected families of Talba were finally resettled, the *barangay* officials who joined them have been able to secure the services of water, electricity and health assistance from the resettlement officials. The organized community was easily mobilized for action by the officials in support of requests made to the resettlement officials. The people's organization and the local authorities complemented each other in acquiring services, ensuring the safety and welfare of the members of the community.

* *Lahar* is an Indonesian term that refers to volcanic debris and molten lava deposits.
Source: Delica (2001) Citizens' Participation Towards Safer Communities

For example, in the Philippines there is a successful network among people's organizations and local and national NGOs. This is the Citizens' Disaster Response Network (CDRN), which was formally established in 1989. Peoples' organizations associated with this network are mainly organized by the poor themselves. They are promoting the organization of grassroots disaster-response mechanisms to plan and implement community vulnerability and risk-reduction measures. For example, in Central Luzon, during the Mount Pinatubo period (before, during and after the eruption in 1991), these mechanisms were responsible for designing evacuation plans and drills, and for emergency-response training.

In other areas covered by this network, people's organizations implement food security and nutrition programmes that include diversification of crops, propagation of resistant crops, seed banking, land-use management, community health, functional literacy and collective marketing of products. Immediately after a hazard strikes, they also undertake some search and rescue work.

During the emergency phase, they organized relief delivery operations in affected areas and erected temporary shelters for those whose houses were damaged through *bayanihan*,[11] organized evacuation and managed evacuation centres. They formed various committees, including health, security, food and livelihood. In Bicol, immediately after the Mount Mayon eruption, TABI, a local NGO, helped the affected and pioneered para-psychosocial first aid. It was also effective in mobilizing the help of the less vulnerable groups.

After disasters, a people's organization within the ambit of this network led the community in repairing and restoring damaged houses. To rebuild their resource base, they implemented the dispersal of seed, farm tools, machinery, fishing equipment, working animals and livestock. Where necessary, they were also involved in restoring community structures, such as the repair of community irrigation facilities, foot bridges and trails, and the installation of the water supply through the repair of pipes and tanks. These examples have proved that vulnerable people are capable of doing many things to make them less vulnerable.

It is heartening to note that there is a rise of a new generation of vulnerability-reduction programmes in some international and national NGOs that focus on the development of community organizations to directly articulate people's needs and priorities instead of only catering to income-generating activities. This is what the poor need most – not resources for safety nets but resources to build their organizational capacity. Advocacy efforts by those organizations supporting the poor and vulnerable must be directed towards ensuring resources for the growth of organizational capacity.

CONCLUSION

Addressing the condition of vulnerability is not an easy task. Vulnerability is multifaceted and addressing it has to be a concerted and sustained effort by all. The role of vulnerable people themselves should never be underestimated or neglected. Their capacity should be recognized and enhanced through a continuing capability-building effort. They are the ones who can personally undertake vulnerability- and risk-reduction measures in their own context, since it is they who are primarily affected.

The complete context needs to be thoroughly understood by anyone who aims to work in vulnerability reduction. As vulnerable people become involved and implement these measures, and as they witness the successful results of their work, they are further encouraged to sustain their cooperation and enthusiasm and to continue to make improvements. Therefore, they need support and encouragement by all who would assist them.

Chapter 11

Macro-economic Concepts of Vulnerability: Dynamics, Complexity and Public Policy

Charlotte Benson

INTRODUCTION

The reported costs of disasters caused by natural hazards have increased significantly during recent decades, with a 14-fold increase between the 1950s and 1990s. During the 1990s, such major catastrophes are reported to have resulted in economic losses averaging an estimated US$54,000 million per annum (in 1999 prices) (Munich Re, 1999). Record losses of some US$198,000 million were recorded in 1995, the year of the Kobe earthquake – equivalent to 0.7 per cent of global gross domestic product (GDP). But what do these figures mean? How were they compiled? Are they accurate? And what do they tell us about vulnerability from an economic perspective, or related appropriate policy response?

MEASURING 'VULNERABILITY'

There have been several recent attempts to distinguish between countries more and less vulnerable to natural hazards for essentially economic purposes. The results, which have been received with much interest, have typically generated a numerical ranking of countries according to relative vulnerability. Indeed, attaching a single quantitative number to a country's level of vulnerability is an appealing notion. Figures on, for example, levels of poverty, provide an immediate indicator of the likely importance of poverty reduction efforts in a particular country and the extent to which poverty factors should be considered and addressed in broad policy. A similar summary indicator of vulnerability could serve to highlight the need to address this, too, and perhaps even bring risk concerns into the heart of government thinking, rather than leaving them on the sidelines as essentially technical problems. However, the usefulness of vulnerability indices hinges on their success in achieving their objective. As a first step, it is therefore useful to examine how each of the ranking exercises measured vulnerability and how successful they were.

The recent flurry of interest in this issue represents part of a wider attempt to measure the extent of vulnerability of individual nations, particularly small states, to various types of external economic shock.[1] This interest has been fuelled, in part, by the fact that many small states have relatively high levels of per capita gross national product (GNP), suggesting economic strength rather than – as is often, in fact, the case – frailty. Focus on their relative wealth, rather than economic stability, has limited their access to concessional aid resources, generating concern that they may require differential treatment by the international development community. Initiatives have therefore been undertaken to develop tools that could generate data on the relative vulnerability of different countries for use in augmenting other factors that determine the allocation of aid resources.[2] The various efforts have focused on structural vulnerability, defined as vulnerability caused by 'factors which are not under the control of national authorities when the shocks occur' (Atkins et al, 2000, p3).

The vulnerability indices that have been developed have been based on a (sometimes weighted) range of components capturing different aspects of vulnerability, including vulnerability relating to natural hazards. However, as discussed below in this section, the way in which vulnerability to natural hazards has been measured has varied between the studies, reflecting significant underlying data constraints. This has resulted in significant differences in their results. More fundamentally, each index has been based entirely on historical data on the impact of past disasters, however defined, ignoring the dynamic nature of vulnerability and the fact that it is a forward-looking concept.

One of the earliest vulnerability indices was developed by Briguglio (1995), based on size (proxied by openness to trade), insularity or remoteness (proxied by transport costs), 'proneness to natural disasters' (his term) and environmental fragility.[3] Proneness to natural disasters was proxied by total damage from significant disaster events (defined as exceeding 1 per cent of GNP) occurring over the period of 1970 to 1989, drawing on earlier disaster analysis by the United Nations Disaster Relief Organization (UNDRO) (1990).[4] The Commonwealth Secretariat has also developed a composite vulnerability index, based on four variables: 'vulnerability to natural disasters' (their term); export dependence; the United Nations Conference on Trade and Development's (UNCTAD's) merchandize export diversification index; and the overall size of GDP of a particular country (Atkins et al, 2000). Measurement of vulnerability to natural disasters was based on the percentage of the population affected by disasters caused by natural hazards over the period of 1970 to 1996, using data provided by the Centre for Research on the Epidemiology of Disasters (CRED) (see section below on Reported 'Costs' of Disasters). The Commonwealth Secretariat is involved in some additional work on developing a composite environmental index, again using 'vulnerability to natural disasters' as one of a number of indicators, but this time defined as the total number of natural disasters over the period of 1970 to 1996, expressed relative to total land area.[5]

Table 11.1 *Top 20 countries 'vulnerable' to natural hazards according to various published indices*

		Basis of disaster index			
Rank	Damage[a] (Source: UNDRO, 1990)		Population affected[b] (Source: Atkins et al, 2000)		Number of disasters relative to land area[c] (Source: Atkins et al, 2000)
1	Vanuatu	228.41	Vanuatu	727.17	Tonga	1.000
2	Nicaragua	206.95	Bangladesh	539.16	St Vincent	0.669
3	Burkina Faso	191.23	Tonga	532.13	Barbados	0.455
4	Dominica	141.30	India	510.67	St Kitts & Nevis	0.453
5	Cook Islands	119.05	Bahamas	491.28	Maldives	0.435
6	Chad	92.04	Mauritania	487.55	St Lucia	0.368
7	Bolivia	84.16	Antigua & Barbuda	430.77	Dominica	0.348
8	St Lucia	81.17	Botswana	418.03	Antigua & Barbuda	0.296
9	Yemen Arab Republic	66.67	Mozambique	361.13	Grenada	0.288
10	Jamaica	64.40	Gambia	339.16	Mauritius	0.224
11	Comoros	61.18	Swaziland	304.31	Comoros	0.161
12	Ethiopia	60.82	Fiji	296.28	São Tomé & Principe	0.170
13	El Salvador	52.32	Dominica	261.97	Cape Verde	0.129
14	Bangladesh	50.32	São Tomé & Principe	245.49	Réunion	0.091
15	Tonga	50.20	Chad	241.60	Kiribati	0.089
16	Tokelau	50.00	Senegal	232.59	Vanuatu	0.080
17	Mauritania	41.15	Grenada	228.26	Jamaica	0.062
18	Mauritius	40.68	China	223.52	Fiji	0.061
19	Antigua and Baruda	38.00	Solomon Islands	213.71	Gambia	0.052
20	St Vincent/Grenadines	35.99	Niger	205.79	Trinidad & Tobago	0.051

Notes: a Index based on total damage from significant disaster events (defined as exceeding 1 per cent of GNP) that occurred over the period of 1970 to 1989
b Index based on percentage of the population affected by disasters caused by natural hazards occurring over the period of 1970 to 1996
c Index based on total number of disasters caused by natural hazards over the period of 1970 to 1996 expressed relative to total land area

The relative ranking of countries according to the different studies has varied substantially, highlighting the sensitivity of such analysis to the choice of indicator.[6] Table 11.1 reports the top 20 countries most 'vulnerable' to natural hazards according to each of the three indices. Table 11.2 takes the top 20 countries as identified by UNDRO (1990) – that is, on the basis of damage – and compares their relative ranking with that derived according to the two Commonwealth Secretariat indices. It also indicates whether or not each of the countries is amongst those 28 reported by Munich Reinsurance as having suffered direct disaster losses exceeding US$1 billion over the period of 1980 to 1989 (as cited in Freeman, 2000). As Tables 11.1 and 11.2 show, all three series highlight the apparently particular vulnerability of (or, perhaps, are biased towards) small island economies. However, they vary considerably even in the relative ranking of this sub-group. For example, St Lucia is placed 8th in terms of the cost of disasters, 37th in terms of population affected and 6th in terms of the number of disasters relative to land area.

Table 11.2 *Comparative ranking of countries to four different indices of national hazard 'vulnerability'*

	Ranking by vulnerability to disasters caused by natural hazards according to			Appears on Munich Re list of countries suffering over US$1 bn direct losses from catastrophes caused by natural hazards over period 1980–1999?
	Damage[a]	Population affected[b]	Number of disasters relative to land area[c]	
Vanuatu	1	1	16	No
Nicaragua	2	54	Joint 44th[d]	Yes
Burkina Faso	3	27	Joint 51st[e]	No
Dominica	4	13	7	No
Cook Islands	5	na	na	No
Chad	6	15	Joint 70th[f]	No
Bolivia	7	38	Joint 70th	No
St Lucia	8	37	6	No
Yemen Arab Republic	9	74	Joint 70th	No
Jamaica	10	30	17	No
Comoros	11	58	12	No
Ethiopia	12	22	Joint 57th[g]	No
El Salvador	13	53	27	Yes
Bangladesh	14	2	23	Yes
Tonga	15	3	1	No
Tokelau	16	na	na	No
Mauritania	17	6	86	No
Mauritius	18	61	10	No
Antigua & Barbuda	19	7	8	No
St Vincent/Grenadines	20	43	2	No

Notes: a Index based on total damage from significant disaster events (defined as exceeding 1 per cent of GNP) that occurred over the period of 1970 to 1989
b Index based on percentage of the population affected by natural disasters occurring over the period of 1970 to 1996
c Index based on total number of hazards caused by natural disasters over the period of 1970 to 1996 expressed relative to total land area
d Four countries are joint 44th
e Three countries are joint 51st
f 30 countries are joint 70th
g 13 countries are joint 57th
Source: UNDRO (1990); Atkins et al (2000); Freeman (2000)

There also appear to be some serious omissions. The Philippines, for instance, is widely acknowledged as one of the most hazard-prone countries in the world; yet, it does not appear at all on the UNDRO ranking of the world's 50 'most disaster-prone' countries, ranks 31st on the Commonwealth Secretariat index based on population affected, and 25th according to the Commonwealth Secretariat index based on number of disasters relative to land mass – that is, not particularly high according to any of the three indices.

Indeed, not only do the indices fail to capture factors that determine future vulnerability, as already noted, they may not even be good indicators of relative historical disaster impact. Any classification or ranking is based on incomplete and partially inaccurate data, reflecting problems outlined below. Any ranking is also sensitive to the period of analysis. Some countries may simply not have experienced a natural hazard event over the period of analysis. In addition, one is not comparing like with like. Different countries face varying types of hazard. For instance, a system of ranking based on physical damage may be biased against more drought-prone countries, where human and macro-economic consequences of hazard events may be high but direct physical damage is limited. The physical and economic size of a country also makes a difference, with hazard events often having little impact on aggregate national indicators in larger countries. However, this makes them affected differently, rather than less affected, than smaller countries.

REPORTED 'COSTS' OF DISASTERS

Nevertheless, in measuring vulnerability, the impact of past hazard events is significant and the above attempts to develop vulnerability indices are at least correct in taking them into account. Comparisons across countries and, within countries, between hazard events helps to build understanding of factors contributing to vulnerability, even if past impacts cannot be directly equated with future vulnerability. Thus, it is worth considering available data on impacts, focusing again upon economic impacts in order to see how complete and reliable the data is. The fact that two of the three indices discussed above were not based on the cost of disasters, despite the fact that they were all calibrated for essentially economic purposes, indicates particular problems with this form of data.

There are three comprehensive international databases on natural disasters, each providing some information on the 'cost' of individual events. In addition, there are numerous national records. However, in practice, the information available on costs is scant. The three international databases are maintained by the Centre for Research on the Epidemiology of Disasters (CRED) of the University of Louvain, Belgium, and by two of the world's largest reinsurance companies, Munich Reinsurance and Swiss Reinsurance, although detailed information from the latter two is not available in the public domain. Although the Office of US Foreign Disaster Assistance (OFDA)/CRED database, covering disasters dating back to 1900, includes information on 'estimated damage', it is only available for 25 per cent of the records (CRED, 2001a).[7] The Munich Reinsurance database contains information on both insured and total losses; but much of the information is little more than an informed guess (ProVention Consortium, 2001). Meanwhile, the Swiss Reinsurance database does not even record total losses, instead covering only data on total insured losses (excluding third-party liability). These figures may be much lower than total loss data, particularly in many developing countries, reflecting limited penetration of catastrophe insurance. Difficulties at an international level reflect similar problems at a national one, relating both to incomplete and partial reporting in many countries.

Thus, data on the cost of disasters is very incomplete. Moreover, even where costs are reported, there are still problems. CRED, for instance, is quick to point out difficulties with the data, relating both to inconsistencies in the way in which losses are valued and the types of losses actually covered (CRED, 2001a).

Data is typically based on damage assessments undertaken in the immediate aftermath of individual disasters, with additional information provided by the insurance industry. These damage assessments may be associated with a number of difficulties. First, many countries still lack standard, comprehensive guidelines for use in estimating the costs of disasters. Even within a particular country, there may be discrepancies between different disasters in terms of the scope of coverage of assessments and the reporting format as many assessors have to hand, at best, only very simplistic guidelines.[8] Moreover, standard social science practices, such as sampling procedures, are often ignored when undertaking damage assessments. Methodologies employed in valuing the damage also vary. For example, some surveys are based entirely on replacement costs and others on present value. In others again, the total cost reported also includes that relating to the upgrading of assets and equipment. These various measures of the cost of a disaster may all be appropriate for specific purposes. However, it is important to understand for what particular purpose cost data have been prepared and on what basis particular figures have been compiled. For example, if the cost of physical damage is being estimated as a basis for calculating the cost of the required reconstruction and rehabilitation effort, then the reconstruction cost is the appropriate pricing basis. In contrast, if the potential economic cost of a hazard is being estimated – as, for example, is required for use in the cost-benefit analysis of mitigation or preparedness projects – then present values should be used.

Second, damage assessments are commonly undertaken by officials and volunteers on the ground, often with little prior specialist training or, perhaps, even experience in general survey techniques. This adds to the uncertainty concerning the accuracy of assessments, particularly where assessors are equipped with only very limited checklists or questionnaires.

Third, there are problems relating to the non-comprehensive scope of coverage. Damage assessments are often undertaken by a range of government, donor and civil society groupings. The various agencies involved often have specific objectives of their own, generally orientated around rehabilitation but reflecting their particular areas of interest (Chardin, 1996). Thus, for example, individual government departments or agencies may be responsible for assessing damage to their respective areas of concern (agriculture, transport, housing and so forth); but damage to the private sector may be partially ignored. Damage that is not eligible for government assistance – for instance, damage experienced by higher-income families – may also be excluded. Certain types of damage may therefore go unreported in official reports, even where efforts are made to combine the various assessments into a more comprehensive overview document. Additional, again contradictory, loss figures may be cited by the insurance industry. Various bodies may also sometimes have reason to either exaggerate or under-report the extent of damage incurred as a consequence of a hazard event.

Fourth, damage assessments are typically completed very rapidly, often only a few months after a disaster. Their basic objective is commonly to provide essential information upon which appropriate and timely responses can be based, addressing both short-term humanitarian and longer-term rehabilitation needs. By definition, such assessments should begin in the immediate aftermath of a disaster and, indeed, the first assessments are typically completed very rapidly, sometimes as little as within seven days of an event. However, although governments may prepare a subsequent report detailing relief and rehabilitation efforts, often no further assessment of the longer-term economic impacts of a disaster is formally required and, therefore, is only very rarely undertaken. Thus, by definition, post-disaster damage assessments often represent little more than stock-taking exercises, focusing on damage to buildings, other infrastructure, capital equipment and standing crops, including, perhaps, surmising the implications for the stream of future production.

Fifth, as well as problems relating to the non-comprehensive scope of coverage indicated above, problems of bias can also result from the mix of expertise included and omitted in the assessment teams, and from the language, gender, ethnic grouping and age of the assessors (Thompson, 1999).

A sixth problem relates to the fact that reported data focuses predominantly on direct costs. Direct costs relate to the physical damage to capital assets, including social infrastructure – that is, stock losses. However, the potential impacts of a hazard event go beyond direct ones to include many flow or knock-on effects, commonly categorized as either indirect or secondary (see, for example, Otero and Marti, 1995). Indirect costs relate to the knock-on disruption to the flow of goods and services, including, for instance, reduced output, loss of earnings and job losses. Secondary effects concern both the short- and long-term impacts of a hazard event on the overall economy and socio-economic conditions, such as on fiscal and monetary performance, levels of indebtedness, the distribution of income, and scale and incidence of poverty.

Thus, for instance, at the macro-level, as well as involving the estimation of a number of incommensurables (that is, losses – most obviously, loss of human life – that cannot be directly quantified, at least not without introducing certain value judgements), a disaster could also result in a shift in fiscal policy or a rise in interest rates. At the household level, it could trigger a change in livelihood patterns or result in increased levels of debt. Again, however, there are measurement problems. For example, a government may take measures to contain the budgetary consequences of a disaster, diverting pre-allocated resources into the relief and rehabilitation efforts. As a consequence, aggregate public expenditure data may not reveal the extent of severity of the budgetary impact of a disaster, although the hidden costs may be substantial. Broad movements in levels of GDP can also underestimate the impact of a disaster.[9] Aggregate figures also fail to capture redistributional impacts – in turn, arising because different groups in society and different economic sectors are differentially vulnerable.

Direct, indirect and secondary costs are not additive and any attempt to aggregate them entails double counting. However, ascertaining the nature of indirect and secondary impacts is, nevertheless, important in understanding the macro-economic significance of direct physical damage. The point is not merely one of quantification, but of understanding processes in order to formulate appropriate policy responses, both *ex ante* and *ex post*.

Thus, in summary, available data on the costs of disasters is often problematic. In some cases, it is not reported at all, while information on others is inaccurate. It is not uncommon to see a range – sometimes, a wide range – of estimates of the cost of a particular disaster.[10] Without detailed knowledge of individual countries, however, it is difficult to ascertain exactly where the difficulties lie or to reconcile differences between the various databases.

In recognition of these various problems, the ProVention Consortium, in collaboration with the Economic Commission for Latin America and the Caribbean (ECLAC), has begun an initiative to improve standards and methodologies, building on an existing manual that ECLAC prepared for use in Latin America. Furthermore, under the auspices of the ProVention Consortium, a working group has also been established to explore the scope for information exchange and consolidation between the four major groups holding data on disasters globally. Both initiatives are important and much needed. Nevertheless, many of the problems with historical data will remain.

As a final note, it should also be remembered that some hazard events are not recorded at all, including many that fall below the arbitrarily defined threshold for an event that can be deemed a 'disaster'. Definitions invariably include criteria such as a minimum of 10 deaths, 100 or more people affected, the declaration of an emergency or appeal for international assistance. Evidence collated by the DesInventar initiative in Latin America on these smaller events suggests that in some countries the impact of these 'everyday disasters' may be much greater than those of the larger events that are formally recorded as disasters (IFRC, 2002).

FACTORS UNDERLYING VULNERABILITY

In attempting to measure vulnerability from a macro-economic perspective, a critical temporal element also needs to be introduced. Vulnerability, by definition, is a forward-looking concept, relating to the potential to suffer harm. Thus, vulnerability cannot be predicated solely on the basis of the impact of past events, even if data on impacts is comprehensive and reliable. Indeed, the nature and scale of vulnerability, whether viewed in economic or other terms, is itself highly dynamic and in constant flux, as various human actions continually interact to alter vulnerability, both at the household and macro-economic level.

Vulnerability to natural hazards is integrally related to prevailing socio-economic, as well as environmental, conditions. Most obviously, it is determined by the extent and nature of human activity and population density in the affected area relative to the nature of potential damage emanating from a hazard event. For example, the choice of crop types grown and cultivation techniques can make a difference. This difference relates not only to potential direct damage, but also to rates of recovery. For instance, banana plantations are highly vulnerable to high winds, which can flatten plants. But new plants can bear fruit in as little as six months. Changes in the agricultural sector can therefore affect the level and nature of vulnerability. Fiji experienced an increase in the economic impact of natural hazards between the 1970s and 1980s, largely reflecting the expansion of the country's important sugar industry onto more marginal lands, where crops were more vulnerable to hazards, combined with the increasing senility of the country's coconut trees, again weakening their hazard tolerance (Benson, 1997a).

The composition of the manufacturing and service sectors also plays a determining role. For example, those based around agro-processing may face particular difficulties post-disaster. But others, such as offshore finance, can be largely unaffected, assuming telecommunication links are re-established relatively quickly and that the sector is not linked to domestic economic performance.

Prevailing global and domestic economic conditions, policies of the incumbent government, demographic growth, unplanned urban expansion and a host of other factors can also affect the nature of vulnerability at a particular moment in time. In terms of the balance of payments, for example, a number of developing countries rely on a handful of commodities for a significant part of their export earnings. Contemporaneous fluctuations in the price of such commodities, as well as of major imports such as oil, can exacerbate or minimize the impact of hazard events, usually by chance timing. Countries already experiencing other adverse economic shocks of one form or another are also typically more vulnerable to natural hazards. The existence and stage of a structural adjustment programme can be a further determining factor.

Vulnerability also needs to be considered in the context of the stage of development of an economy, as defined in terms of factors such as the degree of sectoral and geographical integration, economic specialization, the level of development of the financial sector and government revenue-raising capabilities (Benson and Clay, 2000). Least-developed economies are typically perceived as most vulnerable to natural hazards and other shocks (the case of small island economies being another special category of 'most vulnerable'). However, in its initial stages, increased development may not imply lower vulnerability. Instead, research at a household level suggests that poor and socially disadvantaged groups become more vulnerable initially. Socio-economic change associated with development can lead, for instance, to the breakdown of traditional familial support, declines in traditional coping measures and the increased occupation of marginal lands.

Such patterns may be mirrored at a macro-level. An economy at an intermediate stage of development is more integrated (via transportation and telecommunication links), both between sectors and different geographical regions, thus increasing the multiplier effects of adverse performance in a particular sector or region. Patterns of economic activity are adjusted to benefit from expanded infrastructure networks – for example, to take advantage of improved marketing opportunities. Dependence on physical infrastructure also increases. In the Caribbean island of Dominica, for instance, until the 1950s sea transport had been the primary form of intra-island movement, implying typically rapid post-disaster recovery. The more recent emergence of road transport, coupled with the fact that much of the road network lay along the coast, increased the island's vulnerability to hurricanes, both in terms of their direct and indirect effects (Benson and Clay, 2001).

Intermediate economies generally also have more developed economy-wide financial systems for the flow of funds, including small-scale private savings and transfers, again diffusing the impact of natural hazards more widely via the flow of private funds from non-affected to affected regions. For example, in Zimbabwe the transfer of remittances from urban- to rural-based members of households was facilitated by the well-articulated system for small savings in the aftermath of the 1991 to 1992 drought. This mitigated the impact of the drought on the rural areas, but – at the same time – effectively spread its impact more widely, including into urban areas (Hicks, 1993). Meanwhile, a more developed government is likely to meet a larger share of the costs of the relief and rehabilitation efforts itself, rather than relying almost entirely upon international assistance. This government expenditure will be financed by some combination of the reallocation of planned expenditure, government borrowing and monetary expansion, with various indirect longer-term implications.

Latterly, in the later stages of development, evidence suggests that vulnerability to natural hazards declines again. This partly reflects increased investment in mitigation and preparedness, improved environmental management and a reduction in the incidence of absolute poverty. Moreover, a greater share of economic assets is likely to be held by the private sector and adequately insured against disaster.

Vulnerability is also time dependent in the context of technical and scientific advancement (Benson and Clay, 2000). The role played by the latter relates most obviously to the stage of development of structural mitigation techniques and forecasting technology, as well as to know-how. Application of technical and scientific developments in other fields, such as agriculture, can also determine the impact of a hazard.

Risk perceptions play an additional role. Perceptions influence behaviour and thus, ultimately, vulnerability. For example, a producer may install irrigation facilities to reduce drought-related crop losses; or a household may retrofit its home to enhance its ability to withstand seismic shocks. Similarly, general hazard awareness amongst the community at large can play a significant role in determining political commitment to, and public funding of, risk management activities.

Although perceived or subjective risk is, in part, based on available scientific information, it also reflects other influences. Indeed, subjective perceptions can vary widely between different economic agents, depending upon a complexity of factors. These include the nature of productive and non-productive activities that one engages in, income group and previous hazard experience. Confidence in institutions, credibility of information and underlying attitudes to risk, in turn – sometimes linked to cultural or religious beliefs – can also play a role. In addition, perceptions of risk may be influenced by temporal factors in terms of the length of interval between hazard events. Much lower levels of risk are often attached by a community or government to hazards that have not occurred for several generations. Perceptions of risk are also typically largely based upon past experience and therefore may fail to take into account changes in vulnerability. Evidence from the Caribbean island of Dominica provides a case in point. A number of those interviewed during the course of a recent study of the island stated that the impact of category 4 Hurricane David, in 1979, was, in part, so severe because the island had not experienced a hurricane for 40 years and thus it was caught unawares. Yet, meteorological records show that there had, in fact, been a number of less severe storms over that period. Instead, the island's vulnerability had changed due to various factors, including shifts in the nature and structure of agricultural production, and also, as discussed above, the development of the island's road network. However, people's perception of risk had not caught up (Benson and Clay, 2001).

Attitudes to risk are also important in determining behaviour and, thus, vulnerability. Behaviour, in turn, is, in part, influenced by financial considerations. At a macro-economic level, investments in mitigation and other forms of risk-averting behaviour carry opportunity costs in terms of the alternative use of those resources. The relative opportunity costs may be particularly high in developing countries, where pressures on public resources are often acute and returns to many types of investment high. This, in turn, reflects lower capital stocks and, thus, higher marginal productivity of additional units of investment. At a household level, too, attitudes to risk can also influence behaviour. This knowledge is sometimes expressed in deliberate risk-averting choices to seek lower, more stable, rather than higher, but more volatile, livelihoods. For example, in more typhoon-prone areas of the Philippines, farmers continue to plant traditional varieties of coconut rather than dwarf higher-yielding varieties as the latter have shallower root systems and so are more vulnerable to high winds (Benson, 1997b). In other instances, the poor may choose to accept risk in order to increase economic returns, for instance by occupying and farming fertile floodplains.

POLICY IMPLICATIONS

In summary, there is no single measure of vulnerability from a broad macro-economic perspective. Historical disaster information that does exist is incomplete, while the factors determining the outcome of a future event are highly complex. The impact of, for instance, two identical earthquakes of the same magnitude and same epicentre, but separated by 50 years – or even by one year – in time, will not have the same impact. However, knowledge and understanding of the role played by changing socio-economic and environmental conditions in determining vulnerability remains partial, hampering efforts to assess the precise nature and scale of vulnerability at a particular moment in time.

This presents an immediate obstacle to better policy, particularly regarding decision-making in the context of scarce capital resources. Some overall measure of vulnerability would help to indicate the degree to which overall policies and sectoral strategies need to be sensitized to risk, and efforts to reduce vulnerability need to be explicitly monitored and reported. At an individual project level, it is, of course, possible to build risk considerations into cost-benefit or some other form of analysis. However, even then, there is still an urgent need to emphasize the benefits of considering risks emanating from natural hazards. For instance, the Organization of American States (OAS) found during its Caribbean Disaster Mitigation Programme (CDMP) that:

> *The most common response from the political directorate in the Caribbean to programmes that would reduce vulnerability through more stringent building and development standards remains: 'Our nation is too poor to afford the required standards'* (OAS, 1999).

The OAS continues by stating that 'the challenge of the CDMP and similar programmes that promote safer development consists in debunking this myth by demonstrating that it is cost-effective to invest in mitigation of natural hazards'.

It is even more difficult when it comes to broader policy. Hard choices have to be made, for example, by government and donors about levels of investment in mitigation, both in terms of dedicated infrastructure and the standard to which other facilities are hazard proofed. Similarly, trade-offs have to be made between the quality and quantity of infrastructure provision, more generally. Sectoral and subsectoral strategies also play a role in determining vulnerability, while disasters could affect short- and even longer-term profits in particular areas of the economy. Such decisions regarding the extent to which, and how, vulnerability should be tackled are ideally reached quantitatively. Indeed, as Hood and Jones (1996, p84) state:

> *The argument for quantification [of risk] is that any rational system of risk management must rest on systematic attempts to quantify risks and to assess them against a pre-set array of objectives by methods analogous to cost-benefit analysis.*

Yet, neither risk nor vulnerability emanating from natural hazards can be boiled down to a single numerical (or monetary) figure and directly plugged into decision-making processes. Instead, by default, subjective perceptions play an important role in determining risk-averting behaviour, variously acting to exaggerate or downplay actual risk. Most typically, due to the paucity of data available, they act to downplay risk. More pressing shorter-term demands on public resources also force natural hazards lower down the list of priorities. Will a town mayor, for instance, even want to know, for example, that his municipality could experience severe damage as a consequence of a future earthquake when he is faced with daily difficulties in meeting the costs of sewerage disposal? As a consequence of these various factors, hazards and vulnerability are largely ignored by development planners.

Efforts to measure risk and, particularly, to capture measures of vulnerability in a single aggregate figure also force a simplification of the issue, with indicators inevitably based on direct human and physical losses. This, in turn, contributes to a compartmentalization of risk management, with an emphasis on technocratic solutions rather than a more holistic approach to vulnerability reduction, which seeks to address underlying social, economic and political causes.

There have been some recent attempts to demonstrate the potentially significant adverse impacts of natural hazards and the need for greater risk reduction from another perspective, exploring their long-term effects. Models have been developed to explore the impact of major disaster events on long-term growth (defined in terms of GDP performance), with disaster shocks introduced into the models via a reduction in capital stock (see, for example, MacKellar et al, 1999). Indeed, the basic motivation underlying much of this work has been precisely to force an awakening of governments (and the international community's economists) to the cost of disasters, particularly in the light of an anticipated increase in the incidence of hazard events over the next few decades.

This modelling work has been paralleled by a significant rise in interest in financial risk-transfer mechanisms. Historically, many developing countries have relied upon the international community to meet a significant part of their post-disaster relief and rehabilitation needs. However, donors have recently begun to sit up and notice the significant scale of resources allocated to this end (Arriëns and Benson, 1999; Gilbert and Kreimer, 1999). This, coupled with declining global aid resources and an anticipated increase in the incidence of disasters caused by natural hazards, has stimulated concern about the future financing of post-disaster reconstruction.

In fact, the simultaneity of the two developments – modelling of the long-term impacts of major disasters and increased interest in financial risk-transfer mechanisms – may not be entirely coincidental. The modelling work may have emphasized the adverse long-term economic impact of major disasters. However, it does not shed much light on the causal factors underlying vulnerability; nor, by implication, does it offer many solutions. Thus, rather than trying to address the root cause of the problem – the forms and nature of vulnerability – attention has turned to financial risk-transfer solutions instead.

Disaster-related financial risk-transfer mechanisms involve the establishment of some form of market-based insurance, entailing a large share of reinsurance and therefore transferring risks to the international market. Various permutations exist, in some cases involving conventional catastrophe damage insurance and, in others, using more innovative tools, such as catastrophe bonds (see, for example, Kreimer et al, 1999). Advantages include increased government control over the financing of disasters, possibly including immediate and timely availability of funds (depending upon the precise nature of the scheme); increased capacity for the relevant government to set its own priorities in managing relief and rehabilitation; and greater transparency in the delivery of relief and reconstruction. Increased public insurance, in whatever form, can also stimulate private cover.

Weather index-based insurance offers another alternative. This is a relatively new mechanism, with insurance pay-outs automatic and immediate (typically available within 72 hours) upon the occurrence of the predetermined trigger event, rather than awaiting the outcome of post-disaster damage assessments. Parametric insurance requires a careful assessment of the nature of the hazard event, including sufficient high-quality historical scientific data to enable computation of its probability and, thus, the rate of premium charged. To be economically sensible, the trigger event must also be highly correlated with economic losses, in turn requiring some understanding of the relationship between types of hazard and socio-economic vulnerability – for example, how a particular hazard event would affect crop production. Another option involves the bundling of different types of risk under one contract, potentially reducing premium rates to the extent that better understood risks are bundled with less well understood ones.

There is certain merit in such solutions, as indicated. However, part of this merit relates to the preference of such solutions over and above external assistance, rather than purely for themselves. Missing from much of the discussion, at least at the level recently engaged in by the World Bank and others, has been any mention of the use of insurance in promoting mitigation. For example, premium reductions can be offered against the insurance of properties that have been hazard proofed, as already occurs, for instance, in Fiji on a formal basis and elsewhere on a less formal, individually negotiated level.

Moreover, many developing country governments still need to be convinced of the need to take out some form of financial risk-transfer mechanism themselves, whether it is, for instance, catastrophe insurance on public infrastructure or a weather derivative. Instead, evidence suggests that they are typically more likely to take the view that, in the event of a major disaster, additional external assistance will be forthcoming.

CONCLUSION

The figures on global loss cited at the beginning of this chapter – and equivalent national ones – may demand a call to action. But they tell us relatively little about the precise nature of vulnerability, the factors underlying it or, thus, appropriate ways of supporting a reduction in risk. Measuring vulnerability to natural hazards from an economic perspective is hampered by difficulties. Even data on direct physical losses of past events is incomplete and, possibly, unreliable.

Indeed, efforts, to date, to categorize countries according to 'vulnerability' have perhaps done little more than underline the particular vulnerability of small island states. Yet, one does not need vulnerability indices to know this. Measuring vulnerability or even disaster impacts at an aggregate national level is much more difficult when it comes to much larger countries, such as the Philippines. As already noted, the Philippines did not rank very highly on any of the indices discussed in this chapter. Yet, an average of eight to nine typhoons reach land each year, while the country also experiences earthquakes, volcanic eruptions, floods and droughts. Here, there is more of a problem relating to the fact that the sheer frequency of occurrence of typhoons has clouded recognition by policy-makers and analysts of typhoons as an economic threat. An examination of various commentaries on the Philippines' economic performance since the early 1980s indicated that droughts and major geophysical hazards – that is, hazards that the country does not experience annually – are more likely to be identified than annually occurring typhoons as determinants of annual performance (Benson, 1997b). Yet, typhoons are estimated to cause damage equivalent to 0.6 per cent of GNP annually (ADB, 1994).

Nevertheless, although vulnerability cannot always be easily quantified at a national level, the fact remains that natural hazards can potentially cause enormous economic and human suffering and vulnerability must be addressed. Rather than focusing purely on improving data on the impact of disasters *ex post*, a more rounded approach is required. Reflecting the complex, dynamic nature of vulnerability, more emphasis needs to be placed on *ex ante* examination of the underlying causal factors. Data on short- or even long-term impacts of disasters may or may not impel governments and donors into action, but an in-depth exploration of the complexity of factors determining the outcome of a hazard event would help to identify ways in which risk could be reduced, both through anticipatory mitigation and in responding to individual events.

Policy-makers and others thus need to be equipped with methodological techniques and analytical skills to explore the nature of vulnerability in their economies and to develop appropriate responses. Guidance is also required on the integration of natural hazard risk management within the broader developmental process.

Finally, it needs to be accepted that the vulnerability of an economy cannot be captured in a few quantitative figures. It involves many interactive dynamic factors. By the same token, however, it is important that any attempt to assess vulnerability from a macro-economic perspective is undertaken with a clear eye to policy implications, and that any findings are presented in a form that can be directly drawn upon in determining and justifying policies and actions.

Chapter 12

Gendering Vulnerability Analysis: Towards a More Nuanced Approach

Maureen Fordham

INTRODUCTION: THE VULNERABILITY PERSPECTIVE

The vulnerability perspective (variously elaborated in Hewitt, 1983b; 1997; Winchester, 1992; Blaikie et al, 1994; Varley, 1994; Chambers, 1995; Twigg and Bhatt, 1998; Comfort et al, 2000; Cannon, 2000; and others) has become a significant constituent of hazard and disaster studies in both the developed North and the developing South. It marks a shift from the 'dominant paradigm' (Hewitt, 1983a) of hazards research whose concerns, broadly defined, have been with control of the physical hazard agent rather than disaster – the essentially *social* outcomes and processes of hazardous events – and with individual hazard perception (or misperception) rather than the underlying social structures that create inequalities and vulnerability (Fordham, forthcoming).

The vulnerability perspective also aims to shift the locus of action from post-disaster response to mitigation of the pre-disaster condition and demands a change in current policies that rely heavily on sending assistance only after tragedy has occurred (Comfort et al, 2000). Blaikie et al (1994, p233) argue that:

> *Vulnerability is deeply rooted, and any fundamental solutions involve political change, radical reform of the international economic system, and the development of public policy to protect rather than exploit people and nature.*

It is this fundamental challenge to the status quo that most particularly splits researchers (and practitioners). Resistance remains to a political economy/vulnerability focus from those who criticize the approach (Bryant, 1991) for 'rather stridently expressed views which, at worst, simply call for overall social revolution' (Smith, 1996, p51). Yet, the move from vulnerability to resilience or empowerment cannot be made without critically evaluating social as well as physical structures and processes, or without disturbing the status quo. To return a disaster-struck area to the way in which it was before (notwithstanding the necessity to be sensitive to local demands for the reconstruction of familiar cultural forms and processes) is to risk recreating vulnerable and disaster-prone communities for the future (Fordham, 2000). However, the dominant 'command-and-control' model of disaster management has as a core aim the 'return to normality' (largely undefined) of the affected community. This model, characterized by a response-focused, centralized, hierarchical, 'top-down' bureaucratic structure (Dynes, 1983), is firmly embedded in a dominant masculine culture, which – like the hazards paradigm – places an often inappropriate emphasis on the technical over the social. This can lead to a limited and/or less effective response. Bradley Foerster, from the United Nations Office for the Coordination of Humanitarian Affairs, commenting on the response to the May 1998 earthquake in Afghanistan, concluded that it was a 'Western approach' with an excessive dependence on machines rather than people that was problematic. Responders were obsessed with finding helicopters when engaging local people in assessments and donkey convoys would have been quicker, cheaper and more effective. 'Our Western approach to the problem was give me a machine. The voices of Afghans were not heard' (IFRCa, 1999, p82).

This 'Western' technocratic approach has become increasingly common throughout the world; but challenges to it are becoming more frequent. Alternatives include the Emergent Human Resources Model (EHRM) (Dynes, 1983; Neal and Phillips, 1995), the community engagement model (Buckle, 2001), and others based on less militaristic and more participatory forms, emphasizing flexible, 'bottom-up' organizational structures in which local community groups (usually seen as disruptive within the traditional model) have a clear place (Fordham, 2000).

In line with this more social analytical approach, the vulnerability perspective has usefully shifted some of the attention from the hazard agent, and highlighted underlying social structures and relations that have increased the susceptibility to disaster of the poor, in particular. However, it has been less active (with exceptions) until recently in addressing the conditions and needs of other social groups, or in breaking down monolithic social categories. Too often there has been a blanket use of the term 'victim'; too often, 'the vulnerable' have been represented as an undifferentiated group of passive sufferers in need of external aid and direction. Thus, the term has been disempowering in its inherent denial of agency.

In recent years, the development field, in particular, has provided many useful and increasingly sophisticated additions to disaster theory and practice. This work has highlighted not just the *vulnerability* but also the *capacity* of different social groups (especially women), and has developed participatory approaches to decision-making and policy implementation. These are discussed further below.

This chapter asks three interlinked questions: why single out gender as an analytical category? What is the case for claiming women's greater vulnerability? What is the justification for viewing disaster vulnerability through women's eyes? It then goes on to argue for a more complex and nuanced approach, necessitating a somewhat 'messy' analysis, combining insights and experiences from developing and developed countries.

WHY SINGLE OUT GENDER AS AN ANALYTICAL CATEGORY?

Disasters are not the social levellers that they are sometimes considered to be. Their impacts are felt in specific social and historical contexts and through the parameters of class, race and gender (amongst others) (Enarson and Fordham, 2001). While there has been an acceptance of gender as a key determining variable in social analysis, generally, hazard and disaster research have been largely indifferent to it and disasters have only relatively recently been subject to a gendered analysis. This has been most strongly influenced by work from development studies and practice – of which Boserup's 1970 study of the usually hidden economic role of women was an early example. Alice Fothergill's review (1996; 1998) of disaster research involving some form of gender analysis uncovered around 100 studies, the majority by North American and European researchers. However, in many of these, sex was used as a simple bipolar variable, rather than gender as a central analytical category. The later gender analyses of disaster (see, for example, Enarson and Morrow, 1998) have focused on women's invisibility and have shown them to be often more vulnerable before, during and after disasters, due to a range of factors symptomatic of deep-seated social processes (Fordham, 2000; Enarson and Fordham, 2001).

The dominant hazards paradigm, as a manifestation of dominant masculine (and particularly scientific) culture, can be critiqued from a range of feminist positions, most simply that originating in the feminist environmentalist literature where there is a clear connection between the domination of nature and the domination and control of women (see Mies and Shiva, 1993; Agarwal, 1992; Merchant, 1980). In addition, feminist standpoint theory (Haraway, 1988; 1991; Harding, 1986; 1990; 1991; Smith, 1987; Hekman, 1997; Hartstock, 1998), in its recognition that all knowledge is 'situated' (Haraway, 1988), offers a theoretical justification for the value of women's views from the margins. While it is not to be regarded as a universalist perspective, claiming a single feminist standpoint, it does state that marginalized groups are aware of *both* the constructed account of the world (that of the dominant/ruling groups, who are in the position of not having to see anyone else's 'truth') *and* the deconstructed accounts, as they understand them from their own material experience. Women's varied, but gendered, experiences give them a distinctive starting point for critiquing familiar assumptions from the position of the oppressed. Male-dominated management and universalized experiences of disasters have stimulated most gender research to focus on women specifically (rather than on women *and* men) because of their relative invisibility and their later established greater potential vulnerability.

WHAT IS THE CASE FOR CLAIMING WOMEN'S GREATER VULNERABILITY?

Research from a range of disciplines (not just feminist) and over a considerable period of time has revealed that, in general terms, women and girls are disadvantaged throughout life compared to men and boys. While not wanting to represent women as a victim group, we can say that women, as a group, have fewer opportunities than men, as a group (McDowell, 1999, p25). They more frequently occupy a position of dependence on other persons for at least part of their subsistence. They often have obligations to others that compromise their ability to obtain what they need for themselves. Throughout the world, to varying degrees, women still occupy a (usually invisible) triple role: reproduction, production and community management/activism. What women do – and are – is often hidden behind common sense notions of what is 'natural' for women or men to do and be. In the worst case scenario, females have to face sex-selective abortions, female infanticide and neglect, being sold into slavery and physical and sexual violence. They must deal with reduced educational and employment opportunities, less political representation and power, and fewer civic freedoms. At a higher level of analysis, we can state that widespread patriarchal structures continue to limit women's abilities to obtain equality of opportunity. These combine to make *some* women more vulnerable in *particular locations, situations and times* – the emphasis on specificity is important if over-generalization is to be avoided.

Vulnerability is often – not always – linked to poverty and a significant feminization of poverty has been recognized, particularly through processes of globalization.[1,2] The non-governmental organization (NGO) Social Watch has noted how:

> *Structural adjustment and economic globalization are not gender neutral. In many instances, they are inherently discriminatory against women... In every region of the world, it is women – as workers, producers, consumers, mothers and caretakers – who have been the shock absorbers of adjustment efforts. They bear a disproportionate burden of the costs of economic transition and economic collapse* (Social Watch, 1997).[3]

Women can be made more vulnerable through processes of impoverishment that remain largely hidden. Conventional economic analyses regard the informal sector as marginal; but the vast majority of women in the South work in the informal sector. Women's income from these activities is not a supplement to household income but a vital component of the household's budget that is crucial for its members' survival (Young, 1999, p105). In post-disaster reconstruction, however, it is the formal sector that attracts attention and resources, and is most easily measured.

When gender differentials are found to operate at these fundamental social levels, it is not surprising that they have been found to occur in disasters (Fordham and Ketteridge, 1998), especially if the disaster perspective adopted recognizes that disaster vulnerability cannot be separated from vulnerability in everyday living (Blaikie et al, 1994).

Women's particular needs are not recognized within a male-dominated, official disaster-management domain (Fordham, 1998). Depending upon cultural context, fear and stigma may be attached to rescue/relief centres where women and girls may risk sexual harassment or even shame from being out alone in public places. Male disaster practitioners typically have little awareness of women's particular sanitary and privacy needs, for example, and gender-blind decisions on the siting of latrines and washing facilities in relief camps can increase women's anxiety, add to their work load and enlarge the risk of sexual harassment and violence (Byrne and Baden, 1995). Despite their often widespread presence in lower status positions, women are under-represented in positions of power and responsibility on pre- and post-disaster decision-making committees and organizations (Enarson and Morrow, 1997; Neal and Phillips, 1990). Thus, women are potentially made vulnerable throughout the disaster process.

While the examples above indicate women's greater vulnerability, it is important to underline once again that they are not simply helpless victims – despite often being represented as such in media images. Women also have great capacities to resist and overcome socially constructed disaster impacts.

WHAT IS THE JUSTIFICATION FOR VIEWING DISASTER VULNERABILITY THROUGH WOMEN'S EYES?

It might be argued that a concern with 'gender' is out of date – a preoccupation of the 1980s that has subsequently been dealt with. However, despite many advances for women worldwide, these have been uneven and prejudice and sexism remain firmly embedded in social structures. While the diversity of women is fully acknowledged:

> *There are common patterns in the material conditions of women's everyday lives, including domestic and reproductive labour, care-giving and family support, and vulnerability to sexual and domestic violence. These commonalities afford women a unique angle of vision when natural and technological disasters impact human communities* (Enarson and Fordham, 2001, p43).

However, in addressing gender inequalities, it is all too common to view women and girls as 'special needs' – problematic additions to the universalized needs of men. It is important to move from a notion of women's needs to women's rights (Enarson and Fordham, 2002). And yet, while women's rights have been specifically recognized in the 1993 Convention to End Discrimination against All Women (CEDAW), all too often such laws, treaties and guidelines remain at the level of rhetoric rather than action. Even the task of documenting women's specific experiences in disasters and their contributions to disaster management remains incomplete. In many cases, the move beyond documentation to action has only just begun.

'MESSY' ANALYSIS – A MORE COMPLEX AND NUANCED APPROACH

So far, this chapter has argued for the need to view disaster vulnerability 'through women's eyes', partly to compensate for a universalized masculine perspective that has mitigated against transparency in gender relations. However, this position must now incorporate certain refinements to better approximate what is often a 'messy' reality.

Much of the recent creative thinking in gender and disaster studies and practice is based upon advances in development theory. This has undergone a number of changes in recent years to take account of increasing sophistication in the understanding of gender, development and disaster linkages. These reflect a shift from welfare-based to more transformative approaches, grounded in the need to examine not just women's position but gender *relations* and, indeed, social relations more broadly. Firstly, however, the term 'woman' is problematic since it implies a homogeneous, static and ahistorical category (Maynard, 1997, p2). Its use can be essentializing, obscuring differences between women and focusing on the one thing that women seem to have in common, their biological experiences (Barr and Birke, 1997, p77). Not all women are equal and the universality of women's subordinate position in any society must always be questioned and examined relative to other intersecting axes.

Furthermore, Andrea Cornwell (1997; 2000) has made a notable case for rethinking gender and participatory development (in whose framework disasters must be placed) to more directly address issues of power and powerlessness in the broadest context – which must necessarily include men. Men and masculinities have become an important addition to development studies and practice, based on the argument (amongst others) that men and masculinity need to be studied if power relations between the sexes are to be changed for the better (Sweetman, 1997, p2). Furthermore, focusing simply on women's activities can obscure important dimensions of their livelihood strategies, such as 'vital relations of interdependence between women and men' (Sweetman, 1997, p10). These may go unnoticed or unresearched because they are not recognized within the concerns of particular forms of Western feminist discourse (Mohanty, 1991).

Cornwell (2000) argues that a focus on women can obscure other dimensions of exclusion – powerlessness is not only a female condition:

> *Despite the pervasive use of the term 'gender,' operational frameworks tend to treat 'women' and 'men' as if they constituted immediately identifiable groups by virtue of their sex alone. 'Women' are often represented as if their relationships with men consisted of competing claims and conflicting interests, in which they are invariably the weaker party. 'Men' become powerful, shadowy figures who need somehow to be countered* (Cornwell, 2000, p9).

Mainstream development has been charged with taking men's gender identities for granted and even the move from women in development (WID) to gender and development (GAD) has 'done little to shake the overwhelming preoccupation with women' (White, 1997, p15).[4] It is claimed that 'gender' becomes a shorthand term for 'women' and 'gender relations' refers only to heterosexual relationships – other kinds of male–female relationships are not examined, neither are same-sex relationships of various kinds or inter-generational relationships (Cornwell, 2000, p10). In this analysis, men are as constrained by 'hegemonic masculinity' (Carrigan et al, 1985) as are women.

Dan Connell (1999) illustrates a more complex reality in terms of understanding membership of, and interactions within, a range of primary social, economic, political and cultural categories. He asks:

> *For example, are members of a particular social group – village women, an ethnic minority, a subclan, a caste, landless tenant farmers, farm labourers – present but not truly engaged? Are the opinions which they publicly voice truly their own? Do they say the same things when their husbands or wives or village elders or employers or other authority figures are not present?* (Connell, 1999, p83)

Others, too, while recognizing the value of separating men and women in order to understand their concerns, have called for efforts to reintegrate the two, partly on grounds of efficiency:

> *Despite the many men who now work on gender issues and the many mixed training teams, all too often the issues which effect women most specifically get picked out and dealt with; but men's roles, the asymmetry in power relations and the patriarchy trap for men are little attended to. If this does not change, gender training will continue to argue the case for women and fail to engage men as partners, as change agents and as converts. In practice, development with women will remain development without men, and it will be less effective because of it* (Rowan-Campbell, 1999, p25).

Certainly, the orthodoxy in development thinking – with which disaster thinking has yet to catch up – has shifted to a more masculine-friendly (albeit still critical) position. The question, then, becomes not *whether* to include men and masculinity in the analysis but the *degree of centrality* that they should assume.

But while acknowledging the value – indeed, necessity – of a gender-fair approach to vulnerability analysis, caution must be exercised to avoid, once again, returning women to a subordinate position in which their needs and interests are demoted, particularly when limited resources are available. Male hegemony allows some men to avoid attending to, or participating in, issues relating primarily to the concerns of women. Development initiatives, which are meant to make a constructive difference to the lives of women and men, may be corrupted in the process (Rowan-Campbell, 1999, p12).

Moreover, there has been a degree of backlash against the discourse on gender, particularly in places where men are perceived to be 'losing out' (Byrne et al, 1996; Faludi, 1992). In refocusing a gendered vulnerability analysis to better reflect issues of men and masculinity, there is a danger that this becomes merely a ploy to keep women occupied and diverted. Have men simply (re)captured the agenda for themselves? Might it be that this is representative of a male backlash where men perceive a lessening of attention and demand more, even though they still command the major portion?[5] Will the new emphasis on men in gender and development return us to an earlier mode:

> *There is a real danger that in straying onto male terrain, GAD will stumble into the old tracks, for the resilience of structures of inequality lie precisely in their ability to accommodate new contexts* (White, 2000, p39).

EQUITABLE INEQUALITIES

Ironically, the demand for the inclusion of men and masculinity is being made in the name of an equality that women themselves have yet to achieve. But a distinction has to be made between equality and equity. The two words are not synonymous; rather than striving for equality amongst groups of people reflecting many intersecting axes of difference, we should work towards 'equitable inequalities' that reflect the needs, strengths and relative power of the various groups.[6] Recognizing the often (though not always) subordinate position of many women, it is important to maintain the option of a specific focus on women. As Iris Marion Young has said in reference to *difference* in political movements:

> *If a political movement wishes to address the problems of the truly disadvantaged, it must differentiate the needs and experiences of relatively disadvantaged social groups and persuade the relatively privileged – heterosexual men, white people, younger people, the able-bodied – to recognize the justice of the group-based claims of these oppressed people to specific needs and compensatory benefits* (cited in McDowell, 1997, p333).

CONCLUSION: A MORE NUANCED APPROACH

At the heart of this chapter is a call for *nuanced, critical and reflexive approaches* that go beyond simple checklists of vulnerable groups. While endorsing the validity of certain generalizations (in other words, the notion of certain common experiences between different women), it calls for the *theorizing of gender relations within specific societal and historical contexts*. Importantly, while a gendered perspective is necessary in analysing vulnerability, in any particular context it may not be either sufficient or the most appropriate primary lens. Furthermore, vulnerability analysis is incomplete without an equal focus on capacity.

While leading-edge disaster research and practice in the more developed North is beginning to recognize a broader concept of vulnerability, it has yet to fully grasp the potential of *capacities and vulnerabilities analysis*, which is more closely associated with research in, and on, the South (see Anderson and Woodrow, 1998; 1989; the South Asian 'alternative perspective' in Fernando and Fernando, 1997; and, more broadly, the Food and Agriculture Organization's (FAO's) Socio-Economic and Gender Analysis Programme: http://www.fao.org/sd/2003/PEO507_en.htm). Such an analysis, designed to reflect 'complex reality', if applied to developed countries (and if fully implemented in developing countries) could radically change the process of disaster management. It has the potential to, *inter alia*, fundamentally challenge the (masculine) command-and-control model; build in longer-term aspects; treat disaster mitigation as integral to everyday social and economic development; and develop local community capacities to complement or replace 'official' services through the greater use of, and willingness to work in, equal partnership with NGOs and community-based organizations (CBOs). However, it remains merely an analytical framework like many others and much depends upon the position and intention of those using it.[7] A critical and reflexive approach is essential.

This chapter recommends, somewhat unfashionably, *affirmative action for equitable ends* because women do not participate on an equal basis with men – in the same way that the poor do not participate on an equal basis with the rich – largely due to their pre-existing subordinate positions in society (Connell, 1999, p87):

> *Invariably, if an active intervention is not made to avoid it, those at the bottom of the socio-economic and political ladders will remain where they were...no matter how many members of the community are consulted or involved in project development... Power relationships reproduce themselves, regardless of how 'participatory' or 'democratic' a setting is, unless a conscious, sustained effort is undertaken to avoid them* (Connell, 1999, pp82–3).

Even when stated policy appears gender aware, 'Institutions reproduce the prevailing values of society more often than they challenge them, [and] the power dynamics in mixed settings are generally disadvantageous to women' (Eade, 1999, p8). Thus, *active intervention* is necessary if women are to be not just visible but empowered. However, this does not call for any over-simplified, mechanistic processes of quota attainment; nor does it mean the exclusion of men. Rather, what is recommended is an analysis based on a more transformative socio-economic and gender analysis approach, grounded in the need to examine not just women's position but gender *relations* at all scales. The inclusion of men and masculinities 'should not simply "count men in", but broaden and deepen our understanding of power and inequality' (Cornwell, 1997, p21). The author recommends the use of such situated, critical, reflexive methods of analysis and participatory ways of working. In this way, we move towards a more nuanced approach to a gendered capacities and vulnerabilities analysis.

Chapter 13

Assessment of Capability and Vulnerability

Ben Wisner

INTRODUCTION

The word 'vulnerability' is used in the English hazards and disaster management literature in a large number of ways. This is not necessarily a matter of ambiguity or semantic drift, but disciplinary focus. Essentially, these different uses have invisible, implied adjectives preceding them, hence:

- structural engineering vulnerability;
- lifeline infrastructural vulnerability;
- communications system vulnerability;
- macro-economic vulnerability;
- regional economic vulnerability;
- commercial vulnerability (including insurance exposure);
- social vulnerability.

What they all have in common is the core notion of 'potential for disruption or harm'. Maps and other assessments of such vulnerabilities can then be combined with assessments of hazards that have been identified. Where there is sufficient probabilistic process knowledge of the particular hazards, statements about risk as the probability (not simply potential) for disruption or harm can result, as in the well-known shorthand:

$$\text{Risk} \cong \text{Hazard} \times \text{Vulnerability}.$$

Social vulnerability is one of these categories. The adjective 'social' is more widely made explicit by authors these days. The 'social' is a very large domain. Checklists based on taxonomies are commonly recommended to planners and also to communities as an aid to self-study and action. In this chapter, I review the various ways in which social vulnerability has been theorized and used. I assess the theoretical and practical utility of these formulations and methods to measure or assess social vulnerability.

THE MAIN APPROACHES TO ASSESSING SOCIAL VULNERABILITY

The demographic approach

During the mid-18th century, demography was born of the sovereign's desire to have a complete inventory of wealth in his territory. During the mercantilist period of early capitalist development, the elite began to realize that labour power (as well as potential conscripts into the military forces) was a form of wealth. In a similar way, today there are approaches to vulnerability that lump people in with bridges, financial cyber information systems and strategic petroleum reserves. These are all 'vulnerable elements'.

These approaches continue to follow the former United Nations Disaster Relief Organization (UNDRO) definition (inspired by an engineering approach): 'the potential for damage or loss' (Alexander, 2000). These approaches tend to consider human beings as one of many 'elements' at risk to varying degrees, given hazards with certain characteristics and an array of elements with differing degrees of potential for damage or loss (hence, structural vulnerability of buildings, bridges, health care systems *and* people).

Individual human beings get lost in the process of conceptualizing whole systems. People are enumerated among such 'vulnerable' entities as the banana-exporting economies of the Caribbean; the food systems of Somali pastoralists; physical structures such as in the Andes; bridges; a natural gas pipeline serving Wellington, New Zealand; and administrative networks (for example, the vulnerable health-care delivery system of Los Angeles country, where half of the hospitals could be shut down by the next earthquake).

Moreover, the social vulnerability of groups of people is generally lost in the analytical shuffle by administrators who seek to minimize the 'vulnerability' of systems and things. Such under-appreciated groups who may (or may not) experience increased social vulnerability to the effects of one or another extreme event are very diverse. They include, for example, those who self-identify (for instance, transsexual street youth in West Hollywood) or are identified by language, culture, age (for example, elderly monolingual Russian immigrants in West Hollywood), or who are marginalized in a variety of ways (individuals lacking economic, political or social power and participation). Thus, in the community guidelines for 'hazard vulnerability assessment' provided by the US Federal Emergency Management Agency (FEMA) to its Project Impact communities, there is nowhere reference to any particular group of people with certain characteristics. 'Vulnerability' is used exclusively to refer to such things as water systems. The only place a category of people appears is towards the end when users of this guide are prompted to think about the community's major employers and how their workers get to work.[1]

The taxonomic approach

The second cluster includes approaches that focus on the vulnerability of social groups, and is concerned with the causes of this social vulnerability. These approaches begin from the empirical observation that different groups of human beings often suffer different degrees of death, injury, loss and disruption from the same event, and also experience different degrees of difficulty, success or failure in the process of recovery (Enarson and Morrow, 1997; Hewitt, 1997; Blaikie et al, 1994; Lavell, 1994; Aysan, 1993; Maskrey, 1989). These approaches tend to break vulnerability down into different elements (social, economic, environmental, informational vulnerability, etc), and they tend to work on the basis of empirically developed taxonomies (for example, the vulnerability of women, children, the elderly, the disabled, ethnic/racial/or religious minorities and illegal immigrants).

For example, Morrow (1999, p10) identifies the following groups as typical of the kinds of categories that a vulnerability inventory will reveal in the context of coastal Florida:

- residents of group living facilities;
- the elderly, particularly frail elderly;
- the physically or mentally disabled;
- renters;
- poor households;
- women-headed households;
- ethnic minorities (by language);
- recent residents/immigrants/migrants;
- large households;
- large concentrations of children/youth;
- the homeless;
- tourists and transients.

Surely, the taxonomic approach is a major advance over the conventional use of the term 'vulnerable', which casts a net in a crude and undifferentiated way over things, systems and people. To give one more example of the taxonomic approach, Aysan (1993, p12) identifies eight types of vulnerability. Each of these undermines the capacity for self-protection, blocks or diminishes access to social protection, delays or complicates recovery, or exposes some groups to greater or more frequent hazards than other groups. The usefulness in practical terms of such a list is as a screen to orient the perceptions of planners and service providers and administrators so that relatively 'invisible' or 'voiceless' groups of people are not neglected before, during or after disasters. Aysan's eight types of vulnerability are:

- lack of access to resources (material/economic vulnerability);
- disintegration of social patterns (social vulnerability);
- degradation of the environment and the inability to protect it (ecological vulnerability);
- lack of access to information and knowledge (educational vulnerability);

- lack of public awareness (attitudinal and motivational vulnerability);
- limited access to political power and representation (political vulnerability);
- certain beliefs and customs (cultural vulnerability);
- weak buildings or weak individuals (physical vulnerability).

In a similar way, Lavell (1994, pp52–61) distinguishes among four interrelated kinds of vulnerability: economic, social, educational and informational, and environmental, and Cannon (2000, p47) identifies four 'components of vulnerability':

- initial well-being;
- livelihood resilience;
- self-protection;
- societal protection;
- social capital (social cohesion, rivalries, number and strength of potentially conflicting or cooperating groups).

It was certainly an important advance to rescue human beings from the large amorphous, semantic caldron that mixed the mechanical response of buildings, bridges and natural gas lines with the ability of a single mother to re-establish a home and livelihood after a hurricane. However, analytically these taxonomies and lists are still rather blunt tools. One may ask, is a tourist always socially vulnerable? Doesn't it depend upon the specific hazard and specific circumstances? Does it also not depend upon other characteristics or persons, all of which are capable of change? For example, a tourist who is exhausted after returning from a 50-kilometre hike will be more vulnerable to a flashflood than one who is sitting in an air-conditioned vehicle listening to a flood warning on her radio. The homeless in Tokyo are highly vulnerable to flood emergencies because many of them live along the Sumida River. They are vulnerable to extreme winter weather and typhoons because of their exposure to the elements and their fragile tents (primarily made of blue plastic tarps or cardboard boxes and a collection of umbrellas and blankets). However, they are not highly vulnerable to earthquakes as they are, generally, not exposed to building collapse and are used to the streets and can move easily to the nearest green space where they will be protected from fire (unless they are homeless *and* mentally or physically disabled).

The situational approach

A third kind of approach tries to go beyond these 'laundry lists' and 'taxonomies' (although I will argue later on that they have had a great deal of practical benefit). This approach can be called 'situational'. The key question is not what kind of group a person or family belongs to, but the nature of their daily life and their actual situation (including the way in which it may have changed recently or may be changing). This approach has a lot in common with the analysis of 'household livelihood security' (Sanderson, 2000) or the 'access model' utilized by Blaikie et al (1994; cf Wisner et al, 2003). This approach is based upon a view of disasters that sees them not as 'exceptional' events; rather, they are perceived as extensions of the problems confronted in 'normal' or 'daily' life (Wisner, 1993; Cannon, 2000).

Situational analysis recognizes three kinds of contingency. Firstly, social vulnerability is not a permanent property of a person or group but changes in respect to a particular hazard. Muslim women in Bangladesh never climb trees and are reluctant to leave the seclusion of their homes, so they are more vulnerable than men in a flashflood or storm surge. However, Hindu women in parts of India are more able to cross caste boundaries and do casual work and glean fields at times of food emergency. The second kind of contingency concerns the constantly changing daily, seasonal and yearly circumstances of a person's situation regarding access to resources and power. Such circumstances change dramatically as the life cycle unfolds, as physiological and anatomical changes accompany, for example, childbirth or occupational disease or accident. Finally, there is the contingency born of the complex interaction of particular overlapping identities and forms of empowerment or marginality. It was not simply women who were prominent among the hundreds who died from heat stroke in Chicago in 1995, but elderly women living on their own on limited incomes. They were afraid to come out to shelters, or their lack of mobility inhibited them. They could not afford air conditioning, and they kept their windows closed for fear of thieves (Klinenberg, 2003).

Situational analysis separates human beings – in all of their complexity – and groups of humans from the heterogeneous mass of things and systems said by mainstream planners to be 'vulnerable'. Situational analysis also builds upon the wealth of empirical work that has given rise to the taxonomies and lists of vulnerable groups discussed earlier. However, by recognizing complexity, change and contingency, it provides a more sensitive tool of analysis.

A contextual and proactive approach

Communities and groups may, and increasingly do, appropriate the concept of vulnerability to enquire into their own exposure to damage and loss. This constitutes a radically different, new fourth approach to the assessment of social vulnerability. The concept becomes a tool in the struggle for resources that are allocated politically.

In some parts of Latin America and Southern Africa, such community-based vulnerability assessment has become quite elaborate, utilizing all sorts of techniques to map and make inventories, seasonal calendars and disaster chronologies.[2] Pilot projects have shown that lay people in citizen-based groups are capable of participating in environmental assessments that involve technology not previously accessible to them, such as geographical information systems (GIS) (Pickles, 1995; Levin and Weiner, 1997; Liverman et al, 1998; Maskrey, 1998).

Such community efforts may make use of some checklists that derive from the work of professionals on taxonomies. There are also some ways in which community-based vulnerability assessment resembles situational analysis, as conducted by professional planners or employees of non-governmental organizations (NGOs). However, the main difference is that the community defines its own vulnerabilities and capabilities; outsiders don't. They also decide what risks are acceptable to them and which are not.

As Morrow (1999, p11) remarks:

The proposed identification and targeting of at-risk groups does not imply
helplessness or lack of agency on their part... Just because neighbourhoods have
been disenfranchised in the past does not mean they are unwilling or unable to be
an important part of the process. There are many notable examples of grassroots
action on the part of poor, elderly, women and/or minority communities making
a difference in post-disaster decisions and outcomes. Planners and managers who
make full use of citizen expertise and energy will more effectively improve safety
and survival chances of their communities.

The employment of the concept of social vulnerability as a community tool also
involves a thorough analysis with, and by, the residents of their own resources and
capacities/capabilities. This 'other side' of the vulnerability coin is sometimes
present in checklists, taxonomies and, to a greater degree, externally produced
situational analyses. However, it is in the hands of local people that the logic of
their situation – and the phenomenology of their living over time with risks –
forces them to be aware of, and to discuss, their strengths and capabilities, as well
as their weaknesses and needs (Wisner, 1988; Anderson and Woodrow, 1999).[3]

DISCUSSION OF THE FOUR APPROACHES

What is 'local' knowledge?

The first three of these four approaches are structuralist. As far as I am concerned,
that is excellent. This is not to deny the important contribution of post-
structuralist and post-modern theory to environmental social science. However, I
believe strongly that the constructionist approaches inspired by post-modernism
only have a place in disaster studies and practice as a heuristic or corrective lens
(Harvey, 1989; 1996). For example, during fieldwork in Mexico City between 2000
and 2001, I was told repeatedly that people are more afraid of bottled gas
explosions, violent crime or death in a public transport accident than of
earthquakes. Similar research in Alexandra township in Johannesburg revealed
that domestic violence, dangerous traffic, shack fires and crime were of more
concern to women than flash flooding. It is important to listen to the people
affected and to try to see things from their point of view. However, extreme forms
of post-modern interpretation are not helpful, even absurd. I have heard someone
refer to an earthquake as a 'spectacle'. It well may have that role in the viewer
ratings of CNN, but that in no way erodes the 'reality' of the earthquake disaster
experienced by the people affected in Gujarat, India, or Izmit, Turkey.

The view that the first three interpretations of social vulnerability represent
an imposed Western discourse on reality is, doubtless, true. This kind of 'disaster
discourse' shares much with other forms of 'development discourse' (Rahema
and Bawtree, 1997; Escobar, 1995a; Crush, 1995; Wisner and Yapa, 1995).
However, I would argue that disaster researchers and practitioners who adopt a
social vulnerability perspective are doing something a bit different. As Hewitt puts
it in his excellent essay 'Sustainable Disasters: Perspectives on powers in the
discourse of calamity' (1995, p125):

> *We feel obliged to speak of missing persons or unheard voices; of 'hidden damage' and 'shadow risks' and, more severely, of 'silent' or 'quiet violence'... We identify 'voiceless' and 'invisible' presences; conditions and people ignored or marginalized. Issues are found to be 'hidden', 'masked', 'obfuscated' or redescribed to suit other, also often 'hidden', agendas.*

Despite the difficulties and contradictions involved in 'speaking for' other human beings, much of the work on social vulnerability tries to break out of the hegemonic 'development' and 'disaster' discourses by providing space for alternative subaltern stories and voices. The fourth of these approaches to social vulnerability, the one that seeks to use that concept as a tool for empowerment and self-knowledge, is the best expression of the attempt to break out.

I view social vulnerability, to some extent, as the blockage, erosion or devaluation of local knowledge and coping practices, or – taken together - as local capacity. Vulnerability studies and practice have not given enough attention to local capacity, especially as social capital. In the past, local knowledge, perceptions and coping have been studied ethnographically, but in an individualistic and positivistic manner. At the extreme, vernacular ways of describing hazardous natural events, coping, local knowledge and perceptions have been appropriated by outside agencies seeking to 'package' their standard remedies in language that will make it acceptable to 'recipients' or 'clients'. Earlier models of diffusion innovation and top-down 'extension' remain hidden beneath 'culturally sensitive' veneers.

What is actually needed is an understanding of why and how local knowledge is rendered inappropriate or inaccessible, and of the ways in which people can be empowered to reclaim local knowledge and appreciate its usefulness. Of course, a balanced view of local knowledge is also necessary. Given major rapid changes in environmental conditions, locale (because of migration), population growth or decline (for example, because of HIV/AIDS), and economic and political change, some conventional local knowledge may no longer be applicable. Hybrid knowledge and practices are necessary that combine outside and inside points of view (Wisner et al, 1979; Wisner et al, 1991; Wisner, 1994a; 1994b; 1995a; 1995b).

What also needs to be researched is how groups of people can be motivated to rediscover their own local knowledge or to generate their own knowledge in a cultural environment in which they are told by society that they are 'ignorant', 'superstitious', 'uneducated' or 'incapable'. Unfortunately, these prejudices against the knowledge and capabilities of poor people, working-class people, ethnic minorities, elderly people, youth and children,[4] the disabled[5] and refugees[6] are very common – in subtle and unconscious forms – even universal, in urban and rural areas throughout every country in the world.[7]

In my own work, I was privileged to learn from farmers on the slopes of Mount Kenya 76 different ways that they know of coping with lower than usual rainfall. Recently, in the working-class area of Northwestern Mexico City called Naucalpan, I was told by a school custodian how he had planted trees 20 years previously in order to protect the school children at play from high-tension electrical transmission lines that pass close by the school yard. I am sure that anyone who has done fieldwork among communities and neighbourhoods has had this experience. The creativity of the 'masses' (as they used to be called) is astounding; yet it is seldom tapped because workers, farmers, house-keepers, school children and gang members fear ridicule and manipulation, on the one hand, and appropriation of their knowledge, on the other.

Some practical issues

Typically, the focus of attention of practical tools designed to assess vulnerability in field situations are social characteristics such as gender, age, health status and disability, ethnicity or race or nationality, caste or religion, and socio-economic status. Special-interest NGOs have produced detailed checklists that probe for the special needs and vulnerabilities of, for example, elderly persons, children and unaccompanied children in a post-disaster situation.

These are very useful as *aides memoires* to very busy administrators and case workers in the chaotic situation of a refugee camp or large-scale disaster, such as in Gujarat in 2001 or northwestern Turkey in 1999. For example, an article in the *Guardian Weekly* concerning the effect of religion and caste on distribution of relief aid in the Kutch region of Gujarat stated: 'Foreign aid workers fear that Dalits [a low-caste group] and Muslims may lose out. "The Muslims are very vulnerable. We are worried about what will happen when the monsoon comes", a World Food Programme official said.'[8] In certain situations 'vulnerability' can be addressed in a very straightforward way. For example, just after the volcanic eruption in Eastern Congo that cut the city of Goma in half, Oxfam stated that '[it] is most worried about an estimated 60,000 who are now homeless and living in the densely populated eastern part of the town, cut off from the rest by huge piles of lava rock'.[9]

Such checklists can be very useful. However, the use of checklists does not help one to understand why and how those characteristics have come to be associated with a higher probability of injury, death, livelihood disruption and greater difficulty in the recovery process (Blaikie et al, 1994, p9). The checklists widely used by international agencies and NGOs today are based upon some combination of the agency's own empirical observations and the results of a growing number of post-disaster studies and audits, many of them by sociologists.[10]

But the empirical discovery of an association or correlation does not yet explain the process that gave rise to the association. For example, the finding that domestic violence against women increased after Hurricane Andrew has to be understood in process terms. It is not female gender itself that marks vulnerability, but gender *in a specific situation*. These gender relations were played out in the context of the growth boom of south Florida during the 1980s and early 1990s, weak regulation of the building industry, and down-sizing and restructuring that left many working-class men anxious about future employment (Peacock et al, 1997).

Complexity and contingency

Most situations are very complex and, sometimes, temporary. Situations are rooted in the routines, opportunities and limitations of 'normal' or 'daily' life

(Wisner, 1993) and cannot be disentangled from processes that make the same people vulnerable to a range of risks, including the gamut of social, technological and natural (Wisner, 1999a; 2002b). For example, in 1999 I found in field investigations, together with graduate students at California State University at Long Beach, that there were large numbers of low-income, young, immigrant, non-English-speaking single mothers living in the two census tracts that immediately border San Pedro harbour. This specific geographical location has a higher probability than other parts of San Pedro, or surrounding areas, of cargo explosions, liquefaction and amplified shaking because of soil factors in an earthquake, and exposure to a toxic plume from refinery fires (Wisner, 1999b).

The concatenation of income, age, immigration status, language, single parenthood and gender significantly shifts the meaning of 'gender' as a simple taxonomic indicator of vulnerability. Women in mansions not 3 kilometres distant, overlooking the Pacific Ocean from the heights of Rancho Palos Verde, share the socially constructed identity of 'woman' with these young Guatemalan single mothers. In most other respects, they inhabit separate and parallel universes.

Another limitation of the taxonomic versus the situational approach to vulnerability is that important aspects of vulnerability can always be inadvertently left out. Someone with a mathematical turn of mind or penchant for formal logic might be able to show, as Goedel did for all systems of logic, that completeness and consistency are simultaneously impossible. In other words, lists of socially vulnerable groups are bound to grow indefinitely.

A concrete example is the absence of sexuality or sexual orientation in checklists and post-disaster audits. Yet, in West Hollywood, where I conducted interviews during 2000–2001 as part of a United Nations (UN) university study of urban vulnerability, there is a very substantial population of male to female transgender individuals.[11] They have had a long history of difficult relations with the police and other authorities, and these transsexuals face special needs in medical emergencies and situations requiring mass shelter.

> *My use of the phrase 'special needs' should not be misinterpreted. A critical analysis of the kind of treatment that has been given vulnerability in the past will reveal disciplinary biases. Because of the influence of clinical professions such as public health or social work, 'socially vulnerable groups' tended to be treated as 'special needs groups'. This approach can reduce the individuals concerned, firstly, to passive recipients, even 'victims', and, secondly, to persons without relationships* (Hewitt, 1997).

A richer approach analytically, and a more useful one pragmatically, is to see everyone as having capabilities for self-protection and group action. Capabilities are often latent or unactualized because of external forces, which one might call 'circumstances'. Such capabilities should be seen as going beyond what used to be called 'coping', 'adjustment' and 'adaptation'. Livelihoods and systems of social relations have a coherence and resilience that these earlier terms do not capture. For example, when I visited refugee camps on the Somali–Ethiopian border in

1981, I did not see large numbers of Somali women and children who had been displaced by fighting in the Ogaden merely coping. I saw the women re-weaving their worlds by delimiting home compounds with thorn bush, recreating mutual aid relations among neighbouring women, and defying the authority of the male military camp commanders by sorting themselves out spatially by village of origin (Wisner and Lewis, 1981).

I found another example of local capabilities in the Pico Union district of Los Angeles, just west of the towers of downtown LA. Low income, Hispanic immigrants (many of them undocumented) grouped together in common efforts by more than 30 service NGOs to deliver assistance after the Northridge earthquake. Kilometres distant from the epicentre and area of destruction that was the focus of media and government attention, many of the old tenements and other structures in Pico Union had been damaged. Appeals by local NGOs and churches were not immediately heeded by officials. This self-help process led to the creation of an independent disaster preparedness programme by the NGOs grouped together as the Pico Union Cluster. Resentment and suspicion of racism was so high that it took a very protracted process of negotiation before the Pico Union Cluster agreed to join the official body that the city and county of Los Angeles uses for coordinating NGO response, preparedness and mitigation: the Emergency Network Los Angeles (ENLA).

Threats and opportunities

Until 11 September 2001, it was hard to imagine that the wave of ever-increasing citizen participation in disaster risk management could break, and that the evolution of more and more self-conscious agency by citizens could be turned back. However, there are some very dangerous and troubling signs, at least in the US.

To begin with, even before the attack on the World Trade Center, FEMA had abandoned Project Impact at the national level, leaving it to the states to continue with its participatory citizen-based efforts to create 'disaster-resilient communities'. This was one of the first acts of the new Republican administration of George Bush. Since the terror attack, things have become systematically worse for citizen participation.

After the catastrophic failure of the Union Carbide factory in Bhopal, India, in 1984, there was an upsurge in citizen interest in knowing more about what chemical factories were storing in their communities, what risks they faced and what plans there were to deal with these risks. Legislation was passed in 1987 that asserted the 'citizen's right to know' about these things. A Toxic Release Inventory (TRI) was established by the Federal Environmental Protection Agency. Since 11 September, this information has been removed from the internet and is only available in a limited form at a single designated federal library in each state.

Citizens' and advocate NGOs' access to information of many kinds is being cut back. For example, no longer can one check on the internet if a natural gas pipeline runs under one's children's school or whether such a pipe has been inspected on schedule. The tools for community hazard mapping *by the community* are being stripped away because they may be 'useful to terrorists'.

Such policies are very short-sighted. If the pressure of monitoring by environmental groups, journalists and citizens is removed, more people could die because of toxic emissions and explosions from under-regulated chemical factories than are prevented from dying in a hypothetical terrorist attack. Terrorists already have this information or can get it because they will put the labour time into doing so. The average working-class citizen will not dedicate that kind of time to self-protection (because of the constraints placed by 'normal' life). That is why the web-based information previously available at almost every small town or neighbourhood public library reading room, or high school library, was a vital step towards creating 'a culture of protection' (in the words of the International Decade for Natural Disaster Reduction).

One witnesses an irony of history. Even as citizens' groups in Botswana, Bangladesh and Honduras are actively engaged in producing community hazard maps and vulnerability/capability assessments, citizens in the US are being discouraged from doing so.

Back to 'civil defence'?

David Alexander and Ken Mitchell have pointed out the striking re-adoption of 'command-and-control' approaches to public safety in the US since 11 September (Alexander, 2002; Mitchell, 2003). They document an evolution towards more and more openness, citizen participation and oversight from the days of the Cold War. Major changes in the Federal Emergency Management Agency (FEMA) after Hurricane Andrew in 1991 ushered in a decade of accelerated investment in citizen participation. This was in line with thinking (but, perhaps, not practice) worldwide. In 1995, halfway through the International Decade for Natural Disaster Reduction, the Yokohama message specifically advocated increased citizen participation (Ingleton, 1999, p320). Since the attack on the World Trade Center, there has been a re-militarization and re-centralization of public safety.

The contradictory policies being pursued in the 'war on terrorism' are many and complex. A final example should suffice. In 2001, some US$6000 million was allocated in the federal budget to preparing for chemical and biological terrorism. This money came from *cutting back* on the budget for occupational health and safety and environmental health. Again, it is not hard to imagine how a weak general public health system will allow much more death and disability than a successful bio-terrorist attack.

These policies are not merely panic-inspired mis-steps. They are calculated attacks on the public sector and on corporate regulation. The Republicans in power in 2003 have, for years, opposed the regulation of corporations. They were against releasing 'private' data by companies on their toxic chemical inventories when the 1985 'right to know' legislation was debated and passed. They have consistently promoted the privatization of the health sector in the US and everywhere that US foreign assistance (or, through the US Treasury Department, the World Bank) had influence over other countries.

It is against this kind of thinking and exercise of corporate, military, political and ideological power that the defenders of citizens' participation and control of their own lives must struggle during the early 21st century. Surely, that struggle must, and will, continue.

Conclusion: Vulnerability Analysis as a Means of Strengthening Policy Formulation and Policy Practice

Georg Frerks and Stephen Bender

INTRODUCTION

In an overview article about the state of disaster studies on the occasion of the 20th anniversary of the journal *Disasters* in 1997, David Alexander asserted that the emergence of the notion of vulnerability is one of the most salient achievements in the field during the last decades (Alexander, 1997). Indeed, societal preoccupation with vulnerability and risk to various forms of impact has replaced the earlier global focus upon aspects of wealth as the primary shaper of world development. Exposure to disaster has become recognized as a product of hazard and vulnerability, and the latter is seen, in turn, as actively created by such factors as bad governance, poor development practice, and political and military destabilization. This emphasis on vulnerability is associated with a shift from seeing disaster as an event caused by an external agent to a more sociologically oriented interpretation of disaster as a complex socially (as well as politically, environmentally and economically) constructed process. This view has been promoted by Blaikie et al among others in their well-known model depicting the progression of vulnerability (1994, p23), and reflected in the Cartagena Declaration on Disasters and Development, which helped to shape the International Decade for Natural Disaster Reduction (IDNDR) Yokohama Declaration in 1994.

Simultaneously, many disaster management programmes at field level have reoriented themselves over the last decade from a more reactive stance, emphasizing disaster relief and rescue operations, towards a more proactive effort of vulnerability reduction in the context of development. Both of these programmes and more traditional emergency management command-and-control operations also began to strengthen local capabilities. Similarly, the growing use of vulnerability assessment tools, such as vulnerability and capacity assessments (VCAs), hazard mapping and community profiling, during the 1990s have transformed vulnerability reduction from a concept into a practice (OAS, 1990; IFRC, 1993; Anderson and Woodrow, 1993).

In line with these developments, the authors in this book consider vulnerability as a key to interpreting and mitigating disaster. At the conceptual level, they see vulnerability as an essential link in the nexus between the environment, society and culture, (under) development and poverty, and disaster. They also argue that focusing on vulnerability may well be the single most effective avenue for policy action to reduce the impact of disaster. Vulnerability may have been overlooked in the past, in both theory and practice, due to a preoccupation – if not fascination – with the disaster itself (an event impacting upon a societal unit in such a way that external assistance is needed), the post-World War II military paradigms and the role of the international community in a Cold War context.

Vulnerability analysis, as practised in this book, encompasses different relationships, disciplines, time frames and geographical and institutional levels. As argued by Dorothea Hilhorst and Greg Bankoff in the Introduction, the resulting complexity of vulnerability defies attempts at formulating a general theory or reaching simple solutions. While we may be able to map 'the landscape of vulnerability', there are 'no set routes or fixed destinations'. This offers both potentials and challenges. In Chapter 1, Anthony Oliver-Smith, for example, feels that the field of disaster studies and the notion of vulnerability offer a unique context in which to pursue a theoretical breakthrough in reflecting upon the mutuality of the material and social worlds. Authors in the volume stress the divergence that exists in vulnerability as an idea and a discourse, as well as the lack of common definitions, both scholarly and in practice. At a conceptual level, therefore, the notion of vulnerability definitely offers interesting challenges.

Regarding practice, the authors argue for putting more rights and responsibilities in the hands of the affected people themselves, including the need to develop gender-specific tools to establish the historically and geographically specific vulnerabilities and capacities of women in disasters. In particular, the chapters in this volume show the prevalence of heterogeneity caused by differential patterns of vulnerability linked to household, gender, socio-economic and local or regional variations. Several authors de-emphasize or deny the difference between disaster situations and everyday life (disasters denote dependency, as does underdevelopment). Vulnerability is increasingly seen as being linked to unresolved development problems. Approaches formulated to reduce vulnerability have to take issue with, and be integrated within, 'normal' patterns of development. Further issues discussed include the design of practical diagnostic tools as elements for an integrated approach to risk assessment and management, and the role of the political, policy and organizational context in providing sustainable solutions.

We, indeed, appreciate that the notion of vulnerability holds a certain promise by providing a much-needed conceptual and practical focus that could redirect and improve ongoing efforts at disaster prevention, mitigation and reduction. Yet, vulnerability as an emerging policy approach faces a number of challenges that need to be considered. The authors in this volume have identified a range of biases, weaknesses and omissions. In the following section, we discuss these impediments – and opportunities – to improved policy practice and suggest some ways of dealing with them.

IMPEDIMENTS TO IMPROVED POLICY PRACTICE

The notion of vulnerability carries a number of inherent, problematic aspects that hinder easy application and implementation in policy practice. In addition, working on disaster vulnerability happens in a difficult environment where a number of factors create severe impediments to common approaches and concerted action. The authors in this book have outlined seven major clusters of such impediments.

Definitional heterogeneity

In Chapter 13, Ben Wisner reviews the various ways in which 'social vulnerability' has been used and theorized. He discusses the significance of a shift in vulnerability assessment from taxonomic to situational, to proactive and contextual. The latter assessments are frequently developed through community-based efforts. Though taxonomic approaches ('laundry lists') may give a more precise idea of different types of vulnerability, they are unable to deal with the changing contingencies affecting vulnerabilities in daily life. In Chapters 3 and 4, Omar Cardona and Dorothea Hilhorst stress that there is, as yet, no unifying conception and that actors respond, in practice, from different, sometimes contradictory, frameworks. Similarly, according to Annelies Heijmans in Chapter 8, agencies and populations at the local level lack a common definition of vulnerability and operate from different perspectives. What definition is acceptable and is attached to 'vulnerability' depends upon the user and its role in society.

The implication of this definitional heterogeneity for policy practice is twofold. In the first place, it compounds practical efforts at vulnerability reduction, as diversity and differentiation are usually difficult to implement from a practical perspective. This difficulty is only accentuated in the field of disasters where a tradition exists of hierarchical blueprint approaches that sometimes verge on militaristic organizational practice, as observed by Kenneth Hewitt (1983a) and quoted in the Introduction. Alexander (1997, p291) notes how vulnerability reduction had little success during the 1990s, despite the last decade of the 20th century being declared the IDNDR. He specifically mentions the failure of a coherent academic field to emerge from the welter of disaster-related disciplines. Reasons for this lack include academic over-specialization and a disciplinary training impeding holistic forms of understanding. Moreover, the domination of technocratic disciplines with sophisticated models and analyses does not often correspond to the human situations encountered on the ground, and sometimes evokes a 'siege mentality' among the social sciences. Added to this, as Ian Davis remarks in Chapter 9, is a neglect of social vulnerability analysis caused, among other things, by a bias towards the physical sciences and political concerns. These issues are reflected in the growing recognition of the difference between vulnerability to an event – the expected losses and damage – and vulnerability to the incapacity to respond to the event.

As a consequence, Alexander (1997, pp292–8) notes a lack of consensus on the body of general disaster knowledge, an inhibited development of theory and a lack of holistic analysis. These sentiments are echoed by Cardona in Chapter 3, who also notes the level of fragmentation between the different disciplinary approaches. He states that the absence of a comprehensive theory prevents effective risk management.

From a different angle, however, this heterogeneity may simply be considered a reflection of the multiple realities that make up the life of vulnerable populations around the globe and the difficulties that academicians and practitioners, alike, have in coming to terms with. Instead of considering the lack of definitional consensus only as a handicap, it may also provide a much-needed diversity in order to cope with the challenges of a multifaceted society characterized by divergent interests and perceptions. The simple representation of, or advocacy on behalf of, a variety of such interests and perspectives may already justify exploring a diversified vulnerability landscape. In principle, it could also lead to a more productive cross-fertilization between different concepts and approaches. Allowing for this diversity of definitions and views, perhaps, would also lead to more practicable approaches than the desire to arrive at one overarching model that, by necessity, would have to be broad, abstract, schematic and non-specific. The latter scheme would find it difficult to respond to the variegated requirements of daily practice. We like Allan Lavell's reference to Andrew Maskrey, in Chapter 5, that: 'Homogeneity or preconceived intervention packages tend to be the fodder of risk professionals and technicians and many times deny the social heterogeneity that typifies populations at risk throughout the world.'

From a policy perspective, we conclude that definitional diversity should be welcomed and encouraged – indeed, expected. There is already much evidence that both the private and the public sector are analysing vulnerability and risk with models very specific to the individual decisions to be made. Open and intensive communication will add to cross-fertilization, learning lessons and identifying best practices. Attempts to design, let alone impose, common frameworks are likely to prove futile at the present state of knowledge and institutional compartmentalization. Recognizing diversity comprises a type of middle ground between ineffective fragmentation and the ideal of a holistic perspective, as suggested by Cardona in Chapter 3. Perhaps it also coincides with attempts to relinquish control over the environment in favour of softer management models that stress flexibility, resilience and capacity.

Complexity and dynamism

A second area of concern is the inherently complex and dynamic nature of development, disaster impact and vulnerability. In Chapter 11, Charlotte Benson shows the difficulty, if not the impossibility, of measuring macro-economic vulnerability or of capturing it in a few quantitative figures. Instead, she argues for an *ex ante* in-depth exploration of the complexity of underlying factors. In Chapter 4, Dorothea Hilhorst elaborates the outlines of a 'complexity paradigm' for disaster studies and assesses the resulting unpredictability of causal chains and social change, as well as the uncertainties that it implies for designing required policies. Notions of complexity also call into question ill-conceived ideas of linear development and 'normality' that still pervade much thinking about disaster. Disaster is seen, here, as an abnormality or an aberration (a cycle in and of itself) from a linear path of development, rather than, perhaps, a chronic condition – a constant need for external assistance – as much caused by development as by specific impacting events.

In El Salvador, in fact, risk has increasingly come to be seen as an unresolved development problem. In the Lower Lempa River Valley Project, 'disaster risk' was combined with 'life style' or 'everyday' risk, if not conditioned by it: 'The sum of their permanent living conditions signifies that the poor or destitute live under permanent conditions of disaster.' An important policy implication is the emphasis put on reducing everyday risk and vulnerability as a significant contribution to disaster risk reduction. As noted by Heijmans in Chapter 8, the difference between normal and extreme events, as seen from the scientific or engineering perspectives, is often negligible since both types of events may result in a disaster as a consequence of the conditions under which people live.

Complexity provides similar challenges to policy-makers and practitioners as the issue of definitional heterogeneity and diversity. On the one hand, the emergence of a more sophisticated multidisciplinary approach to disasters, replete with different interrelated levels of analysis linked to natural, environmental, social, cultural and institutional factors – as well as to patterns of vulnerability and overall development – can be considered as progress. Yet, the resulting complexity is difficult to grasp and may yield major problems when applied to the design of policy approaches for implementation. In Chapter 1, for example, Oliver-Smith raises the question of how the linkage between the cultural construction of nature, the social production of disaster, conditions of vulnerability and disaster impact can be theorized. He asserts that globalization may seriously affect the way in which societies address their vulnerability to hazard. 'Today, many local problems, including disasters, may have their root causes and triggering agents and, possibly, their solutions on the other side of the globe. Through this globalization process, problems have become basically non-linear in causation and discontinuous in both space and time, rendering them inherently unpredictable and substantially less amenable to traditional methods of change and adaptation.'

Apart from their complexity *per se*, disaster and vulnerability are also very dynamic processes. Decadal climate variability, as well as human-induced climate change, increase the frequency and strength of the triggers that result in disaster, as shown in a range of recent publications. Figures mentioned in the Introduction to this volume show the increase in the number of disaster events. Another aspect of this dynamism is the historical construction of disaster and vulnerability. Vulnerability is the historical consequence of political, economic and social processes, as Hilhorst and Bankoff remind us. The explanatory model of Blaikie et al (1994) on the progression of vulnerability identifies the processes and forces that impinge upon the changing nature of vulnerability.

The challenge in policy practice is to deal with these non-linear relations between parameters and the resulting complicated patterns of causality. At a general level, the complexity of the interrelations seems to be bewildering, and policy-makers and practitioners appear to be left with the insurmountable task of designing meaningful and effective disaster prevention, mitigation and vulnerability reduction in what Maureen Fordham has called a 'messy reality' in Chapter 12. We believe, however, that a distinction should be made between the comprehensiveness and complexity of the analysis and, by necessity, a more limited focus and scope for action. Not all possible factors and processes are relevant in real life or real time. A distinction must also be made regarding the objective of the policy practice: reduce the likelihood of loss and damage or strengthen the capacity to respond to the misfortune. From a local, institutional, practical or financial perspective, many issues are probably irrelevant, while others evidently deserve to be included.

Perceptions, discourses and attitudes

The persistence of deep-rooted and sometimes biased or 'scientifically incorrect' notions of disaster among the public, at large, and sections of academia and bureaucracy compounds the problem of complexity. The still popular notion of disaster as a purely natural phenomenon caused by an external agent that is considered to be separate from society or the conditions of those affected is one example in this connection. All natural hazard events do not result in disaster. Myths surrounding disaster exemplify such notions.

In Chapter 1, Oliver-Smith asserts that all social characteristics that structure people in society play a role in the way that meanings and explanations of disasters are constructed. They give 'broad disclosure to the internal variance of a community and [are] underscoring the difficulty in determining an absolute or objective determination of the nature of the disaster.' He concludes that there is great variability in the interpretation of threat or the impact of disaster. In Chapter 2, Bankoff pays attention to the existence of a historically rooted discursive framework in which disaster and vulnerability are situated. He claims that tropicality, development and vulnerability all belong to an essentializing and generalizing cultural discourse that denigrates large regions of the world as disease ridden, poverty stricken and disaster prone. Oliver-Smith refers, in this connection, to the Western construction of nature and society or nature and culture as a dichotomy, where it was the human task to dominate and subjugate nature for the purposes of humanity. Disasters or hazards are seen from this perspective as a disorder – a violation by a natural world that is at odds with humanity.

In Chapter 7, Linda Stephen uses discourse analysis to investigate how the food aid discussion is framed in Ethiopia and to show how food insecurity is homogenized in order to fit within the prevailing socio-political setting. The information processing for early warning was shaped by different interpretations paired to particular worldviews about food insecurity and famine, and by a disjuncture between locally situated food insecurity and national decision-making. Likewise, in Chapter 13, Wisner describes the blockage, erosion or devaluation of local knowledge and coping practices by outside agencies seeking to package their standard remedies in language that will make it acceptable to 'recipients ' or 'clients'. In Chapter 6, Roger Pulwarty, Kenneth Broad and Timothy Finan show how drought and El Niño forecasts in, respectively, Brazil and Peru are framed by political and industrial interests, while the plurality of contending (local) perspectives is removed by reducing complex social problems to technical questions.

In Chapter 4, Hilhorst argues that different groups of actors perceive, understand and deal with disaster in fundamentally different ways. She discerns several domains of disaster response (science and disaster management, governance and local) and asserts that these responses often contradict or negate each other. Hilhorst emphasizes that 'although domains imply a shared repertoire of practices and languages…contradictions, conflict and negotiation take place within the domain as much as in interactions with other domains'. In Chapter 3, Cardona adds that even within the group of professionals working in the disaster management area, serious differences impede successful, effective and efficient risk reduction. He also identifies different discourses about vulnerability, risk and disaster between the natural, applied and social sciences and argues for a consistent and coherent holistic theory of risk that could properly inform its management.

In Chapter 10, Zenaida Delica-Willison and Robin Willison observe that vulnerability has been primarily discussed and defined by non-vulnerable people, while 'the vulnerable' themselves use other words to describe their position. Heijmans, in Chapter 8, notes that the experience and understanding of disaster by the very people at risk usually remain invisible in vulnerability assessments. She stresses the importance of knowing what determines their understanding, perceptions and ways of coping. In Chapter 12, Fordham adds gender relations to this conceptualization of vulnerability to better recognize difference and agency. Too often, vulnerability has been used as a blanket term, representing an undifferentiated group of passive sufferers in need of external aid and direction. In fact, this particular use of vulnerability is disempowering in its inherent denial of agency and the specific vulnerability of women. Moreover, dominant hazard paradigms, as a manifestation of masculine culture, can be fruitfully critiqued from a range of feminist positions. At the same time, Fordham signals the need for 'gender-fair' approaches, including analyses of men and masculinity. Notwithstanding these observations, we believe that there is a growing issue that, as the veil of indiscriminate vulnerability is parted, exposing the cause and expected impact on specific vulnerable groups, there is also the challenge of how societies will use this information through policy approaches and implementation.

We believe that the existence of different perceptions, attitudes and discourses about risk, vulnerability and disaster is a highly relevant issue for policy-makers and practitioners. Recognizing these different notions is an initial step towards improved practice. Lack of understanding, on the other hand, renders actions inappropriate and ineffective. It is in this connection that the re-appreciation of local knowledge and gender-specific and bottom-up approaches is to be welcomed. The conventional condescension of local knowledge has done much harm, irrespective of whether such knowledge can be considered as scientifically 'true'. As the construction of vulnerability and the actions taken to reduce it are intimately linked to the perceptions, calculations and activities of stakeholders, it is indispensable to take their views into account. In Chapter 5, Lavell talks, in this connection, about the 'social reading' and 'subjective dimensioning' of risk by social actors and affected populations. He states that 'acceptable and unacceptable risk cease to be technical dimensions and become socially determined variables influenced by different cultural, economic, social, political, institutional and organizational conditioning factors'.

We recommend more academic and applied work to grasp these 'realities'. Hilhorst's work on the social domains of disaster knowledge and action could be fruitfully elaborated by in-depth case studies. Such work will necessarily include the domains of governance, corruption, civil society, public participation, transparency, accountability and local response. Different remarks on the nature, production, 'framing' and utilization of knowledge also invite further thinking about the organizational and policy context of knowledge. Although one may agree upon the desirability of incorporating local knowledge more constructively within implementation than simply ignoring it or brushing it aside as unscientific or 'wrong', existing models find it difficult to realize this. In Chapter 7, Stephen provides the 'extractive vulnerability assessment' in the case of Ethiopia as an example of a largely top-down exercise. Hilhorst, on the other hand, believes that through rival narratives, scenarios or alliances between stakeholders, win–win situations may occur. Apart from academic work to document differentiated perceptions among involved stakeholders, further work is recommended to compare existing practical instruments in order to engage local perspectives or even to design new ones. Lavell's case study of the Lower Lempa River Valley in Chapter 5 contains several examples of such tools, varying from discussion sessions to diagnostic and training workshops and popular consultations.

Homogenization and aggregation

A further issue of policy relevance is in relation to levels of analysis and aggregation. In Chapter 7, Stephen argues that the unit or level of analysis is of primary importance in establishing profiles of vulnerability. Aggregate pictures of vulnerability at national or regional levels often miss the heterogeneity at local and household levels shown by participatory rural appraisals and household surveys in terms of food security, crop production, income and assets. In fact, Stephen states that the emphasis on broad-scale vulnerability is shaped by international and national discourses and is detrimental to realistic appraisal. Apart from the analytical quality, the choice of level or scale also biases how aid is targeted, in practice. Dominant methodologies continue to be assessments of national needs, catering to the needs of donors and governments and not to the needs of local farmers. Empirical evidence showed that spatial and temporal variations in vulnerability bear no relationship to the distribution of food aid. We do recognize, however, that behind the ongoing application of, literally, scores of vulnerability and risk assessment models with varying geographical, hazard, location, population and structural input and output parameters, there are users of the resulting information who are receiving desirable information about specific subjects of interest.

In Chapter 5, Lavell echoes a similar sentiment, asserting that: 'As we aggregate and work at macro-scales, precision is lost. Risk is expressed and can best be measured at the local level, or below, on the geographical and social scales.' This, of course, does not deny the obvious fact that often processes and policies at higher levels reveal certain patterns of risk and vulnerability even if 'the causal space of risk and the territories where loss is suffered are rarely the same'. The emphasis on local perceptions, attitudes, local organization and empowerment, therefore, must coincide with wider conceptual and causal approaches to vulnerability. This sometimes creates problems for local stakeholders from a political, functional and jurisdictional angle.

Stephen recommends approaching vulnerability on the basis of a scientific project with a theoretical framework and suitable data-collection methodologies, where weight should be given to place-based local analyses. The framework must conceptualize the significance of diversity but also explore how socio-political, economic and institutional questions frequently shape homogenized or aggregated policy responses.

From a policy standpoint, the concern about aggregation and the resulting homogenizing tendencies make sense. Aggregated policies may skim over local variations, rendering their measurement imprecise or too loosely targeted. It may be useful, therefore, to enquire into the mechanisms shaping homogenized policy responses and to explore ways of making them more sensitive to local differences. However, it also seems important to consider the organizational and procedural implications of a more localized policy practice in order to avoid the criticism that such a practice is not 'do-able'.

Implementation issues

One of the issues emerging strongly from the chapters is the traditional neglect of local involvement and perspectives when dealing with disaster. The authors are convinced of the need to remedy this. Pulwarty et al, in Chapter 6, note how 'knowledge-based interventions can and do simplify complex situations and strengthen existing assumptions and myths about the "powerlessness" of affected people'. Their study shows the homogenizing assumptions about culture, history and capacity in technocratic approaches to risk assessment and management. Political power and expert-derived power determine which actor is seen as a legitimate developer of risk messages and whose view of reality is represented. These authors recommend that impediments to the flows of disaster knowledge and information are assessed in order to unwrap the particular decision and organizational contexts that determine the development and use of that knowledge. However, this should be combined with an understanding of local contexts and contending perspectives.

In Chapter 13, Wisner observes that there is already a growing tendency of communities and groups appropriating the concept of vulnerability to enquire into their own exposure to damage and loss. Local ownership of vulnerability assessments may also induce a more politically informed approach towards empowerment and change. Wisner asserts that the concept may become a tool in the struggle for resources that are allocated politically. He implies that much work on social vulnerability tries to break out of the hegemonic 'development' and 'disaster' discourses by providing space for alternative subaltern stories and discourses. Similarly, Heijmans, in Chapter 8, identifies the existence of 'development aggression' in the Philippines, where people are the victim of human-induced disaster as a consequence of 'modernization' or 'development' projects. They are displaced, while their livelihoods and disaster-coping mechanisms are undermined, if not annihilated. These people should be given voice through organizational and capacity strengthening, alliance-building and advocacy.

Heijmans suggests the simultaneous promotion of human rights in order to change 'poor victims' and 'passive recipients' into 'powerful claimants'.

Wisner argues for an understanding of why and how local knowledge is rendered inappropriate or inaccessible and the ways in which people can be empowered to reclaim it and appreciate its usefulness. He observes that, as a consequence of the terrorist attacks on the US, information needed for citizens' groups to work on community-based protection has been removed from the public domain out of fear of abuse, leaving citizens ironically more vulnerable than before. He links the re-militarization and re-centralization of public safety to a calculated attack on the public sector and on corporate regulation.

According to Delica-Willison and Willison in Chapter 10, 'the cornerstone of efforts to reduce vulnerability is self-organization of the vulnerable at the local or community level'. Community-based organizations in the Philippines are a positive example of such an approach. Apart from catering to direct and immediate needs, these organizations create community bonding, promote social values, build social entities and give voice to the poor and influence local government. Although the El Salvadoran government and the Inter-American Development Bank were initially hesitant, both eventually embraced notions such as popular participation, local self-awareness, empowerment, negotiating strength and organizational capacity-building in the Lower Lempa Valley project as keys to success. A more participatory approach, however, was also combined with an increased awareness of the dangers posed by unilateral views of disaster risk reduction, based solely on technological as opposed to broader interventions.

Apart from everything else, implementation efforts should incorporate local stakeholders and their views in order to provide contending perspectives on disaster reality. Such efforts need to be combined with awareness, empowerment and capacity-building activities. Community-based organizations and non-governmental organizations (NGOs) can be important partners in these approaches. It is also suggested that local participants should endeavour to 'break out' of hegemonic development and disaster discourses and give voice to their own alternative or subaltern stories.

Tools

In Chapter 9, Ian Davis observes evidence of progress in the development and application of vulnerability and capacity assessments (VCAs). More attention is currently paid to the element of capacity than a decade ago. This makes it necessary not only to assess the vulnerability of populations and the impact on their social and economic infrastructure but also the capacity of society to respond to an emergency. The understanding of local capacities and coping mechanisms should also, now, be incorporated explicitly within disaster planning. Comparative internationally based research is needed to review the different approaches and their results and to identify 'best practice'. In line with the above mentioned notions of popular participation and the importance of local knowledge and action, Davis argues further for a de-professionalization of the VCA process in order to include a range of local and NGO stakeholders. In Chapter 12, Fordham also recognizes the potential of VCAs and argues for a critical, reflexive and transformative approach, combined with participatory ways of working towards a gendered capacities and vulnerabilities analysis.

In the final event, the test of VCA methodologies is whether and how they lead to improved risk-reduction strategies by decreasing different types of (gendered) vulnerability, as well as strengthening local capacities. Although the development of VCAs has definitely shown progress, its impact on disaster risk reduction and on daily management practice still needs further strengthening.

Political and policy context

Stephen Bender argued, during the international conference 'Vulnerability in Disaster Theory and Practice' held at Wageningen University in 2001, that vulnerability reduction to natural hazards is only one of many development concerns requiring attention. Though minimizing risk is a serious concern and challenge for many societies, and is even a condition for future private- and public-sector development, vulnerability reduction of populations and their infrastructure has not been a stated development objective. In fact, development has often generated disaster vulnerability. This has much to do with the way in which development programmes are conceived, funded, executed and evaluated. At present, vulnerability reduction resulting in physical and economic risk reduction has little constituency and, therefore, receives very little funding. The reason for this is partly the lack of a proactive stance among politicians who feel that prevention is an issue beyond their political horizon, and one that, in media terms, may be less conspicuous than immediate palliative action after a disaster. There does exist a small constituency for financial risk reduction, and some international entities are researching and proposing the sale of financial instruments based on risk analysis. Benson arrives at a similar conclusion in Chapter 11 when she argues that natural hazard risks, let alone risk reduction strategies, are rarely, if ever, considered in development and economic policy-making or even in individual projects. She suggests that innovative forms of insurance may be helpful in designing new policy approaches over and above problematic forms of government action or external assistance.

In Chapter 9, Davis observes that a wider application of vulnerability analysis, encompassing root causes and underlying processes, will inevitably encounter the resistance of powerful political and commercial forces as it constitutes a challenge to the status quo. In this sense, improved disaster policy practice necessitates both political advocacy and persuasion to reach its goals.

CONCLUSION

Bankoff and Hilhorst's mapping of the 'vulnerability landscape' as an environment without 'set routes and fixed destinations' will hardly be reassuring for policy-makers and practitioners. They are asked to act in the face of disaster and usually want to know where to go and which path to tread. Although this volume adds to our understanding of mutuality, complexity, heterogeneity, gender specificity and diversity in relation to vulnerability, it also, paradoxically, complicates policy practice. Most of the insights gained are not easy to translate into policy measures, and such measures, in turn, are difficult to implement.

Yet, we know better than before what comprises 'bad' practice. We have also learned that simple or technocratic answers will not do. Neither do generalized or aggregated approaches work; they may, instead, create bias and injustice. Homogenizing tendencies need to be corrected to allow for prevailing differentiation, especially with regard to gender. And we have learned to look for the organizational contexts and policy interests that induce such homogenizing practices. We also know that purely expert knowledge is insufficient, if not inadequate, and that local stakeholders must be involved. Their perceptions, ideas and discourses must be incorporated within our work and our own approaches must, consequently, be de-professionalized.

In this volume, we have also identified some broad guidelines that inform better practice and have acquired better tools to chart the terrain. We accept that definitional diversity must be welcomed, as it represents the divergent realities and interests in society. We have also learned not to exaggerate the differences between specific disaster conditions and those of everyday life. Though we recognize the complexity and dynamism of vulnerability and risk in theory, we have opted for a more limited focus and scope in practice since not all potential factors are relevant from an action perspective. We stress, in the strongest possible terms, the importance of local participation, empowerment, and capacity and organizational strengthening. We are also aware of the political boundaries of action and feel that advocacy is always needed, as is resistance to hegemonic and counterproductive development or disaster discourses in certain other situations. We hope that improved VCA methodologies can help us, in a pragmatic way, to deal with the various challenges outlined above.

In the end, too, we realize that there still remain many open questions and that more work is needed in order to travel safely through the landscape of vulnerability. We recommend further applied research in different actors' domains of knowledge and understanding. We also invite studies on how policy and commercial interests frame different discourses and responses. We endorse the need to make international comparisons between different VCA approaches in an attempt to identify best practices and lessons learned. By way of a final conclusion, we express the hope that this volume comprises a set of helpful signposts to guide and inform those committed to vulnerability reduction and that the map it provides at least includes some coordinates furnished by those most affected by the disasters themselves.

Notes

INTRODUCTION

1   Authors are listed in reverse alphabetical order.
2   All such statistics are 'soft' in that, at best, they only indicate trends.
3   The absence of a historical perspective has not gone completely unnoticed and there have been persuasive calls for a more diachronic approach, most recently by Anthony Oliver-Smith and Susana Hoffman in *The Angry Earth* (1999) and by Kenneth Hewitt in *Regions of Risk* (1997).
4   The conference was organized by Disaster Studies, Centre for Rural Development Sociology, Wageningen University, with the support of the Educational Centre 'Hotel De Wereld' and the Conference Bureau of Wageningen University, and was held in Wageningen, The Netherlands, on 29–30 June 2001.

CHAPTER 1

1   Portions of this chapter have appeared in Oliver-Smith, A (2002) 'Theorizing Disasters: Nature, Power, Culture,' in S M Hoffman and A Oliver-Smith (eds) *Catastrophe and Culture: The Anthropology of Disaster*, SAR Press, Santa Fe.

CHAPTER 2

1   Parts of this chapter have previously appeared in Bankoff, G (2001) 'Rendering the World Unsafe: "Vulnerability" as Western Discourse', *Disasters*, 25(1): 19–35 and Bankoff, G (2002) 'Discoursing Disasters: Paradigms of Risk and Coping', *Trialog: A Journal for Planning and Building in the Third* World, 73(20): 3–7
2   Watts argues that the origins of development lie within modernity, but that modernity itself cannot be unproblematically located within the West: the modern and developed require the non-modern and the undeveloped for the purposes of juxtaposition.
3   The figures include the annual averages between 1990 and 1998.
4   See, in particular, A Sen's classic treatise on famine (Sen, 1981).
5   The concept of vulnerability has also been applied to disadvantaged and marginalized populations within more industrialized nations (Bolin and Stanford, 1999, p89–112).
6   See Bankoff (2003, Chapter 8).

CHAPTER 4

1   The writing of this chapter was made possible through the generous sponsorship of the Netherlands Organisation for Scientific Research (NWO).

CHAPTER 6

1   Winter comprises the period of February to May.
2   From *O Povo* newspapers, 17 January 1992.
3   A total of 484 from six administrative units were surveyed to document levels of use of government initiatives, irrigation access and other coping strategies, such as non-agricultural income.

CHAPTER 7

1   The hierarchy of administrative boundaries is as follows: region, zone, *wereda* and peasant association. The government of Ethiopia collects data down to the peasant association level. Villages and households follow in size after the peasant association.
2   The peasant association is the lowest administrative level where data is collected.
3   Several international development targets (IDTs) were established at the World Summit for Social Development in Copenhagen in 1995. In addition to the reduction in malnutrition, they include gender equity in education, poverty reduction and improvements in maternal and child health. In 1996, the World Food Summit upheld the goal of halving the cases of malnutrition by 2015.
4   Bilateral aid transfers directly from governments in aid-giving countries to governments in developing countries.
5   'Naples terms' are agreements among creditors associated with the Paris Club to implement a new treatment on the debt of the poorest countries. They were agreed in 1994. Under these terms, two substantial enhancements are granted to developing countries on a case-by-case basis, on the level of reduction and the conditions of treatment of the debt. For the poorest and most indebted countries, the level of cancellation is at least 50 per cent and can be raised to 67 per cent of eligible non-overseas development assitance (ODA) credits. Creditors agreed in September 1999 that all Naples terms treatments would carry a 67 per cent debt reduction.
6   The terms of the accord between the Paris Club and Russia call for an upfront discount of 80 per cent on the stock of debt owed and the application of Naples terms to the remaining 20 per cent – in other words, this part is subject to a 67 per cent reduction in net present value terms (*IMF/World Bank Special Programme of Assistance Status Report for Ethiopia*, 1998).
7   NDVI measures various stages of plant formation derived from satellite images covering geographically large areas.
8   The post-modern analysis of food security shifts the focus from macro-economic indicators such as GDP/GNP towards micro-economies and the dynamics of local places. See Maxwell (1994). See, also, the compilation of Foucault's writings (1980), in which he articulates a post-modernist view on the social construction of knowledge, such as the influence of gender and culture on our interpretation of events. See Derrida (1976) for the application of 'deconstruction', a post-modern form of text analysis.
9   Fractals are curves or geometrical figures, each part of which has the same statistical characteristics as the whole. In mapping, the principle is used to recreate textured surfaces such as in physical relief maps.
10 See Clay et al (1999), who explain that conventional wisdom in Ethiopia sets 1680 kilocalories (based on grains alone) as the daily requirement per person, which comes from grains alone. The government's target is 2100 kilocalories from all sources.
11 See discussion in Sharp (1998).

CHAPTER 8

1   It is necessary to distinguish between hazard types, since each hazard has a particular impact upon people's resource base. River erosion, lahar flows and landslides affect people's entitlement to land. Typhoons and floods primarily destroy seasonal crops.

2   As of December 1997, the Philippine government approved that 56,168.53 hectares of prime agricultural lands can be converted. In 1998 alone, 554,350 farmer households lost their primary source of livelihood (IBON, 1998).

3   The term 'development aggression' has been in use among communities and the NGO movement since 1995, when the Philippines started to implement 'development' programmes on a large scale. The Mining Act was approved, the country held the Asia–Pacific Economic Cooperation (APEC) meeting in 1996, and planners set ambitious targets aimed at reaching the status of a newly industrialized country (NIC) by the year 2000.

4   The 'disaster-pressure' model is a very effective instrument to encourage local people to analyse their conditions, to discover root causes of why they endure hardship and to mobilize them for action. It raises people's awareness about the political origins of the disaster and their vulnerability.

5   Given the critique of the disaster-cycle model, and considering the importance of people's participation in the assessment, assessment tools require the following features:

- recognize people's perceptions of risks that go beyond the emergency and disaster paradigm, including a hazard assessment from people's perspective;
- recognize people's capacities and coping mechanisms from a historical perspective;
- identify and analyse the dynamic pressures that deprive the people of their resources to cope with adverse events;
- increase awareness of people about the root causes of vulnerability and future risks;
- encourage transference and application by the community so that it can further improve its expertise in identifying and articulating what it needs to reduce its vulnerability.

CHAPTER 10

1   Some of the devastating earthquakes in recent years were those that hit Gujarat, India, on 26 January 2001; Izmit, Turkey, on 17 August 1999; and Baguio, the Philippines, on 16 July 1990.

2   Discussion with villagers of Barangay Gutad, Floridablanca and Pampanga some time in 1996.

3   Discussion with the villagers of Barangay Talba, Tenejeros and Bacolor in March 1998.

4   A training session was conducted by the Asian Disaster Preparedness Centre (ADPC) in November 1999 in Bangladesh. A participatory risk assessment was undertaken in Sukhar Char, Bangladesh. This is a statement of one of the participants in the assessment. *Bipodepenneta* is a Bangla term for vulnerabilities.

5   'Five-six' refers to a usurious rate of interest for loans where one has to repay 6 pesos for every 5-peso loan. It is a 20 per cent interest on the amount borrowed, to be repaid within a short period of time, usually weekly.

6   Discussion with the villagers of San Mateo, Marikina, the Philippines in September 1998.

7   Fieldwork in Delhi, July 2001.

8 Community-based organizations (CBOs) such as Buklod Tao in Marikina, Metro Manila, and CBOs linked with Tabang sa Biktima sa Bikol (TABI) in Bicol; Montanosa Relief and Rehabilitation Services (MRRS) in Baguio; Pampanga Disaster Response Network (PDRN); CONCERN in Central Luzon.

9 Barangay is the smallest political unit in the Philippines.

10 One of the authors studied the Multi-Purpose Cooperative in Soro-soro, Ibaba and was directly involved in organizing these two cooperatives.

11 *Bayanihan* is a Filipino word for cooperation. It is associated with the collective endeavour of the spirit of cooperation, especially in helping those who are most in need.

CHAPTER 11

1 A notable exception was a study undertaken by the US Agency for International Development's (USAID's) Office of the United States Foreign Disaster Assistance (OFDA) to determine which countries should form the primary focus of its disaster prevention, mitigation and preparedness (PMP) activities (Heyman et al, 1991). This study took into account capacity to cope with hazards, including from institutional and resource availability perspectives, as well as historical data on disaster occurrence. However, an overall ranking of countries was not attempted.

2 Small states face a number of special disadvantages associated with size, insularity and remoteness, which, in turn, result in potential economic sub-optimality, a high degree of openness and limited diversification. These factors render them particularly exposed and vulnerable to a range of external shocks, including natural hazards, causing high volatility in national incomes. Although the range of per capita incomes and rates of growth of small and large developing countries are not significantly different, the standard deviation of real per capita growth is about 25 per cent higher amongst the former (Commonwealth Secretariat and World Bank, 2000).

3 Bruguglio's work was commissioned by the United Nations Conference on Trade and Development (UNCTAD), in accordance with a resolution to construct such an index as agreed at the 1991 International Conference on Islands and Small States in Malta. The importance of a vulnerability index was again recognized at the Barbados Global Conference on Sustainable Development of Small Island Developing States during April to May 1994, leading to a meeting of experts under the auspices of the UN Department of Economic and Social Affairs (ECOSOC) to develop a vulnerability index. Its findings were considered both by the Commission for Sustainable Development and the Committee for Development Planning (CDP) in 1998. The latter recommended that further work again be carried out on the development of a vulnerability index; in 1999, it proposed that the Economic Diversification Index should be replaced by the Economic Vulnerability Index (EVI) as one of the criteria used in identifying less developed countries (LDCs). After an examination of the issues, the CDP recommended that the EVI should reflect relative risk posed to a country's development from two forms of exogenous risk: weather-related ones and those emanating from the external economic environment.

4 The United Nations Disaster Relief Organization (UNDRO, 1990) developed an index of 'disaster proneness', based on 1980 population data, 1980 gross domestic product (GDP) per capita and total gross national product (GNP) significant disaster damage (defined as exceeding 1 per cent of GNP), as well as the number of disaster events occurring between 1970 and 1989. The index was used to identify the 50 'most disaster-prone' countries in the world.

5   At the time of drafting, the United Nations Development Programme (UNDP) was also working on the development of some form of vulnerability indicator. In contrast to previous attempts, however, the UNDP is planning to build in political, social and economic factors that could play a role in determining the level, nature and quality of future mitigation and preparedness efforts.

6   Admittedly, the indices themselves are based on data over slightly different periods.

7   OFDA and the Centre for Research on the Epidemiology of Disasters (CRED) used to maintain their own, separate databases. In 1999, the two organizations agreed an initiative to merge the two.

8   Thus, for instance, in Vietnam local governments sometimes express rice losses in terms of acreage and sometimes in terms of tonnage. As a further example, the Bangladesh *Standing Orders on Disasters* (Bangladesh Government, 1999) includes a basic form for post-disaster assessment of loss and damage to be completed by local government units, including information on the value of various types of loss (for example, crops, livestock, industrial concerns and fish farms). However, there is no indication how losses should be valued, implying potentially considerable internal inconsistencies in the data reported.

9   For example, as a direct consequence of a volcanic crisis, GDP for the island of Montserrat plummeted by 8 per cent, year on year, in 1995, by a further 22 per cent in 1996 and by 21 per cent in 1997. Yet, these figures underestimate the extent of decline as the economy was partly sustained by substantial inflows of assistance, to some extent offsetting the decline in productive activities.

10   To take an example, the old OFDA database reported that the 1986 floods in Northeast China resulted in 80 deaths and losses totalling US$1.5 billion. For the same event, the Munich Reinsurance database reported 260 deaths and US$1.2 billion in damage. As a second example, the OFDA database reported that the November 1980 earthquake in Irpinia, Italy, resulted in 4689 deaths and losses totalling US$20 billion, but Munich Reinsurance reported 3114 deaths and damage totalling US$10 billion. Countless other discrepancies between the various databases also exist.

CHAPTER 12

1   In fact, some forms of poverty reduction can *increase* vulnerability (see Chambers, 1995, for a discussion of the trade-offs that poor people make between income and security) and some increases in poverty can reduce vulnerability (see Jodha's 1988 study of farmers and villagers in Rajasthan whose per capita income had fallen 5 per cent, but who regarded themselves as better off in terms of well-being – some criteria of which can be equated to a reduction in vulnerability; cited in Chambers, 1995).

2   There is some contention about the feminization of poverty. Baden and Milward (1995) have argued that it is difficult to measure satisfactorily; there is little clarity about what it means, or about whether such a trend can be empirically verified.

3   Instituto del Tercer Mundo–Social Watch (www.fp.chasque.apc.org:8081/socwatch) is an NGO watchdog system aimed at monitoring the commitments made by governments at the World Summit for Social Development and the Beijing World Conference on Women.

4   WID, the welfarist position of women in development; GAD, the efficiency and anti-poverty position of gender and development.

5   See Dale Spender's (1982) classic piece of feminist educational research on this topic, as discussed in Eade (1999).

6   Equity is concerned with moral justice and right. Equality concerns the condition of being equal; sameness; evenness.
7   See March et al (1999, pp89–91) for some of its limitations.

CHAPTER 13

1   See www.fema.gov/impact/Chapter2-Assessment.pdf.
2   See Wisner et al (1979); Cuny (1983); Maskrey (1989); Wisner et al (1991); Geilfus (1997); Soto (1998); von Kotze and Holloway (1998); Anderson and Woodrow (1998); Carasco and Garibay (2000); Plummer (2000); Turcios et al (2000); Chiappe and Fernandez (2000); Wilches-Chaux and Wilches-Chaux (2001).
3   See an interesting discussion of poverty as 'capability deprivation' in Sen (2000, pp87–110).
4   See Hart (1997); Johnson et al (1998).
5   See Tierney et al (1988); Helander (1992); Wisner (2002a).
6   Refugees and displaced persons often show great creativity in adapting to their new surroundings and, as recent research has shown, do not necessarily destroy the environment of their new temporary homes (Black, 1998).
7   See Freire (1982); Hall et al (1982); Goonatilake (1984); Scott (1985; 1990); Colburn (1989); Hardoy and Satterthwaite (1989); Marglin and Marglin (1990); Dudley (1993); Eade (1997); Holland and Blackburn (1998); Grenier (1998); Twigg and Bhatt (1998); Peri Peri (1999); Carrasco (2000).
8   Luke Harding (2001) 'Indian quake widens rifts between the castes', *Guardian Weekly*, 22–28 February 2001, p5
9   Oxfam UK on 23 January 2002 via ReliefWeb: www.reliefweb.int/w/ rwb.nsf/480fa8736b88bbc3c12564f6004c8ad5/304aec5eb40e2d2e85256b4a006fac61 ?OpenDocument
10 Studies and post-disaster audits summarized by Wisner, et al (2003), Trujillo et al (2000); Buckle et al (2000); Jaspars and Shoham (1999); Mileti (1999); Bolin and Stanford (1998); Fordham (1998); Fernando and Fernando (1997); Pelling (1997); Enarson and Morrow (1997); Hewitt (1996); Wisner (1996b); Lavell (1994); Blaikie et al (1994); Aysan (1993).
11 The project covers 220 constituent municipalities in six mega-city regions: Los Angeles, Tokyo, Mexico City, Mumbai, Manila and Johannesburg. See Valasquez et al (1999) and Wisner (2002).

References

Aberley, D (ed) (1993) *Boundaries of Home: Mapping for Local Empowerment*, New Society Publishers, Gabriola Island

Adams, J (1995) *Risk*, UCL Press, London

ADB (1994) 'Climate Change in Asia: Philippines Country Report', Regional Study on Global Environmental Issues, Asian Development Bank (ADB), Manila

ADPC (2001) *Training Reports*, Asian Disaster Preparedness Centre (ADPC), Pathumtahni

Agarwal, B (1992) 'The gender and environment debate: Lessons from India', *Feminist Studies*, 18(1): 119–58

Agrawal, A (1995) 'Dismantling the divide between indigenous and scientific knowledge', *Development and Change*, 26: 413–39

Alexander, D (1997) 'The study of natural disasters, 1977–1997: Some reflections on a changing field of knowledge', *Disasters*, 21(4): 283–304

Alexander, D (2000) *Confronting Catastrophe*, Oxford University Press, New York

Alexander, D (2002) 'From Civil Defense to Civil Protection – And Back Again', RADIX Website, www.anglia.ac.uk/geography/radix/reflections3.htm

Altman, D (1998) 'Globalization and the "Aids Industry"', *Contemporary Politics*, 4(3): 233–46

Anderson, M and Woodrow, P (1999) *Rising from the Ashes: Development Strategies in Times of Disaster*, Intermediate Technology Publications, London

Anderson, M (1995) 'Vulnerability to disaster and sustainable development: A general framework for assessing vulnerability', in C Munasinghe (ed) *Disaster Prevention for Sustainable Development*, World Bank, Washington, DC

Anderson, M and Woodrow, P (1989) *Rising from the Ashes: Development Strategies in Times of Disasters*, Westview Press, London

Anderson, M B and Woodrow, P J (1993) 'Reducing vulnerability to drought and famine', in J O Field (ed) *The Challenge of Famine: Recent Experience, Lessons Learned*, Kumarian Press, West Hartford, pp131–46

Anderson, W (1995) 'Where every prospect pleases and only man is vile: Laboratory medicine as colonial discourse', in V Rafael (ed) *Discrepant Histories; Translocal Essays on Filipino Cultures*, Anvil Publishing, Manila

Anderson, W (1996) 'Immunities of empire: Race, disease, and the new tropical medicine, 1900–1920', *Bulletin of the History of Medicine*, 70: 94–118

Annan, K A (1999) 'An increasing vulnerability to natural disasters', *The International Herald Tribune*, 10 September

Appadurai, A (1996) *Modernity at Large: Cultural Dimensions of Globalization*, The University of Minnesota Press, Minneapolis

Appfel-Marglin, F (1996) 'Introduction: Rationality and the world', in F Appfel-Marglin and S A Marglin (eds) *Decolonizing Knowledge: From Development to Dialogue*, Clarendon Press, Oxford

Arce, A and Long, N (1992) 'The dynamics of knowledge: Interfaces between bureaucrats and peasants', in N Long and A Long (eds) *Battlefields of Knowledge: The Interlocking of Theory and Practice in Social Research and Development*, Routledge, London

Arce, A and Long, N (2000) 'Reconfiguring modernity and development from an anthropological persepctive', in A Arce and N Long (eds) *Anthropology, Development and Modernities: Exploring Discourses, Counter-Tendencies and Violence*, Routledge, London and New York

Arkel, K van (2000) 'Social and Political Aftershocks of the Marmara Earthquake on August 17th 1999 in Turkey', MSc thesis, Disaster Studies, Wageningen University, Wageningen, The Netherlands

Arnold, D (1996) 'Tropical medicine before Manson', in D Arnold (ed) *Warm Climates and Western Medicine: The Emergence of Tropical Medicine, 1500–1930*, Rodopi, Amsterdam and Atlanta, Georgia, pp1–19

Arriëns, W T L and Benson, C (1999) 'Post-disaster rehabilitation: The experience of the Asian Development Bank', Paper Prepared for International Decade for Natural Disaster Reduction and UN Economic and Social Commission for Asia and the Pacific (IDNDR–ESCAP) Regional Meeting for Asia: Risk Reduction and Society in the 21st Century, Bangkok, 23–26 February, mimeo, Asian Development Bank, Manila

Asad, T (ed) (1975) *Anthropology and the Colonial Encounter,* Ithaca Press, Cornell

Atkins, J P, Mazzi, S and Easter, C D (2000) 'A commonwealth vulnerability index for developing countries: The position of small states', *Commonwealth Economic Paper Series* 40, Commonwealth Secretariat, London

Aysan, Y (1993) 'Keynote paper: Vulnerability assessment', in P Merriman and C Browitt (eds) *Natural Disasters: Protecting Vulnerable Communities*, Telford, London

Aysan, Y F, Coburn, A W, Davis, I and Spence, R J S (1989) *Mitigation of Urban Seismic Risk: Actions to reduce the impact of earthquakes on highly vulnerable areas of Mexico City*, Report of Bilateral Technical Cooperation Agreement between the Governments of Mexico City and the UK, Disaster Management Centre, Oxford Polytechnic and University of Cambridge, Oxford and Cambridge

Baden, S and Milward, K (1995) 'Gender and poverty', *BRIDGE Report # 30*, Report Commissioned by the Gender Office, Swedish International Development Cooperation Agency (SIDA), Institute of Development Studies, Sussex

Balthazar, C (1979) *Estado, Pesca y Burguesia: 1939–1973*, Realidad y Teoria, Lima

Bangladesh Government (1999) *Standing Orders on Disaster,* Disaster Management Bureau, Ministry of Disaster Management and Relief, Government of Bangladesh, Dhaka

Bankoff, G (1999) 'A history of poverty: The politics of natural disasters in the Phillipines, 1985–1995', *The Pacific Review* 12(3): 381–420

Bankoff, G (2001) 'Rendering the world unsafe: "Vulnerability" as Western discourse', *Disasters*, 25(1): 19–35

Bankoff, G (2002) 'Discoursing disasters: Paradigms of risk and coping', *Trialog A Journal for Planning and Building in the Third World*, 73(2): 3–7

Bankoff, G (2003) *Cultures of Disaster; Society and Natural Hazard in the Philippines*, Routledge Curzon, London

Barber, R and Chavez, F (1983) 'Biological consequences of El Niño', *Science*, 222: 1203–10

Barr, J and Birke, L (1997) 'Women, science and adult education: toward a feminist curriculum?', in M Maynard (ed) *Science and the Construction of Women*, UCL Press, London

Beck, U (1992) *Risk Society: Toward a New Modernity*, Sage, London

Belloni, H, Douma, N, Hilhorst, D, Holla, J and Kuiper, G (2000) 'Journalistig: Weergave van "natuurrampen" in Nederlanse dagbladen', *Disaster Sites* 5, Wageningen University, Wageningen

Bender, S O (1999) 'The Vulnerability Context of Disasters', Contribution to UN–IDNDR and QUIPUNET Internet Conference, 14–25 June 1999, The International Programme Forum: The concluding phase of the UN International Decade for Natural Disaster Reduction, www.quipu.net:1999/

Benson, C (1997a) 'The economic impacts of natural disasters in Fiji', *ODI Working Paper* 97, Overseas Development Institute (ODI), London

Benson, C (1997b) 'The economic impacts of natural disasters in the Philippines', *ODI Working Paper* 99, Overseas Development Institute (ODI), London

Benson, C and Clay, E J (2000) 'Developing countries and the economic impacts of natural disasters', in A Kreimer and M Arnold (eds) *Managing Disaster Risk in Emerging Economies*, Disaster Risk Management Series 2, World Bank, Washington, DC

Benson, C and Clay, E J with F V Michael and A W Robertson (2001) 'Dominica: natural disasters and economic development in a small island state', *Disaster Risk Management Working Paper* Series 2, World Bank, Washington, DC

Benthall, J (1993) *Disasters, Relief and the Media*, I B Taurus and Co Ltd, London

Biersack, A (1999) 'Introduction: From the "new ecology" to the new ecologies', *American Anthropologist*, 101(1): 5–18

Black, R (1998) *Refugees, Environment and Development*, Longman, Harlow/ Essex

Blaikie, P, Cannon, T, Davis I and Wisner, B (1994*) At Risk: Natural Hazards, People's Vulnerability, and Disasters*, Routledge, London and New York (2nd edition, forthcoming 2003)

Blaikie, P, Cannon, T, Davis, I and Wisner, B (1996) *Vulnerabilidad, el Entorno Social de los Desastres*, La Red de Estudios Sociales en Prevención de Desastres en América Latina, La RED/ITDG, Bogotá

Blaut, J (1993) *The Colonizer's Model of the World: Geographical Diffusionism and Eurocentric History*, Guilford, New York

Blockley, D (ed) (1992) *Engineering Safety*, MacGraw-Hill International Series in Civil Engineering, London

Blolong, R R (1996) 'The Ivatan cultural adaptation to typhoons: A portrait of a self-reliant community from the indigenous development perspective', *Aghamtao, Journal of Anthropological Association of the Philippines*, 8: 13–24

Bolin, R and Stanford L (1999) 'Constructing vulnerability in the First World: The Northridge earthquake in Southern California, 1994', in A Oliver-Smith and S Hoffman (eds) *The Angry Earth; Disaster in Anthropological Perspective*, Routledge, New York and London, 89–112

Bolin, R and Stanford, L (1998) *The Northridge Earthquake: Vulnerability and Disaster,* Routledge, London

Boserup, E (1970) *Women's Role in Economic Development,* St Martin's Press, New York

Brand, L A (2001) 'Displacement for development? The impact of changing state–society relations', *World Development*, 29(6): 961–76

Brenner, N (1997) 'State territorial restructuring and the production of spatial scale: Urban and regional planning in the Federal Republic of Germany, 1960–1990', *Political Geography*, 16: 273–306

Briguglio, L (1995) 'Small island developing states and their economic vulnerabilities', *World Development*, 23(9): 1615–32

Broad, K (1999) 'Climate, culture and values: El Niño 1997–1998 and Peruvian fisheries', PhD thesis, Columbia University, New York

Brookesmith, P (1997) *Future Plagues; Biohazard, Disease and Pestilence; Mankind's Battle for Survival*, Blandford, London

Bruin, J (1996) 'Root causes of the global crisis', Women's International League for Peace and Freedom and Inhured International, Nepal

Bruun, O and Kalland, A (eds) (1995) *Asian Perception of Nature: A Critical Approach*, Curzon Press, Richmond

Bryant, E A (1991) *Natural Hazards*, Cambridge University Press, Cambridge

Buckle, P (2001) 'Community-based management: A new approach to managing disasters', Paper Presented at the Disaster and Social Crisis Research Network, Sessions for the

5th European Sociological Association Conference, 28 August–1 September 2001, Helsinki, www.anglia.ac.uk/geography/d&scrn/

Buckle, P, Mars, G and Smale, S (2000) 'New Approaches to Assessing Vulnerability and Resilience', *Australian Journal of Emergency Management*, 15(2): 8–14

Burawoy, M, Blum, J, George, S, Gille, Z, Gowan, T, Haney, L, Klawiter, M, Lopez, S, Riain, S and Thayer, M(2000) *Global Ethnography, Forces, Connections and Imaginations in a Post-modern World,* University of California Press, Berkeley, Los Angeles and London

Burby, R (ed) (1998) *Cooperating with Nature: Confronting Natural Hazards with Land-Use Planning for Sustainable Communities,* Joseph Henry Press, Washington, DC

Burton, I, Kates, R W and White, G F (1978) *The Environment as Hazard,* Oxford University Press, New York

Byrne, B and Baden, S (1995) 'Gender, emergencies and humanitarian assistance', *BRIDGE Report* 33, Institute of Development Studies, Sussex

Byrne, B and Laier, J K, with S Baden and R Marcus (1996) *National Machineries for Women in Development: Experiences, lessons and strategies for institutionalizing gender in development policy and planning,* Report Prepared for the European Commission, Directorate General for Development (DGVIII), Institute of Development Studies, Sussex

Camacho, D (1998) *Environmental Injustices, Political Struggles: Race, Class, and the Environment,* Duke University Press, Durham

Cannon, T (1994) 'Vulnerability analysis and the explanation of "natural" disasters', in A Varley (ed) *Disasters, Development and Environment,* John Wiley and Sons, Chichester, New York, Brisbane, Toronto and Singapore, pp13–29

Cannon, T (2000) 'Vulnerability analysis and disasters', in D Parker (ed) *Flood Hazards and Disasters,* Routledge, London

Cardona, O D (1993) 'Natural disasters, global change and sustainable development: a strategy for reducing effects', III Meeting of the Scientific Advisory Council for the International Geophere–Biosphere Programme, Forum on Earth System Research, ICSU, Ensenada, Baja California, Mexico

Cardona O D (1996) 'Manejo ambiental y prevención de desastres: dos temas asociados', *Ciudades en Riesgo,* in M A Fernández (ed) *Ciudades en Riesgo: Degradación Ambiental, Riesgos Urbanos y Desastres,* La RED, USAID, Lima (reprinted as *Cities at Risk,* A/H Editorial, Quito, Ecuador, 1999)

Cardona, O D (1999) 'Environmental management and disaster prevention: Holistic risk assessment and management', in J Ingleton (ed) *Natural Disaster Management,* Tudor Rose, London

Cardona, O D (2001) *Estimación Holística del Riesgo Sísmico utilizando Sistemas Dinámicos Complejos,* Universidad Politécnica de Cataluña, Barcelona, http://www.desenredando. org/public/varios/2001/ehrisusd/index/html

Carrasco, F (2000) *Participación Comunitaria y Cambio Social,* Instituto de Investigaciones Sociales (UNAM) and Plaza y Valdes Editores, Mexico City

Carrasco, F and Garibay, B (2000) *Guia Communitária para la Prevención de Desastres,* Government of the City of Mexico and Institute of Social Research, National Autonomous University of Mexico (UNAM), Mexico City

Carrigan, T, Connell, R and Lee, J (1985) 'Towards a new sociology of masculinity', *Theory and Society,* 14(5): 551–604

Casiple, R C (1996) 'Human rights versus development aggression: Can development violate human rights?', *Human Rights Forum – Journal for Human Rights Defenders,* VI(1): 37–43

CDRC (2001) *Disasters in the Philippines 2000,* Citizens' Disaster Response Center, Quezon City

Central Statistics Authority (1994) *Ethiopian Census 1990,* Government of Ethiopia, Addis Ababa

Chambers, R (1989) 'Vulnerability, coping and policy', IDS Bulletin 20, Institute of Development Studies, Sussex

Chambers, R (1995) 'Poverty and livelihoods: Whose reality counts?', *IDS Discussion Paper* 347, Institute of Development Studies, Sussex

Chardin, J-P (1996) 'Report on Mission to the Philippines, 10–22 May', mimeo, International Decade for Natural Disaster Reduction Secretariat, Geneva

Checkland, P and Scholes, J (1990) *Soft Systems Methodology in Action*, Wiley, Chichester

Chiappe, I and Fernandez, M (2001) *Manual del Capacitador: 7 Módulos para Capacitadores en Gestión de Riesgo*, Programa Nacional de Prevencion de Riesgos y Atencion de Desastres, La Paz, Bolivia

Clay, D C, Molla, D and Habtewold, D (1999) 'Food aid targeting in Ethiopia: A study of who needs it and who gets it', *Food Policy*, 24: 391–409

Cohen, A (1987) *Whalsay: Symbol, Segment and Boundary in a Shetland Island Community*, Manchester University Press, Manchester

Colburn, F (ed) (1989) *Everyday Forms of Peasant Resistance*, M E Sharpe, Armonk

Coleridge, P (1993) *Disability, Liberation, and Development*, Oxfam Publications, Oxford

Collins, J (1992) 'Marxism confronts the environment', in S Ortiz and S Lees (eds) *Understanding Economic Process*, (Monographs in Economic Anthropology 10), University Press of America, Lanham

Columbus, C (1494) *In Laudem Serenissimi Ferdinandi Hispaniaerum Regis, Bethicae et Regni Granatae, Obsidio, Victoria, et Triuphus, et de Insulis in Mari Indico Nuper Inuentis*, Johann Bergmann de Ople, Basel

Comfort, L (1995) 'Self Organization in Disaster Response and Recovery: The Maharashta, India, Earthquake of September 30, 1993', *Quick Response Reports* 74, Natural Hazards Research and Applications Information Center, University of Colorado, Boulder, Colorado

Comfort, L, Wisner, B, Cutter, S, Pulwarty, R, Hewitt, K, Oliver-Smith, A, Weiner, J, Fordham, M, Peacock, W and Krimgold, F (1999) 'Reframing disaster policy: The global evolution of vulnerable communities', *Environmental Hazards*, 1: 39–44

Committee for the International Decade for Natural Disaster Reduction (IDNDR) *Proceedings of a Workshop at the Royal Society*, London, 19 April

Commonwealth Secretariat/ World Bank (2000) *Small States: Meeting challenges in the global economy*, Report of the Joint Task Force on Small States, London and Washington, DC

Connell, D (1999) 'Participatory development: An approach sensitive to class and gender', in D Eade (ed) *Development with Women*, Oxfam Publication, Oxford

Copans, J (1975) *Secheresses et Famines du Sahel*, Maspero, Paris

Cornwell, A (1997) 'Men, masculinity and "gender in development"', in C Sweetman (ed) *Men and Masculinity*, Oxfam, Oxford

Cornwell, A (2000) 'Making a difference? Gender and participatory development', *IDS Discussion Paper* 378, Institute of Development Studies, Sussex

Covello V T and Mumpower, J (1985) 'Risk analysis and risk management: An historical perspective', *Society for Risk Analysis* 5(2): 103–20

Cowen, M and Shenton R (1995) 'The invention of development', in J Crush (ed) *Power of Development*, Routledge, London and New York, pp27–41

CRED (2001a) 'CRED/OFDA (USAID) – EM–DAT Project', Presentation to Second Technical Advisory Group (TAG) meeting, Washington, DC, 6–8 February, Centre for Research on the Epidemiology of Disasters (CRED), University of Louvain, Brussels

CRED (2001b) *Disaster Database*, Centre for Research on the Epidemiology of Disasters (CRED), University of Louvain, Brussels

Cronon, W (1983) *Changes in the Land: Indians, Colonists, and the Ecology of New England*, Hill and Wang, New York

Crush, J (ed) (1995) *Power of Development*, Routledge, London

Cuny, F (1983) *Disasters and Development*, Oxford University Press, Oxford

Curtin, P (1989) *Death by Migration; Europe's Encounters with the Tropical World in the Nineteenth Century*, Cambridge University Press, Cambridge

Curtis, P (1993) 'Famine household coping strategies: Their usefulness for understanding household responses to armed conflict', Refugees Studies Programme, Oxford, unpublished

Cutter, S L (ed) (1994) *Environmental Risks and Hazards*, Prentice Hall, New Jersey

Cutter, S (1996) 'Vulnerability to environmental hazards', *Progress in Human Geography*, 20(4): 529–39

Da Cunha, E (1902) *Rebellion in the Backlands* (translated by Simon Putnam and reprinted in 1985), University of Chicago Press, Chicago

DAC Informal Network on Poverty Reduction (2000) *DAC Guidelines on Poverty Reduction*, Consolidated test of the draft guidelines submitted for review to the Fourth Meeting of the Implementation Group, OECD, Paris, 2–3 March

Davis, I (1985) 'Shelter after disaster' PhD thesis, University College London (UCL), London

Davis, I (1994) 'Assessing community vulnerability' in UK IDNDR Committee, *Medicine in the International Decade for Natural Disaster Reduction (IDNDR) Research Preparedness and Response for Sudden Impact Disasters in the 1990s*, Proceedings of a workshop at the Royal Society, London 19 April 1993, UK IDNDR Committee, London, pp11–13

Davis, M (2001) *Late Victorian Holocausts: El Niño Famines and the Making of the Third World*, Donelly and Sons, Chicago

Delica, Z (1999) 'Community Mobilization for Early Warning', *Philippine Planning Journal School of Urban and Regional Planning*, 30(2): 30–40

Delica, Z (2001a) 'Citizens participation towards safer communities', Paper presented at the Global Forum on Social Services and Local Governance, Stockholm, May 2000

Delica, Z (2001b) 'Community mobilization for early warning', *Philippine Planning Journal School of Urban and Regional Planning*, 30(2): 30–40

Derrida, J (1976) *Of Grammatology*, first US edition, Johns Hopkins University Press, Baltimore

DFID (1999) *Sustainable Livelihoods Guidance Sheets*, 1,1 –2,2, April

Dia R et al (1986) 'Drought as a social phenomenon in Northeastern Brazil', in R Garcia and J Escudero (eds) *Drought and Man: The Roots of Catastrophe*, Pergamon Press, Oxford

Diaz, H and Markgraf, V (eds) (1992) *El Niño: Historical and Paleoclimatic Aspects of the Southern Oscillation*, Cambridge University Press, Cambridge

Douglas, M (1992) *Risk and Blame: Essays in Cultural Theory*, Routledge, London

Douglas, M and Wildavsky, A (1982) *Risk and Culture, An Essay on the Selection of Technological and Environmental Dangers,* University of California Press, Berkeley, Los Angeles and London

Downing, T E (1991) *Assessing Socio-economic Vulnerability to Famine: Frameworks, Concepts and Applications*, The Alan Shawn Feinstein World Hunger Program Research Report 91–1, Brown University, Providence, Rhode Island

Downing, T E, Rahman, A, Butterfield, R and Stephen, L (1999) 'Climate change and vulnerability: Toward a framework for comparing adaptability to climate change impacts', Paper Prepared for UNEP Workshop on Vulnerability Indicators, 5–6 October 1999

DPPC (1995) *Guidelines for the Early Warning System in Ethiopia*, Disaster Prevention and Preparedness Commission (DPPC), Addis Ababa

DPPC (1997) *Food Supply Prospects – 1998*, Disaster Prevention and Preparedness Commission (DPPC), Addis Ababa

DPPC (1998) *5-Year Plan of the Federal Disaster Prevention and Preparedness Commission, 1998–2002*, Disaster Prevention and Preparedness Commission (DPPC), Addis Ababa

Drabek, T E (1986) *Human Systems Response to Disasters*, Springer Verlag, New York

Drèze, J and Sen A (1989) *Hunger and Public Action,* Clarendon Press, Oxford

Dudley, E (1993) *The Critical Villager: Beyond Community Participation*, Routledge, London

Duffield, M (1993) 'NGOs, disaster relief and asset transfer in the Horn: Political survival in a permanent emergency', *Development and Change*, 24: 131–57

Duncan, R (2001) 'A conceptual framework for designing a country poverty reduction strategy', Paper Delivered at the Asia and Pacific Forum on Poverty, Asian Development Bank (ADB), Padig City, 5–9 February

Dynes, R (1983) 'Problems in emergency planning', *Energy*, 8: 653–60

Eade, D (1997) *Capacity Building: An Approach to People-Centred Development*, Oxfam Publications, Oxford

Eade, D (1999) (ed) *Development With Women*, Oxfam, Oxford

Eele, G and Stephen, L (1998) *The Impact of Food Aid on Developing Country Markets: A report commissioned by the World Food Programme*, Oxford Policy Management, Oxford

Elms, D G (1992) 'Risk Assessment', in D Blockley (ed) *Engineering Safety*, MacGraw-Hill, London

Enarson, E and Fordham, M (2001) 'Lines that divide, ties that bind: race, class, and gender in women's flood recovery in the US and UK', *Australian Journal of Emergency Management*, 15(4): 43–52

Enarson, E and Fordham, M (2002) 'From women's needs to women's rights in disasters', *Environmental Hazards*, 3: 133–6

Enarson, E and Morrow, B H (1997) 'A gendered perspective: the voices of women', in W G Peacock, B H Morrow and H Gladwin (eds) *Hurricane Andrew Ethnicity, Gender and the Sociology of Disasters*, Routledge, London

Enarson, E and Morrow, B H (eds) (1998) *Through Women's Eyes: The Gendered Terrain of Disaster,* Preager, Westport

Escobar, A (1995a) *Encountering Development, The Making and Unmaking of the Third World,* Princeton University Press, Princeton

Escobar, A (1995b) 'Imagining a post-development era', in J Crush (ed) *Power of Development*, Routledge, London and New York, pp211–27

Escobar, A (1999) 'After nature: Steps to an antiessentialist political ecology', *Current Anthropology*, 40(1): 1–30

Escobar, A (2001) 'Culture sits in places: Reflections on globalism and subaltern strategies of localization', *Political Geography*, 20: 139–74

Faber, D (1998) *The Struggle for Ecological Democracy*, Guilford, New York

Fairhead, J (1993) 'Representing knowledge: The "new" farmer in research fashions', in J Pottier (ed) *Practising Development, Social Science Perspectives*, Routledge, London

Faludi, S (1992) *Backlash: The Undeclared War Against American Women*, Anchor Books, New York

FAO (1993) 'Socio-economic and gender analysis programme', Food and Agriculture Organization (FAO), www.fao.org/sd/seaga/main1 en.htm#2

FAO (1998) *Food Outlook*, Report 5, Food and Agriculture Organization (FAO), Rome

Ferguson, J (1997) 'Anthropology and its evil twin', in F Cooper and R Packard (eds) *International Development and the Social Science; Essays on the History and Politics of Knowledge*, University of California Press, Berkeley, Los Angeles and London

Ferguson, J (1999) *Expectations of Modernity; Myths and Meanings of Urban Life on the Zambian Copperbelt*, University of California Press, Berkeley, Los Angeles and London

Fernandez, M A (ed) (1996) *Ciudades en Riesgo: Degradacion Ambiental, Riesgos Urbanos y Desastres*, La RED, Lima

Fernando, P and Fernando, V (1997) *South Asian Women: Facing Disasters, Securing Life*, Duryog Nivaran and Intermediate Technology Group, Colombo

Finan, T (1999) 'Drought and demagoguery: A political ecology of climate variability in Northeast Brazil', Workshop on Public Philosophy, Environment and Social Justice, Carnegie Council on Ethics and International Affairs, New York, 21–22 October

Fleishman, J (1984) 'Personality characteristics and coping patterns', *Journal of Health and Social Behaviour*, 25: 229–44

Fordham, M (1998) 'Making women visible in disasters: Problematizing the private domain', *Disasters*, 22(2):126–43

Fordham, M (2000) 'The place of gender in earthquake vulnerability and mitigation', Second Euro Conference on Global Change and Catastrophic Risk Management: Earthquake Risks in Europe, International Institute of Advanced Systems Analysis, Laxenburg, 6–9 July

Fordham, M (2003) 'Gender, disaster and development: the necessity of integration', in M Pelling (ed) *Natural Disaster and Development in a Globalizing World*, Routledge, London

Fordham, M and Ketteridge, A M (1998) 'Men must work and women must weep: Examining gender stereotypes in disasters', in E Enarson and B Morrow (eds) *Through Women's Eyes: The Gendered Terrain of Disaster*, Praeger, Westport

Forsyth, T (1996) 'Science, myth, and knowledge: Testing Himalayan environmental degradation in Thailand', *Geoforum*, 27: 375–92

Fothergill, A (1996) 'Gender, risk and disaster', *International Journal of Mass Emergencies and Disasters*, 14(1):33–56

Fothergill, A (1998) 'The neglect of gender in disaster work: An overview of the literature', in E Enarson and B Morrow (eds) *The Gendered Terrain of Disaster: Through Women's Eyes*, Praeger, Westport

Fotheringham, S (1997) 'Trends in quantitative methods 1: stressing the local', *Progress in Human Geography*, 21(1): 88–96

Foucault, M (1977) *Discipline and Punish: The Birth of the Prison*, Allen Lane, London

Foucault, M (1980) *Power/ Knowledge: Selected Interviews and other Writings, 1972–1977*, Harvester, Brighton

Fournier d'Albe, M (1985) 'The quantification of seismic hazard for the purposes of risk assessment', International Conference on Reconstruction, Restoration and Urban Planning of Towns and Regions in Seismic Prone Areas, Skopje

Fox J A and Brown, L D (eds) (1998) *The Struggle for Accountability: The World Bank, NGOs and Grass Roots Movements*, MIT Press, Cambridge

Frank, A (1967) *Capitalism and Underdevelopment in Latin America: Historical Studies of Chile and Brazil*, Monthly Review Press, New York

Freeman, P (2000) 'Estimating chronic risk from natural disasters in developing countries: A case study on Honduras', Paper Presented at the Annual Bank Conference on Development Economics – Europe, 'Development Thinking at the Millennium', Paris, 26–28 June, mimeo, International Institute for Applied Systems Analysis, Laxenburg

Freire, P (1982) *Extensão o Comunicação?*, Paz e Terra, São Paulo

Frerks, G (2000) 'Recreating coherence through the perspective of conflict and disaster: The role of local coping capacities', Paper Presented at the Tenth World Congress for Rural Sociology, Rio de Janeiro, 30 July–5 August 2000

Gandy, M (1996) 'Crumbling land: The post-modernity debate and the analysis of environmental problems', *Progress in Human Geography*, 20(1): 23–40

Geilfus, F (1997) *Ochenta Herramientas para el Desarrollo Participativo: Diagnóstico, Planificación, Monitoreo, Evaluación*, Servicio Jesuita a Refugiados (SJR), Bogotá, www.desplazados.org.co

Ghai, D and Vivian, J (eds) (1992) *Grass-roots Environmental Action: People's Participation in Sustainable Development*, Routledge, London

GHI and UNCHD (2001) *Global Earthquake Safety Initiative*, Pilot Project Final Report, Geo Hazards International (GHI) and UN Centre for Human Development (UNCHD), Kobe

Gibbons, M (1999) 'Science's new social contract with society', *Nature*, 402: 81–4

Gilbert, R and Kreimer, A (1999) 'Learning from the World Bank's experience of natural disaster related assistance', *Urban and Local Government Working Paper Series* 2, World Bank, Washington, DC

Glantz, M, (1994) 'Forecasting El Niño: Science's gift to the 21st Century', *EcoDecision*, 12: 78–81

Glantz, M (2001) *Currents of Change*, Cambridge Press, Cambridge

Goldsmith, W and Wilson, R (1991) 'Poverty and distorted industrialization in the Brazilian Northeast', *World Development*, 19: 435–55

Goodman, A and Leatherman, T (1998) *Building a New Biocultural Synthesis: Political Economic Perspectives in Biological Anthropology*, University of Michigan Press, Ann Arbor

Goonatilake, S (1984) *Aborted Discovery: Science and Creativity in the Third World*, Zed Books, London

Gottdiener, M (1995) *Post-modern Semiotics: Material Culture and the Forms of Post-Modern Life*, Blackwell, Oxford

Government of Ethiopia, IMF and World Bank (1998) 'Ethiopia: Enhanced structural adjustment facility medium-term economic and financial policy framework paper', 1998/ 1999–2000/ 2001, Section III, IMF/ World Bank, Washington, DC

Green, C and Warner, J (1999) 'Flood management: Towards a new paradigm', Paper Presented at the Stockholm Water Symposium, Stockholm, 9–12 August

Greenfield, G (1992) 'The great drought and elite discourse in imperial Brazil', *Hispanic American Historical Review*, 72: 375–400

Grenier, L (1998) *Working with Indigenous Knowledge: A Guide for Researchers*, International Development Research Centre (IDRC), Ottawa

Guha, R (1997) *Dominance Without Hegemony; History and Power in Colonial India*, Harvard University Press, Cambridge, Massachusetts and London

Gurr, T (1993) *Minorities at Risk: A Global View of Ethnopolitical Conflicts*, US Institute of Peace Press, Washington, DC

Habermas, J (1970) *Toward a Rational Society: Student Protest, Science, and Politics*, Beacon Press, Boston

Hajer, M (1993) 'The politics of environmental discourse: A study of the acid rain controversy in Great Britain and the Netherlands', DPhil thesis, University of Oxford, Oxford

Hall, B, Gillette, A and Tandon, R (eds) (1982) *Creating Knowledge: A Monopoly?* International Council for Adult Education, Toronto

Handmer J and Wisner, B (1998) 'Hazards, globalization and sustainability', for submission to *Development in Practice*, www.anglia.ac.uk/geography/radix

Haraway, D (1988) 'Situated knowledges: The science question in feminism and the privilege of partial perspective', *Feminist Studies* 14(3): 575–99

Haraway, D (1991) *Simians, Cyborgs and Women: The Reinvention of Nature*, Routledge, New York

Harding, S (1986) *The Science Question in Feminism,* Open University Press, Buckingham

Harding, S (1990) 'Feminism, science and the anti-enlightenment critiques', in L Nicholson (ed) *Feminism/Post-modernism*, Routledge, New York

Harding, S (1991) *Whose Science? Whose Knowledge? Thinking From Women's Lives*, Open University Press, Buckingham

Hardt, M and Negri A (2001) *Empire*, Harvard University Press, Cambridge

Harragin, S and Chol Changath Chol (1998) 'The Southern Sudan vulnerability study', Save the Children Fund, London

Harrison, M (1996) 'The tender frame of man: Disease, climate, and racial difference in India and the West Indies, 1760–1860', *Bulletin of the History of Medicine*, 70: 68–93

Hart, R (1997) *Children's Participation: The Theory and Practice of Involving Young Citizens in Community Development and Environmental Care*, Earthscan and UNICEF, London

Hartsock, N C M (1998) *The Feminist Standpoint Revisited*, Westview Press, Boulder, Colorado

Harvey, D (1989) *The Condition of Post-modernity*, Blackwell, Oxford

Harvey, D (1996) *Justice, Nature and the Geography of Difference*, Blackwell, Oxford

Harwell, E E (2000) 'Remote sensibilities: Discourses of technology and the making of Indonesia's natural disaster', *Development and Change*, 31: 307–40

Heijmans, A and Victoria, L (2001) *Citizenry-Based and Development-Oriented Disaster Response: Experience and Practice in Disaster Management of the Citizens' Disaster Response Network in the Philippines*, Center for Disaster Preparedness, Manila

Hekman, S (1997) 'Truth and method: Feminist standpoint theory revisited', *Signs*, 22(2): 341–65

Helander, E (1992) *Prejudice and Dignity: An Introduction to Community-Based Rehabilitation*, UN Development Programme (UNDP), New York

Herzfeld, M (1992) *The Social Production of Indifference, Exploring the Symbolic Roots of Western Bureaucracy*, Berg Publishers, Oxford/New York

Hewitt, K (1983a) 'The idea of calamity in a technocratic age', in K Hewitt (ed) *Interpretations of Calamity from the Viewpoint of Human Ecology*, Allen and Unwin, Boston

Hewitt, K (ed) (1983b) *Interpretations of Calamity from the Viewpoint of Human Ecology*, Allen and Unwin Inc, London and Sydney

Hewitt, K (1995) 'Sustainable disasters? Perspectives and power in the discourse of calamity', in J Crush (ed) *Power of Development*, Routledge, London and New York, pp115–28

Hewitt, K (1997) *Regions of Risk: A Geographical Introduction to Disasters*, Longman, Harrow and Essex

Heyman, B, Davis, C and Krumpe, P F (1991) 'An assessment of worldwide disaster vulnerability', *Disaster Management*, 4(1): 3–14

Hicks, D (1993) 'An Evaluation of the Zimbabwe drought relief programme 1992/1993: The roles of household level response and decentralized decision-making', mimeo, World Food Programme (WFP), Harare

Hilhorst, D (2000) *Records and Reputations; Everyday Politics of a Philippine Development NGO*, Ponsen and Looyen, Wageningen

Hilhorst, D (2001) 'Village experts and development discourse: "Progress" in a Philippine Igorot village', *Human Organization*, 60(4): 401–14

Hoddinott, J (1999) 'Targeting: Principles and practice', *Technical Guide* 9, International Food Policy Research Institute (IFPRI), Washington, DC

Hoffman, S and Oliver-Smith, A (1999) 'Anthropology and the angry earth: An overview', in A Oliver-Smith and S M Hoffman (eds) *The Angry Earth: Disaster in Anthropological Perspective*, Routledge, London

Holla, J and Vonhof, S (2001) 'One disaster and a multitude of realities: The aftermath of the Mozambican flood: The actors involved in the resettlement project in Xai–Xai', MSc thesis, Wageningen University, Wageningen, The Netherlands

Holland, J and Blackburn, J (1998) *Whose Voice? Participatory Research and Policy Change*, IT Books, London

Holling, C S (1994) 'An ecologist view of the Malthusian conflict', in K Lindahl–Kiessling and H Landberg (eds) *Population, Economic Development, and the Environment*, Oxford University Press, New York

Holling, C, Gunderson, L and Ludwig, D (2002) 'In quest of a theory of adaptive change', in L Gunderson and C Holling (eds) *Panarchy, Understanding Transformations in Human and Natural Systems*, Island Press, Washington, Covelo and London

Hood, C and Jones, D K C (1996) *Accident and Design: Contemporary Debates in Risk Management*, UCL Press, London

Hood, C, Rothstein, H and Baldwin, R (2000) *The Government of Risk: Understanding Risk Regulation Regimes*, Oxford University Press, Oxford

Hoogvelt, A (1997) *Globalization and the Post-Colonial World*, The Johns Hopkins University Press, Baltimore

Horigan, S (1988) *Nature and Culture in Western Discourses*, Routledge, London

House of Commons, International Development Committee (2002) 'Global climate change and sustainable development', Third Report of Session 2001–2002, *Recommendation*, 16(1): 74, The Stationary Office, London

Human Rights Watch (1998) 'Sudan: Global trade, local impact: Arms transfers to all sides of the civil war in Sudan', *Human Rights Watch*, 10(4A), New York

Huntington, S (1968) *Political Order in Changing Societies*, Yale University Press, New Haven

IBON (1998) 'Midyear Briefing, The Estrada Administration: coping with the economic crisis', *IBON Birdtalk*, Manila, 25 June

IBON (2000) 'San Roque Multi-Purpose Dam Project (SRMDP)', Special Release 57, December, Manila

IFRC (1993) *Vulnerability and Capacity Assessment: a Federation Guide,* International Federation of Red Cross and Red Crescent Societies (IFRC), Geneva

IFRC (1999a) 'Two quakes hit the Hindu Kush', *World Disasters Report 1999*, International Red Cross and Red Crescent Societies (IFRC), Geneva, pp69–83

IFRC (1999b) *Vulnerability and capacity assessment, An International Federation Guide*, International Federation of Red Cross and Red Crescent Societies (IFRC), Geneva

IFRC (1999c) *World Disaster Report*, International Federation of Red Cross and Red Crescent Societies (IFRC), Geneva

IFRC (2001) *World Disasters Report: Focusing on Reducing Risk*, International Federation of the Red Cross and Red Crescent Societies (IFRC), Geneva

IFRC (2002) *World Disasters Report 2002*, International Federation of Red Cross and Red Crescent Societies (IFRC), Geneva

IFRC (2002) 'Assessing vulnerabilities and capacities during peace and war', *World Disasters Report 2002*, International Red Cross and Red Crescent Societies (IFRC), Geneva, pp129–147

IMF and World Bank, (1999) 'Special program of assistance status report for Ethiopia, 1998', Africa Live Database, www.4.worldbank.org/afr/stats/ldb.cfm

Ingleton, J (ed) (1999) *Natural Disaster Management,* Tudor Rose, London

Ingold, T (1992) 'Culture and the perception of the environment', in E Croll and D Parkin (eds*) Bush, Base: Forest, Farm*, Routledge, London

Jamieson, D (1999) 'Nature and the limits of justice', Workshop on Public Philosophy, Environment and Social Justice, Carnegie Council on Ethics and International Affairs, New York, 21–22 October

Jansen, K (1998) *Political Ecology, Mountain Agriculture, and Knowledge in Honduras*, Thela, Amsterdam

Jasanoff, S and Wynne, B (1998) 'Scientific knowledge and decision-making', in S Rayner and E Malone (eds) *Human Choice and Climate Change*, Batelle Press, Washington, DC

Jaspars, S and Shoham, J (1999) 'Targeting the vulnerable: A review of the necessity and feasibility of targeting vulnerable households', *Disasters*, 23(4): 359–72

Johnson, B B and Covello, V T (1987) *The Social and Cultural Construction of Risk,* D Reidel Publishing Company, Dordrecht

Johnson, V, Ivan–Smith, E, Gordon, G, Pridmore, P and Scott, P (1998) *Stepping Forward: Children and Young People's Participation in the Development Process,* IT Publications, London

Kates, R W (1971) 'Natural hazard in human ecological perspective: hypotheses and models', *Economic Geography*, 47(3): 438–51

Kates, R W (1978) *Risk Assessment of Environment Hazard*, John Wiley and Sons, New York

Kearney, M (1996) *Reconceptualizing the Peasantry: Anthropology in Global Perspective*, Westview Press, Boulder, Colorado

Klinenberg, E (2002) *Heat Wave: The Social Autopsy of a Disaster*, University of Chicago Press, Chicago

Kotze, A von and Holloway, A (1998) *Reducing Risk: Participatory learning activities for disaster mitigation in southern Africa*, International Federation of Red Cross and Red Crescent Societies (IFRC) and Department of Adult and Community Education, University of Natal, Durban, www.oxfam.org.uk

Kreimer, A, Arnold, M (eds) and World Bank (1999) 'Managing disaster risk in Mexico: Market incentives for mitigation investment', *Disaster Risk Management Series* 1, World Bank, Washington, DC

Kuklick, H (1991) *The Savage Within: The Social History of British Anthropology, 1885–1945*, Cambridge University Press, Cambridge

Kuper, A (1988) *The Invention of Primitive Society: Transformations of an Illusion*, Routledge, London and New York

Lam, N and Quattrochi, D A (1992) 'On the issues of scale, resolution and fractal analysis in the mapping sciences', *The Professional Geographer*, 44(1): 88–98

Latour, B (1987) *Science in Action*, Harvard University Press, Cambridge

Lavell, A (1992) 'Ciencias sociales y desastres naturales en América Latina: Un encuentro inconcluso', Desastres Naturales, Sociedad y Protección Civil, COMECSO, México

Lavell, A (1994) 'Prevention and mitigation of disasters in Central America: Vulnerability to disasters at the local level', in A Varley (ed) *Disasters, Development and Environment*, Wiley, Chichester, pp49–63

Lavell, A (1996) 'Degradación ambiental, riesgo y desastre urbano: Problemas y conceptos', in M A Fernandez (ed) *Ciudades en Riesgo*, La RED, USAID, Lima

Lavell, A (1999) 'The impact of disasters on development gains: Clarity or controversy', Paper Presented at the IDNDR Programme Forum, Geneva, 5–9 July

Lees, S and Bates, D (1984) 'Environmental events and the ecology of cumulative change', in E Moran (ed) *The Ecosystem Concept in Anthropology*, Westview Press, Boulder, Colorado, pp133–59

Lees, S and Bates, D (1990) 'The ecology of cumulative change', in E Moran (ed) *The Ecosystem Approach in Anthropology*, University of Michigan Press, Ann Arbor

Lefebvre, H (1991) *The Production of Space*, Blackwell, Oxford and Cambridge

Lehat, M (1990) 'The International Decade for Natural Disaster Reduction: Background and objectives', *Disasters*, 14(1): 1–6

Lemos, M C (2002) 'A tale of two forecasts: The politics of seasonal climate forecast use in Ceará, Brazil', *Policy Sciences*

Levin, R and Weiner, D (1997) *'No More Tears': Struggles for Land in Mpumalanga, South Africa*, Africa World Press, Trenton

Lewis, J (1999) *Development in Disaster-Prone Places; Studies of Vulnerability*, Intermediate Technology Publications, London

Linde, P van der (2001) 'An evaluation of the flood warning system in the Orange River Basin', MSc thesis, Wageningen University, Wageningen, The Netherlands

List, F (1856) *The National System of Political Economy*, J B Lippincott, Philadelphia

Little, P and Painter M (1995) 'Discourse, politics, and the development process: Reflections on Escobar's anthropology and the development encounter', *American Ethnologist*, 22(3): 606–9

Liverman D M (1990) 'Vulnerability to global environmental change', in K Dow et al (eds) *Understanding Global Environmental Change: The Contributions of Risk Analysis and Management*, Clark University, Worcester, MA

Liverman, D, Moran, E, Rindfuss, R and Stern, P (eds) (1998) *People and Pixels: Linking Remote Sensing and Social Science*, National Academy Press, Washington, DC

Locke, J (1965) *Two Treatises on Government*, New American Library-Mentor, New York

Long, N (1992) 'From paradigm lost to paradigm regained? The case for an actor-oriented sociology of development', in N Long and A Long (eds) *Battlefields of Knowledge: The Interlocking of Theory and Practice in Social Research and Development*, Routledge, London and New York

Long, N (2001) *Development Sociology: Actor Perspectives*, Routledge, London

Long, N and Ploeg, J D van der (1989) 'Demythologizing planned intervention: An actor-oriented perspective', *Sociologia Ruralis*, XXIX(3/4): 226–49

Long, N and Villarreal, M (1993) 'Exploring development interfaces: From the transfer of knowledge to the transformation of meaning', in F Schuurman (ed) *Beyond the Impasse: New Directions in Development Theory*, Zedbooks, London

Luhmann, L (1993) *Risk: A Sociological Theory*, Aldine de Gruyter, New York

MacKellar, L, Freeman, P and Ermolieva, T (1999) 'Estimating natural catastrophic risk exposure and the benefits of risk transfer in developing countries', mimeo, International Institute for Applied Systems Analysis, Laxenburg

Magalhaes, A and Glantz, M (eds) (1992) *Socioeconomic Impacts of Climate Variations and Policy Responses in Brazil*, Esquel Brazil Foundation and UNEP, Brasilia

Mansilla, E (ed) (1996) *Desastres: Modelo para Armar*, La RED, Lima

March, C, Smyth, I and Mukhopadhyay, M (1999) *A Guide to Gender-Analysis Frameworks*, Oxfam, Oxford

Marglin, F and Marglin, S (eds) (1990) *Dominating Knowledge: Development, Culture, and Resistance*, Clarendon Press, Oxford

Marston, S A (2000) 'The social construction of scale', *Progress in Human Geography*, 24(2): 219–42

Maskrey, A (1989) 'Disaster mitigation: A community based approach', *Development Guidelines* 3, Oxfam, Oxford

Maskrey, A (1994) 'Comunidad y desastres en América Latina: Estrategias de intervención', in A Lavell (ed) *Viviendo en Riesgo: Comunidades Vulnerables y Prevención de Desastres en América Latina*, La RED, Tercer Mundo Editores, Bogotá

Maskrey, A (ed) (1998) *Navegando entre Brumas: La Aplicación de los Sistemas de Información Geográfica al Análisis de Riesgo en América Latina*, LA RED and IT Peru, Lima

Maskrey, A (1999) 'Reducing global disasters', in J Ingelton (ed) *Natural Disaster Management*, Tudor Rose, Leicester, pp84–86

Maxwell, D G (1996) 'Measuring food insecurity: the frequency and severity of coping strategies', *Food Policy*, 21(3): 291–303

Maxwell, S (1994) 'Food security: a post-modern perspective', *Working Paper* 9, Institute of Development Studies, IDS Publications, University of Sussex, Brighton

Maynard, M (ed) (1997) *Science and the Construction of Women*, UCL Press, London

McDowell, L (1999) *Gender, Identity and Place: Understanding Feminist Geographies*, Polity Press, Cambridge

McDowell, L (ed) (1997) *Undoing Place? A Geographical Reader*, Arnold, London

Meillassoux, C (1974) 'Development or exploitation: Is the Sahel famine good business?', *Review of African Political Economy*, 1: 27–33]

Merchant, C (1980) *The Death of Nature: Women, Ecology and the Scientific Revolution*, Harper and Row, San Francisco

Mesfin Wolde-Mariam (1986) *Rural Vulnerability to Famine in Ethiopia, 1958–1977*, Intermediate Technology Publications, London

Mies, M and Shiva, V (1993) *Ecofeminism,* Zed Books, London

Mikulecky, D (1997) 'Life, complexity and the edge of chaos: Cognitive aspects of

communication between cells and other components of living systems',
www.griffin.vcu.edu/complex/mikulecky/rev.htm

Mileti, D S (1996) 'Psicología social de las alertas públicas efectivas de desastres, Especial:
Predicciones, Pronósticos, Alertas y Respuestas Sociales, Revista', *Desastres & Sociedad* 6,
La RED, Tarea Gráfica, Lima

Mileti, D (1999) *Disasters by Design: A Reassessment of Natural Hazards in the United States,*
Joseph Henry Press, Washington, DC

Mitchell, J K (2003) '"The fox and the hedgehog: Myopia about homeland vulnerability in
US policies on terrorism" – Terrorism and Disaster: New Threat, New Ideas', *Research
in Social Problems and Public Policy,* 11: 53–72

Moeller, S (1999) *Compassion Fatigue: How the Media Sell Disease, Famine, War and Death,*
Routledge, New York

Mohanty, C T (1991) 'Under Western eyes feminist scholarship and colonial discourses', in
C T Mohanty, A Russo and L Torres (eds) *Third World Women and the Politics of Feminism,*
Indiana University Press, Bloomington and Indianapolis

Morris, D W (1996) 'Ecological scale and habitat use', *Ecology,* 68: 362–9

Morrow, B (1999) 'Identifying and mapping community vulnerability', *Disasters,* 23(1):
1–18

Mudimbe, V (1988) *The Invention of Africa: Gnosis, Philosophy, and the Order of Knowledge,*
University of Indiana Press, Bloomington

Mula, R P (1999) 'Coping with mother nature: Households' livelihood security and coping
strategies in a situation of a continuing disaster in Tarlac', PhD thesis, Wageningen,
The Netherlands

Munich Re (1999) 'A year, a century, and a millennium of natural catastrophes are all
nearing their end', Press Release, 20 December, Munich Reinsurance, Munich

Muñoz-Carmona, F A (1997) 'Notes on communication and volcanic risk', in B M Drottz
Sjoberg (ed) *New Risk Frontiers,* 10th Anniversary, The Society for Risk Analysis –
Europe, Centre for Risk, Stockholm

Murphy, A (1993) 'What is a good forecast? An essay on the nature of goodness in weather
forecasting', *Weather and Forecasting,* 8: 281–93

Murphy, R (1994) *Rationality and Nature,* Westview Press, Boulder, Colorado

Neal, D M and Phillips, B D (1990) 'Female-dominated local social movement
organizations in disaster-threat situations', in G West and R L Blumberg (eds) *Women
and Social Protest,* Oxford Unversity Press, New York

Neal, D M and Phillips, B D (1995) 'Effective emergency management: reconsidering the
bureaucratic approach', *Disasters,* 19(4): 327–37

Nowotny, H, Scott, P and Gibbons, M (2001) *Re-thinking Science: Knowledge Production in an
Age of Uncertainty,* Polity Press, Cambridge

O'Brien, M (2000) *Making Better Environmental Decisions: An Alternative to Risk Assessment,*
MIT Press, Cambridge

OAS/Department of Regional Development and Environment (1990) *Disasters, Planning
and Development: Managing Natural Hazards to Reduce Loss,* Organization of American
States (OAS), Washington, DC

OAS (1999) 'Investing in mitigation: Costs and benefits', Caribbean Disaster Mitigation
Project, OAS website, http://www.oas.org/en/cdmp/costbene.htm

ODI (1998) *The Future of Food Aid: Summary Findings and Recommendations,* Overseas
Development Institute (ODI), London

Oliver-Smith, A (1979) 'The Yungay avalanche of 1970: Anthropological perspectives on
disaster and social change', *Disasters,* 3(1): 95–101

Oliver-Smith, A (1986) 'Disaster context and causation: An overview of changing
perspectives in disaster research', in A Oliver-Smith (ed) *Natural Disasters and Cultural
Responses,* College of William and Mary, Williamsburg, pp1–38

Oliver-Smith, A (1994) 'Peru's five-hundred-year earthquake: Vulnerability in historical context', in A Varley (ed) *Disasters, Development, and Environment,* John Wiley and Sons, Chichester, pp3–48

Oliver-Smith, A (1996) 'Anthropological research on hazards and disasters', *Annual Review of Anthropology,* 25: 303–28

Oliver-Smith, A (1999a) 'What is a disaster?: Anthropological perspectives on a persistent question', in A Oliver-Smith and S M Hoffman (eds) *The Angry Earth: Disaster in Anthropological Perspective,* Routledge, London

Oliver-Smith, A (1999b) 'Peru's five-hundred-year earthquake: Vulnerability in historical context', in A Oliver-Smith and S M Hoffman (eds) *The Angry Earth: Disaster in Anthropological Perspective,* Routledge, London

Oliver-Smith, A (2001) 'Displacement, resistance and the critique of development: From the grass roots to the global', Final Report Prepared for ESCOR R7644 and the Research Programme on Development Induced Displacement and Resettlement, Refugee Studies Centre, University of Oxford, Oxford, www.qeh.ac.uk/rsp/

Oliver-Smith, A and Hoffman, S (eds) (1999) *The Angry Earth; Disaster in Anthropological Perspectives,* Routledge, New York and London

Olson, R, Sarmiento, J, Gawronski, V and Estrada, A (2000) 'The marginalization of disaster response institutions: The 1997–1998 El Niño experience in Peru, Bolivia and Ecuador', *Special Publication 36*, Natural Hazards Research Applications and Information Centre, Boulder, Colorado

Orlove, B and Tosteson, J (1999) 'The application of seasonal to interannual climate forecasts based on ENSO events: Lessons from Australia, Brazil, Ethiopia, Peru, and Zimbabwe', International Studies Working Paper, UC Berkeley Inst, Berkeley

Otero, R C and Marti, R Z (1995)'The impacts of natural disasters on developing economies: Implications for the international development and disaster community', in M Munasinghe and C Clarke (eds) *Disaster Prevention for Sustainable Development: Economic and Policy Issues,* Report from the Yokohama World Conference on Natural Disaster Reduction, 23–27 May 1994, World Bank and International Decade for Natural Disaster Reduction, Washington, DC

Oxfam (2000) *The Sphere Project: The Humanitarian Charter and Minimum Standards in Disaster Response,* www.sphereproject.org

Paine, R (2002) 'Danger and the no risk thesis', in S M Hoffman and A Oliver-Smith (eds) *Catastrophe and Culture: The Anthropology of Disaster,* SAR Press, Santa Fe

Palmer, B (1990) *Descent into Discourse: The Reification of Language and the Writing of Social History,* Temple University Press, Philadelphia

Parker, D and Handmer J (1997) 'The role of unofficial flood forecast warnings', *Journal of Contingencies and Crisis Management,* 6: 45–60

Paulik, G (1971) 'Anchovies, birds and fishermen in the Peru current', in W Murdoch (ed) *Environment: Resources, Pollution and Society,* Sinauer Assoc, Stamford Connecticut

Peacock, W, Morrow, B and Gladwin, H (eds) (1997) *Hurricane Andrew: Ethnicity, Gender, and the Sociology of Disaster,* Routledge, London

Pelling, M (1997) 'What determines vulnerability to floods: A case study in Georgetown, Guyana', *Environment and Urbanisation,* 9(1): 203–26

Peri Peri (ed) (1999) *Risk, Sustainable Development, and Disasters: Southern Perspectives,* Peri Peri Publications and Disaster Mitigation for Sustainable Livelihoods, Department of Environmental and Geographical Sciences, University of Cape Town, Cape Town, www.egs.uct.ac.za/dimp/

Perrow, C (1984) *Normal Accidents: Living with High Risk Technologies,* Princeton University Press, Princeton

Pessoa, D (1987) 'Drought in Northeast Brazil: Impacts and government response', in D Wilhite and W Easterling (eds) *Planning for Drought: Toward a Reduction of Societal*

Vulnerability, Westview Press, Boulder, Colorado

Pfaff, A, Broad, K and Glantz, M (1999) 'Who benefits from climate forecasts?', *Nature*, 397: 645–6

Pickles, J (ed) (1995) *Ground Truth: The Social Implications of Geographic Information Systems*, Guilford, New York

Pieterse, J (1998) 'My paradigm or yours? Alternative development, post-development, reflexive development', *Development and Change*, 29: 343–73

Platt, R (1999) *Disasters and Democracy: The Politics of Extreme Natural Events,* Island Press, Washington, DC

Plummer, J (2000) *Municipalities and Community Participation: A Sourcebook for Capacity Building*, Earthscan, London

Possekel, A (1999) *Living with the Unexpected: Linking Disaster Recovery to Sustainable Development in Montserrat*, Springer-Verlag, Berlin, Heidelberg, New York and Tokyo

Pradervand, P (1989) *Listening to Africa: Developing Africa from the Grass Roots*, Praeger, New York

ProVention Consortium (2001) *ProVention Consortium Disaster Database Working Group Meeting*, Report of Proceedings, Provention Consortium, 5 February, www.provention consortium.org/econanalysis.htm

Pulwarty, R and Redmond, K (1997) 'Climate and salmon restoration in the Columbia River basin: The role and usability of seasonal forecasts', *Bulletin of the American Meteorological Society*, 78: 381–97

Pulwarty, R and Riebsame, W (1997) 'The political ecology of vulnerability to hurricane-related hazards', in H Diaz and R Pulwarty (eds) *Hurricanes: Climate and Socio-economic impacts*, Springer-Verlag, Heidelberg

Quarantelli, E L (1985) 'What is a disaster? The need for clarification in definition and conceptualization in research', in S Solomon (ed) *Disasters and Mental Health: Selected Contemporary Perspectives*, US Government Printing Office, Washington, DC

Quarantelli, E L (1988) 'Disaster studies: An analysis of the social historical factor affecting the development of research in the area', *International Journal of Mass Emergencies*, 5(3): 285–310

Quarantelli, E L (1991) 'More and worse disasters in the future', Paper Presented at the UCLA International Conference on the Impact of Natural Disasters: Agenda for Future Action, Los Angeles, California, 10–12 July

Quarantelli, H (1973) Conversation with I Davis, Columbus Ohio, March 1973

Radder, H (1992) 'Normative reflections on constructivist approaches to science and technology', *Social Studies of Science*, 22: 141–73

Rahnema, M and Bawtree, V (eds) (1997) *The Post-Development Reader*, Zed Books, London

Rawls, J (1971) *A Theory of Justice*, Belknap/Harvard University Press, Cambridge

Redmond, C L (1999) *Human Impact on Ancient Environments*, University of Arizona Press, Tucson

Reis, J (1981) 'Hunger in the Northeast', in S Mitchell (ed) *The Logic of Poverty: The Case of the Brazilian Northeast*, Routledge and Kegan Paul, London

Renn, O (1992) 'Risk communication: Towards a rational discourse with the public', *Journal of Hazardous Materials*, 29: 465

Richards, P (1989) 'Agriculture as a performance', in R Chambers, A Pacey and L A Thrupp (eds) *Farmer First: Farmer Innovation and Agricultural Research*, Intermediate Technology Publications, London

Rijkswaterstaat (2002) 'Ruimte voor de Rivier, Startnotitie MER in het kader van PKB Procedure', Rijkswaterstaat, The Hague

Robben, A C G M (1989) *Sons of the Sea Goddess*, Columbia University Press, New York

Roe, E (1991) 'Development narratives, or making the best of blueprint development', *World Development*, 19(4): 287–300

Rostow, W (1960) *The Stages of Economic Growth: A Non-Communist Manifesto*, Cambridge University Press, Cambridge

Rowan-Campbell, D (1999) 'Development with women', in D Eade (ed) *Development With Women*, Oxfam, Oxford

Said, E (1979) *Orientalism*, Random House, New York

Said, E (1994) *Culture and Imperialism*, Vintage, London

Sanderson, D (2000) 'Cities, disasters and livelihoods', *Environment and Urbanization*, 12(2): 93–102

Schaefer, M (1970) 'Men, birds and anchovies in the Peru Current: Dynamic interactions', *Transactions of the American Fishery Society*, 99: 461–67

Schrijvers, Joke (1991) 'Dialectics of a Dialogue Ideal: Studying Down, Studying Sideways and Studying Up' in Lorrain Nencel and Peter Pels (eds) *Constructing Knowledge: Authority and Critique in Social Science*, Sage, London,Newbury Park, Delhi

Scott, J (1985) *Weapons of the Weak: Everyday Forms of Peasant Resistance*, Yale University Press, New Haven

Scott, J (1990) *Domination and the Arts of Resistance*, Yale University Press, New Haven

Scott, J C (1998) *Seeing Like a State: How Certain Schemes to Improve the Human Condition Have Failed*, Yale University Press, New Haven

Sen, A (1981) *Poverty and Famine: An Essay on Entitlement and Deprivation*, Clarendon, Oxford

Sen, A (2000) *Development as Freedom*, Alfred A Knopf, New York

SERA, PPPD and DPPC (1999) 'National guidelines for vulnerability profile development', Guidelines Prepared by Strengthening Emergency Response Abilities; Policy, Planning and Program Department; and Disaster Prevention and Preparedness Commission, Addis Ababa

Shackley, S, Wynne, B and Waterton, C (1996) 'Imagine complexity: The past, present and future potential of complex thinking', *Futures*, 28(3): 201–25

Sharp, K (1998) 'Between relief and development: Targeting food aid for disaster prevention in Ethiopia', *RRN* 27, Overseas Development Institute (ODI), London

Shukman, D (2001) 'Crying wolf in Africa,' *The Spectator*, 17 March

Slovic, P (1992) 'Perceptions of risk: Reflections on the psychometric paradigm', in S Krimsky and Golding (eds) *Social Theories of Risk*, Praeger, Wesport

Smith, D (1987) *The Everyday World as Problematic: A Feminist Sociology*, Northeastern University, Boston

Smith, K (1996, 1999) *Environmental Hazards: Assessing Risks and Reducing Disaster*, 2nd edition, Routledge, New York, London

Smith, K and Ward, R (1998) *Floods: Physical Processes and Human Impacts*, John Wiley and Sons, Chichester, New York, Wernhem, Brisbane, Singapore and Toronto

Smith, N (1995) 'Remaking scale: Competition and cooperation in pre-national and post-national Europe', in H Eskelinen and G Snickars (eds) *Competitive European Peripheries*, Springer, Berlin, pp59–74

Social Watch–Instituto del Tercer Mundo (1997) www.fp.chasque.apc.org:8081/socwatch/1997/feminiza–poverty.htm

Solomon Islands Government (2000) *Comprehensive Policy for the Mitigation and Management of Civil and Ethnic Unrest for the Solomon Islands Government*, Honiara

Soto, L (1998) *Módolos para la Capacitación: Guia de La RED para la Gestión Local del Riesgo*, La RED and IT Peru, Quito

Souza, I and Filho, J (1983) *Os deagregados, Fillhos da Sec: Uma Analise Socio-Politica das Secas do Nordeste*, Editors Voces, Petropolis

SPHERE Project (2000) *Humanitarian Charter and Minimum Standards in Disaster Response*, SPHERE Project, Geneva, www.sphereproject.org/

Stacey, R, Griffin, D and Shaw, P (2000) *Complexity and Management: Fad or a Radical Challenge to Systems Thinking?* Routledge, London and New York

Starr C (1969) 'Social benefit versus technological risk', *Science*, 165, American Association for the Advancement of Science

Stephen, L J (2002a) 'The complexity of vulnerability', unpublished PhD thesis 'Vulnerability and Food Insecurity in Ethiopia', University of Oxford, Oxford

Stephen, L J (2002b) 'Famine early warning systems as political systems', unpublished PhD thesis 'Vulnerability and Food Insecurity in Ethiopia', University of Oxford, Oxford

Stocking, G (1968) *Race, Culture, and Evolution; Essays in the History of Anthropology*, The Free Press and Collier-Macmillan, New York and London

Stonich, S (1993) *'I Am Destroying the Land!' The Political Ecology of Poverty and Environmental Destruction in Honduras*, Westview Press, Boulder, Colorado

Stonich, S (1999) 'Comments', *Current Anthropology*, 40(1): 23–4

Susman, P, O'Keefe, P and Wisner, B (1983) 'Global disasters: A radical interpretation', in K Hewitt (ed) *Interpretations of Calamity from the Viewpoint of Human Ecology*, Allen and Unwin, Boston, pp264–83

Sweetman, C (ed) (1997) *Men and Masculinity*, Oxfam, Oxford

Tainter, J A (1988) *The Collapse of Complex Societies*, Cambridge University Press, New York

Tester, K (1991) *Animals and Society: The Humanity of Animal Rights* Routledge, London

Thomas, K (1983) *Man and the Natural World: Changing Attitudes in England, 1500–1800*, Allen and Unwin, London

Thompson, P (1999) 'Damage and needs assessments: Ex-post response', mimeo, InterWorks, Madison

Thorp, R and Bertram, G (1978) *Peru 1890–1977: Growth and Policy in an Open Community*, Columbia University Press, New York

Tierney, K, Petak, W and Hahn, H (1988) 'Disabled Persons and Earthquake Hazards', *Monograph* 46, Institute of Behavioral Science, Program on Environment and Behavior, Boulder, Colorado

Timmerman, P (1981) 'Vulnerability, resilience and the collapse of society', *Environmental Monograph* 1, Institute for Environmental Studies, University of Toronto, Toronto

Toulmin, C (1995) 'Tracking through drought: Options for destocking and restocking', in I Scoones (ed) *Living with Uncertainty: New Directions in Pastoral Development in Africa*, Intermediate Technology Publications, London

Trujillo, M, Ordóñez, A and Hernández, C (2000) 'Risk-Mapping and Local Capacities', Oxfam Working Papers, Oxfam Publications, Oxford

Turcios, A, Jaraguin, U and Riviera, D (2000) *Hacia una Gestión Ecológica de los Riesgos: Bases Conceptuales y Metodologicas para un Sistema Nacional de Prevención y Mitigación de Desastres, y de Protección Civil*, Lutheran World Federation and Unidad Ecologica Salvadoreña, San Salvador

Twigg, J and Bhatt, M (1998) *Understanding Vulnerability: South Asian Perspectives*, Intermediate Technology Publications, London and Colombo

Uitto, J I (1998) 'The geography of disaster vulnerability in megacities', *Applied Geography*, 18(1): 7–16

UN International Decade for Natural Disaster Reduction (IDNDR) (1992) *Stop Disasters*, Newsletter

UNDP (UN Development Programme) (1994) *Human Development Report 1994*, UN Development Plan (UNDP), New York

UNDP (2000) *Human Development Report*, Oxford University Press, New York

UNDRO (1990) *Preliminary Study on the Identification of Disaster–Prone Countries Based on Economic Impact,* UN Disaster Relief Organization (UNDRO), New York and Geneva

UNHCR (1994) *Report of the UN Secretary General to the Commission of Human Rights*, UN High Commissioner for Refugees (UNHCR), Geneva

Valasquez, G, Uitto, J, Wisner, B and Takahashi, S (1999) 'A new approach to disaster mitigation and planning in mega-cities: The pivotal role of social vulnerability in disaster risk management', in T Inoguchi, E Newman and G Paoletto (eds) *Cities and the Environment: New Approaches to Eco-Societies*, UN University Press, Tokyo

Vargas Llosa, M (1997) *The War at the End of the World*, Penguin Books, New York

Varley, A (1994a) 'The exceptional and the everyday: Vulnerability in the International Decade for Disaster Reduction', in A Varley (ed) *Disasters, Development and Environment*, John Wiley and Sons, Chichester, pp1–11

Varley, A (ed) (1994b) *Disasters, Development and Environment*, Wiley, London

Vayda, A and McKay, B (1975) 'New directions in ecology and ecological anthropology', *Annual Review of Anthropology*, 4: 293–306

Villarreal, M (1994) 'Wielding and yielding: Power, subordination and gender identity in the context of a Mexican development project', PhD thesis, Wageningen University, Wageningen, The Netherlands

Waal, A de (1997) *Famine Crimes: Politics and the Disaster Relief Industry in Africa*, Africa Rights, International African Institute, and James Currey, London and Oxford

Waldrop, M (1992) *Complexity: The Emerging Science at the Edge of Order and Chaos*, Viking, London

Walker, P (1989) *Famine Early Warning Systems: Victims & Destitution*, Earthscan, London

Walker, P and Walter J (eds) (2000) *World Disasters Report 2000: Focus on Public Health*, International Federation of Red Cross and Red Crescent Societies (IFRC), Geneva

Warner, J, Waalewijn, P and Hilhorst, D (2002) *Public Participation in Disaster-Prone Watersheds: Time for Multi-Stakeholder Platforms?* Disaster Sites 6, Wageningen Disaster Studies, Wageningen

Watts, M (1983) 'On the Poverty of Theory: Natural Hazards Research in Context', in K Hewitt (ed) *Interpretation of Calamity from the Viewpoint of Human Ecology*, Allen and Unwin, Boston

Watts, M (1993) 'Hunger, famine and the space of vulnerability', *GeoJournal*, 30(2): 117–25

Watts, M (1995) 'A new deal in emotions: Theory and practice and the crisis of development', in J Crush (ed) *Power of Development*, Routledge, London and New York, pp44–61

Webb, P, Richardson, E, Seyoum, S and Yisehac, Y (1994) *Vulnerability Mapping and Geographical Targeting: An exploratory methodology applied to Ethiopia*, Report to the US Agency for International Development, Health and Human Resources Analysis for Africa Project, Order 6, IFPRI, Washington, DC

Weiskel, T C and Grey, R A (1992) *Environmental Decline and Public Policy,* The Pierian Press, Ann Arbor

Westgate, K N and O'Keefe, P (1976) 'Some definitions of disaster', *Occasional Paper 4*, Disaster Research Unit, University of Bradford, Bradford

White, G F (1942) 'Human adjustment to floods: A geographical approach to the flood problem in the US', *Research Paper 29*, Department of Geography, University of Chicago, Chicago

White, G F (1973) 'Natural hazards research', in J Chorley (ed) *Directions in Geography*, Methuen, London, pp193–216

White, G F, Kates, R W and Burton, I (2001) 'Knowing better and losing even more: The use of knowledge in hazards management', *Environmental Hazards*, 3(3/4): 81–92

White, L Jr (1967) 'The historical roots of our ecological crisis', *Science*, 155(3767): 1203–7

White, S (1997) 'Men, masculinities and the politics of development, in Sweetman, C (ed) *Men and Masculinity*, Oxfam, Oxford

White, S C (2000) '"Did the earth move?" The hazards of bringing men and masculinities into gender and development', *IDS Bulletin*, 31(2): 33–41

Whitman R V (1975) 'Seismic design decision analysis', *Journal of the Structural Division*, American Society of Civil Engineers (ASCE), New York

Wijkman, A and Timberlake, L (1984) *Natural Disasters: Acts of God or Acts of Man?* Earthscan, Washington, DC

Wilches-Chaux, G (1989) *Desastres, Ecologismo, y Formación Profesional*, Servicio Nacional de Aprendizaje (SENA), Popayán

Wilches-Chaux, G (1998) *Auge, Caida y Levantada de Felipe Pinillo, Mecanico y Soldador, Guia de La RED para la Gestion Local del Riesgo*, La RED, Lima

Wilches-Chaux, G and Wilches-Chaux, S (2001) *¡Ni de Riesgos!* Fondo Para la Reconstucción y Desarrollo de Eje Cafetero, Bogotá,

Wildavsky, A (1991) 'Risk perception', *Risk Analysis*, 11(1)

Williams, R (1980) *Problems in Materialism and Culture*, Verso, New York

Winchester, P (1992) *Power, Choice and Vulnerability: A Case Study in Disaster Mismanagement in South India*, James and James, London

Winterhaler, B (1980) 'Environmental analysis in human evolution and adaptation research', *Human Ecology*, 8: 137–70

Wisner, B (1988) *Power and Need in Africa: Basic Human Needs and Development Policies*, Earthscan and Africa World Press, London and Trenton

Wisner, B (1993) 'Disaster vulnerability: Scale, power and daily life', *GeoJournal*, 30(2): 127–40

Wisner, B (1994a) 'Teaching African science: Notes on common sense, tribal war, and the end of history', in P Allen, D Lloyd and A Samatar (eds) *African Studies and the Undergraduate Curriculum*, Lynne Reinner, Boulder, Colorado

Wisner, B (1994b) '*Jilaal, gu, hagaa*, and *der*: Living with the Somali land, and living well', in A Samatar (ed) *The Somali Challenge: From Catastrophe to Renewal?* Lynne Reinner, Boulder, Colorado

Wisner, B (1995a) 'Bridging expert and local knowledge for counter-disaster planning in urban South Africa', *GeoJournal*, 37(3): 335–48

Wisner, B (1995b) '*Luta*, livelihood, and lifeworld in contemporary Africa', in B Taylor (ed) *Ecological Resistance Movements*, SUNY Press, Albany

Wisner, B (1996a) 'The limitations of carrying capacity, part I', *Political Environments*, 3: 1–6

Wisner, B (1996b) 'The geography of vulnerability', in J Uitto and J Schneider (eds) *Preparing for the Big One in Tokyo: Urban Earthquake Risk Management*, UN University Press, Tokyo

Wisner, B (1997) 'The limitations of carrying capacity, part II', *Political Environments*, 5: S3–S7 and S26–S27

Wisner, B (1998) 'Marginality and vulnerability', *Applied Geography*, 18(1): 25–33

Wisner, B (1999) 'There are worse things than earthquakes: Hazard vulnerability and mitigation in Los Angeles', in J Mitchell (ed) *Crucibles of Hazard: Mega-Cities and Disasters in Transition*, UN University Press, Tokyo, pp375–427

Wisner, B (2000) 'From acts of God to water wars', in D Parker (ed) *Floods*, Routledge, London, Vol 1, pp89–99,

Wisner, B (2001) 'NGOs and the neoliberal state: Why post-Mitch lessons didn't reduce El Salvador's earthquake losses', *Disasters* 25(3): 251–68

Wisner, B (2002) 'Disaster Risk Reduction in Megacities: Making the Most of Human and Social Capital', Paper presented at the workshop The Future of Disaster Risk: Building Safer Cities, Washington, DC, World Bank and the ProVention Consortium, 4–6 December

Wisner, B (2003a) 'Disability and disaster: Victimhood and agency in earthquake risk reduction', in R Rodrigue and E Rovai (eds) *Earthquakes*, Routledge, London (forthcoming)

Wisner, B (2003b) 'Urban social vulnerability to disaster in Greater Los Angeles', in S Sassen (ed) *Cities (Encyclopedia of the Life Support Systems)*, UNESCO, Paris (forthcoming)

Wisner, B, Kruks, S and Stea, D (1991) 'Participatory and action research methods', in E Zube and G Moore (eds) *Advances in Environment, Behavior and Design*, Plenum, New York

Wisner, B, Blaikie, P, Cannon, T and Davis, I (2003) *At Risk: Natural Hazards, People's Vulnerability and Disasters*, (2nd edition) Routledge, London

Wisner, B and Lewis, H (1981) 'Refugee rehabilitation in Somalia', *Consulting Report 6*, Regional Development Project, University of Wisconsin at Madison, Madison

Wisner, B and Yapa, L (1995) 'Building a case against economic development', *GeoJournal*, 35(2): 105–18

Wisner, B et al (1979) 'Designing storage systems with villagers', *African Environment*, 3(3–4): 85–95

Wisner, B et al (1999) *Toward a Culture of Prevention in Two Coastal Communities: A comparison of the hazardousness of San Pedro and Laguna Beach*, Research Report, California State University at Long Beach, Long Beach

Wong, S (2001) *Status Report of Planned Dams in East and Southeast Asia*, RWESA, p49

Woolgar, S (1988) *Science: The Very Idea*, Ellis Harwood and Tavistock, Chichester and London

World Bank (1988) *The Philippines: The Challenge of Poverty*, World Bank, Washington, DC

World Bank (1999) 'World Bank aid flows', www.worldbank.org/data

World Bank (2000) *World Development Report 2000/2001: Attacking Poverty*, Oxford University Press, New York

Wynne, B (1987) *Risk Management and Hazardous Waste: Implementation and the dialectics of credibility*, Springer-Verlag, Berlin

Wynne, B (1994) 'Scientific knowledge and the global environment' in M Redclift and T Benton (eds) *Social Theory and the Global Environment*, Routledge, London

Young, L (1999) 'Gender and hunger: Salvaging essential categories', *Area*, 31(2): 99–109

Zapata, A (1998) *Los Actors de la Pesca Industrial Peruana 1955–97*, Instituto Estudio Peruanos, Lima, Peru

Index